FIRE IT UP

FIRE IT UP

More Than 400 Recipes for Grilling Everything

BY ANDREW SCHLOSS AND DAVID JOACHIM

PHOTOGRAPHS BY ALISON MIKSCH

CHRONICLE BOOKS

SAN FRANCISCO

Text copyright © 2011 by Andrew Schloss and David Joachim.
Photographs copyright © 2011 by Alison Miksch.
All rights reserved. No part of this book may be reproduced in any form
without written permission from the publisher.

Library of Congress Cataloging-in-Publication Data available.
ISBN 978-0-8118-6505-0

Manufactured in China

Design by Wink

10 9 8 7 6 5 4 3 2 1

Chronicle Books LLC
680 Second Street
San Francisco, California 94107
www.chroniclebooks.com

Acknowledgments

It's been a joy to continue exploring the wide world of grilling. Since the fall of 2007 when we began working on this book, we have become indebted to dozens of people who helped us organize our ideas, develop and test recipes, and find oddball ingredients.

We would especially like to thank all of the local farmers, ranchers, and purveyors who provided ingredients. We grilled everything from T-bone steaks to beef cheeks to pork ribs to whole kid to hearts of palm, watermelon, and eggs. Thank you to Rod Wieder of Backyard Bison for bison chuck, sirloin, ribs, and steaks; Steve Shelly of Gottschell Farm for melons, beets, tomatoes, and carrots; Tom Colbaugh of Happy Farms for geese, chicken, and eggs; Chuck Armitage of Lettuce Alone Farm for Brussels sprouts, radicchio, and eggs; Don and George DeVault of Pheasant Hill Farm for fennel, asparagus, and fava beans; Nathan Thomas of Breakaway Farms for grass-fed beef and pastured pork and poultry; as well as the rest of the vendors at our local Emmaus Farmers' Market for inspiring us to fire up the grill as we walk and talk through the market on Sunday afternoons.

Thanks also to Greg Baringer at nearby Baringer Brothers Meats for beef hearts, cheeks, petite shoulder tender, and other oddball cuts of beef and pork; Bill Steele at Mr. Bill's Poultry for quail, duck, and other fine birds; Jim and Nicole Lechner at Goat World Farms for goat racks and whole kid; Jon and Sukey Jamison at Jamison Farm for all manner of lamb, including kidneys, liver, and heart; Terry Koch, the fish market manager at our local Wegman's for tracking down mackerel, opakapaka, and other fish when we needed it; and Mike and Jill Polek for the local venison. Other great purveyors around the United States provided quality ingredients, including venison, elk, and antelope from Broken Arrow Ranch, abalone from Estero Bay Abalone, and alligator tail from Viva Gourmet.

A special thank-you to Mark and Jennifer Bitterman of The Meadow for turning us on to salt blocks for grilling, and providing the most exciting array of artisan salts and rare peppers anywhere. Mark, thanks also for your inimitable contributions to Chef Salt, our line of artisanal spice rubs.

We spent months developing, testing, and refining recipes and would like to thank the many testers and tasters who cheerfully helped along the way, especially Debby and Ned Carol; Phil Schulman; Carol Moore; Catherine Ziff; Melissa Hunter; Dina Kunst; Dana, Ben, and Isaac Schloss; Karen Shain Schloss; Christine Bucher; August and Maddox Joachim; Chuck and Jennifer Weaver; Lora and Jacob Bucher; Barry, Dana, and Micah Bucher; Cathy, Ken, Tomias, Nick, and Tessa Peoples; Jill, Mike, Scott, and Brad Polek; Andrew and Kim Brubaker; Tom Aczel and Michelle Raes; Doug Ashby and Danielle Lubene; Bill Melcher; Mark Bowman; and Mark Taylor.

To capture the infinite variety of ingredients available to grill cooks, we shot the photographs in this book over several seasons. Big thanks to photographer Alison Miksch, photo assistant Jada Voigt, food stylist Michael Pedersen, assistant food stylists Donna Land and Sharon Sanders, and prop stylist Barb Fritz. Thanks also to Hopewell Farms for letting us photograph their cattle; Tom Colbaugh from Happy Farms for letting us photograph his lamb, chickens, and geese; and George Devault of Pheasant Hill Farm for allowing us to chase his pigs with a camera.

None of this would have been possible without our agent Lisa Ekus and our editor Bill LeBlond. Thank you both for guiding this project with wise insights from beginning to end. At Chronicle Books, thanks to Sarah Billingsley for expert editing; Anne Donnard for a stunningly simple design; Deborah Kops for incisive copyediting; Peter Perez and David Hawk for creative PR and marketing; and Doug Ogan, Ann Spradlin, Dean Burrell, and Tera Killip for publishing assistance throughout.

Finally, a big thank-you to Christine Bucher and Karen Shain Schloss for cheering instead of fainting in front of the endless parade of spit-roasting goats, bison ribs, football-size stuffed flank steaks, calf fries nailed to a plank, pork bellies, lardo, gator tails, whole rabbits, pheasant, goose, ostrich, raw tuna on red-hot coals, blue crabs, crawfish, abalone, conch, and all manner of animal organs, including calf's liver, veal sweetbreads, hog kidneys, and lamb's tongue. A vegetarian was never so accommodating! But they both also enjoyed their share of grilled baby artichokes, beets, flame-kissed nopales and cardoons, whole grill-roasted Romanesco, fiddleheads, grilled poblano-stuffed tamales, cheese-filled panini, grilled banana satay, fruit pizzas, watermelon steaks, grilled figs, caramel s'mores, and grilled ice-cream sandwiches.

You both light our fires and we thank you for it.

Table of Contents

Introduction: How to Use This Book

American cooks have rediscovered the joy of good ingredients, simply prepared. We're clamoring for heirloom tomatoes, free-range chicken, and locally grown fingerlings. These days, it's all about the ingredients. And that's the focus of this book. We explain the inner workings of more than 290 common and uncommon ingredients and the best ways to grill them. We've combined America's oldest cooking occasion—grilling outdoors—with its newest cooking obsession: preserving the integrity of high-quality ingredients.

The ins and outs of buying, preparing, and flavoring your favorite ingredients are explained throughout every chapter. To simplify these details, we created at-a-glance charts, which are master guides to everything you would ever want to grill. The charts show the ingredient's different cuts or varieties, alternate names in the marketplace, best grilling methods, and substitutions.

Each chapter opens with a discussion of everything you need to know when buying, handling, and grilling the ingredient you're working with, including straight talk about terms such as wild, farm-raised, ranched, pastured, grass-fed, grain-fed, milk-fed, formula-fed, free-range, water-chilled, air-chilled, natural, organic, and sustainable.

A few other things you'll notice are little tidbits scattered throughout the recipes called "Know-How" and "Keep It Simple." Know-How gives you must-have information like how to butterfly flank steak, or clean an octopus, and it includes step-by-step illustrations when necessary. Keep It Simple shows you alternate ways of preparing recipes in less time, using fewer ingredients. We know that some cooks want to be grill masters and some just want dinner on the table. Tips throughout the book can help you accomplish both.

As devoted farmers'-market and gourmet-market shoppers, we put a premium on high-quality ingredients. We also know that some ingredients, like beef cheeks, can be hard to find. We offer tips throughout the recipes on sourcing oddball ingredients. You can also refer to the list of ingredient sources on page 400.

We hope this book shows you a different way of looking at grilled food. Although the ingredient is the star, and not the grill, we don't leave grilling novices hanging out to dry. Chapter 1: A Primer on Grilling Methods & Equipment, explains everything you need to know to grill successfully. And Chapter 2: How to Build Flavor into Anything Grilled, discusses all manner of marinades, brines, mops, rubs, pastes, and sauces, with 161 mini-recipes and variations, which you can use in the book's recipes or in your own creations. The goal in all this is to help you grill every food imaginable, and do it successfully. Grilling can be about so much more than hot dogs and hamburgers. Here's wishing you newfound joy at the grill and the deepest pleasure possible from every dish you share at your table.

1

A PRIMER ON GRILLING METHODS & EQUIPMENT

Grilling is not simply a matter of tossing food over fire. Rather, grilling is a set of cooking methods made possible by your equipment. In fact, your equipment determines the type of grilling you can do.

Most grills are designed for direct grilling—putting food directly over fire. This basic form of grilling works on all grills, including big and small gas grills, and charcoal and wood grills such as campfire grills, hibachis, and kettle grills.

But add a lid and ample grilling space, and the possibilities expand. Indirect grilling, which means putting food on the grill grate away from the fire and covering the grill, turns a grill into an oven. With the lid down you capture smoke, which infuses your food with its aromas. A lid also allows you to do grill-roasting, grill-braising, grill-baking, and other hybrid forms of grilling.

Here's a look at the various types of live-fire cooking we employ throughout this book:

- **Direct Grilling**
- **Bilevel Grilling**
- **Indirect Grilling**
- **Adding Smoke**
- **Rotisserie Grilling**
- **Grill-Braising and Wrapping**
- **Planking and Blocking**
- **No Grill Grate**

DIRECT GRILLING GUIDE

TEMPERATURE	°F	COAL APPEARANCE	COAL THICKNESS	GRATE HEIGHT	VENTS (% OPEN)	*COUNTING (SECONDS)
High	500° F ↓	Red-hot glow	4"	2"	100% OPEN	2x
Medium-High	450° F ↓	Light ash; orange glow	3" to 4"	3"	80% OPEN	4x
Medium	400° F ↓ 350° F	Medium ash; visible glow	3"	4"	70% OPEN	6x
Medium-Low	↓ 300° F	Medium-thick ash; faint glow	2"	5"	60% OPEN	8x
Low	↓ 250° F	Thick ash; spotty faint glow	1.5"	6"	50% OPEN	10x

*At this temperature, you should be able to hold your hand (palm down) about 4 inches above the grill grate and count, saying "one thousand" after each number ("1 one thousand, 2 one thousand . . .") the number of times listed in the chart without having to withdraw your hand.

Direct Grilling

Light a grill, put food over the fire, and you are direct grilling. Typically the grill grate rests 2 to 6 inches above the flame, and quick-cooking foods are placed on the hot grate. Direct grilling works best for searing small, relatively thin foods that will cook through in less than 30 minutes, including hamburgers, hot dogs, sausages, steaks, chops, poultry parts, small whole fish, fish steaks and fillets, shellfish, sliced or tender vegetables and fruits, flatbreads, and sandwiches.

To set up any grill for direct grilling, preheat it to high with the grill grate in place and the lid down (if you have a lid). Adjust the heat to the appropriate level for the food you are cooking, and then get grilling. The way you adjust the heat will depend upon the type of grill you're using.

To adjust and manage a live fire, keep in mind that fire is, at its core, oxygen combining very rapidly with another substance—so rapidly that it releases heat energy. Managing the temperature of the fire is a matter of controlling the flow of oxygen to the fuel. In a gas grill, the oxygen flow and fuel supply are regulated. Turn the temperature knob up or down, and you get high or low heat. With a charcoal or wood fire, heat adjustment is less automated. The flames are completely dependent upon the air and the fuel that you make available to them. Without oxygen and charcoal or wood, the fire can't breathe and it dies.

That's the real meaning of live-fire cooking. It's up to you to keep the fire alive by adding charcoal or wood and adjusting the air flow with vents or by manually blowing onto the fire. On a charcoal grill, keep the lid off and the vents 100 percent open, and you'll soon get high heat. Keep the lid down and the vents only 50 percent open, and you'll get less oxygen and low heat.

The thickness of your coal bed also determines how hot the fire is. Four inches thick (about a triple layer of charcoal briquettes) and glowing red is best for high heat. A bed 2 inches thick (about a single layer of briquettes) with only a little orange glow is best for medium-low heat. See the chart above for details. Note that in the chart, we give a range of temperatures for each heat level, but in the recipes throughout the book, we specify a temperature within that range.

BILEVEL GRILLING GUIDE

HEAT	TEMPERATURE	COAL APPEARANCE	COAL-BED THICKNESS	VENTS (% OPEN)	**COUNTING (SECONDS)
High/Medium	Direct: 500+/375°F Ambient: 400–450°F	Red-hot glow/ visible glow	4"/3"	90% OPEN	2x/6x
High/Medium-Low	Direct: 500+/325°F Ambient: 350–400°F	Red-hot ash/medium ash; faint glow	4"/2"	80% OPEN	2x/8x
High/Low	Direct: 500+/275°F Ambient: 300–350°F	Red-hot/thick ash; faint glow	4"/1–2"	70% OPEN	2x/10x
Medium-High/ Medium-Low	Direct: 425/325°F Ambient: 350–400°F	Orange glow/ medium ash and faint glow	3"–4"/2"	70% OPEN	4x/8x
Medium-High/Low	Direct: 425/275°F Ambient: 300–350°F	Orange glow/ Thick ash and faint glow	3"–4"/1–2"	60% OPEN	4x/10x
Medium/Low	Direct: 375/275°F Ambient: 250–300°F	Visible glow/thick ash; faint glow	3"/1–2"	50% OPEN	6x/10x

Direct temperature is measured with an oven thermometer placed on the grill grate directly over the fire. Ambient temperature is registered on the thermometer embedded in the grill hood. **At this temperature, you should be able to hold your hand (palm down) about 4 inches above the grill grate and count, saying "one thousand" after each number ("1 one thousand, 2 one thousand . . .") the number of times listed in the chart without having to withdraw your hand.

Bilevel Grilling

When direct grilling over charcoal or wood, it helps to set up two heat levels. Let's say you're cooking a 2-inch thick porterhouse steak. You want to sear both sides over medium-high to high heat, but then you'll need to move it over to medium or medium-low heat so it can cook through without burning on the surface. On a gas grill, you just turn down the temperature knob. But on a charcoal or wood grill, it's best to create two different heat levels. To set up a charcoal or wood grill for bilevel grilling, rake the hot coals into a bed that's 3 to 4 inches thick on one side and 1 to 2 inches thick on the other. Set the grill grate in place, preheat it, and use the higher heat area to sear meats, fish, and vegetables. Use the lower heat area for toasting breads and keeping foods warm. If anything starts to burn over the high-heat area, move it to the low-heat area. See the chart above for details. Again, we give a range of temperatures for each heat level in the chart, but each recipe will specify a temperature within that range.

CROSSHATCH MARKS

Grill grates comes in all configurations these days, but most consist of multiple parallel metal bars. To create a diamond pattern of crosshatch marks with such a grill grate, preheat the grill to high heat, and scrape and oil the grate. Think of the grate as a clock, and set your food on the hot grate, pointing the food to 10 o'clock. When the food is nicely grill-marked, rotate it 45 degrees to 2 o'clock. Cook until nicely grill-marked again. You'll need at least 2 to 3 minutes over high or medium-high heat to create deep grill marks in each direction. That means you'll have to cook the food for at least 4 to 6 minutes per side. If the food will overcook in that time but you really want nice grill marks, create the marks on the first side only, then flip the food and finish cooking. When serving, flip again so that the grill-marked side is faceup.

INDIRECT GRILLING GUIDE

HEAT	TEMPERATURE	COAL APPEARANCE	COAL-BED THICKNESS	GRATE HEIGHT	VENTS (% OPEN)	*COUNTING (SECONDS)
High	400–450°F	Bright orange glow	4" split bed	2"	100% OPEN	4x
Medium-High	350–400°F	Light ash; orange glow	3–4" split bed	3"	80% OPEN	5x
Medium	300–350°F	Medium ash; visible glow	3" split bed	4"	70% OPEN	8x
Medium-Low	250–300°F	Medium-thick ash; faint glow	2" split bed	5"	60% OPEN	10x
Low	225–250°F	Thick ash; spotty faint glow	1½" split bed	6"	50% OPEN	11x

* At this temperature, you should be able to hold your hand (palm down) about 4 inches above the grill grate and count, saying "one thousand" after each number ("1 one thousand, 2 one thousand . . .") the number of times listed in the chart without having to withdraw your hand.

HEATING AND TURNING

When food is grilled, very intense heat hits the food's surface, but the heat slows down dramatically from there. It is only gradually transferred to the center of the food. So the surface of grilled food can burn before the center is done. To solve the problem, start the food over high heat to brown both sides (which creates flavor), then move it to low heat to finish cooking without burning the surface. If you have no low-heat area, then frequent turning will give the surface away from the heat a rest from the intense flame and allow time for the heat retained in the food to make its way to the center. When cooking over a raging fire, turn your food often for a well-browned crust and a center that's not raw.

Indirect Grilling

Direct grilling will burn the surface of big and dense foods that take more than 30 minutes to cook through. Tough cuts and large roasts (like beef brisket, pork shoulder, whole chickens, and turkeys), large whole fish, and dense vegetables (like whole potatoes) require longer cooking with lower heat. For indirect grilling, you put the food away from the heat and close the lid, turning the grill into something closer to an oven. Indirect grilling opens up all kinds of cooking possibilities, such as grill-roasting a whole turkey; grill-braising beef cheeks; and grill-baking an apple, a cake, or a custard.

To set up a gas grill for indirect grilling, light some burners but leave the others off. For a two-burner gas grill, light just one side and put the food over the other, unheated side. If your grill has three or more burners, you can light one side of burners or light the outside burners and put the food over the unheated middle area. We prefer the latter for more even heating.

On a charcoal grill, the principle is the same: set up the grill to create an unheated area for cooking and a heated area for the coals. For the most even cooking, rake the coals to opposite sides of the grill and leave the center unheated. However, if your grill is small, you'll get a larger cooking area by raking the coals to one side of the grill. Either way, to indirect grill, you put your food over the unheated area then close the lid to trap and circulate heat gently around the food. For indirect grilling you need to have the lid down or the food won't cook because most of the heat will escape. It would be like trying to bake cookies with the oven door open. You'll also let out all that wonderful smoke from the coals. See the chart on the facing page for details on setting up your grill for indirect grilling. As in the charts for direct and bilevel grilling, we give a range of temperatures for each heat level, but the recipes in the book specify a temperature within that range.

Setting up a Drip Pan

For fatty meats like pork shoulder, beef brisket, and skin-on duck, you'll need to put a disposable aluminum drip pan beneath the food. A drip pan not only prevents flare-ups but also acts like a roasting pan, catching flavorful juices that can be turned into a sauce when the food is done cooking. On a charcoal grill, set the pan under the grill grate in the bottom of the grill near the coals. On a gas grill, set the pan under the grill grate over the unlit burner(s). Or, use a roasting rack just as you would for roasting in an oven. Put the food on a roasting rack over the unheated area of the grill and set the drip pan directly beneath the roasting rack on the grill grate. With this method, you don't need to lift the hot grill grate and there's little chance of stray charcoal ashes falling into your flavorful juices in the pan. When you want steam for low-moisture foods like pork or to help soften connective tissue in tough cuts like beef brisket or veal breast, fill the drip pan with just enough hot liquid to provide steam, but not so much as to severely dilute the flavorful juices. About a ¼ to ½ inch of liquid in the pan should do it. Start with hot liquid. Cold liquid will increase your cooking time because some of the grill heat will be spent warming up the water. Choose whatever liquid you like. Water is fine for steam alone, but flavorful liquids like beer, wine, stock, fruit juice, or vegetable juice will provide a handy base for a sauce.

Adding Coals

When indirectly grilling on a charcoal grill, you'll need to replenish the coals about once an hour. Adding hot coals works best, so keep some coals at the ready in a chimney starter. If you don't have a chimney starter, put unlit charcoal over the old ones as they begin to die down, and leave off the lid for a few minutes to stoke the fire and help light the new coals. Then replace the lid and adjust the temperature as necessary.

Increasing Your Options

Indirect grilling requires a bit more setup than direct grilling, but it greatly expands the kinds of ingredients you can bring to the grill. We indirectly grill everything from whole chicken, turkey, and duck to pork ribs and pork belly, beef rump roast, veal shanks, marrow bones, rack of goat, ham of boar, whole rabbit, whole red snapper, whole eggplant, whole eggs (yes, eggs), flan, pretzels, shortcake, and corn sticks. And you've still got the hot part of the grill grate available in case you want to directly grill some tender vegetables alongside whatever you're indirectly grilling. You can also sear meat directly over the heat, then move it away from the heat and close the lid to mimic the process of slow-roasting. Avoid lifting the lid. Every time you do, heat escapes, lengthening your total cooking time. Remember, if you're looking, you're not cooking.

RESTING

Grilled food tastes juicier after a brief period of rest. If you cut into a steaming hot steak or roast, the juices readily escape. But as meat cools, the proteins become firmer and better able to retain the juices. Ideally, meat should cool to about 120°F before serving, which may take anywhere from 5 minutes for a thin steak or chop to 15 minutes for a thick roast or whole chicken to 1 hour for a whole lamb or suckling pig. During the resting period, the internal temperature of the meat will continue to rise a few degrees at a rate relative to its density and thickness. For precise doneness, remove thin steaks and chops when they are a few degrees shy of the desired internal temperature, and thick roasts and whole animals when they are 5 to 10 degrees shy of the desired internal temperature.

GRILLING 1-2-3

You can use your grill like an oven or a stove. Your grill grate is essentially a built-in stove-top pan with slats. Treat your grill grate just as you would a pan or baking sheet. The grill grate is your cooking surface, so keep it clean, get it hot, and oil it. If you're using a grill tray, screen, skillet, or basket, then this becomes your cooking surface, and the same rules apply. For successful grilling, follow these simple steps every time you grill:

1. Get it hot. Preheat your grill (gas, charcoal, or wood) on high with the grill grate and/or grill tray in place and the lid down (if you have a lid) for at least 10 minutes. You want your cooking surface to be very hot. Built-in temperature gauges only measure the ambient temperature of the air inside the grill, not the grill grate itself. Any part of the grate directly over the heat should be hot enough to sear food on contact. Hold your hand a few inches above the grate and count "one one thousand, two one thousand. . . . " If you make it to "four one thousand," you've got a medium-high fire on your hands—a good place to start most direct grilling. See the charts on pages 12–14 for more details on grill temperatures. A hot grill grate provides the best sear marks, the most flavor, and the least sticking.

2. Keep it clean. When your grill grate or grill tray is hot, scrape off any debris with a stiff wire brush. A hot cooking surface cleans more easily than a cold one. For the cleanest grill, scrape it twice: once right after food comes off the grill (that's when the burnt-on debris will easily loosen itself from the hot metal) and once again right before you add food to the grill. Once the grill grate or tray cools, any bits of food adhering to the cold metal will be much more difficult to remove.

3. Oil it well. Rub oil or fat over the hot scraped cooking surface. We like to wad up a paper towel and drop it in a little canola or other vegetable oil. Grab the oily towel with your tongs and rub it on the grill grate. You can also use a chunk of fat trimmed from meat. Either way, the fat will pick up some fine soot and create a super-clean grill grate; but more important, it will lubricate your cooking surface, helping to prevent sticking and improving heat transfer to the food's surface for more efficient browning.

Adding Smoke

One of the great advantages of a grill lid is that it captures smoke, which infuses your grilled food with woodsy aromas and flavors. Fat and juices that drip into the fire will send a little bit of smoke back to the food, but most smokiness in grilled food comes from wood. If you grill over a wood fire or very smoky lump charcoal like mesquite, you can get some good smoke flavor in a roast or long-cooking, tough cut of meat. But when grilling over gas or a fire of charcoal briquettes, you'll need to add wood chips or chunks to get a smoky flavor. (You can buy chunks or make them yourself by chopping up appropriate wood.)

To set up a grill for added smoke, soak wood chips or chunks in water for at least 30 minutes so they're wet enough to slowly smolder rather than quickly incinerate. Light your grill and add the soaked chips or chunks as part of the preheating step. On a charcoal grill, toss a handful or two directly onto the hot coals, wait until you see smoke (5 to 10 minutes), then add your food, and close the lid. If you can, position the lid so that the upper air vents are on the opposite side from the lower air vents on the bottom of the grill. This will draw maximum smoke over the food.

On a gas grill, add the soaked chips or chunks to your grill's smoker box or tray. If your gas grill doesn't have a smoking tray, you can make one. Put a single layer of soaked wood in a disposable aluminum pan or wrap it in foil and poke holes in the foil with a fork. Put your foil smoking tray directly over one of the hot burners beneath the grill grate and preheat the grill. When you see smoke, add the food, and close the lid to trap the smoke. Whenever the smoke subsides, add more soaked chips or chunks (usually about once every 45 minutes). The more smoke you see, the more smoke flavor you'll get in the food.

Choose your smoking wood based on the food you're grilling. Mesquite and hickory emit thick, heavy smoke, which works best with robust meats such as beef and game. Oak, alder, and maple produce a medium-bodied smoke, which works well with a wider range of foods like pork, poultry, game, fish, and dense vegetables. Fruit and nut woods like apple, cherry, and pecan give off milder, sweeter smoke, which complements delicate foods like lean fish, shellfish, vegetables, and fruit.

You can also soak leaves, branches, vines, nutshells, herbs, and other plant material in water for smoking. For the most smoke, use green wood or branches rather than dry, seasoned wood. Green wood is moist enough to smolder over a long period, giving off wonderfully fresh-smelling smoke. Green tea leaves lend delicious herbal flavors to Wasabi-Drizzled Mussels with Green Tea Fumes (page 288), and grapevines add sweet and tannic aromas to Vine-Smoked Dungeness Crabs with Preserved Lemon Relish (page 278).

If you have no other source of smoke but really want smoke flavor, cheat by adding liquid smoke to your marinade, baste, or sauce. See page 124 for details on this widely available natural product.

Rotisserie Grilling

Indirect grilling usually requires frequent basting to keep the meat from drying out. A rotisserie does the basting for you. As fat melts from the meat, the rotisserie keeps the melted fat constantly rolling around the meat's surface. Most grills can accommodate a rotisserie assembly, but each one works a little differently. Usually, you slide the spit rod through the center of your bird or roast, secure the meat with thumb-screw skewers or several lashings of kitchen string, then set the meat into the assembly. Before you complete the process make sure there is (1) ample space for rotation, (2) even weight distribution, and (3) a secure and appropriate weight load for your motor. If the food is too heavy or cannot rotate easily, it may burn out your rotisserie motor. On some grills, you'll need to remove the grill grates so that the food can rotate unobstructed. If you can adjust the food's distance from the heat, 4 to 10 inches works best in most cases.

Rotisserie grilling a whole animal is usually referred to as spit-roasting, but the process is the same. It's just done on a large scale. For large whole animals like kid goat, spring lamb, and suckling pig, suspend the meat 1 to 2 feet away from the heat. For heavy animals, you may want to use pliable metal wire (18 to 20 gauge) and secure the backbone to the spit rod to be sure the animal does not spin loose on the rotisserie. To cook large animals evenly with a charcoal rotisserie setup, it helps to make a thicker coal bed beneath the animal's toughest cuts (shoulders and hips) and a thinner coal bed near the tender cuts (along the back). It's also nice to throw some soaked or green-wood chunks in the grill for smoke flavor. Rotisserie grilling may seem like a bother, but once the fire and food are set, it produces self-basting, superior-tasting meat and handily feeds a crowd. For some examples, try the Rotisserie Chicken for Everyone (page 183) and Spit-Roasted Whole Kid Spanish-Style (page 164).

LID UP OR DOWN?

Putting a grill lid down over your food traps heat, moisture, and smoke. By trapping heat, the lid delivers some convection heat currents to the top of your food, which speeds the cooking and offers other advantages such as melting cheese on pizza. By trapping moisture, a lid can help dissolve connective tissue in tough meats and keep them juicy. Finally, a lid traps smoke, which infuses the food over time, enhancing its flavor. For all of these reasons—faster cooking, juicier food, and more smoke flavor—we usually grill with the lid down. However, moisture is the enemy of a crusty surface on foods like grilled steak. If you want a great crust on a steak or if the food will cook through in less than 10 minutes—for example thin, small, and tender foods like asparagus, fish fillets, and chicken cutlets—there is little reason to close the lid.

Grill-Braising and Wrapping

Barbecue pit masters have always struggled to maintain enough moisture in meat to soften the connective tissue in tough cuts like ribs without adding so much moisture that the meat tastes steamed. For big, tough cuts like brisket and ribs, they sometimes wrap the meat in foil about halfway through cooking. That gives the meat enough time near dry heat to form a tasty crust or bark, while retaining moisture during the last half of cooking. Meat juices collect in the foil and simulate the cooking method known as braising, whereby tough meats are slowly cooked in a little liquid in a covered pot. The method works wonders for tough cuts on the grill like beef cheeks, oxtail, and veal shanks. We call it grill-braising because we usually brown the meat over direct heat on the grill, and then wrap it in foil or nest it in a foil pan with some liquid and finish cooking away from the heat. The liquid slowly braises tough meats to melting tenderness and makes a terrific sauce.

You can also wrap just to hold together delicate ingredients. Foil isn't the only wrap for grilling. You can use grape, banana, or lotus leaves; corn husks; or almost any large leaf. These wraps are best for foods like fish or ground meat, which tend to fall apart on the grill. In addition to retaining the food's moisture, wrapping infuses the food with the wrap's subtle flavors. Soak any dry wrapper like dried leaves in water to prevent the wrapper from burning. Use this technique in dishes like Whole Red Snapper Stuffed with Feta Pilaf and Wrapped in Vine Leaves (page 241) and Camembert Wrapped in Grape Leaves Served with Cranberry Mustard Vinaigrette (page 364).

Planking and Blocking

Another way to protect delicate foods on the grill is to set them on a plank of wood or a block of salt. Wood planking is fairly common now and allows you to effortlessly cook a fillet of salmon or a wheel of cheese. Choose a plank that is about ¼ inch thick and wide and long enough to accommodate the food you are grilling. Cedar and alder planks are easy to find, but apple and cherry also work well. In fact, you could use almost any plank of untreated wood. Like chips and chunks, a wood plank should be soaked in water so it smolders instead of incinerates in the grill, but the plank needs to soak for more time, about 1 hour. For the most smoke flavor, char one side of the plank over the fire, then flip it and set the food on the charred side. You'll find a lid helpful here to trap heat and deliver it to the top of the planked food for even cooking. For a novel variation, roll up some food in wood grilling "paper." These extremely thin sheets of cedar or alder can be wrapped around delicate foods and grilled like little food bundles.

To push the grilling possibilities even further, pick up some salt blocks. They are similar to wood planks on the grill, but they get hot enough (up to 650°F) to sear food and also delicately season it. Salt blocks for grilling should be at least 1½ inches thick to prevent cracking. Be sure to slowly heat the block and gradually bring it up to searing temperature. Start the block over low heat on the grill and over a 30-minute period move the block in two steps to high heat. On a charcoal grill, use a bilevel fire to better regulate the heat. Then set the food on the hot block and the food will cook in minutes.

The big advantage to salt blocks is they are reusable dozens of times. After each use, wipe the block clean of debris with a scouring pad, warm water, and gentle pressure. Blot dry and the block is ready to go for next time. Salt blocks work best with thin and delicate foods like fish, shellfish, cheese, and eggs. Bring some fried eggs on a salt bock from the grill to the table, and your guests will surely be impressed. Try the recipe for Pepper and Salt Block Scallops with Grapefruit Mojo (page 293).

No Grill Grate

With indirect grilling, spit-roasting, wrapping, and planking, the food gets progressively farther away from the heat. But we have to confess: we love what fire does to food. Sometimes we dispense with all accessories—even the grill grate—to bring the food closer to the fire. For example, we tested the Preserved Lemon and Lamb Kebobs (page 149) two ways. First we grilled the skewers of ground lamb directly on the grill grate. The next time we made the dish, we removed the grate and suspended the skewers over the fire with the skewer ends resting on bricks. The latter method eliminated sticking and gave the lamb a clean, fire-kissed flavor. On a gas grill, you can remove the grill grate and place the bricks directly on your heat diffuser (the metal plates, flavorizer bars, or lava rocks above the burner); then suspend the skewers over the bricks.

Sometimes "closer to the fire" isn't close enough. Firm vegetables like potatoes, sweet potatoes, and beets taste completely delicious when cooked right in the fire. Nestle these vegetables in hot coals and the skins will blister and char, sending wonderfully smoky aromas deep into the flesh. When it's cooked to fork-tenderness, cut the vegetable in half, dollop with some seasoned butter, and scoop the fire-roasted vegetable from its toasted jacket. Yum! Meat and fish work well on the coals, too. Just be sure to use lump charcoal or a wood fire when you will be eating the surface of the food that has touched the coals. Charcoal briquettes (made from sawdust) leave an unpleasant sooty coating of fine ash on food. However, lump charcoal and wood leave nothing but phenomenal flavor. Check out the recipes for Fire-Roasted Sweet Potatoes with Root Beer–Rum Butter (page 307), Campfire Raclette with New Potatoes Cooked in the Coals (page 360), and Raw Charred Tuna with Green Tea Ponzu Sauce (page 263). We firmly believe that the less that comes between the fire and the food, the better the flavor.

Types of Grills

We mentioned earlier that your equipment determines the type of grilling you can do. The biggest determining factors are the size of your grill, what it's made of, and the type of fuel it uses. If you're buying a new grill, consider all three factors. The grill should have plenty of space for your average grilling session. If you only cook a few steaks, chops, fish fillets, and/or vegetables at a time, a cooking area as small as 150 square inches or 14 inches in diameter may be sufficient. For larger roasts, leg of lamb, and whole turkeys, you'll want at least 400 square inches and preferably 600 square inches of grill space, about the size of an average four-burner gas grill. For large grilling sessions with bigger foods or a greater variety, consider an even larger grill or more than one.

Most grills are made of stainless steel because it's durable, easy to maintain, and fairly lightweight compared to other materials. Ceramic grills like Japanese kamados and Indian tandoors are heavier but retain heat better than steel and use less fuel. Ceramic grills excel at cooking tough cuts of meat for long periods of time.

Apart from the material, the more common concern is the fuel the grill burns. Gas, charcoal, and wood all have advantages and disadvantages. Here's a quick survey of each.

GAS: Turn a knob or push a button, and your gas grill is lit. Turn the knob again, and the flame goes up or down instantly. This convenience has made gas grills the most widely used type of grill in North America. While charcoal aficionados point out that gas grills don't emit smoke to flavor your food, you can always add wood chips to a gas grill for smoky flavor (see page 16). The chief disadvantage with gas grills is moisture. Gas contains about 30 percent moisture, which vaporizes as steam during combustion. For every 10 minutes of cooking on a gas grill, you release about ½ to 1 cup water vapor in your grill. That moisture goes to the surface of your food and prevents the internal temperature from rising as high as it does in a charcoal or wood grill. Water cannot reach temperatures above 212°F (at least not outside a pressure cooker). But browning, the hallmark of grilled flavor, doesn't happen until at least 250°F—which isn't to say that browning doesn't occur in a gas grill. It does. But the average backyard gas grill doesn't get quite as hot as a charcoal or wood grill. If you're a purist about creating a crusty surface on your food, the high and dry heat of charcoal and wood is hard to beat.

CHARCOAL BRIQUETTES: Charcoal comes in two ready-made forms, briquettes and lump charcoal. Both are essentially wood that has been preburned to make it easier to light the fire and get grilling. Briquettes are made from finely ground wood (sawdust) and various ingredients to bind the sawdust into briquettes, help the briquettes light, and make them last a long time. The primary advantages of briquettes are steady burning, fairly high and dry heat (see the discussion at left regarding gas), and a bit of smoky aroma to flavor your food. The chief disadvantage is the mess of handling and cleaning up charcoal. If you love grilling with briquettes, shop around for a good brand. We've found that national and boutique brands perform more consistently than less expensive store brands.

LUMP CHARCOAL: This type of charcoal is closer to real wood in its natural state and we prefer it for most grilling. It looks like rough pieces of burned wood, and that's exactly what it is. The pros and cons are similar to charcoal briquettes with one additional consideration: lump charcoal tends to burn hotter than briquettes. A briquette fire won't burn as hot as one made from mesquite lump charcoal, which burns at around 800°F, and can't come close to the heat of bincho-tan, a dense Japanese oak charcoal that burns at around 1100°F. With lump charcoal, you can count on a great crust and browning on your steak. But the fuel burns out faster, requiring frequent replenishment for long-cooking foods. To get the best of both worlds, we sometimes combine fast-burning, high-heat lump charcoal with steady-burning, medium-heat briquettes.

WOOD: While charcoal has already lost half its potential energy during the preburning process, wood contains all of its potential energy and burns much hotter—a distinct advantage for browning and flavor. Wood also emits billows of smoke, which, given time, thoroughly infuse the food you are cooking. The downside is that wood takes longer to light than charcoal and is less consistent. It scores low on the convenience scale but high on the flavor scale. You make your choice. If it's high heat you're after, choose seasoned (aged) wood, which burns dry and hot. For more smoke, use green or unseasoned wood, which burns wet and slow. Barbecue pit masters often use a combination of the two.

MEAT, GAME, AND FISH DONENESS

MEAT	BLUE	RARE	MEDIUM-RARE	MEDIUM-DONE	MEDIUM-WELL	WELL-DONE
Beef and bison roast and steak	120°F	125°F	135°F	145°F	155°F	170°F
Beef and bison tough cuts	---	---	---	---	155°F	170°F
Ground beef and bison	---	---	---	150°F	155°F	160°F
Venison steak and roast	120°F	125°F	135°F	145°F	155°F	170°F
Venison tough cuts	---	---	---	---	155°F	170°F
Ground venison	---	---	---	150°F	155°F	160°F
Pork and boar chops and roast	---	---	---	145°F	155°F	170°F
Pork and boar roast	---	---	---	145°F	155°F	170°F
Pork and boar shoulder	---	---	---	145°F	165°F	170°F
Ground pork and boar	---	---	---	---	155°F	165°F
Lamb and goat chops and roast	120°F	125°F	135°F	145°F	155°F	170°F
Lamb and goat shoulder	---	---	---	---	155°F	170°F
Ground lamb	---	---	---	---	150°F	160°F
Veal chops and roast	---	---	135°F	145°F	155°F	170°F
Veal shanks	---	---	---	---	155°F	170°F
Ground veal	---	---	---	---	150°F	160°F
Whole chicken and turkey and all dark meat	---	---	---	---	165°F	175°F
Chicken and turkey breast	---	---	---	---	155°F	---
Duck, goose, and game birds	---	140°F	150°F	165°F	170°F	180°F
Rabbit, squirrel, and small game	---	---	---	140°F	150°F	160°F
Alligator	---	---	---	140°F	150°F	160°F
Fish	---	---	125°F	130°F	140°F	150°F

Judging Doneness

Even the most sophisticated grilling technique will be of little consequence if the food is over- or underdone. Burning and overcooking food is the most common grilling mistake. Setting up the grill for bilevel grilling will help. We also give grilling temperatures for the fire and the cooked food in every recipe. But it is helpful to know what food is supposed to look like when it's done. Here's an overview of what happens to food as it cooks and what it should look like at various stages along the way.

The intense heat of a grill causes the molecules in food to move, react with each other, and form new textures and flavors. Water evaporates, causing shrinkage; proteins coagulate and shrink; starches soften and gelatinize; fats melt; and sugars caramelize and brown. All of these changes release volatile aromatic compounds, which make grilled food smell delicious. These changes also show you how far along your food is in the cooking process.

In our recipes, we often give doneness cues like "Cook until nicely grill-marked." What we mean is that the food should bear light to dark brown stripes where it has been seared by the hot metal. For vegetables and fruits, you want only light to medium grill-marking to prevent the soft tissues from becoming flabby, which makes the vegetables or fruit go limp on the plate. Most grilled vegetables like bell peppers and zucchini should still be crisp-tender. For flatbreads like pizza and naan, the bread should blister and brown in spots and look matte rather than shiny on the top side. It will also feel firm to the touch. Fish should have light or medium grill marks and still look quite moist and somewhat filmy in the center.

The doneness of meat depends on factors like muscle density and other breed and genetic considerations, as well as how long the meat was aged, the meat's temperature before cooking, where it comes from on the animal, and its fat and water content. Fat conducts heat more slowly than muscle fiber, so fatty meats cook more slowly than lean meats. Bones also slow down the heat transfer because air within the bone structure conducts heat much more slowly than the bone material itself. Water, on the other hand, speeds up heat transference and conducts heat twice as fast as fat. That's why lean, tender, boneless cuts like beef tenderloin cook very quickly.

Visual or tactile checks and internal temperature are the most reliable methods of testing meat doneness. As meat cooks, it becomes drier, more opaque, browner, and firmer. Meat cooked to a doneness of blue has a red center that's still raw and it feels soft when pressed on the surface. When cooked rare, meat has a deep red center and resists slightly when pressed. Medium-rare meat appears bright red in the center and feels resilient to the touch, while medium is rosy red or pink in the center and feels slightly firm. Medium-well meat retains only a hint of pink in the center and feels firm when pressed, and well-done meat looks tan or gray all the way through and feels stiff.

Judging the doneness of tough and fatty cuts of meat like pork shoulder is a lot easier. Tough cuts are done when they are fork-tender. Period. Most tough meats won't show signs of tenderness until they reach at least 160°F inside. Use the chart on the facing page to familiarize yourself with internal doneness temperatures for various kinds of meat, game, and fish. These temperatures provide an accurate doneness test if you are not confident about what the meat should look like and how it should feel.

When testing internal temperatures, be sure that the thermometer reaches the center of the thickest portion of the food without touching bone (which could give you a false reading). The temperatures below are consistent with how most chefs serve food for the best flavor and texture and to meet consumer expectations. But keep in mind that the U.S. Department of Agriculture (USDA) defines doneness at slightly higher temperatures for enhanced food safety reasons (with a generous margin for user error). For instance, the USDA defines most meats as rare at 135°F, medium-rare at 145°F, medium at 160°F, and well-done at 170°F and above. The USDA also recommends cooking ground meats to 160°F to reduce the risk of illness. However, at those temperatures, the meat will probably be cooked more than you wish. By the time the meat's internal temperature reaches 160°F, most of the moisture and flavor in ground meat will be gone. Use the chart's figures with confidence, but if you have any reason to doubt the safety of your meat, feel free to follow USDA figures. In combination with the visual doneness cues discussed previously and in each ingredient chapter, internal temperatures will help you get a better feel for the doneness of various foods. Soon you'll be able to tell just by looking, and you'll turn out perfectly cooked steaks and grilled vegetables with nothing but tongs.

Chapter 2

HOW TO BUILD FLAVOR INTO ANYTHING GRILLED

A well-built fire and the best ingredients amount to little if the food coming off the grill doesn't taste good. Flavor is the most flexible part of a recipe. A grilled chicken breast is still a grilled chicken breast, whether it is flavored with garlic and extra-virgin olive oil or lemongrass and Thai fish sauce. The main ingredient and the grilling technique don't vary, only the seasoning and the sauce. But what a difference those little changes make.

The Power of Alcohol

The flavorful parts of herbs and spices are fat soluble, but most food is full of water. Since fat and water don't mix, in order to transfer the flavor from seasonings into the fibers of meat or vegetables, it is necessary to include an ingredient that helps bind the two immiscible substances together, and alcohol does just that in many preparations.

One end of an alcohol molecule combines well with fats and oils, while the other end bonds easily with water, making alcohol extremely useful for infusing food with flavor. Its fat-bonding end helps it carry oily aromatic molecules through cell membranes easily, and its water-loving side makes it especially effective at helping those aromatics stick to the cells.

When uncooked, low concentrations of alcohol, 1 percent or less, increase the release of aromatic molecules into the air. So adding a very small amount of alcohol to a glaze or dipping sauce can enhance flavor and aroma perception. At higher levels, above 5 percent, the effect is diminished by the aroma of the alcohol itself.

Alcohol vaporizes more easily than water, and has a lower boiling point (172°F), so much of the alcohol in a mop or basting sauce evaporates during grilling. Tough cuts of meat that are grilled for several hours and basted with an alcohol-based mop absorb much more flavor than those basted with a water-based mop. And by the time they are done grilling, only 5 percent of their initial alcohol content will remain.

Alcohol may also improve the healthfulness of grilled food. According to research conducted at the University of Porto in Portugal in 2008, steak marinated in alcohol and then grilled had reduced levels of heterocyclic amines (HCAs), which are potentially carcinogenic compounds created when meat is cooked over high heat. Researchers found that alcohol-marinated meat produced up to 90 percent fewer HCAs than untreated meat. They hypothesized that the alcohol prevents certain water-soluble molecules from moving to the surface of the steak, where they would be turned into HCAs at high temperatures.

Seasonings

Although there are thousands of seasonings and seasoning blends (see the more than 160 mini-recipes in this chapter for examples), there are only five basic vehicles for delivering these seasonings to grilled food: spice rubs and pastes, brines, marinades, mops, and, finally, glazes and sauces.

Spice Rubs

Spice rubs are the quickest way to flavor a grilled ingredient. When exposed to fire, rubs form an intensely flavored crispy crust on the surface of grilled food. They are the first thing to hit the palate, and they create a dynamic interplay between the relatively untouched moist meaty interior of a chop, steak, or roast and the slightly charred, somewhat salty, wonderfully spicy surface. Rubs are predominantly salt and sugar, as much as 25 percent. The salt affects the surface protein of a piece of meat, causing it to absorb flavors in the rub to about $\frac{1}{16}$ inch. The sugar mixes with the protein and forms a weak chemical structure, which quickly breaks down into hundreds of flavorful compounds when it comes in contact with fire. This series of reactions, known as Maillard reactions, produce the brown grill marks and intense flavor that are the hallmarks of grilled food. For the best results, apply the spice rub, then let the food sit for 10 minutes or so while the grill is heating. The salt and sugar will sink deeper into the food and help to develop a more pronounced crust. Sometimes we let rubbed food refrigerate for more than 24 hours to create the best crust possible.

Rubs made from all dry ingredients, called dry rubs, can be stored in a tightly closed plastic bag or jar in a cabinet for up to a month. Rubs that contain moist or fresh ingredients such as chopped garlic and herbs, called fresh rubs or pastes, should be refrigerated and will last anywhere from a few days to a week, depending on the shelf life of their most perishable ingredient.

Brines

Brining adds moisture and flavor to food. Grilling directly over flame is an intense form of cooking that tends to dehydrate low-moisture, low-fat, delicate ingredients like lean pork and white-meat poultry. Soaking these meats in 5 percent salt brine for as little as 1 hour before grilling can make them noticeably juicier. For the simplest brine, dissolve about 2 tablespoons salt and 1 tablespoon sugar in 2½ cups water or another flavored liquid.

Brines work in two ways: First, salt loosens the muscle fibers that cause muscles to contract. Brine-soaked meat therefore becomes noticeably softer and, if not overcooked, it will taste more tender. Second, salt causes the protein molecules to unfold, exposing more bonding sites for water. That means that brined meat can absorb as much as 10 percent of the moisture from the brine. When meat cooks, it naturally loses some juices (about 20 percent), but by bulking up the moisture in meat through brining, you can effectively cut the net loss of juices by half. The result: juicier-tasting pork, chicken, and other food from your grill.

Brines act as a seasoning as well. When water from the brine enters the meat, any flavorful components from herbs, spices, or flavored liquids dissolved in the brine are also absorbed deep into the meat. And if brine contains about 5 percent alcohol, its flavoring abilities are greatly enhanced (see the discussion about alcohol on the facing page).

Meats absorb brine from the outside in, so the fibers closest to the surface get most of the benefits. But it's the surface that dehydrates most during grilling, so even a short period of brining can make your meat noticeably juicier and more flavorful.

Incomplete brining yields less juicy results, but brining for too long poses far greater problems. Overexposing meats to the salt in brine makes the protein coagulate, which forces moisture out of the muscle tissue. So you end up with meat that is even drier than it was before it went into the brine. This potential drawback makes it especially important to monitor your brining times. The brine's strength and the food's density, size, and shape all affect brining time. Use the chart below as a guide.

Marinades

Marinades are like brines, but they do the job with acid rather than salt. Most ingredients contain acid, but they vary widely in acidity and as a result, so do marinades. Vinegar, citrus or other fruit juice, wine or other alcohols, buttermilk, yogurt, tea, or coffee each bring different flavors and textures to a marinade, but chemically they all work the same way.

Just like salt in brines (see facing page), acids in marinades open the structure of proteins by disrupting their chemical bonds. When a piece of fish or meat is submerged in an acidic marinade, its fibers tenderize, it takes on moisture, and it forms bonds with flavorful elements in the solution. Because acids are less reactive than salts, brines are more effective than marinades at accomplishing these tasks. Unless you inject a marinade deep into the interior of an ingredient, it is difficult for the marinade to have any tenderizing effect deeper than a fraction of an inch without making the finished dish taste overly sour.

As with brines, it is possible to marinate food for too long. When proteins are overexposed to acids, they will stop absorbing liquid from the marinade, and will eventually begin to release juices from the muscle fibers. When this happens, the meat will start to look cooked (brown, dry, and firm) and the marinade will start to become cloudy. Remove the food from the marinade before this starts to happen. If you see that an ingredient is starting to overmarinate or overbrine, simply remove it from the liquid, pat it dry, cover it with plastic wrap or slip it in a zipper-lock bag, and refrigerate it until you are ready to light up the grill. Use the chart below for approximate marinating times.

BRINING AND MARINADING GUIDE

FOOD	BRINING TIME	MARINADING TIME
Small seafood and thin fish (less than 1 inch)	about 30 minutes	about 1 hour
Thick fish (more than 1 inch)	about 1 hour	2 to 4 hours
Boneless poultry pieces, chops, and steaks	2 to 3 hours	3 to 6 hours
Bone-in poultry pieces, chops, and steaks	4 to 6 hours	3 to 6 hours
Roasts (less than 3 pounds) and ribs	4 to 6 hours	8 to 12 hours
Large roasts or whole birds (3 to 6 pounds)	6 to 8 hours	12 to 16 hours
Whole large birds (over 6 pounds) such as turkeys	8 hours to overnight	24 hours

Mops

A mop is a flavorful liquid similar to a marinade or brine, but usually with a lower concentration of acid or salt. Mops are typically drizzled on long-cooking tough meats during indirect grilling or grill-smoking (usually once or twice an hour) to moisten the surface and help tenderize the tough meat fibers. Tough meats contain a network of thick elastic connective tissue, which has to be softened in order to make the meat fork-tender and succulent. Moisture dissolves the connective tissue and transforms it into gelatin, the rich-tasting substance that gives pulled pork, sliced beef brisket, and grill-braised veal shanks their incomparably delicious mouthfeel. Mops deliver some flavor, but only in a supporting role.

Glazes and Sauces

When a thin sauce contains enough sugar to melt across the surface of an ingredient on the grill, it forms a lustrous, lacquered glaze. Unfortunately, the sugar that makes a glaze beautiful and delicious also makes it burn easily. To prevent burning, only brush on glazes during the last few minutes of grilling. Keep in mind that the flavors of a glaze don't have enough time to penetrate the interior of an ingredient. Glazes are most effective as flavorful and textural counterpoints used in conjunction with a rub, brine, or marinade.

Sauces, salsas, chutneys, and other accompaniments work best on the table rather than as grilling ingredients. Like glazes, they often have enough sugar to cause scorching or, like salsas and chutneys, they are so chunky that they fall from the grilling food into the fire. To glaze your food with a sauce, puree some of it and brush it on during the last few minutes of grilling. Serve the reserved chunky portion at the table.

The following recipes for rubs, brines, marinades and mops, and sauces are used in recipes throughout this book. But feel free to cast them in new roles with your favorite grilled foods. We have featured these recipes here for that very purpose. We've also noted which main ingredients (beef, pork, duck, vegetables, etc.) we think they go best with. If you feel inspired to pair them with something that escaped our imaginations, by all means, follow your instincts.

Dry Rubs

Espresso Rub

Best with beef, lamb, duck, game meats
MAKES ¾ CUP

2 tablespoons finely ground dark-roast coffee
2 tablespoons smoked paprika
2 tablespoons dark brown sugar
2 tablespoons coarse salt
2 tablespoons ground black pepper
1 tablespoon ground ancho chile
1 tablespoon finely grated lemon zest

Mix everything together. Store in a tightly closed container in a refrigerator for up to 1 week.

Smokin' Rub

Best with pork, chicken, turkey, rich fish, shellfish
MAKES ½ CUP

2 tablespoons smoked salt
2 tablespoons smoked paprika
1 tablespoon brown sugar, light or dark
2 teaspoons ground chipotle chile
2 teaspoons ground toasted cumin
1 teaspoon ground black pepper

Mix everything together. Store in a tightly closed container for up to 1 month.

Mustard Wasabi Rub

Best with shellfish, fish, chicken, turkey, pork, vegetables
MAKES ¾ CUP

2 tablespoons ground mustard
2 tablespoons wasabi powder
2 tablespoons sesame seeds
2 tablespoons coarse salt
2 tablespoons sugar
2 teaspoons garlic powder
2 teaspoons ground ginger
½ teaspoon cayenne pepper
½ teaspoon ground black pepper

Mix everything together. Store in tightly closed container for up to 1 month.

Umami Rub

Best with chicken, turkey, fish, shellfish, pork, vegetables
MAKES ABOUT ⅓ CUP

1 tablespoon powdered dulse

2 teaspoons ground celery seed

2 teaspoons powdered wild mushrooms, preferably porcini

1 teaspoon sugar

1 teaspoon coarse salt

1 teaspoon dried thyme leaves

1 teaspoon dried savory

1 teaspoon dried basil

½ teaspoon ground ginger

½ teaspoon ground black pepper

½ teaspoon onion powder

½ teaspoon garlic powder

½ teaspoon dried rosemary (crushed)

½ teaspoon dried oregano leaves

½ teaspoon rubbed dried sage

¼ teaspoon ground bay leaf

⅛ teaspoon cayenne pepper

Mix everything together. Store in a tightly closed container for up to 1 month.

Mole Rub

Best with beef, lamb, duck, chicken, turkey, pork, shellfish, rich fish
MAKES ABOUT 1 CUP

¼ cup cocoa powder

2 tablespoons ground ancho chile pepper

2 tablespoons ground guajillo chile pepper

2 tablespoons toasted sesame seeds

2 tablespoons coarse salt

2 tablespoons dark brown sugar

2 teaspoons ground cinnamon

1 tablespoon ground chipotle chile pepper

1 teaspoon ground anise seeds

1 teaspoon garlic powder

1 teaspoon onion powder

1 teaspoon ground black pepper

1 teaspoon dried thyme leaves

1 teaspoon ground dried oregano
Pinch of ground clove

Mix everything together. Store in a tightly closed container for up to 1 month.

Moroccan Rub

Best with chicken, turkey, beef, lamb
MAKES ABOUT ⅓ CUP

2 tablespoons dried thyme leaves

1 tablespoon sugar

2 teaspoons coarse salt

2 teaspoons ground cinnamon

2 teaspoons ground coriander

1 teaspoon ground turmeric

1 teaspoon ground dried lemon peel

1 teaspoon ground black pepper

½ teaspoon ground cumin

½ teaspoon ground ginger

½ teaspoon ground mace or nutmeg

Mix everything together. Store in a tightly closed container for up to 1 month.

Creole Rub

Best with pork, chicken, turkey, shellfish, fish
MAKES ABOUT ⅓ CUP

1 tablespoon paprika

1 tablespoon coarse salt

2 teaspoons ground black pepper

2 teaspoons cayenne pepper

2 teaspoons garlic powder

2 teaspoons onion powder

2 teaspoons dried thyme leaves

1 teaspoon dried oregano leaves

1 teaspoon sugar

Mix everything together. Store in a tightly closed container for up to 1 month.

VARIATION

Chile Rub: (Best with pork, chicken.) Add 1 teaspoon ground ancho chile and ¼ teaspoon ground chipotle chile. Replace the dried thyme with an additional 1 teaspoon dried oregano leaves.

Juniper Rub

Best with beef, veal, pork, game birds, game meats, shellfish
MAKES ABOUT ½ CUP

3 tablespoons juniper berries
1 tablespoon whole almonds
1 teaspoon green peppercorns
2 teaspoons dried thyme leaves
1½ teaspoons ground coriander
1½ teaspoons finely grated lemon zest
1½ teaspoons coarse salt
½ teaspoon ground cloves

Put the juniper berries, almonds, and green peppercorns in a spice grinder and grind coarsely. Or put them in a zipper-lock bag, press out the air, and crush the spices in the bag with the bottom of a heavy skillet. Pour into a cup and mix in the thyme, coriander, lemon zest, salt, and cloves. Store in a tightly closed container for up to 1 month.

Smoked Paprika Rub

Best with beef, veal, pork, lamb, chicken, turkey
MAKES ABOUT ¼ CUP

1 tablespoon smoked paprika
1 tablespoon coarse salt
2 teaspoons dark brown sugar
2 teaspoons ground ancho chile
½ teaspoon ground black pepper

Mix everything together. Store in a tightly closed container for up to 1 month.

VARIATIONS

Smoked Paprika–Saffron Rub: (Best with seafood and beef.) Replace the ground ancho chile with 1 teaspoon crushed saffron threads and 1 teaspoon dried oregano leaves.

Smoked Paprika–Rosemary Rub: (Best with chicken, poultry, pork, veal, lamb.) Replace the ground ancho chile with 1 tablespoon chopped fresh rosemary and 1 teaspoon chopped fresh mint. Add ¼ teaspoon garlic powder and ¼ teaspoon ground cloves.

Coriander Rub

Best with chicken, turkey, pork, lamb
MAKES ABOUT ¼ CUP

1 tablespoon ground coriander
2 teaspoons dried thyme leaves
2 teaspoons paprika
1¼ teaspoons coarse salt
1 teaspoon ground turmeric
¾ teaspoon sugar
¾ teaspoon ground black pepper
½ teaspoon ground cinnamon
¼ teaspoon cayenne pepper

Mix everything together. Store in a tightly closed container for up to 1 month.

VARIATION

Coriander-Ginger Rub: (Best with chicken, turkey, shellfish, fish.) Replace the turmeric with ½ teaspoon ground mustard, ½ teaspoon ground ginger, and ¼ teaspoon ground cloves.

Dukkah

An Egyptian spice and nut blend. Dukkah often features toasted hazelnuts and sesame seeds along with cumin and coriander. We add dried thyme for subtle pine and citrus aromas. Best with chicken, shellfish, fish, vegetables.
MAKES ABOUT ½ CUP

2 tablespoons blanched hazelnuts (skins removed)
¼ cup sesame seeds
2 tablespoons coriander seeds
1 tablespoon cumin seeds
½ teaspoon dried thyme leaves
¼ teaspoon coarse salt
¼ teaspoon black peppercorns

Toast the hazelnuts and sesame, coriander, and cumin seeds in a hot, dry skillet until fragrant, 2 to 3 minutes, shaking the pan often. Let cool and then transfer to a clean spice mill or coffee grinder (or mortar and pestle). Add the thyme, salt, and peppercorns and grind briefly, in batches if necessary, until the mixture is half fine and half coarse. Store in a tightly closed container for up to 1 month.

Bedouin Rub

A fragrant blend that includes spices (such as caraway and cardamom) commonly used among the Arabic desert tribes known as Bedouins. Best with chicken, turkey, lamb, shellfish.

MAKES ABOUT 2 TABLESPOONS

2 teaspoons coarsely ground black pepper

1½ teaspoons caraway seeds

1 teaspoon ground cardamom

½ teaspoon ground turmeric

1 teaspoon coarse salt

1 teaspoon light brown sugar

Mix everything together. Store in a tightly closed container for up to 1 month.

Orange-Cumin Rub

Best with chicken, turkey, shellfish, fish

MAKES ABOUT ¼ CUP

1 tablespoon coarse salt

1 tablespoon paprika

1 tablespoon ground dried orange peel

2 teaspoons ground cumin

1 teaspoon ground chipotle chile

½ teaspoon ground black pepper

½ teaspoon sugar

Mix everything together. Store in a tightly closed container for up to 1 month.

VARIATIONS

Cumin-Oregano Rub: (Best with pork, chicken, turkey.) Omit the orange peel and replace the chipotle chile with 2 teaspoons dried oregano leaves.

Cumin-Thyme Rub: (Best with beef, veal, pork, chicken, turkey, shellfish, fish.) Omit the orange peel and replace the chipotle chile with 2 teaspoons dried thyme leaves. Add ½ teaspoon ground coriander and ½ teaspoon ground cinnamon.

Coarse Cumin Rub: (Best with beef, veal, pork, chicken, turkey, game meats.) Replace the ground cumin with 1 tablespoon whole cumin seeds. Replace the orange peel and chipotle chile with 1 teaspoon whole coriander seeds and 1 teaspoon whole cardamom seeds (removed from the green pods).

Toasted Cumin Rub

Best with beef, pork, chicken, turkey, lamb, game meats

MAKES ABOUT ¼ CUP

1 tablespoon cumin seeds

1 teaspoon coriander seeds

1 teaspoon black peppercorns

1 tablespoon coarse salt or smoked salt

1 tablespoon smoked paprika

½ to 1 teaspoon ground chipotle chile

½ teaspoon sugar

Toast the cumin, coriander, and peppercorns in a dry skillet over medium heat until fragrant, 3 to 4 minutes, and then grind in a spice grinder or with a mortar and pestle. Combine with the salt, smoked paprika, chipotle, and sugar. Store in a tightly closed container for up to 1 month.

Poultry Rub

Best with chicken, turkey, pork

MAKES ½ CUP

2 tablespoons dark brown sugar

2 tablespoons coarse salt

1 tablespoon rubbed dried sage

1 tablespoon dried thyme leaves

2 teaspoons dried marjoram

2 teaspoons dried rosemary (crushed)

2 teaspoons garlic powder

1 teaspoon ground ginger

1 teaspoon ground black pepper

1 teaspoon paprika

½ teaspoon grated nutmeg

Mix everything together. Store in a tightly closed container for up to 1 month.

Seven Pepper Rub

Best with beef, pork, lamb, duck, game meats

MAKES ABOUT ½ CUP

2 tablespoons paprika

2 tablespoons cracked black peppercorns

1 tablespoon cracked green peppercorns

2 teaspoons ground white pepper

2 teaspoons ground ancho pepper

continued →

1 teaspoon ground chipotle pepper

¼ teaspoon cayenne pepper

2 tablespoons coarse salt

2 teaspoons sugar

Mix everything together. Store in tightly closed container for up to 1 month.

Steak House Rub

Best with beef and pork

MAKES ABOUT ½ CUP

2 tablespoons paprika

2 tablespoons cracked black peppercorns

2 teaspoons ground ancho pepper

2 tablespoons coarse salt

2 teaspoons sugar

1 teaspoon ground coriander

1 teaspoon dried thyme leaves

½ teaspoon garlic powder

½ teaspoon onion powder

Mix everything together. Store in a tightly closed container for up to 1 month.

Garam Masala Rub

Best with chicken, turkey, beef, lamb, shellfish, vegetables

MAKES ABOUT ¼ CUP

2 teaspoons cumin seeds

2 teaspoons coriander seeds

2 teaspoons black peppercorns

2 teaspoons cardamom seeds
(removed from about 20 green pods)

1½ teaspoons whole cloves

½ teaspoon fennel seeds

Two 3-inch cinnamon sticks, broken into pieces with a hammer

1 bay leaf

1 teaspoon coarse salt

½ teaspoon sugar

Heat all the spices in a dry medium skillet over medium-high heat until fragrant and toasted, 2 to 3 minutes. Transfer to a plate and cool for 5 minutes. Grind the toasted spices in a spice grinder until fairly fine, like cornmeal. Mix in the salt and sugar. Store in an airtight container for up to 1 month.

Cardamom-Ginger Rub

Best with pork, game meats, lamb, duck, poultry.

MAKES ABOUT ¼ CUP

1 tablespoon ground cardamom

1 tablespoon ground ginger

1 teaspoon ground allspice

1 tablespoon coarse salt

1 tablespoon coarsely ground black pepper

Mix everything together. Store in a tightly closed container for up to 1 month.

Za'atar

Our version of this Middle Eastern spice and herb rub includes aromatic (and perfectly safe) ground sumac berries along with the usual sesame seeds and salt. Look for whole or ground red sumac berries in Middle Eastern markets. Best with chicken, turkey, shellfish, fish, bread.

MAKES ABOUT ¼ CUP

2 tablespoons toasted sesame seeds

2 tablespoons dried thyme leaves

2 teaspoons ground sumac

½ teaspoon coarse salt

Grind the ingredients coarsely with a mortar and pestle or a spice grinder. Store in a tightly closed container for up to 1 month.

Lebanese Rub

Best with beef, lamb, pork, veal, turkey, vegetables

MAKES ABOUT ½ CUP

1 tablespoon ground allspice

1 tablespoon ground cumin

1 tablespoon ground coriander

1 tablespoon grated nutmeg

1 tablespoon ground black pepper

1 tablespoon coarse salt

1½ teaspoons ground sage

1½ teaspoons ground cloves

1½ teaspoons cayenne pepper

1½ teaspoons ground cinnamon

1½ teaspoons ground sumac

Mix everything together. Store in a tightly closed container for up to 1 month.

VARIATION

Silk Road Spice Rub: (Best with chicken, turkey, shellfish, fish.) Omit sage and sumac. Replace with 1 tablespoon ground ginger.

Coriander-Mustard Rub

Best with pork, chicken, turkey
MAKES ABOUT ⅓ CUP

2 tablespoons paprika
2 tablespoons ground coriander
2 tablespoons ground mustard
1 tablespoon ground black pepper
2 teaspoons coarse salt

Mix everything together. Store in a tightly closed container for up to 1 month.

VARIATION

Rosemary-Coriander Rub: (Best with chicken, turkey, pork, lamb, game birds, game meat.) Add 1 tablespoon chopped fresh rosemary and 1 teaspoon ground cumin.

Jamaican Jerk Rub

Best with beef, pork, veal, chicken, turkey
MAKES ABOUT ¼ CUP

1 tablespoon dried thyme leaves
1 tablespoon brown sugar, preferably dark
1½ teaspoons coarse salt
1 teaspoon ground black pepper
1 teaspoon onion powder
½ teaspoon garlic powder
½ teaspoon ground ginger
½ teaspoon ground hot chile powder
½ teaspoon ground allspice
¼ teaspoon ground cinnamon
¼ teaspoon grated nutmeg
½ teaspoon ground coriander

Mix everything together. Store in a tightly closed container for up to 1 month.

Jamaican Curry Powder

Best with veal, pork, chicken, turkey, shellfish, fish
MAKES ABOUT ⅓ CUP

1 tablespoon coriander seeds
1 tablespoon black peppercorns
1 tablespoon fenugreek seeds
1 tablespoon cumin seeds
1 tablespoon brown mustard seeds
2 teaspoons allspice berries
1 teaspoon ground ginger
1 teaspoon ground turmeric

Toast the coriander, peppercorns, fenugreek, cumin, mustard, and allspice in a dry skillet over medium heat until fragrant, 4 to 5 minutes, shaking the pan often. Let cool, and then grind in a spice mill or clean coffee grinder. Stir in the ginger and turmeric. Mix everything together. Store in a tightly closed container for up to 1 month.

Szechuan Anise Rub

Best with beef, lamb, duck, goose, game meats
MAKES ABOUT ¼ CUP

1 tablespoon star anise pieces (pod and seeds)
1½ teaspoons yellow or brown mustard seeds
1 teaspoon Szechuan peppercorns
½ teaspoon anise seeds
¼ teaspoon black peppercorns
¼ teaspoon whole cloves
1 tablespoon dark brown sugar
2 teaspoons coarse salt

Grind the star anise, mustard seeds, Szechuan peppercorns, anise seeds, black peppercorns, and cloves in a spice mill or coffee grinder until finely ground. Combine with the brown sugar and salt. Store in a tightly closed container for up to 1 month.

Smoky Coconut Rub

Best with pork, chicken, turkey, shellfish, fish, vegetables
MAKES ABOUT 1¼ CUPS

1 tablespoon smoked salt
1 tablespoon smoked paprika
1 tablespoon brown sugar, light or dark
¼ to ½ teaspoon ground chipotle chile

continued ➔

½ teaspoon ground coriander

¼ teaspoon ground cinnamon

¼ teaspoon ground ginger

¼ teaspoon ground black pepper, preferably smoked

1 cup unsweetened shredded coconut

Mix everything together. Store in a tightly closed container for up to 1 month.

Shellfish Seasoning

Best with shellfish

MAKES ABOUT ¼ CUP

2 tablespoons celery salt

2 teaspoons ground bay leaf

1 teaspoon ground mustard

1 teaspoon paprika

1 teaspoon ground black pepper

¼ teaspoon ground allspice

¼ teaspoon ground cloves

¼ teaspoon ground ginger

¼ teaspoon ground mace

¼ teaspoon ground cayenne pepper

Pinch of ground cardamom

Pinch of ground cinnamon

Mix everything together. Store in a tightly closed container for up to 1 month.

Fresh Rubs and Pastes

Rosemary-Anise Rub

Best with beef, lamb, game meats, game birds, chicken

MAKES ABOUT ¼ CUP

2 garlic cloves, minced

2 tablespoons chopped fresh rosemary

1½ teaspoons coarse salt

1 teaspoon anise seeds

½ teaspoon ground black pepper

Mix everything together. Store in a tightly closed container in the refrigerator for up to 3 days.

VARIATION

Forest Rub: (Best with game meats, pork, lamb.) Replace the anise seeds with 2 juniper berries, ground in a clean spice mill or coffee grinder.

Fresh Herb Rub

Best with chicken, turkey, shellfish, fish, vegetables, breads

MAKES ABOUT ½ CUP

2 tablespoons chopped fresh flat-leaf parsley

2 tablespoons chopped fresh rosemary

2 tablespoons chopped fresh thyme

2 tablespoons chopped fresh oregano

2 garlic cloves, minced

1 teaspoon coarse salt

½ teaspoon ground black pepper

Mix everything together. Alternatively, if you have a mini-chopper, combine the fresh herb leaves and whole garlic cloves in it and chop all at once. Mix in the salt and pepper. Store in a tightly closed container in the refrigerator for up to 3 days.

VARIATIONS

Dill-Tarragon Rub: (Best with shellfish, fish.) Replace the rosemary with 1 tablespoon chopped fresh dill and the thyme with 1 tablespoon chopped fresh tarragon. Reduce the oregano to 1 tablespoon.

Provençal Rub: (Best with lamb and duck.) Replace 1 tablespoon of the oregano with 2 teaspoons ground fennel seeds and 1 teaspoon dried lavender.

Grill-Roasted Garlic

Good with anything except sweets
MAKES ABOUT ¼ CUP

1 small garlic bulb
1 teaspoon olive oil

Light a grill for direct medium heat, about 375°F (see page 12). Cut the pointed end off the garlic bulb, exposing most of the cloves. Put the garlic bulb, cut-side up, on a 6-inch square of aluminum foil, drizzle with the olive oil, and wrap the foil around the garlic to enclose it. Grill directly over the heat until the cloves are soft, about 30 minutes.

Unwrap the garlic bulb and let cool. Cut the entire bulb in half through its equator, then squeeze the garlic from the skin and mash with a fork. Wrap tightly and store in the refrigerator for up to 4 days.

Zhug

The preferred chile paste in Yemen. Zhug (zoog) adds fresh, warming, and pungent aromas to everything from fish and chicken to pork and vegetables. Think of it as spiced hot sauce mixed with herbal pesto. Best with veal, pork, chicken, turkey, shellfish, fish, vegetables.

MAKES ABOUT 1½ CUPS

3 ounces chile peppers (about 8 jalapeños or 12 serranos), stemmed, seeded, and coarsely chopped
½ cup packed cilantro leaves and small stems
½ cup packed flat-leaf parsley leaves and small stems
¾ teaspoon ground black pepper
¾ teaspoon ground cumin
¾ teaspoon ground caraway seeds
½ teaspoon ground cardamom
½ teaspoon coarse salt
3 garlic cloves
Juice of ½ lemon
¼ cup olive oil, plus more as needed

Combine all of the ingredients in a food processor. Add 1 or 2 more tablespoons oil if necessary to create a loose paste similar to the texture of pesto. Store in a tightly closed container in the refrigerator for up to 2 weeks.

Brines

Espresso Brine

Best with beef, lamb, duck, goose, game meats, game birds
MAKES 3 CUPS

2 cups brewed dark-roast coffee
⅓ cup apple cider vinegar
⅓ cup orange juice
⅓ cup coffee-flavored liqueur
¼ cup Espresso Rub (page 26)

Mix everything together and use as directed in a recipe.

Smokin' Brine

Best with beef, pork, chicken, turkey, duck, goose, game meats, game birds, shellfish, fish
MAKES 3 CUPS

2 cups beer, or ½ cup vodka and 1½ cups water
1 tablespoon liquid smoke
3 tablespoons coarse salt
3 tablespoons sugar
1 cup water

Mix everything together and use as directed in a recipe.

VARIATION

Bourbon Brine: (Best with pork, game meats.) Use bourbon instead of vodka, dark brown sugar for the sugar, and smoked salt for half the salt.

Chile Brine

Best with beef, veal, pork, chicken, turkey
MAKES 3 CUPS

2 cups beer and 1 cup water, or 1 cup rum and 2 cups water
3 tablespoons coarse salt
2 tablespoons brown sugar, light or dark
3 tablespoons chile powder
½ teaspoon finely chopped habanero or Scotch bonnet chile

Mix everything together and use as directed in a recipe.

VARIATION

Ginger Sake Brine: (Best with shellfish and fish.) Substitute sake for rum, granulated sugar for brown sugar, and grated fresh ginger for chile powder.

Riesling Brine

Best with veal, pork, chicken, turkey, shellfish, fish
MAKES ABOUT 1½ CUPS

1 cup mildly sweet Riesling, such as Spätlese or Auslese
1 tablespoon walnut oil
2 tablespoons fresh rosemary leaves (about 3 sprigs), chopped
1 tablespoon anise seeds, crushed
1 tablespoon chopped shallot (about 2 large shallots)
2 teaspoons cracked black pepper
1 tablespoon coarse salt
1 tablespoon white wine vinegar
1 bay leaf, crushed
1 tablespoon sugar

Mix everything together and use as directed in a recipe.

> ### KNOW-HOW: CRUSHING SPICES
>
> Spread out a small amount (1 or 2 tablespoons) of whole spices on a sturdy work surface in a single layer. Cover with a large flat-bladed knife or a small skillet. Press down on the flat surface, moving it back and forth slightly until you hear the spices crack beneath the pressure.

Pineapple Brine

Best with pork, chicken, turkey, shellfish, fish
MAKES ABOUT 2 CUPS

1½ cups pineapple juice
½ cup rum or vodka
2 tablespoons coarse salt
1 tablespoon smoked paprika

Mix everything together and use as directed in a recipe.

Fennel Brine

Best with chicken, turkey, veal, pork, shellfish, fish, vegetables
MAKES ABOUT 2¼ CUPS

2 tablespoons coarse salt
1 tablespoon sugar
2 tablespoon fennel seed, crushed
1 lemon, thinly sliced
¼ cup vodka
1¾ cups cold water

Mix everything together and use as directed in a recipe.

VARIATIONS

Tomato-Basil Brine: (Best with pork, beef, rich fish.) Substitute basil for fennel seeds and add 1 tablespoon tomato paste.

Cardamom Brine: (Best with shellfish, fish.) Substitute 2 tablespoons crushed cardamom seeds for the fennel and add 1 teaspoon dried thyme leaves.

Lemon-Oregano Brine

Best with beef, veal, chicken, turkey, pork
MAKES ABOUT 2½ CUPS

1 cup hot water
3 tablespoons coarse salt
2 tablespoons sugar
1 cup cold water
Zest and juice of 2 lemons
¼ cup chopped fresh oregano
2 tablespoons chopped fresh mint
3 garlic cloves, minced
1½ teaspoons ground cumin
1 teaspoon ground black pepper

Mix together the hot water, salt, and sugar in a medium bowl until the salt and sugar are dissolved. Add the cold water and remaining ingredients. Use as directed in a recipe.

VARIATIONS

Lemon-Rosemary Brine: (Best with lamb, duck, rich fish.) Use the juice of only 1 lemon and eliminate the zest. Replace the oregano and mint with 2 tablespoons chopped fresh rosemary. Omit the cumin, and add 1 tablespoon Pernod or anisette.

Lemon–Black Pepper Brine: (Best with shellfish and fish.) Omit the sugar. Replace the cold water with 1 cup limoncello or 1 cup vodka mixed with 2 tablespoons sugar. Omit the oregano, mint, and cumin. For the black pepper, use 2 tablespoons coarsely ground black pepper.

Lime-Mint Brine: (Best with chicken, turkey, veal, lamb.) Replace the lemons with the zest and juice of 3 limes. Swap the oregano and mint for ¼ cup chopped fresh mint, and add 3 tablespoons chopped fresh rosemary. Omit the cumin and garlic.

Lime-Cilantro Brine: (Best with pork.) Replace the lemons with the zest and juice of 3 limes. Replace the oregano and mint with ¼ cup chopped fresh cilantro.

Lemon-Parsley Brine: (Best with veal, shellfish, fish.) Replace the oregano with parsley.

Mole Brine

Best with turkey, duck, game meats
MAKES ABOUT 3½ CUPS

One 12-ounce bottle beer
1½ cups water
3 tablespoons Mole Rub (page 27)
2 tablespoons coarse salt
¼ cup ketchup

Mix everything together and use as directed in a recipe.

Apple-Sage Brine

Best with chicken, turkey, duck, game meats
MAKES ABOUT 4 CUPS

2 tablespoons coarse salt
2 tablespoons brown sugar, light or dark
2 tablespoons Poultry Rub (page 29)

2 tablespoons rubbed dried sage
3½ cups apple cider
½ cup vodka

Mix everything together and use as directed in a recipe.

VARIATIONS

Apple-Thyme Brine: (Best with chicken, turkey, duck, game meats.) Replace the sage with 2 tablespoons dried thyme leaves.

Sweet Garlic Brine: (Best with chicken, turkey, pork, duck, game meats.) Replace the sage with 6 cloves of garlic, minced.

Molasses Beer Brine

Best with pork, duck, game meats
MAKES ABOUT 2½ CUPS

3 tablespoons coarse salt
¼ cup molasses
1½ cups dark beer
¾ cup water

Mix everything together and use as directed in a recipe.

Orange-Anise Brine

Best with veal, pork, chicken, duck, goose, shellfish, fish
MAKES ABOUT 2 CUPS

2 cups orange juice
2 tablespoons sugar
3 tablespoons coarse salt
½ teaspoon coarsely ground black pepper
2 tablespoons anise seeds

Mix everything together and use as directed in a recipe.

Green Tea Brine

Best with veal, chicken, shellfish, fish
MAKES ABOUT 2 CUPS

1 cup hot brewed green tea
2 tablespoons honey
2 tablespoons coarse salt

continued ➔

½ cup sake

½ cup cold water

1 teaspoon green hot pepper sauce, such as Tabasco's jalapeño

Combine the green tea, honey, and salt in a medium bowl and stir until the honey and salt dissolve. Add the sake, cold water, and green hot sauce. Use as directed in a recipe.

Poultry Brine

Best with chicken and turkey

MAKES ABOUT 3¼ CUPS

3 cups water

3 tablespoons coarse salt

2 tablespoons Poultry Rub (page 29) or Umami Rub (page 27)

2 tablespoons granulated sugar

Mix everything together and use as directed in a recipe.

Coriander Brine

Best with veal, pork, chicken, turkey, shellfish, fish

MAKES ABOUT 2¼ CUPS

¼ cup coriander seeds

2 tablespoons coarse salt

1 teaspoon coarsely ground black pepper

1 tablespoon brown sugar, light or dark

Finely grated zest and juice of 1 lime

2 tablespoons chopped fresh cilantro

¼ cup tequila

1½ cups water

Heat a small skillet over high heat until smoking hot. Remove from the heat and add the coriander seeds; stir until aromatic and lightly toasted, about 30 seconds. Grind in a spice grinder or minichopper. Transfer to a medium bowl and mix in the remaining ingredients. Stir until the salt and sugar dissolve. Use as directed in a recipe.

Juniper Brine

Best with veal, pork, duck, game meats

MAKES ABOUT 1 CUP

2 tablespoons juniper berries, crushed

1 small fresh chile pepper, finely chopped

1 tablespoon coarse salt

2 tablespoons maple syrup

1 tablespoon apple cider vinegar

1 cup water

¼ cup gin

Mix everything together and use as directed in a recipe.

Marinades & a Mop

Honey Marinade

Best with veal, chicken, game birds

MAKES ½ CUP

¼ cup honey

¼ cup apple cider vinegar

2 teaspoons coarse salt

1 teaspoon ground black pepper

1 teaspoon dried thyme leaves

Mix everything together and use as directed in a recipe.

Rosemary Red Wine Marinade

Best with beef, lamb, game meats

MAKES ABOUT 1 CUP

1 cup full-bodied red wine, such as cabernet sauvignon

1 tablespoon red wine vinegar

1 tablespoon olive oil

1 tablespoon chopped fresh rosemary

1 garlic clove, minced

¼ teaspoon coarse salt

⅛ teaspoon ground black pepper

Mix everything together and use as directed in a recipe.

VARIATION

Port Wine Marinade: (Best with lamb, duck, game meats.) Substitute port for the red wine, and increase the quantity of salt to 1 tablespoon.

Buttermilk Marinade

Best with veal, lamb, chicken, turkey, shellfish, fish
MAKES ABOUT 1 CUP

¾ cup buttermilk

2 tablespoons peanut oil or canola oil

2 garlic cloves, minced

2 teaspoons coarse salt

1 teaspoon sugar

1 teaspoon chopped fresh oregano

½ teaspoon ground black pepper

¼ teaspoon cayenne pepper

Mix everything together and use as directed in a recipe.

Adobo Marinade

Best with beef, veal, pork, lamb, poultry
MAKES ABOUT 1½ CUPS

Juice of 1 lemon

Juice of 1 lime

¼ cup orange juice

¼ cup tomato sauce

¼ cup red wine

3 tablespoons olive oil

2 tablespoons mild hot pepper sauce, such as Frank's

2 garlic cloves, minced

2 teaspoons smoked paprika

1 teaspoon coarse salt

Mix everything together and use as directed in a recipe.

Tandoori Yogurt Marinade

Best with veal, chicken, turkey, lamb, vegetables
MAKES ABOUT 1 CUP

¾ cup (6 ounces) plain yogurt

2 tablespoons fresh lemon juice

1 tablespoon minced fresh ginger

2 large garlic cloves, minced

1 tablespoon Garam Masala Rub (page 30)

½ teaspoon ground turmeric

1 tablespoon paprika

1 tablespoon chopped fresh cilantro

1 tablespoon minced fresh onion

½ tsp red food coloring (optional)

Mix everything together and use as directed in a recipe.

Salsa-Beer Marinade

Best with beef, pork, chicken, turkey
MAKES ABOUT 3 CUPS

1½ cups beer (any style)

1 cup salsa (any heat level)

¼ cup apple cider vinegar

2 tablespoons molasses

2 tablespoons Worcestershire sauce

2 teaspoons coarse salt

Mix everything together and use as directed in a recipe.

Korean Barbecue Marinade

Best with beef, pork, lamb, chicken
MAKES ABOUT 1½ CUPS

1 small onion, coarsely chopped

1 medium ripe Asian pear or pear, cored, peeled, and coarsely chopped

6 garlic cloves, coarsely chopped

1 tablespoon chopped fresh ginger

½ cup soy sauce

¼ cup light brown sugar

2 tablespoons honey

2 tablespoons toasted sesame oil

3 scallions (green and white parts), trimmed and thinly sliced

2 tablespoons sake or dry sherry

¼ teaspoon crushed red pepper (optional)

Puree everything in a food processor until relatively smooth. Use as directed in a recipe.

Smoky Coconut Marinade

Best with veal, pork, chicken, turkey, shellfish, fish
MAKES ABOUT 1½ CUPS

1 cup coconut milk
¼ cup coconut rum, such as Malibu
Finely grated zest and juice of 1 lime
1 teaspoon liquid smoke
1 tablespoon chopped fresh cilantro
2 garlic cloves, minced
1 tablespoon minced fresh ginger

Mix everything together and use as directed in a recipe.

VARIATION

Coconut-Thyme Marinade: (Best with veal, pork, chicken, turkey, shellfish, fish.) Omit the liquid smoke and replace the cilantro with fresh thyme.

Lemon Herb Marinade

Best with veal, chicken, turkey, shellfish, fish
MAKES ABOUT 1½ CUPS

Grated zest of 1 lemon
Juice of 2 lemons
½ cup dry white wine
¾ cup olive oil
2 tablespoons Dill-Tarragon Rub (page 32)

Mix everything together and use as directed in a recipe.

Lemon Soy Marinade

Best with fish, shellfish, chicken, beef, pork
MAKES ABOUT 1 CUP

½ cup soy sauce
Grated zest and juice of 1 lemon
2 tablespoons peanut or canola oil
1 tablespoon honey
3 garlic cloves, minced
1 tablespoon minced fresh ginger
2 teaspoons toasted sesame oil
3 scallions (green and white parts), trimmed and chopped

Mix everything together and use as directed in a recipe.

VARIATION

Sweet Mirin Marinade: (Best with fish, shellfish, chicken, beef, pork.) Reduce the soy sauce to ¼ cup. Replace the lemon zest and lemon juice with ¼ cup mirin. Increase the honey to 2 tablespoons.

Sicilian Citrus Marinade

Best with veal, lamb, chicken, turkey, shellfish, fish
MAKES ABOUT 1 CUP

Grated zest and juice of ½ orange
Grated zest and juice of ½ lemon
3 tablespoons red wine vinegar
1 tablespoon tomato juice
½ cup olive oil
1 tablespoon honey
2 garlic cloves, minced
2 canned anchovy fillets, mashed
¼ teaspoon red pepper flakes
1 tablespoon chopped fresh mint

Put the orange zest and juice, lemon zest and juice, red wine vinegar, and tomato juice in a bowl. Whisk in the oil in a thin, steady stream until incorporated. Whisk in the honey, garlic, mashed anchovy, red pepper flakes, and mint. Use as directed in a recipe.

Applejack Mop

Best with beef, pork, game meats
MAKES ABOUT 2⅓ CUPS

¾ cup applejack or Calvados
¾ cup apple cider
¼ cup apple cider vinegar
¼ cup orange juice
¼ cup vegetable oil
2 tablespoons Worcestershire sauce

Mix everything together. Store in a tightly closed container in the refrigerator for up to 1 month.

VARIATION

Bourbon-Cider Mop: (Best with pork and game meat.) Replace the applejack with ¾ cup bourbon.

Sauces

Easy Barbecue Sauce

All-purpose
MAKES ABOUT 2 CUPS

1½ cups ketchup
3 tablespoons unsalted butter
2 tablespoons molasses
2 tablespoons dark brown sugar
2 tablespoons cider vinegar
1 tablespoon yellow mustard
1 tablespoon Worcestershire sauce
1½ teaspoons smoked paprika
1 teaspoon coarse salt
½ teaspoon garlic powder
½ teaspoon onion powder
¼ teaspoon ground black pepper

Combine everything in a medium saucepan and bring to a boil over high heat. Reduce the heat to medium and simmer until slightly thickened, about 20 minutes. Store in a tightly closed container in the refrigerator for up to 1 month.

VARIATIONS

Bourbon Barbecue Sauce: (Best with pork.) Add ½ cup good-quality bourbon.

Applejack Barbecue Sauce: (Best with beef, turkey, chicken.) Add ½ cup applejack or Calvados.

Steak House Barbecue Sauce: (Best with beef.) Add ¾ cup steak sauce, such as A1.

Espresso Grilling Sauce

Best with beef, lamb, duck, game meats
MAKES ABOUT 2⅓ CUPS

1 cup brewed dark-roast coffee
1 cup ketchup
¼ cup dark brown mustard
⅓ cup honey
2 tablespoons citrus juice (lemon, orange, or lime)
2 tablespoons hot pepper sauce
2 teaspoons ground black pepper
2 teaspoons coarse salt

Mix everything together in a medium saucepan. Bring to a boil, lower the heat, and simmer until slightly thickened, about 5 minutes. Store in a tightly closed container for up to 1 month.

Guinness BBQ Sauce

Best with beef, pork, lamb, game meats
MAKES ABOUT 2½ CUPS

2 cups Guinness ale
1 star anise (optional)
1 cup ketchup
¼ cup dark brown mustard
⅓ cup honey
2 tablespoons hot pepper sauce
2 teaspoons coarse salt
2 teaspoons ground black pepper

Boil the Guinness in a saucepan with the star anise (if using) over high heat until reduced by half. Add the remaining ingredients and simmer for 5 minutes, or until thick. Cool and remove the star anise. Store in a tightly closed container in the refrigerator for up to 1 week.

Mole BBQ Sauce

Best with beef, lamb, pork, turkey, duck, game meats
MAKES ABOUT 1½ CUPS

1½ cups chicken broth
1 tablespoon Mole Rub (page 27)
¼ cup golden raisins, finely chopped
½ ounce bittersweet chocolate, finely chopped
1 tablespoon ketchup
1 teaspoon balsamic vinegar
½ teaspoon dried thyme leaves
Coarse salt and ground black pepper

Combine the chicken broth, mole rub, raisins, chocolate, ketchup, vinegar, and thyme in a small saucepan. Bring to a boil, stirring constantly. Simmer until slightly thickened, about 5 minutes. Season with salt and pepper. Store in a tightly closed container in the refrigerator for up to 2 weeks.

Tamarind–Peanut Butter Sauce

Best with chicken, turkey, pork, shellfish, fish, veal
MAKES ABOUT 2¼ CUPS

1¾ cups coconut milk
½ cup peanut butter
1 tablespoon tamarind paste concentrate
1 tablespoon ketchup
2 teaspoons canola oil
2 teaspoons sugar
1 to 2 teaspoons Asian chile paste
2 garlic cloves, minced
2 tablespoons chopped fresh cilantro

Blend the coconut milk, peanut butter, tamarind paste, ketchup, oil, sugar, and chile paste in a blender or food processor. Pour into a bowl and stir in the garlic and cilantro. Store in a tightly closed container in the refrigerator for up to 1 week.

Macadamia Satay Sauce

Best with fish, shellfish, chicken, turkey
MAKES ABOUT 1 CUP

½ cup macadamia nuts
½ cup coconut milk
2 tablespoons fresh lime juice
1 teaspoon sugar
2 teaspoons Asian chile paste
2 garlic cloves, coarsely chopped
2 tablespoons chopped fresh cilantro
Coarse salt and ground black pepper

Grind the macadamia nuts in a food processor until finely chopped. Add the coconut milk, lime juice, sugar, chile paste, and garlic and process into a smooth sauce with the consistency of heavy cream. Stir in the cilantro and season with salt and pepper. Store in a tightly closed container in the refrigerator for up to 1 week.

Herbed Tzatziki

Best with fish, shellfish, chicken, turkey
MAKES ABOUT 1¾ CUPS

1 large cucumber, seeded, peel left on
2 teaspoons coarse salt
1 cup Greek yogurt or drained yogurt
½ cup sour cream
1 tablespoon extra-virgin olive oil
1 tablespoon white wine vinegar
1 large clove garlic, crushed or pressed
1 teaspoon chopped fresh dill
1 teaspoon chopped fresh oregano
1 teaspoon chopped fresh flat-leaf parsley
1 teaspoon chopped fresh mint
Pinch of ground black pepper

Grate the cucumber and place in a colander. Sprinkle with the salt, toss gently, and let stand over a plate or bowl for 1 hour. Press on the cucumber to extract as much liquid as possible, and then combine with the yogurt in a small bowl. Stir in the remaining ingredients. Refrigerate for up to 2 days.

VARIATION

Cucumber-Mint Yogurt: (Best with fish, shellfish, chicken, turkey.) Double the cucumber, eliminate the sour cream, replace the vinegar with 2 tablespoons lemon juice, and substitute 3 tablespoons chopped fresh mint for the dill, oregano, parsley, and mint.

Ginger Yogurt Dip

Best with fish, shellfish, chicken, turkey, lamb
MAKES ABOUT 1¼ CUPS

1 cup vanilla yogurt
¼ cup crème fraîche, or 2 tablespoons sour cream plus 2 tablespoons heavy cream
2 teaspoons minced crystallized ginger
¼ teaspoon ground ginger
⅛ teaspoon ground cinnamon
⅛ teaspoon grated nutmeg
Pinch of coarse salt

Mix the ingredients together. Store in a tightly closed container in the refrigerator for up to 3 days.

Preserved Lemon Yogurt

Best with fish, shellfish, chicken, turkey, lamb
MAKES 2 CUPS

2 preserved lemons, coarsely chopped, seeds discarded (see Know-How on page 149)
½ cup fresh cilantro leaves and stems

4 garlic cloves, coarsely chopped

¼ cup extra-virgin olive oil

1 cup whole-milk yogurt

Process the lemons, cilantro, and garlic in a food processor until finely chopped. Mix in the olive oil and yogurt. Refrigerate in a tightly closed container for up to 2 weeks.

VARIATION

Preserved Lemon Relish: (Best with fish, shellfish, chicken, turkey.) Omit the yogurt. Replace the garlic with 2 tablespoons chopped shallots. For the herbs, replace ¼ cup of the cilantro with ¼ cup parsley, dill, or basil, or a combination. Add a pinch of ground black pepper.

Preserved Lime Yogurt

Best with fish, shellfish, chicken, turkey, veal

MAKES ABOUT 1¼ CUPS

1 cup plain yogurt, preferably Greek

2 tablespoons minced preserved lime (see note)

2 tablespoons finely chopped fresh mint

2 tablespoons olive oil

1 tablespoon minced onion

1 teaspoon fresh lime juice

⅛ teaspoon ground black pepper

Pinch of sugar

Mix the ingredients together and store in a tightly closed container in the refrigerator for at least 1 hour or up to 2 days.

NOTE: To make preserved limes, follow the Know-How on page 149 for preserving lemons. Substitute 5 limes for the lemons and pack them in a wide-mouth pint-size jar.

Orange Vinaigrette

Best with fish, shellfish, chicken, turkey, vegetables

MAKES ABOUT ¾ CUP

2 tablespoons raspberry vinegar or red wine vinegar

¼ cup walnut oil or extra-virgin olive oil

½ cup orange marmalade

½ teaspoon Dijon mustard

½ garlic clove, minced

½ teaspoon coarse salt

¼ teaspoon ground black pepper

1 tablespoon chopped fresh basil

Put the vinegar in a bowl and whisk in the walnut oil in a thin, steady stream until incorporated. Whisk in the remaining ingredients. Store in the refrigerator in a tightly sealed container for up to 2 weeks.

VARIATIONS

Orange-Lime Vinaigrette: (Best with fish, shellfish, chicken, turkey.) Replace 1 tablespoon of the raspberry vinegar with 1 tablespoon fresh lime juice. Replace the basil with 2 teaspoons chopped fresh cilantro and 2 teaspoons chopped fresh mint.

Red Currant Vinaigrette: (Best with fish, shellfish, chicken, turkey, game meats.) Replace the raspberry vinegar with sherry vinegar. Replace the marmalade with red currant preserves.

Cranberry Mustard Vinaigrette: (Best with poultry, pork, and cheese.) Replace the marmalade with whole-berry cranberry sauce, increase the mustard to 1 teaspoon, and replace the basil with rosemary leaves.

Jalapeño-Lime Vinaigrette: (Best with fish, shellfish, chicken, turkey.) Replace the raspberry vinegar with lime juice and the walnut oil with pumpkin seed oil, avocado oil, or fruity olive oil. Replace the marmalade with ⅓ cup jalapeño jelly and the basil with cilantro or mint or a combination.

Red Wine Vinaigrette

Best with beef, veal, lamb, game meats

MAKES ABOUT ¾ CUP

1⅓ cups fruity red wine, such as Syrah or Merlot

3 tablespoon balsamic vinegar

¼ cup extra-virgin olive oil

Coarse salt and ground black pepper

Reduce the wine in a skillet over medium-high heat until thick and there is about ⅓ cup left. Scrape into a small bowl and mix in the balsamic vinegar and olive oil. Season with salt and pepper.

VARIATION

Port Wine Vinaigrette: (Best with game meats.) Substitute port for the red wine.

Pourable Herbed Mayonnaise

Best with beef carpaccio or tartare, shellfish, fish
MAKES ABOUT 1¼ CUPS

1 large fresh egg
2 tablespoons fresh lemon juice
1 teaspoon Dijon mustard
¼ teaspoon coarse salt
Pinch of ground white or black pepper
1 cup extra-virgin olive oil
2 teaspoons finely chopped fresh flat-leaf parsley
1 teaspoon finely chopped fresh tarragon
2 to 4 tablespoons whole milk

Combine the egg, lemon juice, mustard, salt, pepper, and ¼ cup of the oil in a food processor. Process for a few seconds and then, with the machine running, gradually add the remaining oil in a thin, steady steam. Scrape down the sides and process until thickened and smooth, 10 to 15 seconds.

Scrape into a bowl and stir in the parsley, tarragon, and just enough milk to make the sauce pourable. Cover and refrigerate for up to 1 week.

VARIATIONS

Blender Mayonnaise: (Best with shellfish, fish.) Omit the milk, parsley, and tarragon.

Caper Mayonnaise: (Best with shellfish and fish.) Omit the milk. Add 1½ tablespoons small drained capers (chop them if large) and 3 minced garlic cloves along with the herbs.

Tartar Sauce: (Best with shellfish and fish.) Make the Caper Mayonnaise (above) and add 2 tablespoons minced fresh dill or sweet pickles.

Gribiche Sauce

Best with fish, vegetables
MAKES ABOUT 1 CUP

2 tablespoons mayonnaise
2 tablespoons sour cream
2 tablespoons fresh lemon juice
1 hard-cooked large egg, finely chopped
2 tablespoons small drained capers, finely chopped if large
2 tablespoons chopped fresh flat-leaf parsley
1 teaspoon chopped fresh tarragon
1 tablespoon finely chopped shallot
Coarse salt and ground black pepper

Mix everything in a small bowl; cover and refrigerate for up to 2 weeks.

White Steak Sauce

Best with veal, pork, chicken, turkey, shellfish
MAKES ABOUT ¾ CUP

¼ cup Lea & Perrins Marinade for Chicken
1 teaspoon light brown sugar
½ cup mayonnaise
1 teaspoon brown mustard
1 garlic clove, minced
Dash of cayenne pepper
1 tablespoon unsalted butter, melted and still hot

Stir the Worcestershire sauce and sugar together in a small bowl until the sugar dissolves. Mix in the mayonnaise, mustard, garlic, and cayenne, stirring until smooth. Mix in the butter. Use within 2 hours, or cover and refrigerate for up to 1 week. Warm and whisk together before serving.

Grilled Lemon "Tartar" Sauce

Best with shellfish and fish
MAKES ABOUT 1¼ CUPS

1 large lemon, ends removed
2 teaspoons coarse salt
½ teaspoon ground black pepper
¼ cup extra-virgin olive oil
1 small garlic clove
½ cup water
1 teaspoon sugar
1 tablespoon chopped fresh dill, flat-leaf parsley, or marjoram

Light a grill for direct medium-high heat, about 425°F (see page 12).

Cut the whole lemon into ¼-inch-thick slices; remove and discard the seeds. Sprinkle with salt and pepper and set aside for 10 minutes. Blot with paper towels to absorb surface moisture. Coat with 1 tablespoon of the olive oil.

Brush the grill grate and coat with oil. Grill the lemon slices until heavily grill-marked, about 3 minutes per side.

Chop the lemon coarsely and puree in a food processor with the remaining 3 tablespoons oil, the garlic, water, and sugar to form a creamy sauce with bits of lemon peel in it. Transfer to a small bowl and stir in the dill. Store in a tightly closed container in the refrigerator for up to 1 week.

Jalapeño Relish

Best with pork, veal, beef, chicken, turkey, shellfish
MAKES ABOUT 2½ CUPS

1 pound jalapeño peppers (about 12), stemmed, seeded, cored, and chopped (1½ cups)
¾ cup coarsely chopped onion
¾ cup peeled, seeded, and coarsely chopped cucumber
2 tablespoons chopped fresh cilantro
1 garlic clove, chopped
¼ cup olive oil
2 tablespoons orange juice
1 tablespoon fresh lime juice
1 tablespoon agave nectar or honey
½ teaspoon coarse salt

Combine the jalapeños, onion, cucumber, cilantro, garlic, oil, orange juice, lime juice, agave nectar or honey, and salt in a small food processor. Pulse briefly until finely chopped but not pureed. Let stand overnight or up to 5 days in the refrigerator. Return to room temperature before serving.

Cilantro Pesto

Best with veal, chicken, turkey, shellfish, fish, vegetables
MAKES ABOUT ⅓ CUP

4 shelled almonds
1 cup fresh cilantro leaves
1 garlic clove
2 tablespoons extra-virgin olive oil
Coarse salt and ground black pepper

Chop the almonds finely in a food processor or minichopper. Add the cilantro and garlic and process until finely chopped (or chop everything with a knife). Transfer to a small bowl, mix in the oil, and season with salt and pepper. Store in the refrigerator in a tightly closed container for up to 2 days.

Grilled Tomato Chutney

Best with lamb, beef, chicken, turkey, game meats, cheese
MAKES ABOUT 1¼ CUPS

2 garlic cloves
Two ¼-inch-thick slices fresh ginger
½ medium onion, thickly sliced
2 teaspoons canola oil
1 large tomato (about 12 ounces)
2 jalapeño chiles
½ teaspoon ground toasted cumin seeds
½ teaspoon coarse salt
¼ teaspoon ground black pepper
2 tablespoons chopped fresh cilantro
2 tablespoons chopped fresh mint

Light a grill for direct medium-high heat, about 400°F (see page 12). Soak two or three bamboo skewers in water for at least 30 minutes. Thread the garlic cloves, ginger slices, and onion slices on the skewers and coat with a thin film of oil. Brush the grill grate and coat with oil.

Grill the skewers until the vegetables are lightly charred on all sides, about 5 minutes total.

At the same time, place the tomato and jalapeño chiles over the fire and char on all sides, turning every 3 to 4 minutes. Remove the skins from the tomato and chiles with your fingers. Remove the stems, and discard the chile seeds if you want the chutney to be milder.

Chop the garlic, ginger, onion, tomatoes, and chiles finely and combine with the cumin, salt, black pepper, cilantro, and mint. Store in the refrigerator in a tightly closed container for up to 2 weeks.

Grilled Tomato Marmalade

Best with beef, lamb, game birds, duck, goose, cheese, bread
MAKES ABOUT 1½ CUPS

2 pounds plum tomatoes, halved lengthwise
1 tablespoon olive oil
¾ teaspoon coarse salt
¼ teaspoon ground black pepper
½ cup sugar
3 tablespoons sherry vinegar

Light a grill for direct medium-high heat, about 425°F (see page 12).

Scoop out the seeds from the tomato halves, coat the tomatoes with oil, and season with the salt and pepper. Put the tomatoes on the grill, cover the grill, and cook until the tomatoes brown on both sides, about 8 minutes. Cool for a few minutes.

continued

Remove the skins from the tomatoes and discard. Chop the tomato flesh finely and mix with the sugar and vinegar in a saucepan. Simmer over medium heat until the mixture thickens, about 20 minutes, stirring as needed. Store in the refrigerator in a tightly closed container for up to 2 weeks.

Grilled Mango Salsa

Best with shellfish, fish
MAKES ABOUT 2 CUPS

½ small red onion, sliced ½ inch thick

2 large jalapeño chile peppers, stemmed, seeded, and halved lengthwise

1 large garlic clove, unpeeled

2 tablespoons canola or olive oil

1 large ripe mango

1 large ripe tomato, seeded and finely chopped

Finely grated zest and juice of 1 lime

¼ cup chopped fresh cilantro

½ teaspoon coarse salt

¼ teaspoon sugar

Light a grill for direct medium-high heat, about 400°F (see page 12).

Put the onion, jalapeño halves, and garlic in a medium shallow dish. Drizzle with the oil and stir gently to coat all over.

Brush the grill grate and coat with oil. Put the mango, onion, jalapeño, and garlic directly over the heat, reserving the oil in the dish. Grill the mango until soft and charred in spots, 10 to 12 minutes total, turning a few times. Remove to a bowl, cover, and let rest for 10 minutes.

Grill the onion, jalapeño, and garlic until nicely grill-marked, 5 to 6 minutes, turning once. Remove to a cutting board. Peel the garlic, mince, and add to the shallow dish of oil. Finely chop the onion, jalapeño, and the raw tomato. Add to the shallow dish. When the mango is cool enough to handle, peel back the skin, working over the shallow dish to capture any juices and flesh. Discard the skin. Hold the peeled mango over the dish and squeeze between your hands, working the flesh loose with your fingers and letting it drop into the bowl. Chop any large pieces of flesh with a knife. Stir in the lime zest and juice, cilantro, salt, and sugar. Serve warm or refrigerate in a tightly closed container for up to 1 day.

Black Caper Butter

Best with veal, shellfish, fish
MAKES ABOUT ¾ CUP

½ cup (1 stick) unsalted butter

1 tablespoon minced shallot

2 tablespoons dry white wine

2 tablespoons fresh lemon juice

2 tablespoons drained capers, chopped if large

2 tablespoons minced fresh flat-leaf parsley

Melt the butter in a small frying pan over medium heat. When the butter foams, reduce the heat to medium-low and cook until it turns from yellow to medium brown, but not black, 5 to 7 minutes. Watch carefully to keep the butter from burning. Pour the browned butter into a small heat-proof bowl. Add the shallots to the pan and cook for 1 minute. Stir in the wine and lemon juice and simmer for 2 minutes. Reduce the heat to low, pour the browned butter back into the pan, and add the capers and parsley. Serve immediately or keep warm for up to 15 minutes.

VARIATIONS

Parsley-Walnut Sauce: (Best with veal, poultry, seafood.) Before melting the butter, toast ¾ cup walnuts in the skillet over medium heat until fragrant, shaking the pan now and then, 5 minutes. Remove and finely chop. Add 2 minced garlic cloves along with the shallots. Omit the capers and stir in the chopped walnuts along with the parsley. Makes about 1½ cups.

Orange Brown Butter: (Best with shellfish and fish.) Replace the wine and lemon juice with 2 tablespoons orange juice and 2 tablespoons raspberry vinegar or red wine vinegar. Omit the capers. Replace the parsley with mint.

Brown Butter Vinaigrette: (Best with shellfish, fish, vegetables.) Reduce the butter to 4 tablespoons. After browning the butter, remove from the heat and stir in the shallots. Replace the wine and lemon juice with ¼ cup sherry vinegar and whisk the vinegar into the butter along with ½ teaspoon ground mustard. Whisk in ¼ cup extra-virgin olive oil in a slow steady stream until well blended. Whisk in the parsley and omit the capers.

Seafood Butter

Best with shellfish and fish
MAKES ABOUT ⅓ CUP

1 tablespoon fresh thyme leaves

1 tablespoon chopped fresh flat-leaf parsley leaves

2 garlic cloves, minced

⅓ cup unsalted butter, melted

1½ teaspoons fresh lemon juice

½ teaspoon grated lemon zest

¼ teaspoon hot pepper sauce

¼ teaspoon coarse salt, preferably smoked

⅛ teaspoon ground black pepper, preferably smoked

Mix everything together. Use within 1 hour or store in tightly closed container in the refrigerator for up to 1 week. Return to room temperature before serving.

Margarita Butter

Best with pork, chicken, shellfish, fish, vegetables

MAKES ABOUT ½ CUP

3 tablespoons unsalted butter

1 jalapeño chile pepper, stemmed, seeded, and finely diced

1 tablespoon ground coriander

1 tablespoon ground cumin

3 tablespoons tequila

Finely grated zest and juice of 2 limes

1 teaspoon coarse salt

½ teaspoon coarsely ground black pepper

2 tablespoons chopped fresh cilantro

Melt the butter in a small skillet over medium heat. Add the jalapeño and sauté until tender, about 2 minutes. Add the coriander and cumin and sauté for another 30 seconds. Stir in the tequila and bring to a boil. Remove from the heat. Stir in the lime zest, lime juice, salt, pepper, and cilantro. Serve warm. Store in a tightly closed container in the refrigerator for up to 1 week. Warm in a small pan over low heat, stirring often until smooth, before serving.

VARIATION

Coriander Butter Sauce: (Best with pork, chicken, shellfish, fish.) Omit the jalapeño and cumin, and replace the tequila with 1 tablespoon water or vodka.

Poblano-Gorgonzola Butter

Best with lamb and shellfish

MAKES ABOUT ¾ CUP

1 large poblano chile pepper

1 small garlic clove, minced

3 ounces Gorgonzola cheese, without the rind

2 tablespoons unsalted butter, softened

2 tablespoons extra-virgin olive oil

Coarse salt and ground black pepper

Light a grill for direct high heat, about 450°F (see page 12). Put the poblano pepper over the fire, cover the grill and grill until the skin is charred all around, about 10 minutes, turning the pepper about every 3 minutes. Wrap the charred pepper in foil and set aside to cool for about 10 minutes. Rub off the pepper skin with your fingers, cut out the seeds and stem, and mince the pepper.

Mix the minced poblano pepper, the garlic, Gorgonzola, butter, and olive oil in a small bowl until light and fluffy. Season with salt and pepper. Store in a tightly closed container in the refrigerator for up to 1 week. Warm to room temperature before serving.

Black Mustard Butter

Best with lamb and vegetables

MAKES ABOUT ½ CUP

3 tablespoons black mustard seeds

6 tablespoons unsalted butter

1 clove garlic, minced

1 tablespoon finely shredded fresh ginger

2 teaspoons brown mustard

2 tablespoons fresh lime juice

Heat a small skillet over medium heat. Add the mustard seeds and cook until they turn ash gray, about 1 minute. Add the butter and cook until it begins to color, about 4 minutes. Stir in the garlic and ginger. Remove from the heat and stir in the mustard and lime juice. The mixture will immediately turn dark brown. Serve immediately or keep warm for up to 10 minutes.

Coconut Red Curry Sauce

Best with chicken, veal, turkey, shellfish, fish, vegetables, bread

MAKES ABOUT 2 CUPS

1 tablespoon canola oil

½ cup sliced onions (halve the onion and slice to make half-moons)

2 teaspoons minced fresh ginger

2 garlic cloves, minced

1½ cups coconut milk

2 tablespoons Thai red curry paste (see Note)

continued ➔

1 tablespoon brown sugar, light or dark
2 teaspoons Thai fish sauce
2 tablespoons fresh lime juice
2 tablespoons chopped fresh cilantro

Heat the oil in a medium saucepan over medium heat. Add the onions and cook until soft, 4 minutes, breaking them up with a spoon. Add the ginger and garlic and cook until soft, 3 minutes. Stir in the coconut milk, curry paste, brown sugar, fish sauce, and lime juice. Bring to a boil, and then reduce the heat and simmer for 5 minutes. Stir in the cilantro. Use immediately or refrigerate for up to 2 days.

NOTE: Thai red curry paste (or base) is sold in large packets in the international aisle of most grocery stores. You can also use the red curry paste that's available in small jars, but use about half as much because it's twice as potent.

Salsa Ranchero

Best with beef, chicken, shellfish, fish
MAKES ABOUT 1½ CUPS

2 medium tomatoes
1 large red jalapeño chile pepper or 2 serranos
1 small onion, quartered lengthwise
1 large garlic clove, skin left on
2 teaspoons olive oil
2 tablespoons chopped fresh cilantro
Juice of ½ large lime
½ teaspoon coarse salt
⅛ teaspoon ground black pepper

Light a grill for direct medium-high heat, about 450°F (see page 12).

Coat the tomatoes, chiles, onion quarters, and garlic all over with oil. Skewer any vegetables that are in danger of falling through your grill grate or use a grill tray.

Brush the grill grate and coat with oil (coat the grill tray if using). Grill the vegetables directly over the heat until charred all over, 2 to 4 minutes per side (the chiles will be done first, the tomatoes and garlic last).

Remove to a cutting board and peel the garlic. Remove the tomato and chile skins, stems, and cores. Remove as many chile seeds as you like to tame the heat. Coarsely chop the vegetables, and then transfer to a small food processor. Add the cilantro and lime juice and process briefly to a coarse puree.

Transfer to a saucepan and simmer over medium heat until the flavors blend, about 5 minutes. Season with the salt and pepper. Serve immediately or refrigerate for up to 3 days.

Green Tea Ponzu Sauce

Best with shellfish and fish
MAKES ABOUT 1¼ CUP

1 cup brewed green tea
2 teaspoons coarse salt
2 teaspoons light soy sauce
2 teaspoons rice vinegar
¼ cup mirin

Mix everything together. Store in a tightly closed container in the refrigerator for up to 1 week.

Harissa

Best with beef, lamb, chicken, shellfish, fish, vegetables
MAKES ABOUT ½ CUP

¾ cup (about 1 ounce) dried small red chile peppers
1 tablespoon caraway seeds
2 teaspoons coriander seeds
1 teaspoon cumin seeds
6 garlic cloves, coarsely chopped
Coarse salt to taste
Extra-virgin olive oil as needed

Remove the stems from the chiles. Remove as many of the seeds as desired to tame the heat. Soak the chiles in warm water until tender, about 30 minutes. Drain and chop coarsely.

Heat a small heavy skillet over medium-high heat until very hot, about 3 minutes. Add the caraway, coriander, and cumin seeds. Remove from the heat and stir until the spices are aromatic and lightly toasted, about 1 minute.

Grind the toasted seeds, chopped chiles, garlic, and salt in a mortar and pestle, spice grinder, or small food processor to a coarse paste. Add just enough olive oil to make the paste flow, and grind until smooth. Store in a tightly closed container in the refrigerator for up to 1 month.

Chimichurri Sauce

Best with veal, pork, chicken, turkey
MAKES ABOUT 2 CUPS

4 cups fresh flat-leaf parsley leaves and small stems
2 cups fresh cilantro leaves and small stems
5 garlic cloves, coarsely chopped
½ red bell pepper, seeded and coarsely chopped
¼ cup coarsely chopped onion
1 teaspoon dried oregano leaves
1 teaspoon coarse salt
½ teaspoon red pepper flakes
½ teaspoon ground black pepper
⅓ cup sherry vinegar
⅓ cup water
¾ cup extra-virgin olive oil

Combine the parsley, cilantro, garlic, bell pepper, and onion in a food processor. Pulse several times until coarsely chopped. Add the remaining ingredients and pulse until coarsely chopped. Scrape into a bowl and refrigerate for at least 2 hours to blend the flavors. Store in the refrigerator in a tightly closed container for up to 1 week.

Hazelnut Picada

Best with Shellfish, fish, chicken
MAKES ABOUT ⅔ CUP

½ cup finely chopped toasted hazelnuts
Pinch of saffron threads
1 garlic clove, minced
2 tablespoons finely chopped flat-leaf parsley leaves
2 tablespoons water
1 teaspoon fresh lemon juice
Coarse salt to taste
¼ to ⅓ cup extra-virgin olive oil

Grind the hazelnuts, saffron, garlic, and parsley with a mortar and pestle to a coarse paste, adding the water to help the mixture grind more easily. Stir in the lemon juice and salt. Stir in enough olive oil to make a flowing sauce, and set aside. If you don't have a mortar and pestle chop the solid ingredients as finely as possible, but don't use an electric grinder, which would make the picada too smooth. Use within 2 hours or store in the refrigerator in a tightly closed container for up to 1 week.

Muhammara

Best with beef, lamb, chicken, cheese
MAKES ABOUT 1½ CUPS

1 large grill-roasted red pepper (see Know-How, below) or jarred roasted pepper, seeded
⅔ cup walnuts, toasted and coarsely chopped
1 slice bread, lightly toasted, outer crust removed
½ cup extra-virgin olive oil
2 garlic cloves, coarsely chopped
1½ tablespoons pomegranate molasses
2 teaspoons fresh lemon juice
½ to 1 teaspoon red pepper flakes
1 teaspoon ground cumin
½ teaspoon sugar
½ teaspoon coarse salt

Combine everything in a food processor and process briefly to a coarse puree. Let stand at room temperature for 20 minutes to develop the flavors or refrigerate for up to 3 days.

> ### KNOW-HOW:
> ### GRILL-ROASTING PEPPERS
>
> Light a grill for direct medium-high heat, about 425°F (see page 12). Brush the grill grate and coat with oil. Grill the peppers directly over the heat until soft and blackened all over, 4 to 6 minutes per side. Remove to a paper bag or shallow baking dish. Seal the bag or cover the dish and let rest for 15 to 20 minutes. When cool enough to handle, pull out the stems and cores, with their seeds. Cut into the peppers lengthwise and gently scrape away any lingering seeds or ribs. Peel the skin with your fingers or the edge of a paring knife and discard. Cut the pepper lengthwise into halves, quarters, or narrow strips, as desired.

Mustard Butterscotch

Best with pork, game birds, game meats, cheese
MAKES ABOUT ½ CUP

½ cup sugar
¼ cup water
¼ cup whiskey
2 tablespoons spicy brown mustard
2 tablespoons unsalted butter
¼ teaspoon coarse salt

Mix the sugar and water in a small heavy saucepan. Cook over medium-high heat until the sugar melts and the mixture turns pale amber, washing any sugar clinging to the inside of the pan with a damp pastry brush. Stir the whiskey into the pot; the sugar will immediately crystallize. Stir until the sauce becomes smooth again. Remove from the heat and stir in the mustard, butter, and salt. Serve warm. Store in a tightly closed container in the refrigerator for up to 1 week.

Chipotle Chocolate Butter

Best with beef, lamb, duck, berries, cake
MAKES ABOUT ½ CUP

2 ounces semisweet chocolate
6 tablespoons unsalted butter
2 teaspoons honey
⅛ teaspoon ground chipotle chile
⅛ teaspoon medium-coarse sea salt, preferably fleur de sel

Put the chocolate in a small microwave-safe bowl, cover, and cook at full power until half melted, about 1½ minutes. Remove from the microwave, uncover, and add the butter, honey, and chile, stirring until smooth. Stir in the salt. Serve warm. Store in a tightly closed container in the refrigerator for up to 1 week.

Rum Raisin Hard Sauce

Best with cake and fruit
MAKES ABOUT ½ CUP

2 tablespoons raisins, chopped
2 tablespoons dark or golden rum
3 tablespoons honey
½ teaspoon ground cardamom
3 tablespoons unsalted butter

Soak the raisins in rum in a small bowl for 30 minutes. Meanwhile, heat the honey and cardamom in a small saucepan just until warm, about 20 seconds. Remove from the heat and add the butter, stirring until melted. Serve warm. Store in a tightly closed container in the refrigerator for up to 1 week.

VARIATION

Root Beer–Rum Butter: (Best with sweet vegetables and fruit.) Omit the raisins and honey. Bring the rum and 1 cup root beer to a boil in a small saucepan over high heat. Boil until reduced to about ⅓ cup, 10 to 15 minutes. Stir in the cardamom and ½ teaspoon salt. Remove from the heat and add the butter, stirring until melted.

Balsamic Chocolate Drizzle

Best with beef, duck, lamb, strong cheese
MAKES ABOUT ⅓ CUP

½ cup balsamic vinegar
½ ounce bittersweet chocolate

Boil the balsamic vinegar in a small saucepan or skillet until reduced by half. Remove from the heat and add the chocolate, stirring until melted. Keep warm until ready to serve. Store in a tightly closed container in the refrigerator for up to 1 week.

Glazes

Sweet Soy Glaze

Best with pork, beef, chicken
MAKES ABOUT ⅓ CUP

¼ cup kecap manis (sweet soy sauce), or 2 tablespoons tamari soy sauce plus 2 tablespoons molasses
4 teaspoons toasted sesame oil
1 teaspoon rice vinegar
1 teaspoon chile-garlic paste
½ teaspoon Chinese five-spice powder

Whisk all the ingredients together in a small bowl. Store in the refrigerator in a tightly closed container for up to 2 weeks.

Brown Sugar Glaze

Best for pork and poultry
MAKES ABOUT 1 CUP

⅔ cup dark brown sugar
3 tablespoons apple cider vinegar
3 tablespoons water
1 teaspoon coarse salt
½ teaspoon ground black pepper
3 tablespoons unsalted butter

Mix brown sugar, vinegar, water, salt, and pepper in a small saucepan, and bring to a boil over medium heat. Remove from the heat and add the butter, stirring until melted. Use while still warm, or store in a tightly closed container in the refrigerator for up to 2 weeks and rewarm before using.

Maple Lacquer

Best with pork
MAKES ½ CUP

¼ cup maple syrup
1 tablespoon apple cider vinegar
½ teaspoon coarse salt
¼ teaspoon ground black pepper
2 tablespoons unsalted butter

Bring maple syrup, vinegar, salt, and pepper to a boil over medium heat. Remove from the heat and add the butter, stirring until melted. Serve warm. Store in a tightly closed container for up to 2 weeks.

VARIATIONS

Juniper Maple Lacquer: (Best with pork, game meats.) Add 6 juniper berries, finely ground, to the maple syrup.

Mustard Maple Glaze: (Best with pork, poultry, game meats.) Add 2 teaspoons brown mustard with the butter.

Spiced Cider Syrup: (Best with pork, poultry, game meats.) Reduce the quantity of maple syrup to 2 tablespoons. Add ½ cup apple cider, ½ teaspoon pumpkin pie spice (see Note), and ¼ teaspoon ground mustard along with the 2 tablespoons syrup, the vinegar, salt, and pepper. Boil until reduced to about ⅓ cup. Remove from the heat and stir in the butter.

NOTE: If you don't have pumpkin pie spice you can replace it with ¼ teaspoon ground cinnamon, ⅛ teaspoon grated nutmeg, ⅛ teaspoon ground ginger, and a pinch of ground cloves.

White Balsamic Citrus Glaze

Best with veal, chicken, turkey, fruit
MAKES ABOUT ½ CUP

½ cup white balsamic vinegar
½ cup white wine
2 tablespoons fresh lemon juice
1 teaspoon sugar

Combine everything in a small saucepan and boil over high heat until reduced and syrupy, about 5 minutes. Cool and store in the refrigerator for up to 1 week.

Agave Glaze

Best with pork, chicken, vegetables, fruit
MAKES ABOUT 1¼ CUPS

2 dried ancho chile peppers
1 garlic clove, skin left on
¾ cup tequila
½ cup water
⅓ cup agave nectar
2 tablespoons olive oil

continued

 50

FIRE IT UP

Light a grill for direct medium heat, about 400°F (see page 12). Discard the stems and seeds from the chiles, then tear them open and flatten with the palm of your hand. Brush the grill grate and coat with oil. Toast the chiles directly over the heat, flattening them with a spatula, until browned in spots, about 10 seconds per side. Transfer to a bowl, cover with hot water, and soak for 30 minutes. Coat the unpeeled garlic with oil and grill directly over the heat until blacked in spots, about 5 minutes, turning once or twice. Let cool, and then peel.

While the chiles are soaking, pour the tequila into a small saucepan and bring to a boil over high heat. Continue boiling until reduced to about ½ cup.

Drain the chiles and discard the water. Transfer the chiles and peeled garlic to a blender or small food processor and add the ½ cup water. Process until smooth. Remove the tequila from the heat, scrape the chile puree into the saucepan, and stir in the agave nectar and oil. Simmer over low heat for 5 minutes.

VARIATION

Agave Lime Glaze: (Best with shellfish.) Omit the chiles and chop the fresh garlic. When boiling the tequila, cook it down to ⅓ cup. Remove from the heat and stir in the garlic, agave nectar, oil, and 1 teaspoon fresh lime juice. Simmer for 5 minutes.

Thai Red Curry Lacquer

Best with beef, lamb, chicken, game meats
MAKES ABOUT ½ CUP

2 tablespoons Thai red curry paste (see Note, page 46)
2 tablespoons ketchup
2 tablespoons canola oil
2 tablespoons water
1 tablespoon brown sugar, light or dark

Mix the ingredients together. Store in the refrigerator in a tightly closed container for up to 2 weeks.

Teriyaki Plum Glaze

Best with pork, chicken, game birds
MAKES ABOUT ⅓ CUP

3 tablespoons plum preserves, preferably damson
1 tablespoon balsamic vinegar
1½ tablespoons soy sauce
¼ teaspoon hot pepper sauce, such as Tabasco

Mix the ingredients together. Store in the refrigerator in a tightly closed container for up to 2 weeks.

Sweet Ginger Glaze

Best with shellfish, fish, chicken
MAKES ABOUT ½ CUP

¼ cup ginger preserves
¼ cup white wine vinegar
½ teaspoon coarse salt
¼ teaspoon ground black pepper
1 garlic clove, minced

Mix the ingredients together. Store in the refrigerator in a tightly closed container for up to 2 weeks

VARIATION

Brandied Ginger Glaze: (Best with beef.) Sauté the garlic in 1 teaspoon olive oil over medium heat. Add 1 tablespoon brandy and simmer until most of the liquid evaporates. Add the vinegar, simmer for 1 minute, then remove from the heat. Stir in the preserves, salt, pepper, and 1 tablespoon hazelnut oil or walnut oil.

Balsamic Syrup

Best with veal, chicken, cheese, vegetables
MAKES ABOUT ⅓ CUP

1 cup balsamic vinegar
1 teaspoon soy sauce
1 teaspoon dark brown sugar

Boil the balsamic vinegar in a skillet over high heat until slightly thickened and reduced to about ⅓ cup. Stir in the soy sauce and sugar. Store in the refrigerator in a tightly closed container for up to 2 weeks.

Grilled Tomato Oil

Best with veal, pork, chicken, shellfish, fish
MAKES ABOUT 1 CUP

4 ripe plum tomatoes, halved
½ cup best-quality extra-virgin olive oil
1 garlic clove, coarsely chopped
1 large sprig fresh oregano or thyme
½ teaspoon honey
¼ teaspoon coarse salt

Light a grill for direct medium-high heat, about 425°F (see page 12). In a small bowl, toss the tomatoes with 1 tablespoon of the oil. Brush the grill grate and coat with oil. Grill the tomatoes, cut-side down, directly over the heat until nicely grill-marked, 3 to 4 minutes. Flip and grill until the other side is nicely marked, about 3 minutes more. Return to the bowl.

Transfer the grilled tomatoes and oil to a small food processor and puree until fairly smooth. Strain the sauce through a food mill or push gently through a fine-mesh sieve into a small saucepan, leaving behind much of the solids. Add the garlic and oregano to the pan and bring to a boil over high heat. Reduce the heat to a simmer and cook until the liquid is reduced by half, about 10 minutes. Remove from the heat and strain the liquid into a small container with a tight-fitting lid, such as a canning jar. Add the honey and salt, stirring until dissolved. Let cool, then whisk in the remaining olive oil. Refrigerate for up to 4 days. If the cold oil becomes cloudy, it will clear when returned to room temperature.

Pineapple-Rum Glaze

Best with pork, chicken, shellfish, fish, fruit
MAKES ABOUT ⅔ CUP

½ cup coconut rum, such as Malibu
¼ cup pineapple juice
1½ tablespoons molasses
1 tablespoon fresh lime juice
½ to 1 teaspoon habanero hot pepper sauce
½ teaspoon ground cardamom
¼ teaspoon coarse salt
Pinch of allspice
6 tablespoons unsalted butter, cut into 12 pieces

Combine everything but the butter in a small saucepan and bring to a boil over medium heat. Boil until reduced to about ⅓ cup in volume. Remove from the heat and stir in the butter. Serve warm. Store in the refrigerator in a tightly closed container for up to 2 days.

Saffron Butter

Best with shellfish and fish
MAKES ABOUT ⅓ CUP

1 tablespoon fresh lemon juice
1 teaspoon saffron threads
5 tablespoons unsalted butter, melted

¼ teaspoon coarse salt
Dash of cayenne pepper

Pour the lemon juice into a small bowl. Crumble the saffron threads between your fingers into the lemon juice and set aside for 10 minutes. Whisk in the butter, and season with salt and cayenne. Keep warm until ready to serve. Store in the refrigerator in a tightly closed container for up to 2 days.

VARIATION

Curried Saffron Butter: (Best with shellfish and fish.) Add ½ teaspoon garam masala or Madras curry powder to the lemon juice along with the saffron.

Poppy Seed Syrup

Best with vegetables and fruit
MAKES ABOUT 2 CUPS

2 cups water
2½ cups sugar
1 thumb-sized knob fresh ginger, peel left on, sliced ¼ inch thick
½ teaspoon whole cloves
Juice of ½ small lemon
1 tablespoon kirsch or white rum
1 teaspoon vanilla extract
1 teaspoon poppy seeds

Combine the water, sugar, ginger, and cloves in a small saucepan. Bring to a boil over medium heat, and then reduce the heat to medium-low and simmer until slightly thickened and syrupy, 3 to 5 minutes. Remove from the heat and strain into a large bowl. Stir in the lemon juice, kirsch, vanilla, and poppy seeds and let cool. The syrup will keep at room temperature for several hours. Or store in the refrigerator for up to 1 week in a tightly closed container.

Spicy Orange Honey

Best with fruit and cheese
MAKES ABOUT ½ CUP

¼ cup honey
1½ tablespoons orange juice
1 teaspoon hot pepper sauce, such as Tabasco

Mix everything together. The honey will keep at room temperature for several hours. Store in the refrigerator in a tightly closed container for up to 1 week.

Chapter 3

BEEF

We love beef. And we're not alone. Worldwide, more land is used to raise cattle than all other domesticated animals and crops combined. Americans eat about 28 billion pounds of beef every year. Cattle occupy most U.S. farms and ranches, and there are about 100 million head of cattle on American soil at any given time.

The biggest factors influencing the taste of beef are cattle breed, diet, marbling or grade, stress on the animal, and aging. Most U.S. beef comes from hybrid cattle that combine the blocky meatiness of British breeds like Hereford and Durham with the drought-resistant hardiness of Asian breeds like Brahman. Premium beef comes from purebreds like Italian Chianina and Japanese Kobe (also known as wagyu), or from hybrids of top breeds such as Chiangus, a combination of Chianina and Angus. If you're looking for a particular breed, ask for it by name.

RIB

A sought-after middle cut from the steer's back, capturing ribs 6 to 12 and featuring a long rib-eye muscle, which is cut into roasts like prime rib, steaks like rib-eye, and back (dinosaur) ribs.

CHUCK

A 90-pound section of shoulder (including the foreleg), encompassing several roasts and steaks, such as chuck roast, shoulder tender, flat iron steak, and other chuck steaks.

SIRLOIN

Just forward of the steer's haunches, the sirloin contains flavorful meat that's cut into top and bottom sirloin roasts and steaks, and tri-tip roast.

SHORT LOIN

Also called the strip loin, this pricey primal lies between the rib and sirloin. It includes the tenderloin and is cut into strip roasts, strip steaks, T-bone, and porterhouse steaks.

ROUND

An 80-pound upper section of leg cut into lean, medium-tough top and bottom round roasts and steaks, rump roast, and knuckle or round tip (ball tip) roasts and steaks.

CHUCK
26%

RIB
9.5%

SHORT
LOIN
8%

SIRLOIN
9%

ROUND
27%

BRISKET
6%

FORE-
SHANK
4%

SHORT PLATE
5.5%

FLANK
4%

PLATE

The belly of the beast, including skirt steak and short ribs.

BRISKET

The sturdy chest of the steer from between the shoulders to the plate (belly).

FLANK

The underside of the steer farther back from the belly, consisting of coarse, long, parallel muscle fibers cut into flank steak or ground for hamburger.

BEEF

INGREDIENT / PRIMAL CUT	OTHER NAMES	HOW TO GRILL	SUBSTITUTIONS
BRISKET / BRISKET	First-cut, center cut, thin cut, second cut, deckle point, thick cut	INDIRECT medium-low	Chuck
CHUCK STEAK / CHUCK	Shoulder steak, flat-iron steak, blade steak, 7-bone steak, Texas broil, cross-rib steak, patio steak	INDIRECT medium-low	Brisket
SHOULDER TENDER / CHUCK	Shoulder tender roast, chuck shoulder steak, petite fillet, butcher's steak	DIRECT medium-high	Tenderloin
FLANK STEAK / FLANK	London broil, bavette	DIRECT medium-high to high	Skirt steak, top round
GROUND BEEF / CHUCK, ROUND, OR SIRLOIN	Hamburger, Salisbury steak	DIRECT medium-high	Ground round, chuck, or sirloin
HANGER STEAK / PLATE	Hanging tender, flap meat, butcher's steak	DIRECT medium-high	Flank steak, skirt steak
RIB ROAST / RIB	Prime rib, rib-eye roast	INDIRECT medium	Whole sirloin, strip loin
RIB STEAK / RIB	Delmonico steak, entrecote, rib-eye steak, shell steak	BILEVEL medium-high/medium-low	Sirloin steak, strip steak, fillet steak
SHORT RIBS / PLATE	Asian-style short ribs, Korean short ribs, cross-cut ribs, flanken	INDIRECT high / DIRECT medium	Back ribs, hanger steak, skirt steak
BACK RIBS / RIB	Dinosaur ribs	INDIRECT medium	Short ribs
SKIRT STEAK / PLATE	Fajita steak, bavette	DIRECT medium-high	Hanger steak, short ribs
T-BONE / SHORT LOIN	Porterhouse	BILEVEL high/low	Porterhouse, sirloin, fillet steak
PORTERHOUSE / SHORT LOIN	T-bone	BILEVEL high/low	T-bone, Sirloin, fillet steak
LOIN ROAST / SHORT LOIN	Strip roast, shell roast, top loin roast, short loin roast, center-cut loin roast	BILEVEL high/low	Rib eye roast, Tenderloin
TENDERLOIN ROAST / SHORT LOIN	Fillet, filet mignon	DIRECT medium high	Center-cut boneless rib-eye roast

Grain-Fed, Grass-Fed, and Organic Beef

Beginning around the 1950s, high demand for beef led to streamlined and concentrated methods of meat production. Since then, almost all cattle raised in the United States have developed at least 30 percent of their weight by being fed grain (mostly corn) in large feedlots. This production system allows meat producers to standardize flavor and tenderness by feeding the animals a consistent diet and discouraging exercise, and to minimize the time and expense it takes to bring them to market. The tightly packed quarters of the feedlot also force most producers to pump cattle with antibiotics to keep their meat safe. By law, cattle stop receiving antibiotics three days before slaughter to ensure that antibiotics are not in the meat at the time the beef is butchered and sold.

In other countries, raising an animal completely on grass is the norm. Pasture-fed Argentinean beef is world-famous, but in the United States, the grass-fed movement is still relatively small. Typically, feedlot cattle are grazed on grass for about six to eight months, and then "finished" on grain. Opponents of this system point out that keeping an animal on grass throughout its entire life gives its meat a stronger flavor, sweeter aroma, meatier texture, less fat, and more nutrients beneficial to human health. But grass-fed beef costs more to produce, so relatively few U.S. producers have developed grass-feeding systems.

In the meantime, to help identify grass-fed beef and prevent mislabeling, the U.S. Department of Agriculture (USDA) sponsors a voluntary beef inspection program, which verifies and labels 100 percent grass-fed beef. The label only verifies the cattle's diet and does not include criteria about housing, hormones, or antibiotics. Apart from the USDA label, the term "grass-fed" is largely unregulated. Do not confuse grass-fed beef with meat labeled "organic." Certified organic meat is not necessarily grass-fed. It must only meet the USDA National Organic Program standards, insuring that it is

- **fed on 100 percent organic feed (vitamin and mineral supplements are allowed)**

- **not given hormones to promote growth, or antibiotics to prevent disease**

- **given "access" to pasture (certified organic beef can be fed on grain in feedlots, but for no more than 200 days, and its feed must be organic)**

Beef Grades

The USDA grading program, which judges meat for quality (not safety), is voluntary. Because meat producers have to pay to have carcasses graded, only the best meats go through the grading process. Grades are based on conformation (shape and form), color, texture, firmness of the lean meat, and the degree of marbling (intramuscular fat) running through it. There are eight grades for beef—prime, choice, select, standard, commercial, utility, cutter, and canner. Only the top three grades are sold in retail markets.

Choice is the most common grade, and almost all beef for retail sale is raised to be choice. Only 2 percent of cattle meet the standards for prime. The most important characteristic of prime beef is its high degree of marbling. When grilled, the strands of fat striated throughout the lean melt, yielding rich, moist, succulent results. Marbling also tenderizes by separating muscle fibers, making them easier to chew.

Select grade beef can have as little as 3 percent marbling, which is why most supermarkets label it "extra-lean" and tack on a premium price for health-minded consumers. It is lower in fat, but extra-lean beef dries out easily when overcooked, especially on the grill.

Aged Beef

Aging makes beef more tender and flavorful. It is done under special high-humidity refrigeration to keep muscle enzymes in the meat active. The enzymes break down proteins and fat, and they attack the connective tissue between muscle fibers, causing muscle fibers to relax, tenderizing the meat.

During the weeks it takes to dry age meat a lot of water is lost, which concentrates flavor, but can result in a weight loss of up to 20 percent. That's why dry-aged beef costs more.

The Tender and the Tough

Cattle are gigantic animals, some weighing in at almost a ton. It would be impossible to grill the creature whole, not only because of its size but also because its different parts don't cook at the same rate, and they don't all benefit from the same grilling method. To facilitate cooking, a beef carcass is divided into eight primal cuts, and more than thirty retail cuts of steaks, chops, roasts, ribs, stewing cubes, and ground beef.

Tender cuts come from the primal muscle groups that get the least amount of exercise, which run along the center back of the cattle—the rib (rib cage), short loin (center back), and sirloin (lower back). Tougher meats are from the primals that move or support the body—the chuck (shoulder and foreleg), brisket (chest), plate (diaphragm), flank (abdomen), and round (hind leg).

You know that the more you exercise, the bigger and harder your muscles get. The same goes for beef. But while exercise may make you stronger and more fit, too much exercise just makes a butchered cow a bunch of tough meat. Here's how to separate the tough from the tender:

Muscles have two parts: (1) muscle fibers, the red bulky part, and 2) connective tissue, the transparent membrane that surrounds the fibers, giving the muscle shape and definition. As a muscle is exercised, the fibers take on protein, making the muscle bigger, redder, and more flavorful, and the connective tissue thickens, making the muscle harder and tougher.

The first rule for picking beef is to look at the red parts. If the surface looks rough, like coarsely woven cloth, its connective tissue is thick and the meat will be tough. A smooth, silken appearance means there's not enough connective tissue to worry about and the meat will be tender.

How to Grill Beef

When meat cooks two things happen: (1) the protein in the muscle fibers becomes drier, firmer, and more opaque, and (2) the connective tissue melts. Tender cuts like steaks and chops are done when the protein is cooked to the desired degree of doneness (see the chart on page 20). The hotter the meat gets, the drier, firmer, and browner it becomes, allowing you to judge internal temperature by the look and feel of the grilled beef. Tough cuts, on the other hand, are done when the connective tissue has softened enough to pierce the meat easily with a fork. Period. There is no such thing as medium-rare brisket or blood-rare barbecued beef. For that reason, you don't need to take the temperature of tough meat to test its doneness; if it is tender, it is ready.

Grinding beef automatically tenderizes it by breaking the connective tissue into small pieces. Since tough meat is flavorful and grinding tenderizes meat, the best cuts for flavorful ground beef are tough cuts like chuck. Take care when cooking ground beef. During grinding, the surface and interior of a piece of meat are mixed together, causing bacteria on the surface to become dispersed throughout the batch. It is not advisable to eat any ground beef that is not cooked to a temperature of at least 145°F. The USDA recommends 160°F to ensure that all areas of the food have reached a temperature of 140°F or higher, but we have found that at that temperature, all of the moisture is gone as well. We prefer to stop cooking beef burgers at an internal temperature of 150°F; the meat will be slightly pink in the center, and still relatively juicy.

Grill tender steaks and ground beef over direct medium-high to high heat (see page 12), determining the heat level by how much you want your steaks or burgers cooked. An intense fire will give you a great crust while leaving the interior of the meat relatively rare. If you like your beef more cooked, a medium fire will give a steak time to cook through without scorching the surface. For the best of both worlds, brown the beef over high heat, and then move it to medium-low heat to finish cooking the interior without burning the outside.

While most grilling is done over direct heat, beef roasts thicker than 2 inches need to cook over indirect heat (see page 14) to give them time to reach the desired internal temperature before the surface burns.

BRISKET/BRISKET

Espresso-Powered Barbecued Brisket

MAKES 6 SERVINGS

Brisket is a large, tough cut, which takes hours of cooking over a low, slow fire to reach tenderness. The extended grilling time (at least an hour per pound) allows incredible flavor to permeate deep into the meat. We start by massaging the beef with a rub of hot pepper and dark-roast coffee. If you're new to coffee on beef, the combination is fantastic. It works because all roasted ingredients share a common browned flavor, regardless of whether the browning is on dark-roasted coffee or fire-flecked beef. Roasted or browned flavors are what we've come to love about barbecued meat, which is why roasted coffee beans have the surprising effect of making beef taste meatier. We enhance the phenomenon by drizzling a coffee-infused mop over the roasting brisket with enough frequency to help soften its tough fibers, as the flavor of dark-roast coffee pervades the meat. The finished brisket is sliced and served with a bittersweet barbecue sauce for dipping.

INGREDIENTS:

Juice of 2 lemons

2 cups strong brewed coffee, preferably espresso roast

¼ cup molasses

2 tablespoons aged balsamic vinegar

2 teaspoons coarse salt

¾ cup Espresso Rub (page 26)

1 flat or center-cut beef brisket (3 to 4 pounds), trimmed, with ¼ inch of fat on one side

1 cup Espresso Grilling Sauce (page 39)

DIRECTIONS:

Mix the lemon juice, coffee, molasses, balsamic vinegar, salt, and 1 tablespoon of the rub in a small bowl. Set aside.

Rub the remaining spice rub all over the brisket. Cover tightly in plastic wrap and refrigerate for at least 8 hours.

Rest the meat at room temperature before grilling, about 1 hour. Light a grill for indirect medium-low heat, about 250°F (see page 14). Brush the grill grate and coat with oil.

Put the brisket, fatty-side up, on the grill away from the heat, and cover the grill. Cook until severely browned and blackened in spots or very well-done (about 170°F on an instant read thermometer), 4 to 6 hours total. Mop or drizzle the brisket with the espresso mop on both sides whenever the surface looks dry, every 45 minutes during the entire cooking time. After 2 hours of cooking, put the brisket in an aluminum foil pan and return the pan of brisket to the grill away from the heat. Cover the grill and continue cooking. The pan helps to retain moisture in the brisket. Once the brisket is in the pan, you only need to mop the top, fatty side. If your grill has a temperature gauge, it should stay around 250°F during the entire cooking time. If using charcoal, add fresh coals about once an hour during cooking.

Remove the pan of brisket from the heat and let rest for 20 minutes.

While the meat is resting, make the grilling sauce. Trim any excess fat from the brisket and slice across the grain (don't trim too much fat, though; the crispy bits taste great). Serve with the grilling sauce.

CHUCK STEAK/CHUCK

Herb-Crusted Chuck Steak and Slow-Baked Potatoes

MAKES 4 SERVINGS

What's so great about chuck steak? Rich, beefy flavor. The chuck or shoulder is the most exercised muscle group on a steer, and exercise is what develops a complex, meaty taste. Any bone-in or boneless chuck steak will do, such as seven-bone, blade, flat iron, Denver, or chuck-eye steak. Depending on how they are cut, chuck steaks can be tender or somewhat chewy, so we sear them over medium-high heat, and then move them over to low heat to finish cooking slowly. Our favorite for this recipe is flat iron steak because it has a deep, brawny flavor.

INGREDIENTS:

3 cups Salsa-Beer Marinade (page 37)

1½ to 2 pounds chuck steaks, about 1 inch thick

4 russet or other baking potatoes, scrubbed

3 tablespoons olive oil

1 teaspoon coarse salt

2 tablespoons Dijon mustard

½ cup Fresh Herb Rub (page 32)

1 cup salsa (any heat level)

6 tablespoons unsalted butter, cut into pieces

Sour cream or butter for the potatoes (optional)

DIRECTIONS:

Put the marinade and steaks in a 1-gallon zipper-lock bag. Press out the air, seal, and refrigerate for 6 to 8 hours.

Light a grill for bilevel medium-high/low heat, about 425/275°F (see page 13). Brush the grill grate and coat with oil. Pat the potatoes dry, then prick each about 6 times with a fork. Coat with about 1 tablespoon of the oil and sprinkle with the salt. Put the potatoes on the grill as far away from the heat as possible, cover, and cook until tender, about 1 to 1½ hours.

About an hour before serving, remove the steaks from the marinade and discard the marinade. Pat the steaks dry and spread all over with the mustard. Combine the herb rub and the remaining 2 tablespoons oil and spread over the mustard. Let stand at room temperature for 30 minutes.

Simmer the salsa in a small saucepan over medium heat until most of the liquid is gone, about 5 minutes. Reduce the heat to low and whisk in the butter. Keep warm.

When the potatoes are nearly done, grill the steaks directly over medium-high heat until nicely grill-marked, about 3 to 4 minutes per side. Reduce the heat to low on a gas grill or move the steaks to the low-heat area on a charcoal or wood grill. Cover and cook to an internal temperature of 135 to 145°F for medium-rare to medium, about 5 to 7 minutes more. Remove and let rest about 5 minutes.

Using a fork, make a lengthwise line of prick marks on one side of each potato. Squeeze the ends toward the middle to crack open. Serve the steak with the salsa butter. If you like, serve the potatoes with sour cream or butter.

SHOULDER TENDER / CHUCK

Grilled Carpaccio
of Shoulder Tender

MAKES 4 TO 6 SERVINGS

Shoulder tender (a.k.a. petite tender or clod tender) comes from the beef chuck and rests on top of the shoulder, near the top blade. It's a fairly narrow strip of beef similar in size and shape to pork tenderloin. Thank God butchers figured out how to separate this one shoulder muscle from the many others in the beef chuck. It's a rarity because it's both tender and flavorful, making shoulder tender excellent served raw. But it's somewhat uncommon, so hunt around for a butcher who can cut it for you. If you can't find it, use the same weight of beef tenderloin. It goes without saying that you should buy the best-quality beef from a reputable butcher or rancher, especially for raw carpaccio. But even if you buy supermarket beef, you can rest easy. Most bacteria reside on the surface of meat, and brief searing not only improves flavor but also kills surface bacteria. A drizzle of quickly made, pourable mayonnaise lends some creaminess to the paper-thin beef. For additional garnishes, serve the carpaccio with grilled ramps and shaved Parmesan.

INGREDIENTS:

1 beef shoulder tender roast (about 1 pound)

1 tablespoon extra-virgin olive oil

½ teaspoon coarse salt

¼ teaspoon ground black pepper

¾ cup baby arugula or microgreens

½ teaspoon minced shallots

½ teaspoon fresh lemon juice

¼ cup Pourable Herbed Mayonnaise (page 42)

1½ tablespoons drained small capers

DIRECTIONS:

Light a grill for direct high heat, about 450°F (see page 12). Keep the roast cold until just before grilling, and then coat the cold roast with about 1 teaspoon of the olive oil and season with the salt and pepper. Brush the grill grate and coat with oil. Grill the roast directly over the heat just until grill-marked on all sides, 4 to 5 minutes total. The center should remain raw.

Quickly chill the roast in the refrigerator, then wrap tightly in plastic and freeze until partially frozen, about 1 hour. Slice paper-thin on a meat slicer. Or slice thinly by hand, and then sandwich each slice between two sheets of plastic wrap and pound until paper-thin.

Arrange the slices on chilled plates. Toss the arugula or microgreens with the shallots, lemon juice, and remaining 2 teaspoons olive oil. Mound a small portion of the greens in the center of each plate. Drizzle lightly with the thinned mayonnaise and garnish with the capers.

Ultimate Cheeseburger

MAKES 6 SERVINGS

The best beef burgers are all about the meat itself instead of fancy toppings. And not all ground beef is created equal. You need some fat or the burger will be dry. You also want flavor, which means choosing meat ground from a well-exercised muscle group such as the chuck. We prefer ground chuck with a meat-to-fat ratio of about 4 to 1 (80 percent lean). Don't skimp on the fat. Many of the flavorful compounds in beef are fat-soluble and you need fat to carry that flavor. You also need some fat for moistness.

Burgers taste best when the meat is ground just before cooking. If you have a grinder or grinder attachment for your mixer at home, cut the meat into thick strips or chunks, and chill it in the freezer until very cold or partially frozen. Then grind it twice. The next best thing is to buy a chuck roast, and have your butcher grind it the same day you plan to cook the burgers. In last place is supermarket beef that has been sitting in plastic for a few days, which yields the blandest, driest burgers because so many of the juices have drained away.

We know that some people like a rounder burger to keep the center rare and red, while others prefer a flatter burger to provide a stable shelf for toppings. Either way, ground meat will swell up slightly in the center during grilling because the meat shrinks around the circumference of the burger, where the heat is highest, squeezing the cooler center and puffing it outward. If you like a rounder, puffier cooked burger, gently shape the raw meat into flat or discus-shaped patties that taper to the edge. If you like a flat cooked burger, make a slight depression in the center of the patty when shaping. It will swell and form a flat surface as the burger cooks.

INGREDIENTS:

2 pounds cold freshly ground beef chuck, 80 percent lean

⅓ cup ice-cold water

¾ teaspoon coarse salt

½ teaspoon ground black pepper

4 to 5 ounces cold cheddar, Swiss, Jack, or blue cheese, shredded or crumbled

Butter for the rolls (optional)

6 crusty yet soft rolls, such as kaiser, split

DIRECTIONS:

Light a grill for direct medium-high heat, about 425°F (see page 12). Using your hands and a light touch, mix together the beef, water, salt, pepper, and cheese. Gently shape into 6 patties no more than 1 inch thick. Refrigerate the burgers until the grill is ready.

Brush the grill grate and coat with oil. Put the burgers directly over the heat, cover, and grill for 7 minutes, flipping after about 4 minutes for medium-done (150°F, slightly pink).

Add a minute per side for well-done. Avoid pressing down on the burgers, which squeezes out moisture and makes them dry.

If you like, butter the rolls before grilling. Grill the rolls, cut-sides down, directly over the heat until toasted, about 1 minute. If serving the burgers directly from the grill, serve on the buns. If the burgers will sit, even for a few minutes, keep the rolls and burgers separate until just before eating.

Cilantro-Lime London Broil

MAKES 6 SERVINGS

Flank steak was the original London broil, a tough, flavorful cut that could be grilled or broiled like more tender steaks, and then sliced against its completely uniform grain to tenderize it. Now it is more common to see London broil cut from the round (leg). But the muscle fibers are not parallel in a round steak, as they are in flank steak, making it impossible to consistently slice against the grain. That's why London broil made from the round is unreliable in texture, and why recipes often direct you to marinate the meat for a day or more in an attempt to tenderize it. Do yourself a favor and use the real London broil—flank steak. In this recipe, we marinate for flavor. Soaking the beef in coriander and lime infuses the flank with a fresh fajita fragrance in just a few hours. Unlike other tough cuts of beef, which require hours of slow indirect grilling, this flank is ready in just 10 minutes. We serve it gilded with cilantro-lime butter sauce.

INGREDIENTS:

1 tablespoon ground cumin

1 tablespoon ground coriander

Coarse salt

Ground black pepper

1 tablespoon sugar

Finely grated zest and juice of 4 limes

½ cup water

2 pounds flank steak

6 tablespoons unsalted butter

1 garlic clove, minced

⅓ cup chopped fresh cilantro

DIRECTIONS:

Combine the cumin, coriander, 1 tablespoon salt, 1 teaspoon pepper, the sugar, the zest and juice of 3 of the limes, and the water in a zipper-lock bag; seal and shake until the salt and sugar dissolve, about 30 seconds. Add the flank steak, press out the air, seal, and refrigerate for at least 2 hours or up to 12 hours if you like.

Remove the steak from the marinade and bring to room temperature before grilling, about 1 hour. Discard the marinade.

Light a grill for direct high heat, about 500°F (see page 12).

Melt the butter in a small frying pan over medium heat, add the garlic, and cook until the garlic sizzles. Stir in the remaining zest and juice of 1 lime and heat to boiling. Remove from the heat and stir in the cilantro, and season with salt and pepper. Keep warm while you grill the steak.

Brush the grill grate and coat with oil. Put the steak on the grill and cook for about 8 to 10 minutes per side for medium-rare to medium-done (135 to 145°F).

Allow to rest for 5 minutes before slicing. Cut against the grain on the diagonal into thin slices. Serve the steak drizzled with some of the cilantro-lime butter sauce; serve the rest of the sauce on the side.

Argentine Stuffed Flank Steak

MAKES 6 MAIN-COURSE OR 10 TO 12 APPETIZER SERVINGS

In Argentina, this stuffed and rolled beef dish is known as matambre, or "hunger killer." Made with eggs, bacon, and beef, it's certainly not for the fainthearted. But sliced crosswise, it makes an impressive presentation. Spinach and carrots are traditional vegetables for the stuffing, and we've used them here. If you prefer, use almost any vegetable combination you like. Grill cooks at parrillas (traditional Argentine grills) sometimes wrap the meat roll in foil and cook it indirectly to mimic a roasting method. But foil prevents the flavor of the fire from getting on the meat, so we like to brown the roll over direct heat first, and then move it away from the heat to continue grill-roasting the beef to tender doneness. Garlicky, colorful chimichurri sauce keeps the meat moist as it cooks and then serves as a sauce on the plate.

INGREDIENTS:

4 small carrots, trimmed and peeled

4 slices bacon

1 thick flank steak (about 2½ pounds), butterflied (see Know-How, below)

1 teaspoon coarse salt

½ teaspoon ground black pepper

½ teaspoon ground cumin

1 tablespoon chopped fresh oregano

2 cups Chimichurri Sauce (page 47)

4 ounces baby spinach leaves

1 small onion, thinly sliced

2 Smoked Eggs (page 367) or hard-cooked eggs, peeled and halved lengthwise

½ red bell pepper, seeded and cut lengthwise into thin strips

DIRECTIONS:

Bring a wide saucepan of salted water to a boil. Add the carrots and cook until beginning to get tender, about 5 minutes. Drain and set aside. Meanwhile, cook the bacon in a skillet over medium heat until crisp, about 5 minutes. Transfer to paper towels and reserve the drippings.

Light a grill for indirect medium-high heat, about 400°F (see page 14).

Stand facing your work surface and position the butterflied steak with the grain running horizontally. Gently pound the steak to an even thickness of ¼ to ½ inch. Mix together the salt, pepper, cumin, and oregano, and then season both sides of the steak with the spice mixture. Reposition so that the cut side is up and the grain is running horizontally.

Spoon ¾ cup of the chimichurri sauce into a bowl and stir in 2 tablespoons of the reserved bacon drippings. Reserve the remaining chimichurri. Brush about half of the chimichurri-drippings mixture over the top of the steak. Arrange half the spinach in a narrow horizontal row close to the edge of the steak nearest you. Crumble half the bacon and half the onion over the spinach. Make three more rows above the spinach: a row of carrots, then eggs, then bell pepper. Position

KNOW-HOW: BUTTERFLYING FLANK STEAK

Stand facing your work surface and position the steak with the roughest side up. The goal is to cut the steak through the side and open it up like a book, so that you end up with a larger, thinner square of meat. Using a sharp, thin knife like a boning knife, make small slashing cuts to slice through one of the longest sides of the steak. Lift the top of the steak as you cut and begin opening it up, taking care to keep the knife level with the cutting surface to make an even horizontal cut all the way across the steak. Stop cutting just before you reach the other end of the meat and open up the butterflied steak so that it lies flat.

continued ➡

the pieces end to end as necessary to create long, horizontal rows. Repeat the rows of spinach/onions/bacon, carrots, eggs, and bell pepper, leaving a 1-inch border of uncovered meat at the top. Drizzle some of the chimichurri-drippings mixture over the stuffing, and then roll the steak from bottom to top into a compact roast. Using kitchen string, tie the roast crosswise at 2-inch intervals. Brush all over with the chimichurri-drippings mixture.

Brush the grill grate and coat with oil. Grill the roast directly over the heat until browned all over, 8 to 10 minutes total. Use tongs and a spatula to move the roast to the unheated area of the grill, and close the lid. Cook until the internal temperature of the meat registers 130°F, 20 to 25 minutes total. During cooking, turn the roast once and baste once or twice with the chimichurri-drippings mixture.

Remove to a cutting board and let stand for 20 minutes. Cut crosswise across the grain into slices about ½ to ¾ inch thick, removing the string as you go. Serve with the reserved chimichurri. The roast can also be chilled and sliced cold.

BACK RIBS/RIB

Pepper-Cured Beef Back Ribs

MAKES 4 SERVINGS

When you finish a meal of back ribs, you feel somewhat like a caveman or Fred Flintstone facing a pile of cartoonishly large beef bones on the table. No wonder they're dubbed dinosaur ribs. Don't be fooled by the prehistoric moniker; back ribs are the most expensive beef ribs you can buy, and their rich, full flavor is worth every penny. They are essentially what remains after rib-eye steaks are made boneless. If your butcher has back ribs, snatch them up for this peppery preparation, finished with tongue-bracing, vinegar-laced barbecue sauce. You can also use short ribs, which are, naturally, smaller. Short ribs will taste good, but the resulting mound of diminutive bones may not satisfy the caveman (or woman) in you.

INGREDIENTS:

8 beef back ribs (about 10 ounces each)

1 tablespoon garlic-flavored oil, homemade (see Know-How, below) or purchased

¼ cup Seven Pepper Rub (page 29)

1 cup Steak House Barbecue Sauce (page 39)

DIRECTIONS:

Coat the ribs all over with the garlic oil, and then sprinkle with the rub. Let stand for 1 hour at room temperature.

Light a grill for indirect medium-high heat, about 375°F (see page 14). Brush the grill grate and coat with oil. Put the ribs on the grill away from the heat, cover, and cook until the thickest piece of meat can be easily pierced with a fork, about 30 minutes, turning after 15 minutes. Baste frequently with the barbecue sauce during the last 10 minutes of cooking.

Remove to a platter and a serve.

KNOW-HOW: MAKING GARLIC OIL

To makes 2 cups, peel and crush the cloves from 1 garlic bulb and combine with 2 cups olive oil in a small saucepan. Warm over medium-low heat until the garlic starts to bubble, about 8 minutes. Cool to room temperature. Strain and store in a closed container in the refrigerator for up to 2 months.

SKIRT STEAK/PLATE

Multipepper Skirt Steak Fajitas

MAKES 8 FAJITAS

Many beef cuts have obscure names, but some are simple and direct like T-bone and skirt steak. Skirt is the perfect name for this long, flat strip of meat cut from the diaphragm of a steer. It's dense, tough, and full of deep, meaty flavor. Fortunately, it's also thin, so it cooks quickly and can be cut across the grain to help tenderize it. That's traditionally how beef fajitas are made, and ours get extra juiciness from a lime, tequila, and coriander brine and a slew of peppers, both hot and sweet. On the downside, skirt steak can be long and unwieldy. To keep it manageable on the grill, cut the skirt into 1-foot lengths, which you can easily flip with tongs.

INGREDIENTS:

2¼ cups Coriander Brine (page 36)

2 garlic cloves, minced

2 pounds beef skirt steak

1 teaspoon ground chipotle chile

¼ cup Cumin-Oregano Rub (page 29)

1 tablespoon canola oil

1 poblano chile, halved lengthwise, stemmed, and seeded

1 Anaheim chile, halved lengthwise, stemmed, and seeded

1 red bell pepper, quartered lengthwise, stemmed, and seeded

1 large onion, sliced ½ inch thick

8 flour tortillas (fajita size)

2 cups of your favorite salsa

4 lime wedges for serving

¾ cup sour cream for serving (optional)

DIRECTIONS:

Combine the brine, garlic, and beef in a 1-gallon zipper-lock bag. Press out the air, seal, and refrigerate for 3 to 4 hours.

Remove the beef from the marinade and pat dry. Mix the chipotle chile into the rub and sprinkle the rub all over the beef. Let stand at room temperature for 30 minutes. Oil the peppers and onion slices and set aside. Spritz the tortillas with a little water and wrap in foil.

Light a grill for bilevel high/medium heat, about 500+/375°F (see page 13). Brush the grill grate and coat with oil. Grill the steak directly over high heat for 5 to 8 minutes per side for medium-rare to medium-done (135 to 145°F on an instant-read thermometer). Remove from the heat and let rest for 5 minutes.

Meanwhile, lower the heat on a gas grill to medium-high, or on a wood or charcoal grill, place the peppers and onion slices over the medium heat. Grill until blackened in spots but still a bit crunchy, about 5 minutes total, flipping the onion slices carefully with a spatula. Grill the foil pack of tortillas directly over medium heat until heated through, about 2 minutes per side. Set aside and keep warm. Remove the peppers and onions from the heat and slice into thin strips. Arrange on a platter.

Cut the steak across the grain on the diagonal into thin slices and arrange on the platter along with the lime wedges. Allow guests to roll up the beef, peppers, and onions in tortillas with the salsa, sour cream (if desired), and a squeeze of lime.

Rosemary Hanger Steaks Crusted in Mustard and Gruyère

MAKES 6 SERVINGS

Hanger steaks are cut from the plate of a steer, just below the chest. These relatively narrow, long strips of meat hang from the skirt steak (diaphragm) and have a chewy texture and rich, beefy taste. A full-bodied red wine marinade intensifies the flavor. To keep the meat from toughening, hanger steak is best grilled quickly over a hot fire. We like to envelop the steak in herbed mustard with a little Gruyère cheese, which melts, dries, and forms a delicious crust.

INGREDIENTS:

1 cup Rosemary Red Wine Marinade (page 36)

1 large hanger steak (about 1½ pounds)

Mustard Gruyère Paste:

⅓ cup finely grated Gruyère cheese

¼ cup whole-grain mustard

2 tablespoons finely chopped fresh parsley

1 tablespoon olive oil

¼ teaspoon salt

⅛ teaspoon freshly ground black pepper

5 tablespoons unsalted butter

6 shallots, thinly sliced

DIRECTIONS:

Pour the marinade into a 1-gallon zipper-lock bag, drop in the steak, press out the air, seal, and refrigerate for at least 8 hours, and up to 16 hours, turning occasionally.

For the paste: Combine the Gruyère, mustard, parsley, oil, salt, and pepper to make a paste.

Light a grill for direct high heat, about 475°F (see page 12). Remove the steak from the marinade and reserve the marinade. Pat the steak dry and coat all over with the paste.

Brush the grill grate and coat with oil. Grill the steak directly over the heat for 5 to 7 minutes per side for rare to medium-rare (125 to 135°F on an instant-read thermometer). Remove and let rest for 5 minutes. Slice across the grain on a diagonal into thin strips.

While the steak is grilling, heat 1 tablespoon of the butter in a small saucepan over medium heat. Add the shallots and sauté until tender but not browned, about 5 minutes. Add the reserved marinade and boil until reduced by about half, at least 5 minutes. Stir in the remaining 4 tablespoons butter. Serve with the steak.

Kalbi with Three Dipping Sauces

MAKES 4 TO 6 SERVINGS

Kalbi (or galbi) are Korean short ribs cut from various sections of the ribs running from shoulder to loin on the steer. Look for ribs with at least 1 inch of meat on the bones because you'll be cutting the meat into a thinner, quick-cooking section for this recipe. Have your butcher remove the silver skin and fat from the ribs and cut the rib bones crosswise into 2-inch lengths. Some Koreans marinate short ribs in cola or lemon-lime soda (the Koreans David grew up with used Sprite), but we prefer a more traditional Korean marinade made with Asian pears, ginger, and soy sauce. Short ribs are best grilled over charcoal for a satisfying, smoky crust. In Korean restaurants, diners cook their meat to taste on a communal charcoal grill in the center of the table. You could set up a similar arrangement at home with a hibachi on a picnic table. If you happen to have 12 little bowls or ramekins, set up the three sauces like they do in restaurants, dividing the sauces among the bowls so everybody gets an individual bowl for dipping. Serve with white rice and kimchi.

INGREDIENTS:

Short Ribs:

3 pounds English-style short ribs, cut into 2-inch lengths and butterflied (see Know-How, facing page)

1½ cups Korean Barbecue Marinade (page 37)

1 tablespoon toasted sesame seeds

3 scallions (green part only), thinly sliced

Asian Pear Dipping Sauce:

⅓ cup soy sauce

⅓ cup rice wine, such as Korean Cheongju or Japanese sake or dry sherry

½ Asian pear, peeled, cored, and very finely chopped

2 scallions (green part only), finely chopped

2 tablespoons honey

Ginger Dipping Sauce:

⅓ cup soy sauce

⅓ cup rice vinegar

1 tablespoon sugar

2 teaspoons grated fresh ginger

Hot Sesame Dipping Sauce:

⅓ cup soy sauce

⅓ cup rice vinegar

1 tablespoon toasted sesame oil

1 tablespoon chile-garlic paste

2 teaspoon toasted sesame seeds

6 to 8 romaine lettuce leaves for wrapping

DIRECTIONS:

For the short ribs: After butterflying the meat, tenderize each section by pounding it lightly with a textured meat mallet or the back of a heavy knife. Combine the meat and marinade in 1-gallon zipper-lock bags. Press out the air, seal, and refrigerate for at least 6 hours or up to 1 day.

For the dipping sauces: Combine the ingredients for each sauce in a separate bowl. Let stand at room temperature for up to 3 hours or refrigerate for up to 1 day. Bring to room temperature before serving.

Remove the meat from the marinade and let stand at room temperature for 20 to 30 minutes. Light a grill for direct high heat, about 500°F (see page 12). Brush the grill grate and coat with oil. Grill the rib sections directly over the heat, turning now and then, until nicely grill-marked, about 2 to 3 minutes per side. Remove to a platter and scatter the sesame seeds and scallions on top.

To serve, allow diners to cut pieces of meat off the bone, wrap the meat in a lettuce leaf, and dip into one of the sauces. When the meat is gone, gnaw on the bones.

KNOW-HOW: BUTTERFLYING SHORT RIBS

Position a rib section, meaty-side up, on a cutting board. The goal is to remove the meaty side from the bone, then cut lengthwise into the meaty side several times to open it out, almost as you would a brochure with several folds. It should be uniformly ¼ inch thick. (See illustrations.)

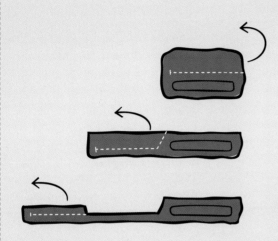

1. Using a sharp, thin-bladed knife, start by cutting through the longest side of the meat along the top side of the bone almost, but not all the way, through the other side. Open up flat like a book.

2. Make an L-shaped cut down into the chunk of meat near the bone, turning your knife so that it becomes parallel to the board about ¼ inch from the bottom of the meat, and cut through almost to the other side. Open the meat up. You will have a strip of meat that is thicker on one side than the other.

3. Make a horizontal cut through the thick piece ¼ inch from the bottom; open it up. Continue until you have a uniform ¼-inch strip of meat attached to the bone on one side.

Beef Rib Roast with White Beans and Moroccan Rub

MAKES 4 TO 8 SERVINGS

Although this recipe is spectacular with any grade of beef, use it as an excuse to treat yourself to real prime rib. Only 2 percent of the beef in the United States is graded prime, and most of that never reaches the retail market. So you will have to seek it out. A trusted butcher can order it for you even if it is something he doesn't normally carry. Ask your butcher to cut the meat from the bone along the ribs, but leave it attached at its widest end. This cut allows the seductive aroma of Moroccan spices like coriander, thyme, and lemon to reach nearly all surfaces of the meat, while retaining the bone for flavor.

INGREDIENTS:

4-bone standing beef rib roast (about 6 to 8 pounds), preferably prime

¼ cup olive oil

½ cup Moroccan Rub (page 27)

1 pound dry white beans, such as great Northern, soaked overnight and drained (see Know-How, below)

1 medium onion, finely chopped

3 garlic cloves, minced

1 teaspoon grated fresh ginger

3 ripe tomatoes, cored, seeded, and coarsely chopped

2 tablespoons chopped fresh flat-leaf parsley

Pinch of cayenne pepper

DIRECTIONS:

If the meat was not cut from the bone when you purchased it (see the recipe introduction), do this yourself, leaving it attached at its widest end. Pat the roast dry and then coat all over with 2 tablespoons of the oil and all but 1 tablespoon of the rub. Include the underside, where roast is sitting on the bones. Let stand at room temperature for at least 1 hour.

Light a grill for indirect medium heat, about 325°F (see page 14). Brush the grill grate and coat with oil. Put the roast, bone-side down, away from the heat over a drip pan (page 15). Cover and grill-roast to an internal temperature of 125 to 135°F for rare to medium-rare, about 1½ hours to 2 hours.

Meanwhile, put the beans in a medium saucepan with enough water to cover by about 2 inches. Bring to a boil, then reduce the heat so that the liquid simmers and cook until the beans are tender, about 1½ hours. About 10 minutes before the beans are done, heat the remaining 2 tablespoons oil in a skillet over medium-low heat. Add the onions, garlic, and ginger and cook until softened, about 5 minutes. Add the tomatoes, parsley, cayenne, and remaining 1 tablespoon Moroccan Rub and cook for 2 minutes. Drain the beans, add to the vegetables, and simmer for 10 to 15 minutes.

Remove the beef to a large carving board, cover loosely with foil, and let rest for 20 minutes. Run your knife parallel to the ribs and separate the big rib-eye section of meat from the rib bones. Cut between the ribs to serve the individual ribs. Slice the roast into thick or thin slices and serve along with the beans.

KNOW-HOW: SOAKING DRIED BEANS

Hydrating beans before cooking reduces cooking time and removes some hard-to-digest carbohydrates, which can cause flatulence. To hydrate them, soak the beans for about 10 hours or overnight in enough water to cover the beans by 3 inches. Drain the soaking water, rinse the beans, and proceed with the recipe. To shorten the soaking time, put the beans and water in a saucepan, bring to a boil, and boil for 2 minutes. Remove from the heat, cover, and let the beans stand in the water for 1 hour. Drain the soaking water, rinse the beans, and proceed with the recipe.

Toasted Cumin Rib Steaks with Chorizo Salsa

MAKES 4 SERVINGS

When taken from prime-grade beef and left whole, the rib roast is known as prime rib. Cut it into steaks, and you've got rib steaks, each including a large rounded "eye" muscle and a few smaller muscles surrounding it. Bone-in rib-eye steaks are called "cowboy steaks" and boneless ones may be called "shell steaks" or *entrecôte*, French for "between the ribs," meaning the steak was cut from between ribs 9 to 11 on the steer. Rib steaks are among steak lovers' favorite cuts for their balance of taste and tenderness. They pack a hefty flavor, so we simply add a spice rub of toasted cumin, coriander, and paprika. A little chipotle chile in the rub ties the flavors with the chorizo salsa served on the side.

INGREDIENTS:

Chorizo Salsa:

6 ounces fresh Mexican chorizo, removed from the casing

2 ripe medium tomatoes, cored, seeded, and finely chopped

2 large jalapeño chile peppers, seeded and finely chopped

1 garlic clove, minced

¼ cup finely chopped red onion

¼ cup chopped fresh cilantro

Juice of 1 lime

Coarse salt

4 boneless beef rib-eye steaks (8 to 10 ounces each), about 1 inch thick (see Know-How, below)

½ cup Toasted Cumin Rub (page 29)

DIRECTIONS:

For the salsa: Crumble the chorizo into a medium skillet and cook over medium heat until browned, about 5 minutes, breaking up the meat with a spoon. Add the tomatoes, chiles, garlic, onion, cilantro, and lime juice; season with salt; and cook until the vegetables just begin to soften, 2 to 3 minutes. Cool to room temperature while you prepare the steaks.

Pat the steaks dry, and then sprinkle with the rub. Let stand at room temperature for about 30 minutes.

Light a grill for bilevel medium-high/medium-low heat, about 425/325°F (see page 13).

Brush the grill grate and coat with oil. Grill the steaks directly over medium-high heat until nicely grill-marked, about 3 to 4 minutes per side. Reduce the heat to medium-low on a gas grill or move the steaks to the medium-low heat area on a charcoal or wood grill. Cover and grill for another 3 to 4 minutes per side for medium-rare to medium-done (135 to 145°F). Transfer to a platter and let rest for 5 minutes. Serve with the salsa.

KNOW-HOW: BONING A RIB ROAST FOR SEASONING

Slip a thin blade boning knife between the meat and the bone at the narrow end of a rib roast. Keeping the side of the knife against bone, cut the roast off the rib bones, stopping just before you reach the widest end.

T-BONE/SHORT LOIN

Gin and Juniper T-Bone with Green Olive Tapenade

MAKES 4 SERVINGS

A spice rub and a sauce are enough to make grilled T-bone taste great. But in this recipe, the rub is a head-spinning mixture of crushed juniper berries, almonds, green peppercorns, thyme, coriander, lemon zest, and cloves. And the sauce is rich with green olives, pine nuts, and extra-virgin olive oil, with a few briny capers for a sharp counterpoint to the rub's exhilarating aromas. The whole effect was so deliriously good the first time we made this dish that the next time we deepened the forest flavors by marinating the steak in gin. That just sent us over the top.

INGREDIENTS:

½ cup Juniper Rub (page 28)

¾ cup gin

1 large T-bone steak (2½ to 3 pounds), about 2 inches thick

3 tablespoons olive oil

Green Olive Tapenade:

1½ cups fresh flat-leaf parsley leaves and small stems

1 cup pitted brine-cured green olives such as Arauco, Sicilian, or Spanish olives

½ cup pine nuts

¼ cup extra-virgin olive oil

2 tablespoons drained capers

1 garlic clove, coarsely chopped

1 tablespoon fresh lemon juice

1 teaspoon fresh thyme leaves

¼ teaspoon coarse salt

¼ teaspoon ground black pepper

DIRECTIONS:

Spoon 2 tablespoons of the rub into a 1-gallon zipper-lock bag. Add all but 1 tablespoon of the gin. Drop in the steak and press the air out of the bag. Seal and refrigerate for 4 to 8 hours, turning occasionally.

For the tapenade: Combine all of the ingredients in a food processor. Pulse until the ingredients are finely minced but not pureed into a paste, 10 to 15 seconds.

Remove the steak from the marinade and pat dry. Coat all over with 2 tablespoons of the olive oil, and then sprinkle the remaining rub all over the steak. Let stand at room temperature for 30 minutes before grilling.

Light a grill for bilevel high/low heat, about 500+/275°F (see page 13). Brush the grill grate and coat with oil. Grill the steak directly over high heat until darkly crusted, 4 to 6 minutes per side. Reduce the heat to low on a gas grill, or move the steak to the low-heat area on a wood or charcoal grill. Cover and grill for another 10 to 15 minutes for medium-rare to medium (135 to 145°F). Transfer to a platter and let rest for 5 minutes.

Douse the steak with the remaining 1 tablespoon gin and 1 tablespoon olive oil. Make 4 servings by cutting the meat from each side of the bone and dividing each section of meat into 4 pieces. Or, you can slice the meat ¼ inch to ½ inch thick, and then divide the slices so each guest receives some tenderloin and some top loin. Serve with the tapenade.

Porterhouse Rubbed with Smoked Salt and Szechuan Pepper

MAKES 4 SERVINGS

The difference between porterhouse and T-bone steak is a matter of where the steak is cut from the loin. Both steaks include a T-shaped bone, a cross section of the spine that divides the smaller, tenderloin meat on one side from the larger, more flavorful strip loin meat on the other. But T-bone steaks are cut from a section of the loin approaching the front of the steer, closer to the ribs, and they include smaller portions of tenderloin and strip loin. Porterhouse steaks are cut from a section approaching the rear of the animal and include larger portions of tenderloin and strip loin.

In this recipe, we call for a 2-inch-thick porterhouse. Most butchers don't stock steaks this thick, so call ahead to order it. We've kept the seasoning simple to emphasize the meat and let the unique taste of Szechuan peppercorns shine through. Unrelated to black peppercorns, Szechuan peppercorns have a warm, floral aroma, similar to cardamom. They're not spicy-hot, but the dried berries cause a buzzing, numbing sensation on your tongue, similar to what you would feel if you pressed your tongue onto the terminals of a 9-volt battery. Sanshool is the active chemical compound, and it's completely stimulating and utterly delicious. For additional smokiness in the steaks, grill over lump charcoal and set up your grill with wood chips (see page 16). A knob of butter or crumbled blue cheese finishes the steak nicely. The drink of choice is, naturally, porter, such as Fuller's London Porter or Samuel Smith's Taddy Porter, styles of beer that originated in taverns selling dark ale and a thick loin steak that eventually came to be called the porterhouse steak.

INGREDIENTS:

4 teaspoons Szechuan peppercorns

1½ teaspoons black peppercorns

1 teaspoon coarse smoked salt

¼ teaspoon sugar

1 large porterhouse steak
(2½ to 3 pounds), about 2 inches thick

1 tablespoon olive oil

DIRECTIONS:

Crack the Szechuan and black peppercorns with a mortar and pestle, or place in a zipper-lock bag and crush with a heavy skillet. Mix in the coarse salt and sugar.

Pat the steak dry and then coat all over with the olive oil. Press the spice rub into both sides of the meat. Let rest at room temperature for 1 hour.

Light a grill for bilevel high/low heat, about 500+/275°F (see page 13). Brush the grill grate and coat with oil. Grill the steak directly over high heat until nicely grill-marked, 4 to 6 minutes per side. Reduce the heat to low on a gas grill or move the steak to the low-heat area on a wood or charcoal grill. Cover and grill for another 10 to 15 minutes for medium-rare to medium-done (135 to 145°F). Remove to a platter and let rest for 5 minutes before slicing.

Make 4 servings by cutting the meat from each side of the bone and dividing each section of meat into 4 pieces. Or, you can slice the meat ¼ inch to ½ inch thick, and then divide the slices so each guest receives some tenderloin and some top loin.

LOIN ROAST / SHORT LOIN

Seared Beef Strip Loin
with Seven Pepper Rub

MAKES 8 TO 10 SERVINGS

Here's a cut of meat for a special occasion. The strip loin is the entire loin of beef from which individual strip steaks are cut. It's pricey but feeds a crowd handily, and it makes a striking presentation. If you like, buy a large roast on sale, cut a few strip steaks from it for the future, and use the rest for this recipe. Either way, leave the "tail" on the strip loin for roasting. It's a little fatty but gives the roast a nice appearance on the table. A strip loin roast is all about the beef, so we simply rub this one with oil, garlic, parsley, and a coarse rub of multicolored peppercorns and chiles.

INGREDIENTS:

1 boneless beef strip loin roast (center-cut, about 5 pounds), fat trimmed to ¼ inch

2 tablespoons olive oil

2 garlic cloves, minced

¼ cup chopped fresh flat-leaf parsley

½ cup Seven Pepper Rub (page 29)

DIRECTIONS:

Pat the roast dry. Combine the oil, garlic, parsley, and rub in a cup. Rub the mixture all over the roast, cover, and refrigerate for at least 8 or up to 16 hours. Remove the roast from the refrigerator and let stand for about 1 hour.

Light a grill for indirect high heat, about 425°F (see page 14). Brush the grill grate and coat with oil. Grill the roast directly over the heat until browned all over, 10 to 15 minutes total, turning every 3 to 5 minutes. On a gas grill reduce the grill heat to about 350°F. Use a spatula and tongs to move the roast over to the unheated area of the grill, fat-side up. Cover and cook to an internal temperature of 125 to 135°F for rare to medium-rare, about 35 to 40 minutes. Remove to a platter and let stand for 20 minutes. Cut crosswise into slices about ¼ to ½ inch thick.

TENDERLOIN ROAST / SHORT LOIN

Whole Grilled Tenderloin Larded with
Gorgonzola and Roasted Garlic

MAKES 8 SERVINGS

Just as strip steaks are cut from the strip loin roast, filet mignon steaks are cut from the tenderloin roast. This baseball-bat-shaped muscle runs on either side of the steer's backbone beneath the ribs. Its anatomical function is to allow the animal to straighten its back when standing upright, something that cattle never do. Thus, it's the least exercised and most meltingly tender part of the animal. There are only two tenderloins per steer. The short supply and high demand makes tenderloin the most expensive beef cut on the market. But if it's tenderness you're after, it doesn't get any better than this. Here we grill the whole tenderloin with a stuffing of blue cheese and roasted garlic and a soothing wrap of fresh herbs. In the next few recipes, we cook from the small end of the tenderloin, from the shoulder (filet mignon) to the tender center (tournedos) to the larger butt end (chateaubriand).

continued

INGREDIENTS:

5 ounces aged Gorgonzola cheese

¼ cup Grill-Roasted Garlic (page 33)

3 tablespoons unsalted butter, softened

3 tablespoons fresh flat-leaf parsley leaves and small stems

¼ teaspoon kosher salt

¼ teaspoon ground black pepper

½ cup Fresh Herb Rub (page 32)

3 tablespoons olive oil

1 beef tenderloin roast (about 3 pounds), trimmed and tied

DIRECTIONS:

Process the cheese, garlic, butter, parsley, salt, and pepper in a food processor until finely chopped and well blended. Combine the rub with the olive oil and set aside.

Make a hole down the center of the tenderloin with a sharpening steel. Push it through the thicker end until its tip comes out the other side. Remove the steel. Insert a thin, long-bladed knife, making shallow slits to enlarge the hole. Spoon the Gorgonzola mixture deep into the hole. When half of the stuffing has been used, fill the hole from the other side.

Spread the herb mixture all over the tenderloin, cover with plastic wrap, and let stand at room temperature for 30 minutes. Or refrigerate for up to 1 day, and then let stand at room temperature for 30 minutes before grilling.

Light a grill for direct medium-high heat, about 425°F (see page 12). Brush the grill grate and coat with oil. Put the tenderloin directly over the heat and close the lid. Grill until browned on all sides, about 5 minutes per side for medium-rare (an internal temperature of 125°F). Remove and let rest for 5 minutes, and then slice ½ inch thick.

FILLET STEAK/SHORT LOIN

Rosemary-Speared Fillet Steaks with Red Wine Butter Sauce

MAKES 4 SERVINGS

Make these steaks the centerpiece of a quick, elegant meal. You'll need sturdy sprigs of rosemary to act as skewers, which flavor the meat and look great on the plate. Even with a simple pan sauce, this dish is on the table in less than 45 minutes. And to go one better, sprinkle crumbled blue cheese over each steak as soon as it comes off the grill. The cheese will melt and lend a sharp edge to the meaty taste.

INGREDIENTS:

4 beef tenderloin fillet steaks 1½ to 2 inches thick

5 long, sturdy sprigs fresh rosemary

1 tablespoon olive oil

½ cup Steak House Rub (page 30)

¾ cup full-bodied red wine

2 tablespoons red wine vinegar

1 small shallot, minced

½ teaspoon honey

¾ cup cold unsalted butter, cut into pieces

DIRECTIONS:

Cut a narrow slit from one side of each steak all the way through to the other with a thin, sharp knife. Spear each fillet with a sprig of rosemary, inserting the rosemary, tough-

end first, into the slit. Reserve the remaining rosemary sprig. Coat the steaks with the oil and with all but 1 tablespoon of the rub. Let stand at room temperature for 30 to 40 minutes.

Light a grill for bilevel high and medium-low heat, about 500+/325°F (see page 13). Brush the grill grate and coat with oil. Grill the steaks directly over high heat until grill-marked, 2 to 3 minutes per side. Reduce the heat to medium-low on a gas grill or move the steaks to the low-heat area on a charcoal or wood grill. Cover and grill for another 3 to 4 minutes per side for medium-rare to medium-done (an internal temperature of 135 to 145°F). Remove to warm plates and cover with foil to keep warm for 5 minutes.

While the steak cooks, combine the wine, vinegar, shallot, and remaining 1 tablespoon rub in a small saucepan. Bring to a boil over high heat, and then reduce the heat slightly and simmer vigorously until the liquid is reduced to about 2 tablespoons in volume, 6 to 8 minutes. Meanwhile, finely chop the leaves from the remaining sprig of rosemary and add to the pan along with the honey. When the liquid is reduced, whisk in the butter, a piece or two at a time, until incorporated. Serve with the steaks or, for a smoother sauce, strain before serving.

TOURNEDOS/SHORT LOIN

Tournedos and Mushroom Skewers

MAKES 6 SERVINGS

Tournedos are small round slices of beef cut from the center or narrow end of the tenderloin. It's an elegant cut deserving an elegant treatment. It's also quite lean and benefits from rich accompaniments like the béarnaise sauce served here. If you like, serve these stylish skewers with Grilled Potato Cakes (page 307).

INGREDIENTS:

8 small bamboo or metal skewers

1½ pounds beef tenderloin, cut into 8 equal pieces, each at least 1½ inches thick

8 ounces cremini mushrooms, brushed clean

1 tablespoon olive oil

¼ cup Steak House Rub (page 30)

Béarnaise Sauce:

2 tablespoons dry white wine

2 tablespoons white wine vinegar

1 tablespoon chopped shallot

4 sprigs fresh tarragon

2 large egg yolks

1 teaspoon water

½ cup melted unsalted butter

¼ teaspoon coarse salt

⅛ teaspoon ground white or black pepper

DIRECTIONS:

If you are grilling with bamboo skewers, soak them in water for 30 minutes. Toss the beef pieces and mushrooms with the oil. Thread the beef onto four of the skewers and the mushrooms onto the four remaining skewers. Sprinkle the rub all over the beef and mushrooms. Let stand at room temperature for 30 minutes.

Light a grill for direct medium-high heat, about 450°F (see page 12).

For the béarnaise sauce: Combine the wine, vinegar, shallots, and 3 sprigs of the tarragon in a small saucepan. Bring to a simmer over medium heat and continue simmering until reduced by about half. Remove the tarragon and let the mixture cool to lukewarm.

Put the egg yolks and water in the top of a double boiler or in a stainless-steel bowl and whisk until frothy. Set the top of the double boiler or the bowl over gently simmering water, whisk in the vinegar mixture, and continue whisking until the eggs are slightly thickened, 2 to 3 minutes. Remove from the heat and gradually whisk in the melted butter in a steady stream.

continued

Chop the leaves from the remaining sprig of tarragon and stir into the sauce. Season with the salt and pepper, cover, and keep warm until ready to serve.

Brush the grill grate and coat with oil. Grill the skewers directly over the heat until the mushrooms are hot and the meat is browned on all sides and firm to the touch, about 8 minutes, turning every few minutes. Remove to plates, serving one beef and one mushroom skewer per person. Accompany with the béarnaise sauce.

STRIP STEAK/SHORT LOIN

Cumin-Crusted Strip Steak with Sweet Onion Chutney

MAKES 4 TO 6 SERVINGS

When filet mignon steaks are cut from one side of the T-bone, what's left on the other side of the bone is called a strip steak. This reliable piece of sirloin strikes a balance of tenderness and flavor that pleases the masses. It takes to almost any combination of marinades, rubs, and sauces. We take these steaks on a ride toward Mumbai with a crusty coating of aromatic whole cumin, coriander, and cardamom seeds. Onion chutney made with cilantro, mint, and serrano chiles rounds out the flavors. For a more fiery chutney, leave the seeds in the chiles.

INGREDIENTS:

4 boneless strip steaks
(6 to 8 ounces each),
fat trimmed to ¼ inch

Canola oil or olive oil for the steaks

¼ cup Coarse Cumin Rub
(page 29)

Sweet Onion Chutney:

2 thick slices sweet onion, such as Vidalia

¼ cup fresh cilantro leaves

2 tablespoons fresh mint leaves

2 serrano or jalapeño chile peppers,
stemmed and seeded

1 tablespoon sugar

1 teaspoon coarse salt

2 tablespoons Worcestershire sauce

DIRECTIONS:

Light a grill for direct medium-high heat, about 450°F (see page 12). Let the steaks rest at room temperature for at least 15 minutes. Pat the steaks dry, and then coat all over with oil. Sprinkle with the cumin rub. Brush the grill grate and coat with oil. Grill the steaks directly over the heat for 3 to 5 minutes per side for medium-rare to medium-done (an internal temperature of 135 to 145°F). Remove and let rest for 5 minutes.

For the chutney: While the steak cooks, put the onion slabs on the grill near the steak and cook until nicely grill-marked, about 3 minutes per side. Remove the grilled onions to a food processor along with the cilantro, mint, chiles, sugar, salt, and Worcestershire sauce. Pulse until chunky. Serve the chutney with the steak.

Smoky Top Sirloin with Homemade Steak Sauce

MAKES 4 TO 6 SERVINGS

On the back of a steer, the sirloin is a transition area between the tender short loin (home of tenderloin and filet mignon) and the much tougher rump. For that reason, buying steak labeled simply "sirloin" is a gamble. It could be tough and gristly or rather tender and beefy tasting. Ask for top sirloin butt steak, a beefy-tasting cut that veers toward tenderness. We like them at least 1½ inches thick, which could be a special order if your butcher routinely cuts thinner steaks. To enhance the full taste of sirloin, we pile on the smokiness with liquid smoke in the brine; smoked salt, smoked paprika, and chipotle chiles in the rub; and smoldering wood chips in the grill. This spice rub has quite a kick. For less heat, use half the amount of chipotle chile.

INGREDIENTS:

2 cups wood chips, such as hickory, oak, or mesquite, soaked in water for 30 minutes

3 cups Smokin' Brine (page 33)

2 to 2½ pounds boneless top sirloin butt steak, about 1½ inches thick

¼ cup Smokin' Rub (page 26)

Homemade Steak Sauce:

4-inch strip orange zest and juice of ¼ orange

3 tablespoons balsamic vinegar

3 tablespoons apple cider vinegar

3 tablespoons water

2 tablespoons tomato paste

2 tablespoons soy sauce

1 tablespoon finely chopped onion

1 tablespoon Dijon mustard

1 tablespoon molasses

1 tablespoon chopped raisins

½ tablespoon honey

1 teaspoon tamarind paste concentrate

1 small garlic clove, smashed but left in one piece

1 bay leaf

Pinch of dried thyme leaves

Pinch of ground coriander

Pinch of ground cloves

Pinch of ground cinnamon

Pinch of ground ginger

Pinch of cayenne pepper

Coarse salt to taste

DIRECTIONS:

Combine the brine and steak in a 1-gallon zipper-lock bag. Press out the air, seal, and refrigerate for 2 hours. Drain and pat the steak dry with paper towels. Sprinkle with the rub and let stand at room temperature for 45 minutes.

For the steak sauce: Place all of the ingredients for the steak sauce in a small saucepan and stir until smooth over medium heat. Bring to a simmer, and then reduce the heat to low and simmer gently until thick, 10 to 15 minutes. Fish out and discard the orange zest and bay leaf. Cool slightly, and then transfer the mixture to a food processor and puree until very smooth, scraping down the sides once or twice. Taste and add more salt if necessary. Cool.

Light a grill for bilevel high/medium-low heat with smoke, about 500+/325°F (see pages 13 and 16). Add the wood chips and when you see smoke, brush the grill grate, and coat with oil. Grill the steak directly over high heat until nicely grill-marked, about 3 to 5 minutes per side. Reduce the heat on a gas grill to medium-low, or move the steak to the medium-low-heat area on a wood or charcoal grill. Cover and cook for another 8 to 10 minutes for medium-rare to medium-done (an internal temperature of 135°F to 145°F). Transfer to a platter and let rest for 5 minutes before slicing. Serve with the steak sauce.

BOTTOM SIRLOIN/SIRLOIN

Chimichurri Beef Kebabs with Yams and Chorizo

MAKES 4 SERVINGS

A little tougher than top sirloin, bottom sirloin makes great kebabs because the tough connective tissue is cut in several places, making the meat easier to chew. Here we pair the sirloin with an Argentinean chimichurri that explodes with the bright green flavors of parsley and cilantro along with sharp sherry vinegar, rich virgin olive oil, and a modicum of hot pepper flakes for kick. If you're skeptical of yams with beef, consider their molasses-like sweetness and how it caramelizes on the grill and provides a sunburst of flavor to complement the roasted meat. It works, and the paprika-spiked sausage heightens the sensation on all levels.

INGREDIENTS:

4 bamboo or metal skewers

2 cups Chimichurri Sauce (page 47)

¼ cup Smoked Paprika Rub (page 28)

1 pound trimmed bottom sirloin, cut into 1½-inch cubes

12 ounces yams or orange-flesh sweet potatoes, peeled and cut into 1½-inch cubes

2 teaspoons olive oil

8 ounces cured chorizo sausage, sliced diagonally about ½ inch thick

DIRECTIONS:

Make the sauce and rub. Let the steak stand at room temperature for 30 minutes before grilling. If you are grilling with bamboo skewers, soak them in water for 30 minutes.

Toss the yams with the oil in a microwaveable dish. Cover and microwave at full power until barely tender, 2 to 3 minutes. In a large bowl, gently toss the parcooked yams with the steak, chorizo, and paprika rub until evenly coated. Thread the yams, steak, and chorzo alternately on the skewers, leaving a little space beween each piece.

Light a grill for direct medium-high heat, about 425°F (see page 12). Brush the grill grate and coat with oil. Grill the kebabs directly over the heat until the beef is browned on all sides and firm to the touch, about 10 minutes total, turning every few minutes. Serve with the chimichurri.

Spit-Roasted Brazilian Picanha

MAKES 4 TO 6 SERVINGS

Picanha (pee-KAHN-yay) is the Brazilian term for a flavorful cut of meat known in North America as top sirloin cap or coulotte. It's the classic cut of meat grilled in Brazilian rodizio or churrascuria steak houses around the world, where an endless parade of grilled meats is brought to the table and cut straight from metal swords, which function as skewers.

The most popular meat is a C-shaped piece of picanha from the top of the sirloin. When shopping for it, tell the butcher you want top sirloin cap. If you can't get it, ask for tri-tip instead. True picanha is so flavorful (and sensibly priced) that it needs little seasoning—traditionally only sea salt. We add some garlic and briefly cure the salted meat at room temperature, and use a rotisserie so the meat is self-basting. If you don't have a rotisserie, use large metal skewers and position them 2 to 3 inches above the fire. The molho à campanha is a rustic Brazilian "country sauce" similar to Mexican salsa.

INGREDIENTS:

Picanha:

2 to 3 pounds beef top sirloin cap or tri-tip, fat trimmed to ¼ inch

6 garlic cloves, mashed or pressed

⅓ cup coarse sea salt

¼ cup olive oil

Molho à Campanha:

3 tomatoes, cored, seeded, and finely chopped

1 small green bell pepper, cored, seeded, and finely chopped

1 small red chile pepper, such a malagueta, serrano, or jalapeño, seeded and minced

½ cup finely chopped red onion

¼ cup finely chopped fresh flat-leaf parsley or cilantro

2 tablespoons red wine vinegar

2 tablespoons extra-virgin olive oil

½ teaspoon coarse salt

DIRECTIONS:

For the picanha: Cut the beef across the grain into pieces about 2 inches thick. Combine the garlic, salt, and oil to make a paste. Slather the paste all over the meat and let rest at room temperature for 1 hour.

For the molho à campanha: Combine all of the ingredients in a serving bowl and let stand at room temperature until ready to serve. Or cover and refrigerate for up to 2 days and return to room temperature before serving.

Light a grill for direct medium-high heat, about 450°F, with a rotisserie in place (see pages 12 and 17). Brush most of the salt off the meat. To skewer each piece, push the rotisserie spit through the fat on one end of a piece then bend the meat into a C shape and push the spit through the meat and fat on the other end. You should end up with a C-shaped piece of meat with the fat layer pierced on either end and bent round in the middle of the C. Repeat with the remaining pieces, positioning them close together on the spit. Secure according to the rotisserie directions and place the spit in the rotisserie assembly. The meat should rotate about 4 inches above the heat source. Cook to an internal temperature for 125 to 135°F for rare to medium-rare, about 10 to 14 minutes.

Remove the spit from the rotisserie assembly. For an authentic presentation, bring the spit to the table and carve ¼-inch-thick slices off the side of the meat for your guests (use thick grill gloves if necessary). If the meat is too rare for your taste, return it to the rotisserie for further grilling. Serve with the molho à campanha.

Beer-Buttered Rump

MAKES 6 TO 8 SERVINGS

The wedge-shaped rump roast includes meat from both the round and the sirloin. This makes it somewhat tough but also very tasty. Rump is more flavorful than bottom round and eye of round roast, and it's best suited to cooking with some kind of liquid to help break down tough connective tissue. We like to grill rump on a rotisserie to keep the meat moist with constantly rolling rivulets of a beer-and-butter-based mop. If you don't have a rotisserie, see the alternate instructions. Either way, the molasses brine ensures juicy roast beef while the rub of coriander and mustard deepens the beefy flavor.

INGREDIENTS:

4 cups Molasses Beer Brine (page 35)

1 cup chopped onion

3 garlic cloves, minced

2 bay leaves

½ teaspoon cracked black pepper

1 boneless beef rump roast (about 4 to 5 pounds)

2 tablespoons Coriander-Mustard Rub (page 31)

Beer Butter Mop:

4 tablespoons unsalted butter, melted

¾ cup beer, preferably dark

¼ cup apple cider vinegar

2 tablespoons Worcestershire sauce

DIRECTIONS:

Combine the brine, onion, garlic, bay leaves, and black pepper in a 2-gallon zipper-lock bag. Add the rump, press out the air, seal, and refrigerate for 4 to 6 hours.

Remove the rump from the brine, pat dry, and sprinkle the rub all over. Let stand at room temperature for 1 hour.

For the beer butter mop: Combine the ingredients in a small bowl.

Light a grill for indirect medium-low heat, about 300°F, with a rotisserie in place (see pages 14 and 17). Push the spit through the center of the roast and secure according to the rotisserie directions. Place the spit in the rotisserie assembly. The meat should rotate 4 to 5 inches from the heat source. Cover

and cook to an internal temperature of 125 to 135°F for rare to medium-rare, about 1 to 1¼ hours. After the first 15 minutes of cooking, drizzle the roast generously every 15 minutes or so with the mop.

If you don't have a rotisserie, use a covered grill set up for indirect medium-low heat. Sear the roast directly over the heat for about 5 minutes per side, then move the roast away from the heat, cover, and grill for about 50 minutes more, basting and turning the roast every 15 minutes or so.

Remove the spit from the rotisserie assembly and remove the roast from the spit to a platter. Let rest for 15 to 20 minutes. Thinly slice across the grain.

Barbecued Beef Cheeks

MAKES 4 SERVINGS

Beef cheeks are tough meat. As cattle chew cud all day, their cheeks develop thick muscle fibers, which only taste good when slowly cooked until they are fall-apart tender. Time is your biggest ally. Barbecuing and braising are the traditional cooking methods for tough meats, and this recipe combines them both. The cheeks are marinated in red wine infused with rosemary for a day, and then browned over direct heat and returned to the marinade to finish cooking away from the heat. Call them "grill-braised" if you like. The moisture helps to dissolve the cheeks' tough connective tissue and melt its gelatin, creating a mouth-filling sauce. Like most braised dishes, this one tastes even better when made a couple of days ahead, cooled in the sauce, and then reheated in the sauce before serving. We like to serve the cheeks with a spoonful of mashed celeriac potatoes spiked with horseradish. You could also serve them with polenta.

INGREDIENTS:

4 cups wood chips, such as hickory, mesquite, or oak, soaked in water for 30 minutes

2 cups Rosemary Red Wine Marinade (page 36)

1 small onion, finely chopped

1 small leek (light green and white parts), finely chopped

1 medium carrot, finely chopped

½ celery rib, finely chopped

1 garlic clove, minced

1 tablespoon chopped fresh flat-leaf parsley

1 bay leaf

4 small trimmed beef cheeks (about 3 to 4 pounds total)

½ teaspoon coarse salt

¼ teaspoon ground black pepper

1 can (15 ounces) peeled chopped tomatoes, with juice (about 1¾ cups)

Celeriac Potato Mash:

1½ pounds celeriac

8 ounces russet potatoes

Kosher salt

3 tablespoons unsalted butter

⅔ cup light cream

1 tablespoon finely grated fresh horseradish root

Ground white or black pepper

½ ounce dried porcini mushrooms

1 cup beef broth

DIRECTIONS:

Combine the marinade, onion, leek, carrot, celery, garlic, parsley, and bay leaf in a 1-gallon zipper-lock bag. Add the beef, press out the air, seal, and refrigerate for 1 day.

Remove the beef from the marinade and pat dry. Reserve the marinade. Season the beef with the salt and pepper and let stand for 10 to 15 minutes.

Light a grill for indirect high heat, about 425°F, with smoke (see pages 12 and 16). Drain the water from about 1 cup of the chips and add to the grill. Brush the grill grate and coat with oil.

Grill the beef directly over the heat until lightly browned on all sides, 8 to 10 minutes total. Meanwhile, combine the tomatoes (with their juice) and the reserved marinade with its vegetables in a medium saucepan. Bring to a boil over high heat and continue boiling for 5 minutes.

Position a medium-large disposable aluminum pan (just big enough to hold the beef) over the unheated part of the grill and transfer the browned beef to the pan. Reduce the grill heat to low, about 250°F. Pour enough of the marinade and vegetables into the pan to come about halfway up the meat. Reserve any remaining marinade. Cover and grill the beef

continued ➡

in the pan away from the heat until fork-tender, about 3½ to 4 hours. Turn over the meat in the liquid about halfway through the cooking. On a charcoal grill, add fresh wood chips and coals when the old ones die out, about once an hour. To remove the pan from the grill, carefully slide a wooden board or a metal tray beneath it to stabilize it, and lift the pan with the board or tray. Let the beef cool in the liquid until warm.

For the celeriac potato mash: Meanwhile, peel and trim the celeriac and potatoes, and then cut into 1-inch cubes. Put in a medium saucepan, cover with cold water, and season the water with salt. Cover and bring to a boil. Reduce the heat to medium, partially cover, and cook until the potatoes are tender when pierced with a knife, about 20 minutes. Drain in a colander and return the empty pan to low heat. Add the butter, cream, and horseradish and cook until combined, 1 to 2 minutes. Add the celeriac and potatoes and mash with a potato masher or food mill (avoid a food processor or blender, which will make the mixture gluey). Season with salt and pepper and keep warm.

Remove the beef from the liquid, set aside, and cover to keep warm. Strain the liquid into a medium saucepan and spoon off any excess fat. Add the dried mushrooms and the beef broth to the liquid. Bring to a boil over high heat and boil until the liquid reduces to a medium-thick sauce, about 15 minutes. Strain again and season the sauce with salt and pepper if necessary. Serve the sauce in shallow bowls, alongside the beef cheeks and celeriac potato mash.

HEART / VARIETY MEAT

Beef Heart Kebabs with Fire-Roasted Yellow Pepper Sauce

MAKES 4 SERVINGS

You might think hearts are soft, tender things. But the heart of a steer is a strong muscle that pumps vigorously around the clock to keep this enormous animal alive. It's tough, but also extremely flavorful. In Peru beef hearts are skewered and grilled by street vendors everywhere. They're as common as soft pretzels in New York City. These anticuchos (Quechua for "kebabs") feature the hot, sunny flavor of aji amarillo, a spicy yellow chile pepper in a dried and ground form that infuses the meat. If you have access to a good Latin American market, ground aji amarillo is worth seeking out. If not, use a combination of smoked paprika and ground chipotle chile. Don't be tempted to skip the ground annatto seeds (also called achiote seeds); they deliver a distinctive musky aroma and gorgeous yellow color. McCormick sells them in most grocery stores. If you can find only whole seeds, grind them in a spice grinder or coffee mill. For a late-summer meal, serve the beef kebabs with grilled corn on the cob and Grilled Potato Cakes (page 307).

INGREDIENTS:

4 bamboo or metal skewers

Beef Heart:

1½ pounds beef heart, cleaned of veins and fat

⅔ cup olive oil

⅓ cup red wine vinegar

Juice of ½ lemon

2 garlic cloves, minced

1 tablespoon ground aji amarillo, or 2 teaspoons smoked paprika plus 1 teaspoon ground chipotle chile

1 teaspoon ground annatto seeds

1 teaspoon ground cumin

1 teaspoon coarse salt

½ teaspoon ground black pepper

½ teaspoon ground turmeric

2 tablespoons chopped fresh flat-leaf parsley

Fire-Roasted Yellow Pepper Sauce:

1 yellow bell pepper

1 scallion, trimmed

1 large garlic clove, skin on

1 tablespoon white wine vinegar

Juice of ½ lemon

2 tablespoons olive oil

1 teaspoon ground cumin

1 teaspoon ground aji amarillo, or ¾ teaspoon smoked paprika plus ¼ teaspoon ground chipotle chile

½ teaspoon ground turmeric

¼ teaspoon sugar

¼ teaspoon coarse salt

¼ teaspoon ground black pepper

DIRECTIONS:

For the beef heart: Cut the cleaned beef heart into 1½- to 2-inch squares and set aside. In a 1-gallon zipper-lock plastic bag, combine the oil, vinegar, lemon juice, garlic, aji amarillo, ground annatto, cumin, salt, pepper, and turmeric. Stir to combine. Pour ¼ cup of the marinade into a small bowl and stir in the parsley. Cover and set aside. Add the beef heart to the marinade in the bag. Press out the air, seal, and refrigerate for 3 hours.

For the sauce: Light a grill for direct medium-high heat, about 425°F (see page 12). Brush the grill grate and coat with oil. Grill the yellow pepper directly over the heat until blacked all over, 4 to 6 minutes per side. Transfer to a paper bag or small bowl. Seal the bag or cover the bowl and let rest for 15 to 20 minutes. Meanwhile, grill the scallion and garlic directly over the heat until charred in spots, 4 to

6 minutes. Peel the garlic, and then transfer it and the scallion to a food processor. When the pepper is cool enough to handle, pull out the stem and core with the seeds. Tear the pepper in half lengthwise and gently scrape off any lingering seeds or ribs. Peel and discard the skin with your fingers or the edge of a paring knife. Transfer the roasted pepper to the food processor along with the vinegar, lemon juice, olive oil, cumin, ground aji amarillo, turmeric, sugar, salt, and pepper. Process until relatively smooth.

If you are grilling with bamboo skewers, soak them in water for at least 30 minutes. Remove the beef heart from the marinade and thread on the skewers. Grill directly over the heat until nicely grill-marked, about 3 to 4 minutes per side, brushing almost constantly with the reserved ¼ cup marinade. Remove to plates and serve with the yellow pepper sauce.

MARROW BONES/VARIETY MEAT

Bourbon-Braised Marrow Bones with Parsley Salad

MAKES 4 SERVINGS

Here's our take on the roasted marrow bones that Fergus Henderson popularized at St. John restaurant in London. We grill-braise the bones in foil with a couple of shots of bourbon for sweet, caramel-y flavor. The parsley salad adds bright saltiness, and nutty aromas of walnut oil commingle with the bourbon and bones. Scooping the softened marrow onto toast makes a snack of ritualistic satisfaction. If you absolutely love marrow, be sure to also try the Grilled Veal Sweetbreads with Grilled Marrow on Toast (page 107).

INGREDIENTS:

Marrow Bones:

¼ cup walnut oil

¼ cup bourbon

2 teaspoons chopped fresh rosemary

2 garlic cloves, minced

¼ teaspoon coarse sea salt

⅛ teaspoon ground black pepper

8 center-cut beef marrow bones, each about 3 inches

4 slices from a large round loaf of crusty bread, each about ¼ to ½ inch thick

2 tablespoons extra-virgin olive oil

continued →

Parsley Salad:

1 cup loosely packed fresh flat-leaf parsley leaves, coarsely chopped

1 tablespoon minced shallot

1 tablespoon drained capers, chopped if large

2 tablespoons plump, buttery, oil-cured black olives, pitted and finely chopped

2 canned anchovy fillets, chopped

¼ cup walnut oil

Juice of ½ lemon

Pinch of coarse sea salt

Pinch of ground black pepper

DIRECTIONS:

For the marrow bones: Combine the walnut oil, bourbon, rosemary, garlic, salt, and pepper in a large bowl. Add the bones and toss to coat. Cover with plastic and refrigerate for 6 to 8 hours.

Remove the marinating bones from the refrigerator and let stand at room temperature for 30 minutes.

Light a grill for indirect medium-high heat, about 375°F (see page 14). Wrap the bones in heavy-duty foil, about 2 bones per bundle, topping each with some marinade. Put the foil bundles on the grill away from the heat, cover, and cook until the marrow is warm, about 20 minutes. Open the foil bundles and keep warm.

Cut the bread slices in half crosswise on a diagonal, then brush with the olive oil. Grill the bread directly over the heat until lightly toasted, 1 to 2 minutes per side.

For the parsley salad: Toss the parsley, shallot, capers, olives, and anchovies in a medium bowl. Just before serving, drizzle with the oil and lemon juice, sprinkle with a little salt and pepper, and toss.

To serve, scoop out the marrow from the bone, spread on the grilled toast, and top with parsley salad.

OXTAIL/VARIETY MEAT

Barbecued Oxtail in Mole Sauce

MAKES 4 TO 6 SERVINGS

The tail of an ox is packed with connective tissue that, given time and gentle heat, transforms into the most unctuous, mouth-filling substance to ever pass your lips—gelatin. An oxtail's dark red meat has deep, beefy flavor. Together, the dark flavor and rich texture of slow-cooked oxtail scream for chocolate. We turned to Mexico's chile-rich mole for help. Toasted and rehydrated ancho and guajillo chiles, along with grill-blistered tomatoes and garlic, meld into a pureed sauce that finds balance from flowing melted chocolate. We call for Mexican chocolate, such as Ibarra, which is flavored with cinnamon, almonds, vanilla, and sugar and is widely available. But if you can't find it, use semisweet chocolate and add ½ teaspoon ground cinnamon along with a few drops each of vanilla and almond extracts. Serve the oxtail with plenty of rice to soak up the sumptuous sauce.

INGREDIENTS:

3 cups wood chips,
such as hickory or oak,
soaked in water for
30 minutes

Oxtails:

¼ cup Mole Rub (page 27)

3 tablespoons canola oil

5 pounds oxtails, cut into 2-inch pieces

Mole Sauce:

3 ounces dried ancho chiles (about 6)

1 ounce dried guajillo chiles (about 4)

3 large ripe plum tomatoes

4 garlic cloves, skins on

¼ cup chopped Mexican chocolate (about 1 ounce)

2 tablespoons almonds

1 teaspoon dried oregano leaves

½ teaspoon ground cumin

½ teaspoon ground cinnamon

¼ teaspoon ground black pepper

4 cups beef broth

DIRECTIONS:

For the oxtails: Combine the spice rub and oil in a 1-gallon zipper-lock bag. Add the oxtails, press out the air, and seal the bag. Refrigerate for 8 hours.

For the mole sauce: Light a grill for indirect medium heat, about 300°F, with smoke (see pages 14 and 16). Brush the grill grate and coat with oil. Tear open the chiles and discard the stems and seeds. Open up the chiles and press flat with the palm of your hand. Brush the grill grate and coat with oil. Grill the chiles directly over the heat, holding them flat with a spatula, until charred in spots, about 30 seconds per side. Remove to a bowl and cover with hot water. Let soak for 30 minutes.

Meanwhile, grill the tomatoes and garlic directly over the heat until the skins are blackened, about 10 minutes, turning now and then. When cool enough to handle, peel the tomatoes and garlic and transfer to a food processor. Pluck the rehydrated chiles from the liquid and add to the processor along with the chocolate, almonds, oregano, cumin, cinnamon, black pepper, and 2 cups of the broth. Process until very smooth, and then press the mixture through a mesh strainer into a bowl. Stir in 1½ cups of the remaining broth and set aside.

Remove the beef from the marinade, pat dry, and let stand at room temperature for 15 minutes. Grill the oxtails directly over the heat until browned all over, 10 to 15 minutes total. Meanwhile, pour the mole sauce into a medium-large disposable aluminum pan (just big enough to hold the oxtails) and put directly over the heat. Simmer for 5 minutes. Drain 1 cup of the wood chips and add to the grill. Transfer the browned oxtails to the pan and move the pan away from the heat. At this point, you should start to see smoke from the wood chips in the grill. Cover the grill and cook until the oxtails are tender, about 2½ hours, adding a handful of the remaining wood chips about once an hour. Add broth to the pan as necessary to keep the liquid level about halfway up the meat.

To remove the pan from the grill, carefully slide a wooden board or a metal tray beneath it to stabilize it, and lift the pan with the board or tray. Let the oxtails cool in the liquid until warm.

Remove the warm oxtails from the liquid, set aside, and cover to keep warm. Pour the liquid into a medium saucepan, let it settle for a few minutes, and then spoon off any excess fat from the surface. Bring to a boil over high heat and boil until the liquid reduces to a medium-thick sauce, 5 to 10 minutes. Serve with the oxtails.

VEAL

Food lovers have always exalted young, tender foods like baby vegetables, kid goat, and baby beef or veal. "The more tender the better" has been the mantra, and the veal industry has been happy to oblige. Veal has historically been the apotheosis of tender meat. In North America, most veal producers rely upon the dairy industry to develop their special brand of luscious meat.

Dairy cows must bear calves once a year to produce sufficient quantities of milk, and those male calves not used for breeding are sold and raised for the veal market. To keep the meat creamy, veal calves are typically fed a diet of up to 70 percent milk products, such as whey and whey protein concentrate, which also comes from the cheese and dairy industry. Technically, any calf slaughtered before nine months of age can be called veal, but most veal comes from male dairy cattle brought to slaughter at five months of age or less.

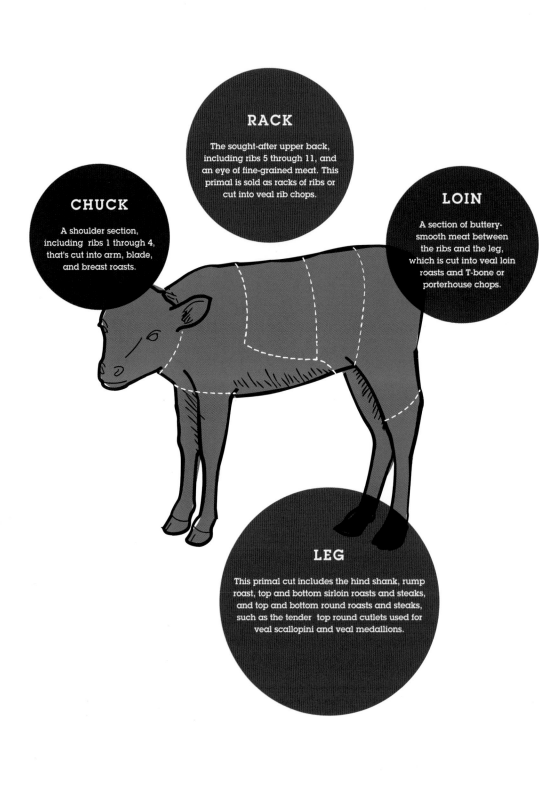

RACK

The sought-after upper back, including ribs 5 through 11, and an eye of fine-grained meat. This primal is sold as racks of ribs or cut into veal rib chops.

CHUCK

A shoulder section, including ribs 1 through 4, that's cut into arm, blade, and breast roasts.

LOIN

A section of buttery-smooth meat between the ribs and the leg, which is cut into veal loin roasts and T-bone or porterhouse chops.

LEG

This primal cut includes the hind shank, rump roast, top and bottom sirloin roasts and steaks, and top and bottom round roasts and steaks, such as the tender top round cutlets used for veal scallopini and veal medallions.

VEAL

INGREDIENT / PRIMAL CUT	OTHER NAMES	HOW TO GRILL	SUBSTITUTIONS
SHOULDER ROAST / CHUCK	Chuck roast, arm roast	INDIRECT medium-low	Blade roast
BREAST / CHUCK	Brisket, flank	INDIRECT medium-low	Veal shoulder arm or blade roast
CROWN ROAST / RACK	---	INDIRECT medium	Lamb crown roast
RIB CHOPS / RACK	Rib eye	DIRECT medium-high	Loin chop
T-BONE CHOP / LOIN	Porterhouse chop; loin chop	BILEVEL medium-low	Rib chop
TOP ROUND CUTLET / LEG	Veal scallopini, escalopes de veau, veal scallops, leg cutlet	DIRECT high	Thin, boneless lamb leg steak
SHANK / LEG OR SHOULDER	Hindshank (leg), foreshank (shoulder)	INDIRECT medium-low	Beef shanks, lamb shanks, veal arm roast
CALF'S LIVER / VARIETY MEAT	Veal liver	DIRECT medium	Lamb liver, beef liver
SWEETBREADS / VARIETY MEAT	Thymus, pancreas	DIRECT medium	Brains
BRATWURST / VARIETY MEAT	---	DIRECT medium	Weisswurst (veal sausage) or other sausage links
FRIES / VARIETY MEAT	Testicles	DIRECT high	Lamb or beef testicles

Milk-Fed, Grain-Fed, Grass-Fed, and Natural Veal

All veal is young, but the quality of the meat has more to do with exercise and feed than age. As North American veal producers improved and streamlined production, they found it advantageous to confine young calves to stalls. Individual veal crates became the norm to restrict the calves' movement, prevent muscle development, and keep the meat ultra-tender and mild in flavor. Velvety soft, finely grained meat is the hallmark of milk-fed veal, and consumers pay a high price for it. But animal protection groups raised enough red flags about production methods to split the veal industry into two primary camps, which now produce two distinct types of veal: milk-fed veal and a broader category of "natural" veal.

For milk-fed or white veal, the calves have historically been confined to stalls or crates just large enough for them to stand, stretch, and lie down. They are fed a nutritionally balanced yet iron-free formula of milk products. (In the Netherlands, the calves are fed skim milk, whey, and fat to produce even larger retail cuts with exceptional tenderness, known as Dutch Provimi veal.) A steady diet of iron-free formula prevents the calves' muscles from developing myoglobin, the red muscle pigment, leaving the meat pale pink in color, rather than dark red like mature beef. Because of the calves' solitary confinement, lack of space, and poor diet, the production methods for milk-fed veal have been under scrutiny for decades. Pressure to improve the standards of the animals' welfare finally prompted the U.S. veal industry's primary advocacy group, the American Veal Association (AVA), to phase out solitary veal crates and stalls by 2017. The AVA now advocates a move to group housing instead.

Group housing has long been a mainstay of European veal production. It is also the cornerstone of natural or red veal, the second type of North American domestic veal. Methods for raising natural veal hearken back to the days prior to the 1950s, before cattle production was streamlined and concentrated. Back then, calves were raised on grass with their mothers, like the fatted calf mentioned in the Bible. Natural veal production dispenses with solitary crates. The calves are essentially free-range, feeding on grass, grain, or a combination of the two. To meet USDA regulations for the term "natural," calves must not be given hormones or antibiotics. Natural operations also allow the calves to forage on pasture—sometimes in grouped pens. The additional exercise and grain in the diet gives natural veal deep pink meat with a beefy flavor. When the two types of veal are tasted side by side, natural veal will taste assertive and meaty, with a satisfying chew; milk-fed veal will taste mildly sweet and much more tender. The choice is yours. We tend to prefer natural veal for grilling because its richer flavor and firmer texture take better to the grill. The delicacy of milk-fed veal is often overshadowed by strong grill flavors.

How to Grill Veal

Grilling veal is mostly a matter of knowing where on the animal the cut comes from and how thick the piece of meat is. As immature cattle, calves have the same body parts as mature beef, but butchers make fewer primal cuts. The sirloin is included with the veal leg, and the plate, flank, and brisket are included in the breast, which is part of the shoulder primal.

As with all animals, the calf's muscles that get the most exercise have the most flavor, but they are also the toughest. Veal breast and other roasts from the chuck tend to be thick and tough, requiring indirect grilling and mopping or other forms of moisture to dissolve tough connective tissue and become fork-tender. Veal chops, top round cutlets, and other small cuts from the rack and upper leg are thinner and have more tender, fine-grained meat. These cuts can be grilled directly over medium or high heat.

The one thing to keep in mind whenever you grill veal is this: avoid overcooking. The youth of the animal ensures tenderness but also means a minimum of intramuscular marbling. Particularly in milk-fed veal, the lack of iron in the diet limits the development of saturated fat. Veal is much leaner than beef, containing about 50 percent less fat and 25 percent fewer calories on average. That means veal can easily dry out on the grill. We like to cook veal chops and most roasts to medium-rare or medium doneness (135 to 145°F). For added moisture, we serve tender cuts like chops and leg cutlets with rich sauces. When slow-grilling tough cuts like veal shank, shoulder, and breast, we use brines and mops for extra juiciness.

T-Bone of Veal au Poivre

MAKES 4 SERVINGS

T-bone veal chops are cut from the loin. Unlike veal rib chops, they include some tenderloin on one side of the bone. We marinate the T-bone in white wine and fresh herbs, grill it quickly in a crust of cracked peppercorns, then finish it with brandy cream sauce on the plate.

INGREDIENTS:

1 cup dry white wine

½ cup olive oil

2 tablespoons Fresh Herb Rub (page 32)

4 veal T-bone chops, about 1½ inches thick, fat trimmed to ¼ inch

1 teaspoon coarse salt

3 tablespoons mixed peppercorns (black, green, red, and white), cracked (see Note)

3 tablespoons unsalted butter

1 large shallot, minced

½ cup Cognac

½ cup heavy cream

DIRECTIONS:

Combine the wine, olive oil, and herb rub in 1-gallon zipper-lock plastic bags. Drop in the veal chops, press out the air, seal, and refrigerate for 4 to 6 hours.

Remove the chops from the marinade and pat dry with paper towels. It's okay if some of the herbs and garlic cling to the meat. Sprinkle with 1 teaspoon salt and the cracked pepper and let stand at room temperature for 1 hour.

Light a grill for bilevel high/medium-low heat, about 375°F ambient temperature (see page 13). Brush the grill grate and coat with oil. Grill the chops directly over high heat until darkly crusted, 4 to 5 minutes per side. Reduce the heat to medium-low on a gas grill or move the chops to the medium-low-heat area on a charcoal or wood grill and cook to an internal temperature of 135 to 145°F for medium-rare to medium-done, about 5 minutes more per side. Remove to a platter and let rest for 5 minutes.

Melt the butter in a skillet over medium-low heat. Add the shallot and cook until softened, 1 to 2 minutes. Add the Cognac and increase the heat to high. Boil until reduced by about half. Stir in the cream and any accumulated juices from the veal platter. Return to a boil and boil until slightly thickened, 2 to 3 minutes. Season with salt and serve with the veal.

Note: Crush the peppercorns coarsely under a heavy frying pan, or buy cracked peppercorns.

Veal Rib Chops with Coriander Rub

MAKES 4 SERVINGS

Ground coriander does magical things to veal. It walks the line between savory and sweet, deepening veal's mild flavor without overpowering its tender texture. Rubbed with coriander and grilled in about 10 minutes, these rib chops need only a dollop of preserved lime (or preserved lemon) yogurt for a tart and briny counterpoint. Grilled onions and sweet potatoes would make good dinner companions here. When buying the veal, keep in mind that chops cut from the shoulder end of the rack are larger, with a smaller eye of tender meat and more tough, flavorful cap muscles. Chops from the loin end have a larger eye of tender, mild-flavored meat.

INGREDIENTS:

4 veal rib chops (10 to 12 ounces each), 1 to 1½ inches thick

¼ cup Coriander Rub (page 28)

1¼ cups Preserved Lime Yogurt (page 41)

DIRECTIONS:

Trim the surface fat on the veal chops to about ¼-inch thickness. Sprinkle the rub over the chops. Let stand at room temperature for 45 minutes.

Light a grill for direct medium-high heat, about 425°F (see page 12). Brush the grill grate and coat with oil. Grill directly over the heat for 5 to 6 minutes per side for medium-rare (an internal temperature of 135°F). Remove to a platter, cover loosely with foil, and let rest for 5 minutes.

Serve the chops with the preserved lime yogurt.

Paillards of Veal Scallopini with Black Caper Butter

MAKES 4 SERVINGS

If you need a quick, elegant weeknight dish, this is it. Top round cutlets of veal leg pounded into thin paillards cook so fast, you need only grill one side. The greater surface area exposes more of the meat to the fire, giving the veal deeper browned flavors. Black caper butter (deeply browned, but not actually black) is often served on fish, but here it lends moisture and succulence to the lean veal.

INGREDIENTS:

4 veal top round steaks (cutlets, 4 to 5 ounces each)

1 tablespoon olive oil

½ teaspoon coarse salt

¼ teaspoon ground black pepper

¾ cup Black Caper Butter (page 44)

continued

DIRECTIONS:

For each paillard, sprinkle a veal cutlet with a little water and place between sheets of plastic wrap. Pound with a flat meat mallet or heavy frying pan to an even thickness of between ⅛ and ¼ inch. Coat the paillards all over with oil and sprinkle with the salt and pepper. Let stand at room temperature while you heat the grill and make the caper butter.

Light a grill for direct high heat, about 450°F (see page 12).

Brush the grill grate and coat with oil. Grill the paillards directly over the heat until nicely grill-marked on one side, about 1 to 2 minutes. Remove to plates with the grilled side up and pour on the black caper butter.

SHANK/LEG

Veal Shanks Mopped with Bourbon Cider

MAKES 4 TO 8 SERVINGS

The first time you eat a veal shank, it tastes unlike any meat you've ever eaten, so soft it nearly melts in your mouth like butter. That's because veal shanks contain a generous amount of collagen, a miraculous protein that melts into mouth-filling gelatin when given gentle, sustained heat and moisture. Hence the popularity of osso buco, Italy's classic dish of braised veal shanks. For this recipe, we use whole veal shanks, not crosscut pieces as in osso buco, and we grill-roast the shanks until they reach fall-apart tenderness. Keep ashes and debris out of the drip pan as you grill the shanks; you'll need the drippings to make the mushroom-bourbon-cider sauce. On a charcoal grill, put the charcoal on one side of the grill and the drip pan on the other to keep the drip pan clean.

INGREDIENTS:

3 cups wood chips, such as apple or cherry, soaked in water for 30 minutes

¼ cup Smoked Paprika–Rosemary Rub (page 28)

2 whole veal shanks (about 4 pounds total)

1 cup Bourbon-Cider Mop (page 38)

3 tablespoons unsalted butter

1 large shallot, minced

4 ounces small cremini mushrooms, sliced

½ cup good-quality bourbon

½ cup heavy cream

2 teaspoons chopped fresh rosemary

Coarse salt

DIRECTIONS:

Sprinkle all but 1 tablespoon of the rub over the shanks and let stand at room temperature for 1 hour. Stir the remaining 1 tablespoon rub into the mop.

Light a grill for indirect medium-low heat, about 300°F, with smoke (see pages 14 and 16). Brush the grill grate and coat with oil. Grill the shanks directly over the heat until browned all over, 8 to 10 minutes. Drain 1 cup of the wood chips and add to the grill. When you see smoke, move the shanks away from the heat and place over a drip pan filled with ¼ inch of water. Cover the grill and cook for 1½ hours, drizzling the meat generously with the mop every 30 minutes. Replenish the charcoal and wood chips as necessary to maintain heat and smoke in the grill, about once an hour. After 1½ hours of cooking, place the shanks on a large sheet of heavy-duty foil, fold up the edges slightly, and drizzle again with the

mop. Wrap the shanks with foil. Remove the drip pan from the grill and set aside. Cover the grill and continue cooking until the meat is fork-tender and the internal temperature is about 185°F, about 1 to 1½ hours more.

Pour the juices from the drip pan into a measuring cup. If necessary, add water to so you have about ½ cup liquid. Return to the drip pan and boil over high heat for 5 minutes, stirring gently to loosen the browned bits; avoid scraping the bottom of the pan if heavily burnt.

Remove the shanks to a platter and unwrap, drizzling any juices onto the platter. Let stand for 20 minutes.

Melt the butter in a medium skillet over medium heat. Add the shallot and mushrooms and cook until softened, 4 to 5 minutes. Add the bourbon, the drippings from the drip

pan, and ½ cup of the accumulated juices from the platter. Increase the heat to high and boil until reduced by about half. Skim any excess fat from the surface. Stir in the cream, return to a boil, and boil until slightly thickened, 2 to 3 minutes. Add the rosemary and season with salt.

Carve the meat from the bone and serve with the sauce. Don't forget to extract the softened marrow from the bones with a narrow utensil. It's unforgettably delicious.

SHOULDER/CHUCK

Pulled Veal Shoulder Sandwiches with Cumin Mop

MAKES 8 TO 10 SERVINGS

Like pork shoulder, veal shoulder is a tough cut, riddled with connective tissue, and rich in flavor. But veal contains even more collagen, which melts into delicious, velvety gelatin. Slow-roasting veal shoulder on the grill and mopping it with cumin-scented sherry vinegar renders it fall-apart tender and perfumed with aromas of smoke and spice. The drip-pan drippings are used to create a sauce for the sandwiches, so keep the pan free of ashes and debris as the veal cooks. In a charcoal grill, the easiest way to keep the pan clean is to put the coals on one side of the grill and the drip pan on the other.

INGREDIENTS:

3 cups wood chips, such as cherry, apple, or oak, soaked in water for 30 minutes

1 boneless veal shoulder roast (5 to 6 pounds)

6 tablespoons Cumin-Thyme Rub (page 29)

1½ cups sherry vinegar or white wine vinegar

¼ cup fresh lemon juice

¼ cup olive oil

2 tablespoons honey

1 shallot, finely chopped

1 cup Easy Barbecue Sauce (page 39) or your favorite sauce

8 to 10 sandwich rolls

DIRECTIONS:

Coat the veal all over with 4 tablespoons of the rub. Cover and refrigerate for 8 hours or up to 24 hours.

Remove the veal from the refrigerator and let stand at room temperature for 1 hour.

Meanwhile, make a mop by combining the vinegar, lemon juice, oil, honey, shallot, and the remaining 2 tablespoons spice rub.

Light a grill for indirect medium-low heat, about 300°F, with smoke (see pages 14 and 16). Brush the grill grate and coat with oil. Grill the veal directly over the heat until nicely grill-marked all over, about 15 minutes total. Drain 1 cup wood chips and put in the grill. Move the veal away from the heat, and place over a drip pan filled with ¼ inch of hot water. Close the lid and cook until the veal is fork-tender, about 3 to 3½ hours. Drizzle with the mop every 30 minutes or so and replenish the wood chips whenever the old ones die out.

Remove the veal to a platter and let stand for 20 to 30 minutes. Shred the meat with a fork and mix with 1 cup of drippings from the drip pan.

To make a sauce, combine another 1 cup of drippings from the drip pan with the cup of barbecue sauce. Serve on the rolls with the sauce.

Breast of Veal Stuffed with Sweet Sausage and Apple

MAKES 8 SERVINGS

Veal breast is roughly equivalent to beef brisket. It's cut from the chest area and contains both lean and fatty muscle and a thin cover of fat. On the grill, this inexpensive cut must be cooked with indirect heat to make it tender. You can buy veal breast with or without the rib bones. It's often stuffed by cutting a pocket between the ribs and meat.

INGREDIENTS:

3 cups wood chips, such as apple or cherry, soaked in water for 30 minutes

1 boneless veal breast (3½ pounds)

¼ cup plus 2 tablespoons Coriander-Ginger Rub (page 28)

2 cups fresh bread cubes (about ½-inch square)

1 tablespoon olive oil

8 ounces loose sweet Italian sausage

½ cup finely chopped onion

½ cup finely chopped celery

½ cup finely chopped apple

1 garlic clove, minced

1 teaspoon grated fresh ginger

2 large eggs, beaten

½ cup heavy cream

1½ cups chicken broth

½ cup apple cider

½ cup apple cider vinegar

1 cup dry white wine

2 teaspoons cornstarch

2 teaspoons cold water

DIRECTIONS:

Cut a horizontal pocket in the veal breast, starting at the thickest end and leaving a 1-inch border of meat. Sprinkle ¼ cup of the rub all over the inside and outside of the veal. Let stand at room temperature for 1 hour.

Light a grill for indirect medium-low heat, about 300°F, with smoke (see pages 14 and 16). Put the bread cubes on a grill tray, put the tray on the grill away from the heat, and toast until the bread is dry, about 15 minutes.

Meanwhile, heat the oil in a medium skillet over medium heat. Add the sausage and cook until lightly browned all over, 6 to 8 minutes, breaking up the meat with a spoon. Remove to a plate. Add the onion and celery to the skillet and cook until softened, 5 minutes. Add the apple, garlic, ginger, and 1 tablespoon of the remaining spice rub and cook for 3 to 4 minutes. Remove from the heat.

Beat the eggs in a large bowl and stir in the cream and ½ cup of the broth. Stir in the sausage, apple mixture, and toasted bread cubes. Let stand until the bread absorbs the liquid, about 10 minutes.

Spoon the stuffing into the veal pocket and tie with kitchen string to help close the opening.

Combine the cider, cider vinegar, and remaining 1 table-spoon rub in a cup for a mop sauce.

Brush the grill grate and coat with oil. Put 1½ cups of the wood chips in the grill. When you see smoke, put the stuffed veal, fatty-side up, on the grill away from the heat and over a drip pan filled with ¼ inch hot water. Cover the grill and cook for 2 hours. After the first 45 minutes, drizzle with the mop sauce, then drizzle about every 30 minutes after that. Replenish the wood chips when the old ones die out, about once an hour. After 2 hours of cooking, wrap the veal breast in heavy-duty foil and return to the grill. Cover and cook until fork-tender, 1 to 1½ hours more.

Remove the veal to a platter and unwrap. Let rest for 20 minutes. Meanwhile, drain any liquid from the foil or plat-ter into a small saucepan. Add the drippings from the drip pan, the remaining 1 cup chicken broth, and the wine. Boil until reduced by one-third. Whisk together the cornstarch and water in a cup, then whisk the mixture into the liquid broth and cook until thickened, about 2 minutes.

Cut the veal into slices about ½ inch thick, removing the string as you go. Serve with the sauce.

Calf's Liver Skewers with Pancetta and Cipolline

MAKES 4 SERVINGS

Calf's liver is the gateway drug of organ meats. Tender and rich-tasting, it leads to further experimentation with sweetbreads, brains, and calf fries. Don't be alarmed. It is just food that tastes great; it won't hurt you. Italians often grill skewers of calf's liver, and here's our take on that preparation. We cut the liver into thumb-size pieces, wrap them with sage leaves and pancetta, and spear them, along with tiny cipolline onions. A reduction sauce of Madeira, balsamic, and peach preserves adds just enough sweetness and spark. Be sure to remove the thin membrane from the liver. Butchers sometimes do this for you, but if not, do it yourself or the membrane will toughen on the grill. The liver itself can also overcook easily, leaving you with a dry slab of shoe leather. Cook only until it's slightly pink in the center. Basic Grilled Polenta (page 382) makes a good accompaniment.

INGREDIENTS:

4 bamboo or metal skewers

1 pound calf's liver

16 thin slices pancetta

16 small sage leaves (or half-leaves if large)

8 small cipolline onions, peeled

2 tablespoons olive oil

¾ teaspoon kosher salt

¼ teaspoon ground black pepper

1 cup dry Madeira or Marsala

2 tablespoons balsamic vinegar

¼ cup peach preserves

3 tablespoons cold unsalted butter, cut into pieces

DIRECTIONS:

If you are grilling with bamboo skewers, soak them in water for at least 30 minutes.

If the liver still has its thin outer membrane, remove it. Cut the liver into pieces about 1 by 2 inches, removing and discarding any veins. Wrap each piece of liver in a slice of pancetta, tucking in a small sage leaf as you wrap. Thread the liver pieces and cipolline alternately onto skewers, threading the cipolline through the ends so that the sides will rest on the grill. Coat all over with the oil and sprinkle with ½ teaspoon of the salt and the pepper. Let stand until the grill is ready.

Light a grill for direct medium heat, about 375°F (see page 12).

As the grill heats up, pour the Madeira and balsamic into a small saucepan and bring to a boil over high heat. Boil until the liquid is reduced by half, 5 to 8 minutes. Reduce the heat to low, stir in the preserves, and simmer for 1 minute. Whisk in the butter and season with the remaining ¼ teaspoon salt and a pinch more pepper. Keep warm.

Brush the grill grate and coat with oil. Grill the skewers directly over the heat until the onions are tender and the liver is nicely browned but still pink inside, about 4 to 5 minutes per side. Serve with the sauce.

Grilled Veal Sweetbreads with Grilled Marrow on Toast

MAKES 4 SERVINGS

Sweetbreads bear no relation to bread and are no sweeter than any other part of an animal. They are pancreas and thymus glands—two glands that reside near the stomach and in the throat of the animal—and they taste absolutely wonderful. Seek out pancreas (stomach or "heart") sweetbreads, which are rounded and have a creamier texture and more delicate flavor than narrow, elongated throat sweetbreads. This recipe has a few separate elements, but smart timing turns them all out at once and makes a great first course. First marinate the marrow bones. Next soak and poach the sweetbreads. Once your grill is lit, put the bones on first, away from the heat. The sweetbreads are grilled directly over the heat and go on when you're about halfway through cooking the bones. When the bones and sweetbreads come off the grill, the bread goes on for toasting.

INGREDIENTS:

4 large bamboo or metal skewers

Grilled Marrow:

¼ cup olive oil

2 teaspoons chopped fresh sage

2 garlic cloves, minced

¼ teaspoon kosher salt

⅛ teaspoon ground black pepper

8 center-cut veal marrow bones, about 2 inches each

Sweetbreads:

1 pound fresh veal sweetbreads, preferably pancreas

1 gallon water

½ cup white wine

½ cup distilled white vinegar

1 large garlic clove, minced

1 teaspoon black peppercorns

1 bay leaf

A few sprigs fresh flat-leaf parsley

A few sprigs fresh thyme

3½ teaspoons salt

2 tablespoons olive oil

¼ teaspoon ground black pepper

¼ cup White Balsamic Citrus Glaze (page 49)

4 slices from a large round loaf of crusty bread, each about ¼ to ½ inches thick

DIRECTIONS:

For the grilled marrow: Combine the oil, sage, garlic, salt, and pepper in a bowl. Add the bones and toss to coat. Cover with plastic and refrigerate for 8 to 16 hours.

Remove the marinating bones from the refrigerator and let stand at room temperature for 30 minutes.

For the sweetbreads: While the bones are marinating, soak the sweetbreads in cold water for 4 hours. Rinse in cold water until the water is clear. Put the gallon of water, the wine, vinegar, garlic, peppercorns, bay leaf, parsley, thyme, and 3 teaspoons of the salt in a large pot. Bring to a boil over high heat, and then reduce the heat so that the mixture barely simmers. Add the sweetbreads and poach until they begin to feel firm, about 5 minutes. Turn off the heat and let

stand in the poaching liquid for 5 minutes. Remove from the poaching liquid and soak in ice water until cool enough to handle. Pat dry, and then remove the membrane and separate into 2-inch pieces. Toss the pieces in a bowl with the oil and thread onto the skewers. Season with the remaining ½ teaspoon salt and the pepper.

If you are grilling with bamboo skewers, soak them in water for at least 30 minutes. Light a grill for indirect medium-high heat, about 375°F (see page 14). Wrap the bones in heavy-duty foil, using about 2 bones per bundle and scraping some of the marinade into each. Put the foil bundles on the grill away from the heat, cover, and cook until the marrow is warm, about 20 minutes. Open the foil bundles and keep warm.

continued ➡

Lower the grill heat to medium. Brush the grill grate and coat with oil. Grill the skewers directly over medium heat until nicely grill-marked, about 5 to 6 minutes total, turning once or twice. Brush with the glaze during the last minute of cooking. Let rest for 2 to 3 minutes before serving.

Cut the bread slices in half crosswise, then dip a brush into the marinade in the foil pouches. Brush the bread slices on both sides with some of the marinade. Grill the bread directly over the heat until lightly toasted, 1 to 2 minutes per side.

Arrange the bones, toast, and skewers on a platter or divide among plates, serving 2 bones, 2 toast halves, and 1 skewer per plate. Provide long, narrow utensils to allow your guests to scrape the marrow onto the toast.

BRATWURST/GROUND VEAL

Bratwurst with the Works

MAKES 10 BRATS

Sheboygan, Wisconsin, is home to Bratwurst Day, held every year on the first Saturday of August. The special dish? Veal bratwurst with the works—two grilled brats served on a big buttered, cornmeal-dusted bun topped with whole-grain mustard, onions, ketchup, and pickles. Yum! We go over the top by adding sauerkraut and cheese to the mix. When buying your brats, keep in mind the two varieties: fresh and cooked. Fresh brats need thorough cooking, while the precooked variety just needs to be browned on the grill. We prefer fresh brats. If you're grilling up a big batch of them and need to hold them, a pan of beer keeps the veal sausages cozy and warm until serving time.

INGREDIENTS:

2½ pounds fresh veal-based bratwurst (about 10 links)

One 12-ounce bottle or can of beer, preferably German bock

2 cups chilled sauerkraut, drained

1 onion, thinly sliced

4 tablespoons unsalted butter

10 crusty sausage or steak rolls

6 ounces thinly sliced Alsatian munster or emmentaler cheese

½ cup ketchup

½ cup whole-grain German mustard

½ cup thinly sliced dill pickle rounds

DIRECTIONS:

Light a grill for direct medium heat, about 350°F (see page 12). Brush the grill grate and coat with oil. Grill the brats directly over the heat until nicely browned (not burnt) all over and the internal temperature is 155°F, about 20 minutes total, turning them often. Meanwhile, combine the beer, sauerkraut, onions, and butter in a disposable aluminum pan. Cook directly over the heat on the grill until warmed through, about 15 minutes. Line a roll with some cheese and add a cooked brat. Top with some of the sauerkraut mixture as well as some ketchup, mustard, and pickles. To hold the grilled brats, nestle in the beer and sauerkraut mixture and keep warm on the grill.

Chapter 5

PORK

Swine are omnivorous scavengers, gorging on practically anything that crosses their path. This ability to thrive on practically anything made them an easy mark for domestication, and they were one of the first wild animals to be domesticated for meat. Neolithic farmers fed feral pigs in order to harvest their meat as long ago as the fourth millennium BCE. We've been doing it ever since.

Swine are classified by sex and age. A pig is a young animal, between six and eight months old, usually weighing between 120 and 180 pounds. Young pigs for roasting whole are under six months and can weigh between 20 and 60 pounds. A hog is a mature pig over eight months, weighing over 180 pounds.

Pork, the meat of swine, is graded 1 through 4, based on the ratio of lean meat to fat on the carcass, with number 1 yielding the highest proportion of lean. Unlike beef and veal, the grades of pork are not marketed to the public. Almost all pork sold to consumers is number 1 grade, and all number 1 grade pork comes from male swine.

LOIN

It runs between the shoulder and the leg and includes four areas from which chops are taken—blade-end, ribs, loin, and sirloin. It also includes the tenderloin.

SHOULDER

Composed of two sections: the upper shoulder and the arm. The upper shoulder, called the Boston butt, is the larger of the two. The arm section is sold as picnic ham.

LEG

Comprises the ham (thigh) and the hind shank (lower leg). A whole ham is composed of three muscle groups, which can be sold separately as inside round, outside round, and knuckle.

BELLY

Comprises the diaphragm and flank muscles, the ends of the rib cage, and large areas of fat. Bacon and spareribs come from the belly.

PORK

INGREDIENT / PRIMAL CUT	OTHER NAMES	HOW TO GRILL	SUBSTITUTIONS
RACK OF PORK / LOIN	Pork rib roast, center-cut rib roast	INDIRECT medium	Bone-in loin
LARDO / LOIN	Cured fat back	DIRECT high	Fat back
CHOPS / LOIN	Rib chops, loin chops, center-cut chop	DIRECT medium-high	Loin chops
LOIN, BONE-IN / LOIN	Rib end loin roast, center-cut pork roast	INDIRECT medium	Rack, rib roast
BONELESS PORK LOIN / LOIN	Center-cut boneless pork roast or chop	DIRECT medium-high	---
CANADIAN BACON / LOIN	Loin bacon, Irish bacon	DIRECT medium	---
TENDERLOIN / LOIN	Filet	INDIRECT low / BILEVEL medium-high	Loin
BACK RIBS / LOIN	Baby back ribs, loin ribs, riblets	INDIRECT low / brined or basted	Other ribs
HAM (FRESH) / LEG	Fresh ham	INDIRECT medium	Sirloin
SIRLOIN / LEG	Sirloin chop, steak, or roast, butt, sirloin end roast, hip-bone roast	INDIRECT medium	Fresh ham
HAM (CURED) / LEG	Canned ham, baked ham	DIRECT medium-high	Canadian bacon
SHANKS / SHOULDER OR LEG	Fore shank, hind shank, hock	INDIRECT low / frequent basting	Ribs
UPPER SHOULDER, LOWER SHOULDER / SHOULDER	Boston butt, picnic ham, shoulder roast	INDIRECT low / frequent basting	Fresh ham
COUNTRY-STYLE RIBS / SHOULDER	Blade end ribs, flatbone ribs	INDIRECT low / brined or basted	Other ribs
SPARERIBS / BELLY	Kansas City ribs, St. Louis ribs	INDIRECT low / brined or basted	Other ribs
PORK BELLY / BELLY	Pancetta, bacon	INDIRECT medium	---
SUCKLING PIG / WHOLE	Piglet	INDIRECT medium-low	---
SAUSAGE / GROUND PORK	Bockwurst, bratwurst, breakfast sausage, chaurice, chorizo, frankfurter, hot dog, Italian sausage, knockwurst	DIRECT high	---
GROUND PORK	Minced pork	INDIRECT medium	Ground veal

Heritage Breeds vs. the Other White Meat

Although there are many pig breeds, only a few are raised commercially for meat. These tend to be fast-growing muscular breeds like Landrace, the pig of Danish bacon fame, and Duroc, an American breed that is used extensively in crossbreeding. Most of the commercially raised pork in North America is a cross between Duroc, Yorkshire, and Hampshire breeds.

In recent years, legendary pig breeds that were considered noncommercial because of their small size and slow growth have come to be valued for the quality of their meat. Berkshire pigs, the oldest continuously bred pigs in the world, are valued for abundant, fine-grained marbling. Their rich firm flesh contrasts sharply with the overtly mild and spartanly lean meat that comes from most commercially raised pigs. Berkshires (called *Kurobuta* in Japan) are now being marketed as an heirloom breed, grown mostly by small producers and fed sustainably on corn and soy.

Although modern demand for lean meat has changed how all livestock are bred, raised, and fattened, pork has been changed most dramatically. Thirty years ago a full-grown hog typically weighed over 300 pounds. Today the top weight is closer to 240 pounds, which yields a carcass of about 180 pounds and a little more than 100 pounds of edible meat. Today's mass-market pig has less fat—about 1 inch along the back, compared with several inches in the past—and larger, leaner muscles.

All of these changes have made lean cuts of pork very similar to chicken in overall content of fat, saturated fat, cholesterol, and calories. But it has also made grilling pork much more difficult.

Grilling Pork

As with all meats, the primary way of deciding how to cook a cut of pork starts with knowing where on the animal the cut came from. The more exercise the muscle got (shoulders and legs), the tougher and more flavorful it will be. Muscles along the back, which move less, produce more tender, milder-tasting meat.

Pork is naturally low in moisture (about 55 percent of its weight, as opposed to chicken, which is closer to 70 percent water). In the past abundant fat deposits dispersed within its lean parts melted into the meat as it grilled and kept it juicy. Now that these fat deposits have been diminished, pork can be unpalatably dry when grilled at too high a heat or for too long. Brining (see page 24), which can increase the moisture content of lean meat by 10 percent, is particularly effective at raising the perception of juiciness in lean cuts of pork.

Long ago pork commonly harbored trichina, the parasite responsible for trichinosis. The threat of trichinosis compelled older pork recipes to recommend cooking pork to 180°F, a temperature at which all of its moisture disappeared. Now the threat of trichinosis has been all but eradicated from commercially raised pork. There are only a few cases of trichinosis reported each year in the United States, and all of these are traced to homegrown pigs that were not inspected or to hunted animals, like wild boar and bear. Trichinae are killed at 140°F.

The tough, dry pork encountered on many tables is largely due to overcooking. The U.S. National Pork Board advises cooking pork to 154°F, but most chefs recommend cooking lean, tender cuts like chops, loin, and tenderloin closer to 150°F, so that it is still slightly pink in the center, and fattier large cuts, like shoulder and fresh ham, to around 160°F.

Pork chops and steaks can be grilled directly, but larger cuts and tougher cuts of pork need lower heat and more time so they tenderize without becoming dry.

When grilling beef and lamb, it's easy to sear the outside of a steak or chop and leave the interior perfectly done, because these meats are often served rare or medium-rare. Pork needs to be more thoroughly cooked, which makes it more difficult to retain the meat's moistness and avoid charring the surface. For this reason, far more cuts of pork are cooked with indirect or lower fires than other meats. Thick pork chops benefit from grilling over a bilevel fire—slightly higher heat for browning and lower heat for cooking the meat through.

All pork benefits from brining, and tougher cuts are frequently mopped (or basted) during grilling. Sweet barbecue sauces are usually served at the table or applied to the meat only after it is done cooking. Premature basting with barbecue sauce is the main cause of incinerated pork (because the sugar in the sauce burns).

Buying Pork

Color and firmness are the most important factors in judging the quality of pork. Look for firm, finely grained, moist meat that has a reddish-pink tint. Pale grayish-pink pork will tend to be dry and flavorless. The more exercised cuts (from the shoulder and leg) will tend to have darker-colored meat than tender cuts. The fat should be white, firm, smooth, and slightly moist.

Try to use pork within 3 days of purchase and store, preferably wrapped in clean butcher or wax paper, in the refrigerator.

Pork Tenderloin with Candied Clementine and Rosemary

MAKES 4 SERVINGS

As we've noted before, the most tender meat comes from muscles that are rarely used. On four-legged animals, that means the twin muscles that run on either side of the spine inside the rib cage, which control the ability of the animal to arch its back, something four-legged animals never do. Hence the name tenderloin, the most tender and most desirable cut on any animal. As one would expect from an unused muscle group, tenderloins are relatively small in relation to the total weight of an animal. In pork, the whole tenderloin weighs less than a pound, just enough for two portions. Like boneless skinless chicken breasts, pork tenderloins are easy to prepare, cook quickly, and marry well with a range of flavors. In this recipe, we brine them in wine and herbs, and flavor them with orange and Provençal herbs. The grilled pork is served with a bittersweet compote of slow-simmered clementines and pine-fresh rosemary leaves

INGREDIENTS:

1½ cups Riesling Brine (page 34)

2 pork tenderloins, trimmed of silver skin (12 to 16 ounces each; see Know-How, below)

2 tablespoons fresh rosemary leaves, finely chopped

1 teaspoon anise seeds, crushed

1 teaspoon cracked pepper

½ teaspoon dried thyme leaves

1 teaspoon garlic salt

3 clementines, sliced and seeded

⅓ cup sugar

1 tablespoon plus 1 teaspoon extra-virgin olive oil

DIRECTIONS:

Combine the brine and tenderloins in a 1-gallon zipper-lock bag, press out the air, seal, and refrigerate for 2 to 3 hours.

While the tenderloins are brining, mix half the rosemary, the anise seeds, pepper, thyme, and garlic salt in a small bowl; set aside.

Coarsely chop the sliced clementines, retaining as much of the juice as possible. Combine the clementine pieces and sugar in a small saucepan, and cook slowly over low heat until tender, stirring often, about 20 minutes. Stir in 1 teaspoon of the olive oil and the remaining rosemary and cool.

Remove the tenderloins from the brine and pat dry. Rub the tenderloins all over with the remaining tablespoon olive oil and the rosemary and anise seed rub. Loosely cover with foil and let the meat rest for about 1 hour at room temperature.

Light a grill for bilevel high/medium heat, 500/375°F (see page 13).

Brush the grill grate and coat with oil. Put the pork over the high heat and grill until browned all over, about 1 minute on each of the four sides. Reduce the heat to medium on a gas grill or move the pork to the lower heat on a charcoal or wood grill. Cover the grill and cook until the meat is just firm when poked, and an instant read thermometer registers 145°F, another 4 to 5 minutes.

Transfer to a platter, cover loosely with foil, and let rest for 5 minutes. Slice and serve with the candied clementines.

**KNOW-HOW:
TRIMMING TENDERLOINS**

Although pork tenderloin is a boneless cut with a minimum of tendon, it is covered with a thin, shiny membrane called the silver skin. If left on, the silver skin can cause the tenderloin to curl up during cooking. Remove the silver skin by grabbing it at the thick end of the meat and shaving it off the meat with a small knife.

RACK/LOIN

....

Mustard and Pistachio–Crusted
Pork Rib Roast

MAKES 4 SERVINGS

....

A full rib roast of pork, also called a rack, is composed of eight ribs (eleven if you include the tapering ribs, which extend into the loin). You should estimate one rib per person, and purchase the roast by the number of ribs, rather than by weight. Because of the configuration of the roast (a long row of ribs), heat from the grill penetrates the meat at the same rate, regardless of the size of the roast. So a four-rib roast will cook in about the same amount of time as an eight-rib specimen. The smallest rib roast is three ribs; smaller than that is a double pork chop.

INGREDIENTS:

One 14-rib pork rib roast (rack of pork, about 3½ pounds)

3 cups Lemon–Black Pepper Brine (page 35)

2 tablespoons spicy brown mustard

2 garlic cloves, minced

Finely grated zest of 1 lemon

½ teaspoon ground black pepper

⅔ cup finely ground pistachio nuts

⅓ cup dry breadcrumbs

¼ cup finely chopped fresh flat-leaf parsley

DIRECTIONS:

If the chine bones, which come off the ends of the ribs at a near right angle, are still attached, make a cut between the bones and the meat. This will make the roast much easier to carve after grilling. Put the pork in a jumbo (2-gallon) zipper-lock bag. Add the brine to the bag, press out the air, and seal. Make sure the meaty parts of the roast are all submerged in brine; if not, massage the bag to distribute the brine more evenly. Refrigerate for 6 hours or overnight.

Light a grill for indirect medium heat, about 325°F (see page 14).

Remove the pork from the brine and pat dry with paper towels.

Mix the mustard, garlic, lemon zest, and pepper in a small bowl. Set the pork roast, meaty side up, on a sheet tray or flat platter. Using a pastry brush, coat the pork roast with a thick layer of the mustard mixture.

Combine the ground pistachios, breadcrumbs, and parsley in another small bowl. Pack the crumb mixture all over the mustard-coated pork roast.

Brush and oil the grill grate. Put the pork roast, meaty-side up, on the grill away from the fire. Close the lid and cook until the eye of the roast registers 150°F on an instant-read thermometer (make sure the thermometer is not touching bone), 1¼ to 1½ hours.

Remove the roast to a carving board and let rest for at least 15 minutes. Carve into chops and serve.

RACK/LOIN

Smoked Pork Chops

MAKES 4 SERVINGS

....

You really need a smoking rig to permeate pork chops with smoke. The heat in a grill is so high that pork chops will overcook before they take on much smoky flavor. To overcome the smoking limitations of the grill, we get the smoke into the chops with a smoke-laden brine and a smoky grill rub before they ever hit the heat.

continued

INGREDIENTS:

3 cups hardwood chips, soaked in water for 30 minutes

2 cups Smokin' Brine (page 33)

4 bone-in rib pork chops (about 3 pounds), at least 1 inch thick

1 tablespoons canola oil

2 tablespoons Smokin' Rub (page 26)

DIRECTIONS:

Combine the brine and pork in a 1-gallon zipper-lock bag. Press out the air and seal the bag. Refrigerate for at least 4 hours or as long as 8 hours.

Light a grill for bilevel direct medium-high/low heat, 425/275 °F, with smoke (see pages 13 and 16).

Remove the pork from the brine and pat dry; coat with the oil and season on both sides with the rub. Let rest for 10 minutes.

Brush the grill grate and coat with oil. Add the wood chips to the grill. When you begin to see smoke, put the pork on the grill directly over the high heat, cover the grill, and cook until browned on both sides, about 10 minutes. Reduce the heat to low on a gas grill. On a charcoal or wood grill, move the chops to the low-heat area. Cover the grill, and cook until the chops are 150°F, about 5 minutes more. Let rest for 5 minutes before serving.

BACK RIBS/LOIN

Baby Back Ribs with Brown Sugar Glaze

MAKES 4 SERVINGS

Back ribs don't come from baby pigs. They're simply small. Taken from either side of the spine along the loin, they are the tapered ribs near the back end of the rib cage. A slab of baby backs has at least eight ribs, and as many as thirteen. The lean meat is coarse but plentiful and the striation of fat is minimal. Because these ribs are small, they are a favorite with little kids. The sweet, simple flavors in this recipe are meant to appeal to young rib pickers.

INGREDIENTS:

2 racks baby back pork ribs (about 4 pounds total)

2½ cups Molasses Beer Brine (page 35)

1 cup Brown Sugar Glaze (page 49)

DIRECTIONS:

Cut the racks in half. Combine in a 1-gallon zipper-lock bag with the brine. Press out the air, seal the bag, and refrigerate for 6 to 12 hours.

Light a grill for indirect medium heat, about 325°F (see page 14).

Brush the grill grate and coat with oil. Put the ribs on the grill away from the heat, cover the grill, and cook until an instant-read thermometer inserted into the thickest part of the ribs registers about 155°F (make sure the thermometer is not touching bone), about 1 hour.

Brush the ribs with half of the glaze, turn, close the lid, and cook for 3 minutes.

Brush with the remaining glaze, turn, cover the grill, and cook for another 3 minutes.

Remove the ribs to a large serving platter, and cut into 1- or 2-rib sections.

CENTER-CUT LOIN/LOIN

Horseradish-Brined Pork Loin
with Cranberry Glaze

MAKES 6 SERVINGS

The long cylindrical muscles that run down the back of a pig on either side of the spine are tough and sinewy at their ends, at the shoulder and hip, and tender and meaty in the center, along the rib and loin. In this recipe a center-cut bone-in pork loin, which comes from the end of the loin closest to the rib, is brined with lemon, horseradish, chiles, and vodka. The alcohol insures that a maximum amount of flavor enters deeply into the structure of the protein, so that every bite delivers some seasoning. It is complemented by a sweet and pungent cranberry crust on the surface of the roast.

INGREDIENTS:

Horseradish Brine:

¼ cup plus 2 tablespoons prepared horseradish

1 small fresh chile pepper, finely chopped

2 tablespoons coarse salt

1½ cups water

½ cup vodka

Finely grated zest and juice from ½ lemon

6-bone center-cut pork loin (about 4 pounds)

1½ cups cranberries

1 cup sugar

Juice of ½ lemon or 1 lime

1 tablespoon canola oil

Coarse salt and ground black pepper

DIRECTIONS:

For the horseradish brine: combine all the ingredients in a 1-gallon zipper-lock bag.

Add the pork, press out the air, seal, and refrigerate for 6 to 8 hours.

Light a grill for indirect medium heat, about 350°F (see page 14).

Mix the cranberries, sugar, and lemon juice in a small saucepan. Cook over medium heat, stirring often, until boiling and the cranberries begin to burst. Crush the cranberries with a fork or vegetable masher, and set aside to cool.

Remove the pork from the brine and pat dry with paper towels. Coat with the oil and season with salt and pepper.

Brush and oil the grill grate. Put the pork roast on the grill so the bone side faces up. Close the lid and cook until the center of the roast registers 150°F on an instant-read thermometer, about 55 minutes, basting with the glaze every 10 minutes or so.

Remove the roast to a carving board and let rest for at least 15 minutes. Carve into ½-inch-thick slices, and serve.

Roasted Beet and Chicory Salad with Charred Lardo

MAKES 4 SERVINGS

Lardo is pure white pig back fat that's been packed in salt to purge any moisture that might dilute its luxury. Grilled lardo is gloriously good sprinkled with forest herbs, like rosemary and thyme. But it's a real bitch to grill. Its very substance is fuel for fire, so it readily bursts into flames. But if you are diligent, chilling it thoroughly before putting it near the fire, and leaving it over the heat just long enough to curl its corners and fleck its edges with char, you and your guests will have the opportunity to taste a truly remarkable grilled tidbit. In this recipe we serve grilled lardo strips on a salad of grilled beets and endive, with a simple orange juice vinaigrette.

INGREDIENTS:

2 beets (about 12 ounces total), well scrubbed

2 tablespoons olive oil

¾ teaspoon coarse salt

¼ teaspoon ground black pepper

1 small head radicchio (about 8 ounces)

2 small heads Belgian endive (about 8 ounces total)

1 cup Orange Vinaigrette (page 41)

6 ounces very cold lardo

1 small scallion (green and white parts), thinly sliced

DIRECTIONS:

Heat a grill for indirect medium-high heat, about 375°F (see page 14). Prick the scrubbed beets all over with a fork. Rub with 1 teaspoon of the oil, then sprinkle with ¼ teaspoon of the salt and ⅛ teaspoon of the pepper. Put the beets over the unheated part of the grill, cover, and cook until tender, 45 to 50 minutes. A skewer should slide in and out easily. Let cool for a few minutes, then cut each beet into 8 wedges.

While the beets cook, cut the radicchio through the core into eighths. Cut the endive in half lengthwise. Brush all over with the remaining 5 teaspoons olive oil and sprinkle with the remaining ½ teaspoon salt and ⅛ teaspoon pepper. During the last 15 minutes of cooking for the beets, brush the heated part of the grill grate and coat with oil. Put the radicchio and endive directly over the heat on the grill until nicely grill-marked, 3 to 4 minutes per side.

Arrange the beets, radicchio, and endive on a platter. Drizzle with the vinaigrette.

Increase the grill heat to high, about 500°F (see page 14), and let the grill grate preheat for 10 minutes. Slice the cold lardo through its widest side into large rectangles about 4 by 3 inches, about ⅛ inch thick. At the last minute, grill the lardo slices directly over the heat until the lardo begins to melt and the edges curl up and char, about 20 to 30 seconds. Flip with tongs and char the other side briefly. Transfer to a bowl to capture the melting fat. Cut into strips and scatter the strips over the salad. Sprinkle with the sliced scallion and drizzle with the fat from the bowl.

HAM/LEG

Barbecued Fresh Ham Larded with Pecans and Garlic, Drizzled with Mustard Butterscotch

MAKES 6 SERVINGS

A whole fresh ham (an entire leg) is huge, weighing in at around 20 pounds. Unless you are feeding a horde, it's probably more than you want to tackle. Fortunately, there are many smaller cuts. A whole boneless ham that is netted and tied weighs about 10 pounds. For most of us, though, a 2- to 3-pound ham, which will serve 6 to 8, is preferable. So we usually look for a boneless inside or outside round, which comes from the inside and the outside of the leg, respectively. Both are easy to slice. The outside round has more flavor and more fat, which makes it good for slow low-heat grilling. In this recipe the pork is brined in garlic-infused apple cider, larded with a paste of minced garlic and pecans, and served with a palate-blowing concoction of home-made butterscotch bedeviled by mustard.

INGREDIENTS:

2½ cups Sweet Garlic Brine (page 35)

1 boneless fresh ham, inside or outside round (about 2 pounds)

⅓ cup chopped pecans

1 garlic clove, minced

¼ cup chopped fresh flat-leaf parsley

1 teaspoon sugar

½ teaspoon coarse salt

¼ teaspoon ground black pepper

1 tablespoon olive oil

½ cup Mustard Butterscotch (page 48)

DIRECTIONS:

Combine the brine and pork in a 1-gallon zipper-lock bag. Press out the air, seal, and refrigerate for at least 6 hours or as long as overnight.

Light a grill for indirect medium heat, about 325°F (see page 14).

Mix together the pecans, garlic, parsley, sugar, salt, pepper, and 1 teaspoon of the olive oil in a small bowl. Remove the pork from the brine and pat dry. Poke three deep holes with a long, thin-bladed knife into each end of the ham and stuff the holes with the pecan mixture. Rub the outside of the ham with the remaining 2 teaspoons of olive oil.

Brush the grill grate and coat with oil. Put the pork on the grill away from the heat, cover the grill, and cook until the center of the pork registers 150°F on an instant-read thermometer, about 1½ hours, turning once halfway through.

In the last minutes of grilling, brush the ham with ¼ cup of the mustard butterscotch. Transfer to a cutting board and let rest for 10 minutes. Slice the ham and drizzle with remaining mustard butterscotch. Serve immediately.

KEEPING IT SIMPLE:

- Use the pecan-garlic mixture as a garnish instead of stuffing it into the ham.

- Use ½ cup honey mustard instead of the mustard butterscotch (although the mustard butterscotch is really worth the extra effort).

SIRLOIN/LEG

Orange Anise Pork Sirloin Roast

MAKES 4 SERVINGS

The sirloin comprises the wide end of a fresh ham, which is the part that corresponds to the hip section of the pig. It gets a lot of exercise and therefore develops a good deal of flavor. The sirloin includes several muscle groups and bones, so a boneless sirloin is much easier to carve than one with the bones in. Because the sirloin is pretty lean, it is important to not overcook it. Brining and mopping it during roasting helps it to retain juiciness.

INGREDIENTS:

2 cups Orange-Anise Brine (page 35)

2 pounds pork sirloin, tied into a compact roast

1 tablespoon olive oil

4 tablespoons Rosemary-Anise Rub (page 32)

1 cup orange juice

2 tablespoons white wine vinegar

DIRECTIONS:

Combine the brine and pork in a 1-gallon zipper-lock bag. Press out the air, seal, and refrigerate for at least 6 hours or as long as overnight.

Light a grill for indirect medium heat, about 325°F (see page 14).

Remove the pork from the brine and pat dry. Coat with oil and season on both sides with 3 tablespoons of the rub. Let rest for 10 minutes.

Mix up a mop of the orange juice, vinegar, and the remaining tablespoon of the rub.

Brush the grill grate and coat with oil. Put the pork on the grill away from the heat, cover the grill, and cook until the center of the pork registers 150°F on an instant-read thermometer, about for 1 hour, turning every 15 minutes and basting liberally with the mop after each turn, Transfer to a cutting board, let rest for 10 minutes, and slice.

SHOULDER ROAST/SHOULDER

Fire-Braised Pulled BBQ Pork Shoulder

MAKES ABOUT 10 SERVINGS

Its tough meat fibers and rich fatty layers make pork shoulder a prime candidate for slow, smoky barbecuing. The only problem is that grills aren't very good at inundating meat with smoke. That job is done better in a smoking rig or BBQ pit. We have found that to get a pronounced flavor of smoke on a grill, it's necessary to add smoke in the seasoning as well as in the fire. In this recipe the smoke comes from multiple directions—a brine flavored with liquid smoke (see below), a rub of smoked paprika and smoked chiles, a mop flavored with a smoky hot sauce, as well as some wood chips in the fire.

INGREDIENTS:

5 cups hardwood chips, soaked in water for 30 minutes

1 bone-in pork shoulder roast (about 5 pounds)

3 cups Smokin' Brine, made with beer (page 33)

1 tablespoon canola oil

½ cup Smokin' Rub (page 26)

1 cup Applejack Mop (page 38)

10 to 12 soft rolls

DIRECTIONS:

Put the pork shoulder in a jumbo (2-gallon) zipper-lock bag. If you only have 1-gallon bags, cut the shoulder in half and use two bags. Add the brine to the bag(s), press out the air, seal, and refrigerate for at least 8 hours or overnight.

Light a grill for indirect low heat, about 225°F, with smoke (see pages 14 and 16). The pork will need to cook for more than 2 hours, so if you are using charcoal or wood, you will need to light additional coals or add more wood to replenish the fire.

Remove the pork from the brine and pat dry with paper towels. Coat with the oil and sprinkle with the rub; set aside for 15 minutes.

Brush the grill grate and coat with oil. Add a handful or two of the wood chips. When you see smoke, put the pork on the grill away from the fire. Close the lid and cook for 1 hour. Add more wood chips and if you are using charcoal or wood, replenish the coals.

Transfer the pork to a disposable or metal roasting pan large enough to hold it comfortably, and put on the grill away from the fire. Mix up the mop ingredients and spoon one-third of it over the pork. Cover the pan with foil and grill for another hour. Uncover and spoon half of the remaining mop over the pork, re-cover, and cook until the pork can be easily pierced with a fork (about 190°F on an instant-read thermometer), 1½ to 2 more hours, basting with the mop every 30 to 45 minutes. Cool for 15 minutes.

Warm the rolls.

Pour any meat juices in the pan into a bowl and set aside. Remove the bones from the pork and cut the meat into 1½-inch-thick slices. Shred the slices using two forks to pull the meat apart. Skim as much fat off the meat juices as possible and mix the remaining juices into the meat.

Serve with the rolls.

WHAT IS LIQUID SMOKE?

Liquid smoke, which is basically smoke-flavored water, is a convenient way to enhance the smoky flavor of smoke-grilled ingredients. Smoke consists of two main components known as phases: the first phase is made up of microscopic oily particles, which appear as a haze. These oily particles are dispersed in the second phase, which is an invisible gas made up of aromatic, water-soluble molecules. Liquid smoke is largely made of trapped smoke vapor from the gaseous phase. Since many of the toxic components of smoke (including most tars and polycyclic aromatic hydrocarbons or PAHs) are in the oily phase, liquid smoke is relatively safe to use. The smoke flavor in liquid smoke is quite concentrated, so the product should be used judiciously.

SHOULDER HAM/SHOULDER

Picnic Ham Smoke-Braised with Hard Cider Mop

MAKES 8 SERVINGS

Picnic ham, the bottom half of the shoulder, is a tough, flavorful cut, riddled with pockets of fat and built for long, slow smoking. Infusing the meat with smoke and grilling the pork slowly enough to melt its tough tissue into gloriously gelatinous globs requires the lowest possible heat. That usually means that the fire is built away from the cooking chamber in a smoker rig. When smoking this cut on a grill you will need to use a form of indirect grilling that uses a small, hot fire able to generate lots of smoke and moderate ambient heat. This means you will use just one burner on a three- or four-burner gas grill, or only half a charcoal chimney's worth of charcoal or wood for a live fire. The trick is to keep the area of the fire so small that the amount of heat it throws out into the interior of the grill is kept at around 225°F.

INGREDIENTS:

4 to 6 cups hickory or fruitwood chips, soaked in water for 30 minutes

3 cups Bourbon Brine (page 33)

1 bone-in picnic ham (3 to 4 pounds)

¼ cup plus 1 tablespoon Smokin' Rub (page 26)

2⅓ cups Bourbon-Cider Mop (page 38)

DIRECTIONS:

Combine the brine and pork in a 1-gallon zipper-lock bag. Press out the air, seal, and refrigerate at least 6 hours or as long as overnight.

Light a grill for indirect low heat, about 225°F, with smoke (see pages 14 and 16). Brush the grill grate and coat with oil.

Remove the meat from the brine, and discard the brine. Pat the meat dry with paper towels and season all over with ¼ cup of the rub.

Mix the remaining 1 tablespoon of rub into the mop in a small bowl.

Drain 1 cup of the wood chips and add to the grill. When you see smoke, put the ham on the grill as far away from the fire as possible. Close the grill lid and cook until the internal temperature of the meat is 160°F and the meat is easily pierced with a fork, 3½ to 4 hours. Baste with the mop every 20 minutes after the first hour of cooking. Add another cup of wood chips to grill whenever the old ones burn out and you no longer see smoke coming from the grill.

Transfer the ham to a cutting board and set aside for 10 minutes before serving. Carve against the grain into ¼-inch-thick slices.

COUNTRY-STYLE RIBS/SHOULDER

Apple-Brined Country-Style Pork Ribs

MAKES 6 SERVINGS

Country-style ribs come from the shoulder and are the meatiest of all pork ribs. This is mostly because they are not really ribs. They are butterflied shoulder blade chops, which is why they look different from spareribs or baby backs. Country-style ribs are a great buy, with more meat and less bone per pound than other rib cuts, but because of the placement of the bone, they are not good for picking up and eating with your fingers.

INGREDIENTS:

3 cups Apple-Thyme Brine (page 35)

6 country-style pork ribs (about 3 pounds total), about 1 inch thick

1 tablespoon canola oil

2 tablespoons Poultry Rub (page 29)

⅔ cup apple cider vinegar

2 tablespoons sugar

1 tablespoon spicy brown mustard

½ teaspoon hot pepper sauce, such as Tabasco

DIRECTIONS:

Combine the brine and pork in a 1-gallon zipper-lock bag. Press out the air, seal the bag, and refrigerate for at least 6 hours or as long as overnight.

Light a grill for indirect medium heat, about 325°F (page 14).

Remove the pork from the brine and pat dry. Coat with the oil and season on both sides with the poultry rub. Let rest for 10 minutes.

Mix up a mop of the cider vinegar, sugar, mustard, and Tabasco.

Brush the grill grate and coat with oil. Put the pork on the grill away from the heat, cover the grill, and cook for about 45 minutes, turning every 15 minutes and basting liberally with mop after each turn, until the pork is very tender, about 190°F (make sure the thermometer is not touching bone).

SPARERIBS/BELLY

Coriander Spareribs with Lime Brine

MAKES 6 SERVINGS

Spareribs, which are cut from the belly, come in a slab of at least eleven bones. The slab tapers at one end and has a flap of tough brisket meat attached along the edge of the wide end. St. Louis ribs are trimmed into a rough rectangle, with the brisket and shorter ribs removed, to make the ribs more uniform. It is the cut we prefer because it grills more evenly, and it is easier to separate into individual ribs. These ribs are brined with a lot of cilantro (coriander leaf) and basted with a composed butter flavored with coriander seeds and more fresh cilantro. The result is lean and fragrant, quite different from a traditional sweet-sour-spicy ketchup-sauced BBQ rib rack.

INGREDIENTS:

2 slabs St. Louis–cut spareribs (about 4 pounds total)

2¼ cups Lime-Cilantro Brine (page 35)

⅓ cup Coriander Butter Sauce (page 45)

DIRECTIONS:

Cut the racks in half, put in a 1-gallon zipper-lock bag, and add the brine. Press out the air, seal, and refrigerate for 6 to 12 hours.

Light a grill for indirect medium heat, about 325°F (see page 14).

Brush the grill grate and coat with oil. Remove the ribs from the brine and discard the brine. Pat the ribs dry with paper towels and put on the grill away from the heat. Cover the grill

and cook until an instant-read thermometer inserted into the thickest part of the ribs registers about 155°F (make sure the thermometer is not touching bone), about 1 hour.

Brush the ribs with half of the butter sauce, turn, and brush with the rest of the butter sauce.

Remove the ribs to a large serving platter and cut into 1- or 2-rib sections.

PORK BELLY / BELLY

Pig Candy

MAKES 4 SERVINGS

A pig's belly is striated with fat and thick slabs of lean meat, which run in ragged, parallel stripes. Think bacon and then think again. The layering is not unlike petit four pastry or ribbon candy—the perfect image for conjuring up this dementedly delicious piggy sweet meat. A slab of pork belly with its rind removed is soaked in a pineapple brine. (The rind is a layer of skin that helps the belly hold its shape for butchering, but becomes as tough as tanned leather during cooking.) Bromelain, a protein-digesting enzyme in fresh pineapple juice, helps to tenderize the lean meat of the belly. The brined belly is then grilled slowly with smoke over an indirect fire until it just about melts. Then it is cut into small squares, rolled in habanero-tinged cinnamon sugar, and quickly grilled to caramelize its surface. The result is a meaty, fatty, sugary, spicy mouth explosion. Garnish with curls of cooked onion, if desired.

INGREDIENTS:

3 cups hardwood chips, such as hickory or fruitwood, soaked in water for 30 minutes

2 cups Pineapple Brine (page 34)

1½ pounds pork belly with rind removed, about 2 inches thick

1 large onion, sliced ¼ inch thick

½ cup light brown sugar

½ teaspoon ground cinnamon

Pinch of ground habanero or another chile pepper

DIRECTIONS:

Combine the brine and pork in a 1-gallon zipper-lock bag. Press out the air, seal the bag, and refrigerate for 12 hours or overnight.

Light a grill for indirect medium heat, about 325°F, with smoke (see pages 14 and 16). Because the pork belly will need to cook for about 2 hours, if you are using charcoal or wood, you might need to light additional coals or add more wood to replenish the fire.

Layer the onion slices over the bottom of a small roasting pan just large enough to hold the pork belly. Remove the pork belly from the brine and discard the remaining brine. Pat the pork belly dry and place on top of the onions.

Drain the wood chips and put in the grill. Place the pan on the grill grate away from the fire, cover the grill, and cook until the meat is fork-tender or an instant-read thermometer inserted in the center of the meat registers 180°F, about 1½ to 2 hours.

Remove the pan from the grill, transfer the pork to a cutting board, and let rest for at least 10 minutes. Reserve the onions if desired. Keep the fire going.

Mix the brown sugar, cinnamon, and chile pepper. Push through a strainer (to remove any lumps) onto a sheet of aluminum foil or plastic wrap. Cut the pork belly into four slices, about 1 inch thick. Cut each slice into four pieces, each approximately 1 by 1 by 2 inches. Roll the pork belly pieces in the brown sugar mixture, coating them evenly and thoroughly. Transfer to a plate or pan large enough to hold in a single layer.

Brush the grill grate and coat with oil. Grill the sugar-coated pork belly pieces directly over the fire until the meat is grill-marked and the sugar melts and bubbles, 10 to 15 seconds per side. Transfer to a platter and serve with toothpicks.

WHOLE PIG

Mustard-Rosemary Suckling Pig Stuffed with Cheddar Grits

MAKES ABOUT 15 SERVINGS

Beyond question, the most opulent of pig presentations—a whole roasted suckling pig glistening with fragrant glaze, belly bulging with cheesy grits, and a garland of rosemary branches crowning its placid, porcine visage—arrives at a table to cheers. And you, its creator, will glow from pride. Hail the grill master!

If you don't have a large grill rig, you will have to be careful about the size of the pig you procure (see the Know-How, page 131). Even a small suckling pig (under 20 pounds) will take up at least 2 feet of grill space, which means you will need a large barrel-shaped grill, or a gas grill with at least that much space between its outside burners to cook the pig correctly. If any part of the pig hangs directly over the fire, it will scorch. Wrapping the overhanging parts in heavy-duty foil helps, but it will not completely solve the problem.

INGREDIENTS:

For the Grits:

2½ cups milk

2½ cups water

2 cups fine grits

2 teaspoons coarse salt

1 teaspoon ground black pepper

2 cups (8 ounces) shredded sharp cheddar cheese

For the Pig:

⅓ cup Smoked Paprika–Rosemary Rub (page 28)

1 suckling pig, dressed (about 20 pounds)

12 large rosemary twigs, plus more for garnish

1 cup Mustard Butterscotch (page 48)

½ cup hot water

DIRECTIONS:

For the grits: Mix the milk, water, grits, salt, and pepper in a medium saucepan until the grits are moistened. Heat to a simmer, stirring constantly, about 10 minutes.

Reduce the heat to low and simmer until a skin forms across the bottom of the pot and the grits pull away from the sides, stirring often, about 30 minutes. Remove from the heat and stir in the cheese; set aside to cool.

For the pig: Light a large grill for indirect low heat, about 225°F (see page 14).

Season the interior of the cavity of the pig with ¼ cup of the rub. Loosely fill the cavity with grits and sew the cavity shut with kitchen twine.

Position the legs under the pig (the pig might come this way from the butcher). The front legs should rest under the chin and the hind legs should be set forward, bent from the hip, not the knee, so they extend along the belly. Tie the hind legs in place with several lengths of twine. Position the ears so that they cover the pig's eyes and tie twine over the ears to hold them in place. Cover the snout and tail with aluminum foil. Place a double thickness of foil around the front feet, and under the loin and the back feet in center of the pig.

Spread a triple layer of heavy-duty aluminum foil on the grill grate so it covers the area that is not directly over the heat. Scatter the 12 rosemary twigs over the foil, and put the pig, right-side up, on top of the rosemary. Cover the grill and cook until the skin is golden brown and an instant-read thermometer inserted into the thickest part of one of the thighs registers 150°F, making sure that the thermometer is not touching bone, about 3 hours. If you are using charcoal or wood you will need to restock the coals after the first hour.

While the pig is roasting, mix the mustard butterscotch with the hot water and remaining spice rub.

Snip the twine and remove from the pig. Coat the outside of the pig with half of the mustard mixture, cover the grill, and cook until an instant-read thermometer inserted into the thickest part of one of the thighs registers 160°F, about 30 minutes more, brushing with the remaining glaze halfway through, and trying to keep the grill temperature at about 225°F.

Remove the pig to a large carving board and let rest. This is best done by two people wearing grill gloves, using the foil to raise the pig, while a third person slips the carving board underneath. Allow the pig to cool for about 10 minutes, and then slip the foil out from underneath. Garnish with more rosemary branches, or if you want, tie them together into a horseshoe shape and slip over the neck of the pig before serving.

To carve, pull out the thread from the belly of the pig. Remove the stuffing from the cavity. Cut the pig into leg and shoulder sections, and carve the meat from the bone. Cut the ribs into 2-rib sections. Serve the meat with stuffing.

KNOW-HOW: PROCURING A PIG

A suckling pig is not just a small pig; it is an infant. The North American Meat Processors Association has developed guidelines for butchering and sizing animals, to which all North American butchers subscribe. Under these guidelines animals are categorized by sizes A through D. Unless you have a gargantuan grill, you want to purchase a pig in the A-weight range, which is 12 to 24 pounds. (These will cost much more per pound than larger pigs.) Most supermarket meat departments will not be able to get an item this specific, so we suggest you look for a good Italian or Hispanic butcher. You can also order frozen suckling pigs online.

GROUND PORK

Sage Pork Burgers

MAKES 4 SERVINGS

Ground pork is naturally sweeter and lighter than ground beef, which can make it bland when it's on its own. In this recipe we've reinforced it with about 30 percent ground beef, an herb rub, sage, and apple cider. In addition to adding a little tartness (a flavor enhancer), the apple cider adds some needed liquid, which helps to make these burgers extra juicy. Although hamburgers are often cooked to 160°F for safety reasons, we have found that they dry out miserably at that temperature. And since all harmful bacteria are killed at 140°F, we have found a better compromise between safety and succulence to be closer to 150°F.

INGREDIENTS:

1 pound ground pork, preferably 83 percent lean

½ pound ground beef, preferably 85 percent lean

3 ounces (3 to 4 strips) bacon, finely chopped

2 tablespoons Poultry Rub (page 29)

1 teaspoon rubbed sage

½ cup apple juice or apple cider

1 tablespoon canola oil

6 hamburger buns, split

DIRECTIONS:

Light a grill for direct medium heat, about 375°F (see page 12).

Mix together the pork, beef, bacon, rub, sage, and apple juice in a large bowl until well blended. Form into 6 burgers, about 5 ounces each, and ¼ inch thick. Coat the burgers with oil.

Brush the grill grate and coat with oil. Put the burgers on the grill, cover the grill, and cook the burgers until an instant-read thermometer inserted into the center of a burger through the side registers 150°F, about 6 minutes per side.

Toast the buns on the grill during the last minute of cooking the burgers.

If serving the burgers directly from the grill, serve on the buns. If the burgers will sit, even for a few minutes, keep the burgers and buns separate until just before serving.

SAUSAGE/GROUND PORK

Grilled Knockwurst and Cheddar with Roasted Garlic and Peppers and Malt Vinegar Syrup

MAKES 6 SERVINGS

Knockwurst (or knackwurst) are fatter and stubbier than hot dogs, which they resemble in both looks and flavor. They are fully cooked, but are made juicier by a brief period of boiling before they go on the grill. Knockwurst get their name from the German word for "crack," alluding to the snapping sound they make when bitten in to. They are typically flavored with cumin and a good dose of garlic. In this recipe, that flavor profile is reinforced with a condiment of roasted garlic and peppers and broadened with a sweet tangy syrup, made by reducing malt vinegar down to a glaze.

INGREDIENTS:

¼ cup Grill-Roasted Garlic (page 33), mashed

1 grill-roasted red pepper
(see Know-How, page 47)
or jarred red pepper, stemmed, seeded, and finely diced

1 tablespoon olive oil

1 tablespoon finely chopped fresh flat-leaf parsley

Coarse salt and ground black pepper

¾ cup malt vinegar

2 tablespoons sugar

6 knockwurst

2 ounces cheddar cheese, cut into paper-thin ½-inch-wide strips

6 split hot dog rolls

DIRECTIONS:

Mash the roasted garlic into a paste using the back of a fork, and mix together with the diced roasted pepper, olive oil, and parsley in a small mixing bowl. Season with salt and pepper and set aside.

Mix the vinegar and sugar in a small skillet and boil over medium-high heat until reduced to ¼ cup, about 5 minutes, stirring briefly near the end; set aside.

Light a grill for direct medium-high heat, 400 to 450°F (see page 12). Brush the grill grate and coat with oil.

Put the knockwurst in a small saucepan. Add enough cold water to cover, cover the pot, and bring to a boil over medium-high heat. Remove from the heat and let rest for at least 8 minutes, or keep the hot dogs warm in the hot water over low heat for up to 30 minutes.

Shortly before serving, split the boiled knockwurst lengthwise almost in half. Open like a book and grill over a medium-high fire on their split side until grill-marked, about 1 minute. Turn, lay the cheddar cheese on the split side, cover the grill, and grill until the cheese is melted, 1 to 2 minutes.

Toast the cut sides of the hot dog rolls on the grill during the last minute of grilling.

Put a knockwurst in a hot dog roll and top each with 1 tablespoon of the roasted garlic and pepper mixture and about 2 teaspoons of the malt vinegar syrup.

Chapter 6

LAMB

Sheep were one of the first domesticated animals, and remain a primary livestock animal in many parts of the world. Unlike cattle, they can live on sparse ranges and rocky landscapes, and their natural tendency to flock makes them easy to herd. But it is the mild, earthy, faintly gamy flavor of baby sheep that has made lamb one of the most popular meats in the world, though not in the United States.

In the land of American meat eaters, lamb seems to be an acquired taste. Americans only eat about a pound of lamb per person per year, and most of that is eaten in ethnic communities. Middle Eastern, Indian, and Mediterranean populations value lamb over all other meats, and it is largely the flavors of those cuisines that we find reflected in lamb recipes.

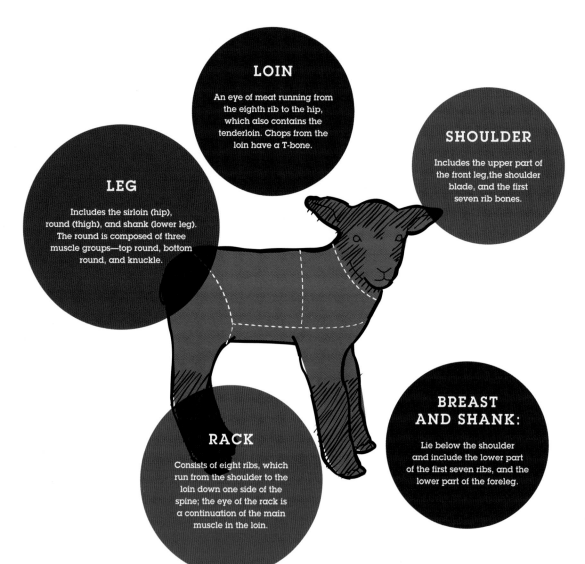

LOIN

An eye of meat running from the eighth rib to the hip, which also contains the tenderloin. Chops from the loin have a T-bone.

SHOULDER

Includes the upper part of the front leg, the shoulder blade, and the first seven rib bones.

LEG

Includes the sirloin (hip), round (thigh), and shank (lower leg). The round is composed of three muscle groups—top round, bottom round, and knuckle.

RACK

Consists of eight ribs, which run from the shoulder to the loin down one side of the spine; the eye of the rack is a continuation of the main muscle in the loin.

BREAST AND SHANK:

Lie below the shoulder and include the lower part of the first seven ribs, and the lower part of the foreleg.

LAMB

INGREDIENT / PRIMAL CUT	OTHER NAMES	HOW TO GRILL	SUBSTITUTIONS
CROWN / RACK	Rack	INDIRECT medium	Rack of lamb
RACK / RACK	Carré, rib roast, rack of lamb, rack roast	INDIRECT high	---
SADDLE / RACK	Foresaddle, double rack	INDIRECT medium	Rack of lamb
RIB CHOPS RACK	English chop	BILEVEL medium-high / medium	Loin chops
LOIN CHOPS / LOIN	T-bone steak or chop	BILEVEL medium-high / medium	Rib chops
NOISETTE / LOIN	Boneless loin, medallions, short loin	DIRECT high	---
TENDERLOIN / LOIN	Filet, tender	DIRECT high	Loin
LEG / LEG	Bone-in leg, boneless leg (BRT), butterflied leg, whole (or full) leg, steamship	INDIRECT medium	---
LEG – SHORT / LEG	Half leg sirloin end or shank end, haunch	INDIRECT medium	---
LEG STEAKS / LEG	Lamb sirloin steaks, lamb steak, leg steak,	DIRECT medium-high	Shoulder chops
SHANK / LEG	Foreshank, hind shank, trotter	INDIRECT medium / frequent basting	---
CUBES / LEG OR SHOULDER	Lamb stew meat	DIRECT medium	Beef cubes
GROUND / SHOULDER, BREAST, OR SHANK	Lamb patties	DIRECT medium or medium-high	Ground beef
SHOULDER ROAST – SQUARE CUT / SHOULDER	Blade roast, shoulder roast	INDIRECT low for smoke / frequent basting	Half leg shank end
SHOULDER ROAST – BONELESS / SHOULDER	Cushion, rolled shoulder, clod	INDIRECT low for smoke / frequent basting	Half leg shank end
SHOULDER CHOPS – ARM OR BLADE / SHOULDER	Arm chop, blade chop, block chop, round bone chop	DIRECT medium	Leg steak
BREAST / SPARERIBS / BREAST	Lamb ribs, Denver ribs	INDIRECT barbeque	Lamb shoulder steak Lamb sirloin steak
RIBLETS / BREAST	Lamb ribs	INDIRECT barbeque	Lamb shoulder steak Lamb sirloin steak
SUCKLING / WHOLE	Baby lamb, milk-fed lamb	INDIRECT medium / frequent basting *preferably rotisserie or spit*	---
HEART / VARIETY MEAT	---	DIRECT medium	Tongue
KIDNEYS / VARIETY MEAT	---	DIRECT medium	---
LIVER / VARIETY MEAT	---	DIRECT medium or medium-high	---

From Spring Lamb to Mutton

Lamb quality is categorized by age and feed. Milk-fed lamb comes from animals that have not been weaned, usually six to eight weeks old, and is called baby lamb. The carcass is tiny, weighing less than 20 pounds, with a rack (rib section) that weighs less than 1 pound and a leg that is less than 2 pounds. True milk-fed lamb is rare in North America, where it is considered an uneconomical way to raise lamb, and where the tiny cuts are seen as skimpy. Along the Mediterranean coast of Europe, milk-fed lamb is highly prized, especially at Easter. (Unlike calves raised for milk-fed veal, milk-fed lambs are not tethered.)

Most of the lamb in North America is slaughtered between three and five months of age, and is known as spring lamb. Spring lamb is small enough to spit-roast whole or halved. A whole spring lamb will feed about 15 people.

Sheep are seasonal breeders, and follow a similar reproductive pattern to other herd animals. The ewes of an entire flock are impregnated in a short period of time by a single ram, selected either by dominance or by the rancher. For most breeds of sheep, breeding naturally happens in the early fall, so that lambs dropped in early spring have the benefit of feeding on lush spring pasturage. Today sheep are bred year-round, and consequently "spring" lamb is no longer seasonal. The U.S. Department of Agriculture identifies spring lamb as lamb that is slaughtered between the first Monday in March and the first Monday in October.

Since almost all lamb meat comes from animals of the same age, they are often identified by place of origin. The most common types are New Zealand lamb, Australian lamb, Icelandic lamb, and American lamb, in that order. These are not necessarily the largest lamb- and sheep-producing countries in the world, but they are the ones with the best marketing and distribution systems for lamb meat. The New Zealand and Australian lamb industries are the most well established, and they export more lamb than all other countries combined. Inroads have been made by Iceland and the U.S. in recent years. Iceland produces lamb that is mild-tasting, and it is grown in a completely sustainable agricultural system that is devoid of feedlots, antibiotics, and growth hormones.

American lamb is also quite mild, but its real distinction is its size. American spring lamb cuts are typically twice the size of spring lamb from other countries, mostly because they spend time bulking up on grain before slaughter. Bigger cuts mean a better meat-to-bone ratio, which means more edible meat per pound.

Grilling Lamb

Unlike beef, veal, and pork, lambs are still delivered whole to some butchers. They are cut in-house, so good butcher shops will sell all parts of the animal.

As with other four-legged animals, the most tender cuts of lamb come from the rib and loin. But because lambs are fairly young and tender throughout, far more of a lamb can be grilled over direct heat like the most expensive cuts of beef and veal. Still, most people want lamb ribs (either as racks or cut into chops), loin chops, legs, and whole loins, so these cuts tend to be high-priced and more readily available.

Most cuts of lamb are surrounded by a layer of fat, which is covered in a papery film called the fell. Since removing the fell from a leg or shoulder can cause a roast to lose its shape, it is advisable when grill-roasting whole cuts to leave the fell intact. But trim the fell from lamb chops or steaks, because it contracts when exposed to high heat and can cause the meat to curl.

Because lamb is assertively flavored, you can spice it assertively without fear of overpowering it. Many of the countries that consume a lot of lamb have cuisines known for sophisticated spicing. Frequently they infuse lamb meat with spices by stewing it in curries and tagines. Because stewing requires simmering the meat in liquid, it isn't appropriate for grilling. But we use rubs, brines, marinades, and sauces for a similar flavor barrage.

Buying Lamb

High-quality lamb meat is light red and finely grained. It has moderately thick layers of dry white fat surrounding the meat, but not a great deal of marbling. Young lamb bones are moist and slightly pink. As lamb gets older, the color of the meat darkens to purple, the cuts of meat get larger with more pronounced marbling, the fat darkens toward yellow and becomes softer and moister, and the bones become hard, dry, and white.

Lamb freezes well, and some of the best buys on quality lamb are frozen products. Although lamb is becoming increasingly popular, Americans don't consume much. So producers find it economical to freeze a sizable proportion of their product in order to give it a longer shelf life. Industrially frozen lamb, if stored properly, will stay in good condition for about 12 months. If you freeze lamb at home, you can keep it for up to 6 months.

The Flavor of Lamb

Lamb has a reputation for being strongly flavored. Pasture feeding lambs, particularly on alfalfa and clover, encourages the development of skatole, an aromatic chemical in lamb fat and meat with a strong aroma. Skatole can be floral and sweet at low levels, but turns fecal when concentrated. It is the reason that pasture-raised mutton is an acquired taste, and why feed and age are important factors for determining lamb flavor. American lamb remains mild even though it is typically slaughtered past six months, because the animals' grain-supplemented diet discourages the development of skatole. Icelandic and New Zealand lambs are fed heavily on alfalfa and are typically slaughtered at four months, before the level of skatole in their meat becomes unpleasant.

KNOW-HOW: FRENCHING A RACK

A frenched rack of lamb is one in which the meat, fat, and membrane from the ends of the rib bones have been stripped away, exposing about 2 inches of cleaned bare bone, which can be used as a handle when eating lamb chops. Frenched racks are readily available, but if you want to french a rack yourself, here's how:

Make a 2-inch-long slit in the meat on each side of each rib bone. Cut out the meat that has been separated from the bone.

Scrape the membrane, fat, and strands of meat from the exposed part of the bones, trying to get the bones as clean as possible.

KNOW-HOW: TYING A CROWN ROAST

Most butchers will be happy to assemble a crown roast for you, but if you want to do it yourself. You will need:

- Heavy-duty thread (or thin, sturdy twine)

- A large needle with a large eye, preferably curved (an upholstery needle works great)

- Heavy cotton twine

- 2 to 3 racks of lamb, frenched (see above)

On the non-meaty side of the racks make small slits in the meat between the ends of bones (no more than ½ inch long and ¼ inch deep). These slits will spread open when the rack is curved into a crown.

Butt the end of one rack up against another. Using the bones as anchors, sew the ends together, using as few stitches as possible. Repeat with as many racks as you are using.

Stand the sewn racks so that the cleaned ends of the bones are pointing up. Bend the meat into a ring, with the meaty side facing in. As the ring forms, the rib bones will arch outward, looking like the points on a crown. To close the ring, tie the ends together using the bones as anchors; stitch as needed to secure in place.

RACK/RACK

Grill-Roasted Rack of Lamb with Wasabi Panko Crumbs

MAKES 2 SERVINGS

A rack of lamb is a lamb rib roast, and it looks a lot like a standing rib roast of beef shrunk to Lilliputian dimensions. Because the meat is delicate, it is often breaded to help protect it from direct heat. In this recipe the meaty parts of the rack are crusted with a mixture of mustard and wasabi (Japanese horseradish) and panko, which are Japanese-style breadcrumbs. To keep the breadcrumbs from blistering off the lamb as it roasts, the meat is first dusted with flour or cornstarch. The starch absorbs any surface moisture from the meat, which would otherwise steam, causing the casing of breadcrumbs and mustard to become unglued. Panko bread crumbs are chunkier than other bread crumbs, and they are also lighter and crispier. This is because panko crumbs are made from highly aerated bread, yielding crumbs riddled with hundreds of tiny holes. When the crumbs are baked, hot air circulates more completely through the breadcrumbs, causing them to toast inside and out.

INGREDIENTS:

3 tablespoons prepared wasabi, or 2 tablespoons powdered wasabi mixed with 3 tablespoons water

1 tablespoon Dijon mustard

⅓ cup panko breadcrumbs

1 tablespoon Mustard Wasabi Rub (page 26)

1 roast-ready rack of lamb (about 1½ pounds), frenched (see Know-How, page 139), excess fat removed

Kosher salt and pepper

1 tablespoon all-purpose flour or cornstarch

DIRECTIONS:

Mix the wasabi and mustard in a small bowl and set aside.

Mix the panko breadcrumbs and rub on a plate and set aside.

Season the meaty parts of the lamb with salt and pepper and coat with flour or cornstarch. Pat off any excess and brush with a thick coating of the mustard mixture. Roll in the seasoned breadcrumbs until thoroughly coated. Wrap the bones with foil to keep them from burning, and set the lamb aside to rest for 30 minutes to set the crumbs.

Light a grill for indirect high heat, about 425°F (see page 14).

Brush the grill grate and coat with oil. Put the lamb on the grill away from the fire, meaty-side up, and grill until an instant-read thermometer inserted into the center of the meat registers 130°F, 20 to 25 minutes (make sure the thermometer is not touching bone). Remove with a wide spatula and set on a cutting board. Let rest for 5 minutes and slice into chops.

KEEP IT SIMPLE:

Substitute regular breadcrumbs for the panko crumbs. The result will be slightly less crispy.

If you don't have wasabi (or don't like it), use 2 tablespoons mustard and omit the wasabi.

SADDLE/RACK

Grill-Roasted Saddle of Lamb with Banana Mustard

MAKES 6 SERVINGS

A saddle of lamb is a specialty cut consisting of the entire rib cage of the animal. Less delicate than a rack of lamb (one side of a saddle), and less ostentatious than a crown roast (several racks tied together in a circle), the presentation of a whole saddle is at once grand and basic, showcasing the natural configuration of the animal's rib section. It is in all respects a primal roast. Because the saddle has two sets of arching rib bones, it will sit securely on a grill grate with the eye of the roast raised away from the fire, allowing it to roast evenly without scorching. This recipe alters the typical herbal palette for lamb with some exotic flavors. The rub has the rich, chocolaty chile character of Mexican mole, and the accompanying condiment is a revelatory blend of pungent banana and sinus-searing mustard vying for your olfactory attention.

INGREDIENTS:

Banana Mustard:

2 tablespoons molasses

½ cup brown mustard

1 ripe banana, mashed

½ teaspoon coarse salt

¼ to ½ teaspoon Asian hot sauce, such as Sriracha

1 lamb saddle (double rack, about 4 pounds), trimmed of excess fat

¼ cup Mole Rub (page 27)

3 tablespoons breadcrumbs

continued →

DIRECTIONS:

Light a grill for indirect medium heat, about 325°F (see page 14).

For the banana mustard: Mix the molasses, mustard, mashed bananas, salt, and hot sauce in a small bowl. Set aside.

With the saddle placed bone-side down, separate the eyes of meat from the vertebrae that run down the center of the roast by making a cut on either side of the spine. You should feel the knife moving along the bone. The meat will now be separated from the vertebrae, but will still be attached to the rib bones running along the bottom of the roast.

Brush the meat, including the parts separated from the vertebrae, with ½ cup of the mustard mixture.

Mix the mole rub and breadcrumbs. Pat all over the outside parts of the roast on the outside. Let rest for about 20 minutes.

Brush the grill grate and coat with oil. Put the roast on the grill away from the heat, cover, and cook until an instant-read thermometer inserted into a thick part of the meat registers about 130°F (make sure the thermometer is not touching bone), about 50 minutes.

Remove the roast to a large serving platter, and let rest for 10 minutes. Carve the lamb from either side of the spine in thin slices. Serve with the remaining ½ cup banana mustard.

KEEP IT SIMPLE:

If you can't get a saddle, use 2 racks of lamb and cut the cooking time in half.

RIB CHOPS/RACK

Mint-Brined Lamb Rib Chops with Red Currant Vinaigrette

MAKES 4 SERVINGS

Lamb rib chops are the most elegant of finger foods. No more than a few bites of delicate meat perched on a natural bone handle, they are the perfect quick-and-easy dinner when you don't want to fuss, but you definitely want to impress. In order to ensure that the meat develops a good crust during grilling but stays juicy in the center, you will need thick chops, about ¾ inch. Depending on the kind of lamb you purchase, you will either need double-rib chops (for Icelandic, New Zealand, or Australian lamb) or single-rib chops (for American lamb).

INGREDIENTS:

2½ cups Lime-Mint Brine (page 35)

8 lamb chops (about 4 ounces each), at least ¾ inch thick

1 tablespoon olive oil

Kosher salt and ground black pepper

1 cup Red Currant Vinaigrette (page 41)

DIRECTIONS:

Combine the brine and lamb chops in a 1-gallon zipper-lock bag. Press out the air, seal the bag, and refrigerate for 2 to 6 hours.

Light a grill for bilevel medium-high/medium-low heat, about 425/325°F (see page 13).

Remove the lamb from the marinade and pat dry. Coat with olive oil and season with salt and pepper.

Brush grill grate and coat with oil. Brown the chops over medium-high heat, about 3 minutes per side. Lower the heat to medium on a gas grill, or transfer the lamb to the lower-heat area on a charcoal or wood grill. Cover the grill and cook until the chops are about 130°F (make sure the thermometer is not touching bone), about 2 minutes more per side.

Serve drizzled with the vinaigrette.

TENDERLOIN/LOIN

Grilled Lamb Tenderloin with Arugula and Chèvre

MAKES 4 SERVINGS

Lamb tenderloins are teeny. Weighing in at about 6 ounces, and only about an inch in diameter, a whole lamb tenderloin provides but a single serving. As its name implies, the tenderloin is buttery soft, and very lean. Don't grill it past medium-done, because it dries out easily. You may have to special-order this cut. Most of the market supply is sold to restaurants, so if there is a butcher in your area who sells to chefs, he or she might be your best bet for a ready supply and a good price.

INGREDIENTS:

2 garlic cloves, minced

¼ cup red wine vinegar

3 tablespoons extra-virgin olive oil

3 tablespoons grape seed or canola oil

Coarse salt

Coarsely ground black pepper

4 boneless lamb tenderloins (about 1½ pounds total), trimmed of excess fat

2 tablespoons chopped fresh rosemary

5 ounces baby arugula

2 ounces fresh chèvre, broken into small pieces

DIRECTIONS:

Mix half the garlic, the red wine vinegar, the two oils, ½ teaspoon salt, and ¼ teaspoon pepper in a small bowl with a whisk. Brush ¼ cup of the vinaigrette over the lamb. Press the rosemary and the remaining minced garlic into the surface of the lamb and season with salt and pepper. Wrap in plastic wrap and refrigerate for 4 to 6 hours.

Light a grill for direct medium-high heat, about 450°F (see page 12).

Brush the grill grate and coat with oil. Unwrap the lamb and grill directly over the fire until an instant-read thermometer registers 130°F (for medium-rare), about 8 minutes, turning halfway through. Transfer to a platter, loosely cover with foil, and let rest for 3 to 5 minutes.

Slice each tenderloin diagonally into three or four thick slices. Drizzle with ¼ cup of the vinaigrette. Toss the remaining vinaigrette with the arugula. Arrange two medallions on each plate, nestled into a mound of the arugula. Scatter the chèvre over the top. Serve immediately.

Lamb Noisettes with Poblano-Gorgonzola Butter

MAKES 4 SERVINGS

If you do not worship lamb with all your heart, and all your soul, and all your disposable income, you should probably move on to another recipe. Lamb noisettes, mined from the very heart of a lamb loin—with all bone, fat, sinew, cartilage, and silver skin peeled away—are the very essence of why we love lamb. And we are willing to pay dearly for it. Because of the large percentage of inedible parts on a rack of lamb, this one pound of completely delectable pristine meat will cost the same as almost four pounds of rack. It's worth it. To secure your investment, we top this lamb with a truly decadent composed butter, combining the fresh green fire of New World poblano chiles with the moldy Old World debauchery of Gorgonzola dolce. We didn't quite know what we were doing when we introduced these two. It was a crazy hunch, and we think it paid off.

INGREDIENTS:

2 teaspoons cardamom seeds

2 teaspoons dried thyme leaves

1 small garlic clove, minced

½ teaspoon kosher salt

½ teaspoon ground black pepper

1 pound boneless lamb rib-eye, silver skin trimmed

2 teaspoons olive oil

½ cup Poblano-Gorgonzola Butter (page 45)

DIRECTIONS:

Light a grill for direct high heat, about 500°F (see page 12).

Spread out the cardamom seeds on a heavy-duty work surface and pound with the bottom of a small frying pan, a meat pounder, or the flat side of a heavy knife until partially cracked. Transfer to a small bowl and add the thyme, garlic, salt, and pepper.

Cut the lamb loin crosswise into eight thick pieces. Flatten each one gently between your hands to an even thickness of about 1½ inches. Rub with the olive oil and season with the cardamom mixture.

Brush and oil the grill grate. Grill the lamb to rare or medium-rare (125 to 130°F on an instant-read thermometer), turning only once. When done, the noisettes will be slightly crusty on the surface and still soft in the center. Do not cover the grill and do not walk away. Noisettes are small and tender, and can overcook easily. They will only take about 2 to 3 minutes per side.

Serve 2 noisettes per person, topped with a generous dollop of Gorgonzola butter. Serve immediately.

Guinness-Brined BBQ Lamb Steaks

MAKES 4 SERVINGS

Guinness, the Irish stout, gives the brine for these simple barbecued lamb steaks much of its punch. Like most dark beers, Guinness has a bittersweet molasses flavor, which is great with lamb. But the hidden power of a Guinness brine is its alcohol content (about 4 percent). Alcohol accelerates the absorption of flavorful components directly into the protein structure of meat, yielding a steak that not only retains about 10 percent more moisture, but also is able to deliver a hit of seasoning with every bite. The flavors of chipotle chiles and cumin in the brine are reinforced with a smoky rub and a dark, pungent Guinness BBQ sauce. A word of warning: the sauce burns easily, so only brush it on the meat at the very end of grilling. In fact it is more flavorful served as a table sauce, although the steaks do look nice varnished with glaze.

INGREDIENTS:

2 cups Guinness ale

1 tablespoon coarse salt

¼ cup sugar

1 cup water

3 tablespoons Smokin' Rub (page 26)

3 pounds bone-in lamb leg steaks (see Know-How, below)

1 tablespoon canola oil

1½ cups Guinness BBQ Sauce (page 39)

DIRECTIONS:

Combine the Guinness, salt, sugar, water, and 2 tablespoons spice rub in a 1-gallon zipper-lock bag. Drop in the lamb steaks, press out the air, and seal. Refrigerate for 2 to 6 hours.

Light a grill for direct medium-high heat, about 425°F (see page 12).

Remove the lamb from the brine and pat dry. Discard the brine. Coat the lamb with the oil and season with the remaining rub. Set aside for 10 minutes.

Brush the grill grate and rub with oil. Grill the steaks for about 7 minutes per side for medium-rare (135°F on an instant-read thermometer). Baste with a thin layer of the sauce during the last minute of grilling.

Rest the meat for 5 minutes before serving. Serve the steaks with the remaining sauce on the side.

KEEP IT SIMPLE:

Substitute any kind of chile rub or Cajun seasoning for the Smokin' Rub.

Substitute prepared BBQ sauce spiked with a tablespoon of instant powdered espresso for the grilling sauce.

Use lamb shoulder chops instead of lamb leg steaks.

KNOW-HOW: MAKING LAMB STEAKS

If you can't find lamb leg steaks, you can get the same cut by slicing a boneless leg of lamb ½ inch thick.

Leg of Lamb Roasted with Rosemary

MAKES 10 SERVINGS

The leg of lamb is one of the most versatile cuts for grilling, providing everything from mammoth feast-worthy roasts to quick-cooking steaks, lamb cubes for skewering, and even some ground lamb. A whole leg typically weighs about 12 pounds. For this recipe you want a steamship leg, which includes all of the meatiest parts of the leg, but without the aitchbone (hip bone), which can make a full leg cumbersome to carve. A steamship leg of lamb still retains the major leg bone, which means that grill-roasting a leg will take a little longer than grilling boneless lamb, but the results are more flavorful and much juicier. Bones, particularly leg bones, have an insulating effect on the meat that surrounds them, giving credence to the old adage, "tender at the bone."

INGREDIENTS:

2 cups Rosemary Red Wine Marinade (page 36)

1 leg of lamb, steamship, aitchbone removed (about 6 pounds)

Coarse salt and ground black pepper

4 tablespoons unsalted butter

2 tablespoons extra-virgin olive oil

¼ cup fresh rosemary leaves, chopped

¼ cup molasses

2 tablespoons spicy brown mustard

2 tablespoons soy sauce

DIRECTIONS:

Combine the marinade and lamb in a jumbo (2-gallon) zipper-lock bag. Press out the air, seal, and refrigerate for 12 hours or overnight.

Light a grill for indirect medium heat, about 300°F (see page 14).

Remove the lamb from the marinade and pat dry. Discard the marinade. Season the lamb with salt and pepper, and set on a rack in a large disposable roasting pan.

Put the pan on the grill away from the heat, cover the grill, and roast until the lamb is browned and an instant-read thermometer inserted into the center registers 130°F, about 1½ hours.

Once the lamb is grilling, melt the butter in a skillet over medium heat. Add the olive oil and rosemary and heat until fragrant, about 1 minute. Remove from the heat and stir in the molasses, mustard, and soy sauce. Set aside

After the first 45 minutes of grilling, baste the lamb with ¾ cup of the rosemary mixture, brushing on a thin coat every 15 minutes.

Put the lamb on a carving board and let rest for 10 minutes. Slice against the grain, starting at the wider end and working your way around the central leg bone. Drizzle the remaining ¼ cup rosemary mixture over the top.

LAMB CUBES/LEG

Preserved Lemon and Lamb Kebabs

MAKES 4 SERVINGS

The lamb cubes that you find in the supermarket meat case are most often cut from the shoulder. It's great meat for stew, but too tough for kebabs. For this recipe you want cubes cut from the lamb leg, which means you will either have to ask the butcher to cut them specially or cut up the leg yourself (not difficult at all). The lamb is marinated in yogurt that has been lavishly studded with preserved lemon and thinned with vodka. The preserved lemon provides the seasoning, and the vodka insures maximum saturation. You can buy jarred preserved lemons in the ethnic section of many grocery stores. We make our own.

INGREDIENTS:

4 long bamboo or metal skewers

2 cups Preserved Lemon Yogurt (page 40)

⅓ cup vodka

1½ pounds boneless leg of lamb, cut into 1½-inch cubes

1 preserved lemon, rinsed and cut into 8 wedges (see Know-How, below)

8 medium garlic cloves, peeled

DIRECTIONS:

Mix 1 cup of the preserved lemon yogurt and the vodka in a 1-gallon zipper-lock bag. Add the lamb cubes and toss to coat. Press out the air from the bag and seal. Refrigerate for 3 to 6 hours.

If you are grilling with bamboo skewers, soak them in water for at least 30 minutes. Light a grill for direct medium heat, about 350°F (see page 12).

Remove the lamb from the marinade, discard the marinade, and pat the lamb dry. On each skewer thread 1 preserved lemon wedge, 2 lamb cubes, 1 garlic clove, 2 more lamb cubes, 1 more garlic clove, 2 more lamb cubes, and another preserved lemon wedge.

Brush and oil the grill grate and grill the kebabs until browned and the meat is barely firm (145°F on an instant-read thermometer), about 15 to 20 minutes, turning the skewers about every 4 to 5 minutes. Serve with the remaining cup of preserved lemon yogurt for dipping.

KNOW-HOW: MAKING PRESERVED LEMONS

Preserved lemons are also available at many specialty groceries and on the Internet.

Makes 1 quart

INGREDIENTS:
10 lemons, scrubbed clean
Kosher salt
Fresh lemon juice, as needed

Cut the tips off the ends of the lemons. Cut each lemon into quarters lengthwise, leaving them attached at one end. Pack the lemons with as much salt as they will hold.

Put the lemons in a sterilized wide-mouth quart-size jar, packing them in as tightly as possible. As you push the lemons into the jar, some juice will be squeezed from them. When the jar is full, the juice should cover the lemons; if it doesn't, add some fresh lemon juice.

Seal the jar and set aside for 3 to 4 weeks, until the lemon rinds become soft, shaking the jar every day to keep the salt well distributed. The lemons should be covered with juice at all times; add more as needed. Rinse the lemons before using.

Lamb Shanks Slow-Cooked with Za'atar

MAKES 4 SERVINGS

Shanks come from the lower half of the leg, fore and hind. Hind shanks are meatier, and therefore preferable. Unlike the shanks of pork and veal, which are so large they need to be sawed into cross sections for serving, lamb shanks are served whole—one shank per person. Eating lamb shanks feels a little medieval, but more than half the weight is taken up by bone, so the portion is not quite as humongous as it seems. These shanks are coated with za'atar, an Arab spice blend of thyme, sumac, pepper, and sesame, and are served with the hot, all-purpose Arab condiment, harissa.

INGREDIENTS:

½ cup vodka

1½ cups vegetable juice, such as V8

¼ cup Worcestershire sauce

¼ cup prepared horseradish

¼ cup fresh lime juice

1 tablespoon coarse salt

1 tablespoon coarsely ground black pepper

1 teaspoon hot pepper sauce

4 lamb shanks (about 1 pound each)

¼ cup olive oil

¼ cup Za'atar (page 30)

¼ cup fresh thyme leaves

¼ to ½ cup Harissa (page 46)

DIRECTIONS:

Combine the vodka, vegetable juice, Worcestershire sauce, horseradish, lime juice, salt, pepper, and hot sauce in a 1-gallon zipper-lock bag. Add the lamb shanks, press out the air, seal, and refrigerate for 8 hours or overnight.

Light a grill for indirect medium heat, about 300°F (see page 14).

Remove the lamb from the marinade, reserving the marinade, and pat dry with paper towels. Coat the lamb with half the oil and sprinkle with half the za'atar. Combine the thyme leaves and leftover marinade in a saucepan. Bring to a boil, boil for 2 minutes, and remove from the heat. Stir in the remaining oil and za'atar and set aside.

Brush the grill grate and coat with oil. Put the lamb shanks on the grill away from the heat. Close the grill and cook until the thickest part of the largest shank is fork-tender and an instant-read thermometer registers about 180°F, about 1½ hours, basting the meat with the boiled marinade every 15 minutes.

Serve 1 shank per person with harissa.

KEEP IT SIMPLE

Use prepared za'atar and harissa instead of homemade.

BONELESS SHOULDER/SHOULDER

Cardamom-Ginger Pulled Lamb with Grilled Flatbread

MAKES 8 SERVINGS

Pulled pork and beef are barbecue icons, famous for their smoky, spicy, sweet, tart, and tangy flavors and falling-off-the-bone tenderness. This slow-grilled lamb shoulder has the same succulence, but with a totally different flavor profile. Its spices come from the Arab palate, a mixture of cardamom, ginger, and thyme. They flavor the brine and the rub, infusing the meat and crusting on its surface. Za'atar, a blend of thyme, sesame seeds, and ground sumac popular in the Middle East, is scattered on the grilled flatbread that accompanies the mound of pulled meat.

INGREDIENTS:

2¼ cups Cardamom Brine (page 34)

3 pounds boneless lamb shoulder, rolled and tied

2 tablespoons olive oil

¼ cup Cardamom-Ginger Rub (page 30)

1¼ cups apple cider vinegar

¾ cup water

¼ cup grated ginger

1 tablespoon coarse salt

2 tablespoons light brown sugar

1 recipe Khubz Za'atar (page 378), or 8 pita breads

2 cups Preserved Lemon Yogurt (page 40; optional)

DIRECTIONS:

Combine the brine and lamb in a 1-gallon zipper-lock bag. Press out the air and seal the bag. Refrigerate for at least 8 hours or overnight.

Light a grill for low indirect heat, about 225°F (see page 14).

Remove the meat from the brine. Discard the used brine and pat the meat dry. Rub the meat with olive oil and season with the spice rub. Set aside for about 10 minutes.

Brush and oil the grill grate and put the lamb on the grill as far away from the fire as possible. Cover the grill and cook until an instant-read thermometer inserted into the center of the meat registers 170°F, about 3½ hours. If using charcoal or wood, you will need to replenish the coals about every hour.

During the first hour of grilling, heat the vinegar, water, ginger, salt, and sugar in a small saucepan, stirring until the sugar and salt dissolve. Baste the lamb with the vinegar mixture every 15 minutes after the first hour of grilling.

Remove the lamb to a cutting board and let rest for 10 minutes. Slice the lamb into 1-inch-thick slices and shred into bite-size pieces, using two forks.

While the meat rests, grill the flatbreads on both sides until toasted, about 1 minute per side; keep warm. Serve the pulled lamb with the warm flatbread and the yogurt, if desired.

KEEP IT SIMPLE:

Replace the preserved lemon yogurt with 2 cups plain yogurt mixed with 1 tablespoon lemon juice, 1 minced garlic clove, and salt and pepper to taste.

Substitute purchased pita for the khubz.

Lamb Shoulder Chops Grilled with Escarole and Cracked Pepper

MAKES 4 SERVINGS

Shoulder chops are an economical and flavorful alternative to rib or loin lamb chops. It is a strange quirk of meat pricing that the most flavorful meat is also the cheapest. This is because flavor and tenderness are inversely proportional. Since meat prices are mostly determined by a cut's degree of tenderness, tough, flavorful cuts, like lamb shoulder, are a great buy. The main difference between grilling shoulder chops and more expensive lamb chops is the level of heat. Keep the heat relatively low, no more than medium, and turn the chops several times to keep the heat distribution even.

INGREDIENTS:

½ cup olive oil

6 garlic cloves, minced

2 tablespoons balsamic vinegar

4 bone-in lamb shoulder chops (about 8 ounces each)

1 large head escarole

½ teaspoon coarse salt

¼ teaspoon ground black pepper

2 tablespoons cracked black pepper

1 lemon, cut into 4 wedges (optional)

DIRECTIONS:

Combine the olive oil, garlic, and vinegar in a shallow dish. Coat the lamb steaks with half the olive oil mixture and set aside for 30 minutes.

Light a grill for direct medium heat, about 375°F (see page 12).

Trim the outer dark green leaves from the escarole. Cut the head in half lengthwise and hold under cold running water to wash away any dirt trapped between the leaves. Cut each half lengthwise into 4 wedges, making sure that each wedge contains a piece of core holding the wedge together. Add the salt and ground black pepper to the remaining olive oil mixture, and toss the escarole wedges to coat.

Season the lamb steaks on both sides with the cracked pepper.

Brush the grill grate and coat with oil. Put the lamb steaks on the grill, cover the grill, and cook until browned on both sides and resilient to the touch, about 30 minutes, turning the lamb about every 8 minutes. (An instant-read thermometer inserted horizontally into the center of the thickest chop should register about 155°F.)

During the last 8 minutes of grilling, put the escarole wedges on the grill and cook until grill-marked and tender, about 4 minutes per side.

Serve each lamb steak with 2 wedges of escarole and a wedge of lemon, if desired.

Moroccan Lamb Riblets with Red Onion Raita

MAKES 4 SERVINGS

When a lamb breast has been cut into individual ribs, they are sold as riblets. Lamb riblets have the same over-the-top lusciousness as the breast, but grill in a fraction of the time. In this recipe the riblets are infused with exotic North African spices in a buttermilk marinade. Buttermilk is mildly acidic, delivering a subtle tang and gentle creaminess to the meat. The grilled riblets are served with a salad-like condiment of red onion, lime juice, and cilantro.

INGREDIENTS:

2 cups Buttermilk Marinade (page 37)

3 tablespoons Moroccan Rub (page 27)

3 pounds rack of lamb riblets, cut into individual riblets

1 red onion, finely diced

Pinch of red pepper flakes

1 garlic clove, minced

2 tablespoons chopped fresh cilantro

Finely grated zest and juice of 1 lime

2 tablespoons olive oil

DIRECTIONS:

Mix the marinade and 2 tablespoons of the rub in a 1-gallon zipper-lock bag. Add the riblets, coat with the marinade, press out the air, and seal the bag. Refrigerate for 6 to 12 hours.

Light a grill for indirect medium-high heat, about 375°F (see page 14).

Toss the red onion, the remaining tablespoon of rub, and the red pepper flakes in a small bowl. Set aside for 10 minutes. Add the garlic, cilantro, lime zest and juice, and 2 teaspoons of the olive oil. Set aside.

Remove the riblets from the marinade and pat dry; discard the marinade. Drizzle the riblets with the remaining 4 teaspoons olive oil.

Brush the grill grate and coat with oil. Put the riblets on the grill away from the heat, cover the grill, and cook until an instant-read thermometer inserted into the thickest rib registers 145°F (make sure the thermometer is not touching bone), about 30 minutes.

If your grill has a temperature gauge, it should stay around 375°F. Serve the lamb riblets with the onion raita.

ORGANS/VARIETY MEATS

Mixed Grill of Lamb Unmentionables —Kidneys, Liver, and Heart

MAKES 4 SERVINGS

Not every carnivore is truly carnivorous. Most draw the line at steaks and chops and roasts. The more serious meat eater might stop at sweetbreads or liver. But this recipe asks a bit more; it is a feast for the committed meat fanatic, for whom every organ is fair game. Lamb hearts, kidneys, liver, and intestine (sausage) are some of the most readily available lamb organ meats, and they grill similarly, which simplifies timing. Their textures range from creamy (liver) to pleasantly chewy (heart), and their flavors are assertive, especially the kidney. Kidneys can have a pungent uric flavor, which we tame with a buttermilk marinade. The collection of offal is served en masse, drizzled with a sweet rich glaze. Use either the Balsamic Chocolate Drizzle or the Mole BBQ sauce. They both taste great.

INGREDIENTS:

¾ cup Buttermilk Marinade (page 37)

1 tablespoon fresh rosemary leaves, coarsely chopped

2 lamb hearts (about 6 ounces each), trimmed of veins and excess fat and opened out flat

3 lamb kidneys (about 3 ounces each), halved lengthwise and fat core removed

10 ounces lamb liver, central vein removed, cut into ½-inch-thick slices

3 tablespoons olive oil

8 ounces lamb sausage, any type, cut into 4 equal pieces

⅔ cup Balsamic Chocolate Drizzle (page 48), or 1 cup Mole BBQ Sauce (page 39)

Coarsely ground black pepper and coarse sea salt

DIRECTIONS:

Combine the marinade and 2 teaspoons of the rosemary in a 1-gallon zipper-lock bag. Add the hearts, kidneys, and liver, press out the air, and seal. Refrigerate for at least 4 hours or as long as 24 hours.

Light a grill for direct medium-high heat, about 425°F (see page 12).

Remove the meat from the marinade and pat dry. Discard the marinade. Coat the marinated meat with olive oil.

Brush the grill grate and coat with oil. Put the heart on the grill and cook until browned on both sides and resilient to the touch, about 10 minutes, turning halfway through. Add the sausage to the grill about 2 minutes after you put on the heart, and turn with the heart. The sausage is done when it is brown and firm. Remove both to a platter and keep warm.

Brush the grill grate again and recoat with oil. Grill the kidneys and liver just until browned and resilient to the touch, about 4 minutes, turning halfway through. Do not overcook.

Warm the drizzle or sauce. Cut the hearts and sausage into thick slices. Arrange on a platter with the liver and kidneys. Pour half the sauce over the top and serve the remainder on the side. Season with the remaining teaspoon rosemary and a liberal sprinkling of pepper and salt.

KEEP IT SIMPLE:

Prepare fewer types of meat: choose any one or any combination.

GOAT, BISON & OTHER GAME MEAT

Most people think of game meat in a nostalgic way, with mental images of wild buffalo, antelope, and boar roaming the prairie or hunted in the untamed woods. That's the original definition, which distinguishes the meat of domesticated animals like cattle and pigs from the meat of wild animals hunted for sport. However, most game meat is now semi-domesticated as well. The majority of bison, boar, antelope, and alligator sold in the United States is farm-raised or ranched and is not truly wild. Among big game, some of the only truly wild game meat left is bear and moose, both of which are difficult to come by. Even small game like rabbit and hare are primarily farmed.

BISON

Wild, Ranched, Farm-Raised

GOAT

Ranched, Farm-Raised

DEER (VENISON)

Wild, Ranched, Farm-Raised

BOAR

Wild, Ranched, Farm-Raised

HARE, RABBIT

Wild, Farm-Raised

GATOR

Wild, Ranched, Farm-Raised

GOAT, BISON, AND OTHER GAME MEAT

INGREDIENT / PRIMAL CUT	CLASSIFICATION	HOW TO GRILL	SUBSTITUTIONS
GOAT SHOULDER (CHEVON) / CHUCK	Ranched or Farm-Raised	Indirect, medium-low heat	Lamb shoulder
RACK OF GOAT (CABRITO) / RACK	Ranched or Farm-Raised	Indirect, medium heat	Rack of lamb
GOAT LOIN (CABRITO) / LOIN	Ranched or Farm-Raised	Bilevel or indirect, medium heat	Lamb loin
WHOLE KID (CHEVON OR CABRITO) / WHOLE	Ranched or Farm-Raised	Indirect, medium heat; preferably spit-roasted	Whole lamb
BISON RIBS / RIB	Ranched or Farm-Raised	Indirect, medium-low heat	Beefalo or beef back ribs
GROUND BISON / CHUCK, SIRLOIN, TRIMMINGS	Ranched or Farm-Raised	Direct, medium heat	Ground beefalo or beef chuck
BEEFALO RIB-EYE STEAK / RIB	Ranched or Farm-Raised	Direct, medium heat or bilevel	Bison or beef rib-eye steak
GATOR TAIL / TAIL	Wild or Farm-Raised	Direct, medium heat	Boneless loin of hare or rabbit
BOAR RIBS / RIB	Wild, Ranched, or Farm-Raised	Indirect, low heat	Pork spareribs
HAM OF BOAR / LEG	Wild, Ranched, or Farm-Raised	Bilevel or indirect medium heat	Ham of pork
HARE (JACKRABBIT) / WHOLE	Wild or Farm-Raised	Indirect, medium heat	Whole rabbit or whole chicken
RABBIT / WHOLE	Wild or Farm-Raised	Indirect, medium heat	Whole hare, squirrel, or chicken
MUSKRAT (MARSH RABBIT) / WHOLE	Wild	Indirect, medium-low heat	Rabbit, squirrel, pheasant, or chicken
SQUIRREL / WHOLE	Wild	Indirect, medium-low heat	Whole hare, rabbit, or chicken
MOOSE SHOULDER / CHUCK	Wild	Indirect, low heat	Elk, antelope, caribou, moose or other deer shoulder
VENISON SHOULDER / CHUCK	Wild, Ranched, or Farm-Raised	Indirect, medium-low heat	Antelope, caribou, elk, moose, or other deer shoulder
GROUND VENISON / CHUCK	Wild, Ranched, or Farm-Raised	Direct, medium or bilevel heat	Ground anelope, elk, caribou, moose, or other deer
DEER RIB ROAST / RIB	Wild, Ranched, or Farm-Raised	Indirect, medium heat	Antelope, caribou, elk, moose, or other deer rib roast
ELK FILLET STEAK / LOIN	Ranched or Farm-Raised	Direct, medium-high heat	Moose, caribou, antelope, or other deer fillet steak
ANTELOPE CHOPS / RACK OR SADDLE	Farm-raised	Bilevel medium-high/ low heat	Caribou, elk, moose, or other deer loin chops

Wild, Ranched, and Farm-Raised

Game is available in varying degrees of domestication. Truly wild game animals live a natural life with little human intervention until they are killed and eaten by hunters. But the meat of wild animals is not inspected and therefore banned from commerce and restaurants in North America. The game meat available to most cooks and consumers is from animals that have been ranched or farm-raised. Ranched game animals are essentially free-range, roaming acres of ranch land and consuming a diet of forage. The animals are not intensively bred, so they are genetically similar to their wild counterparts. They are hunted or trapped and then slaughtered, and their meat is processed in sanitary facilities similar to those used for domesticated animals such as beef cattle. Ranched game meat like venison, wild boar, and elk is about as close to wild game meat as most of us can get.

Farm-raised game tends to bear a more noticeable mark of human intervention. The animals are bred and raised under human control with a standardized diet to produce a more consistent product. They are semi-domesticated, meaning the animals still resemble their wild counterparts but have also been bred for valuable traits. Farm-raised game meat may even come from hybrid species such as beefalo, a hybrid of domesticated cattle and American bison. But most ranched and farm-raised meat retains the robust flavor associated with wild game.

Big and Small Game

Game is classified by size for the purpose of hunting. Large game includes animals like deer, bear, and antelope. Small game refers mostly to small mammals like rabbit, squirrel, and muskrat. The most common game meats are:

Goat: Among the first animals to be domesticated, goat meat is still considered by some North Americans to taste gamy (see box, facing page). Goats are related to sheep, and goat meat tastes similar to lamb, but it's a bit more barnyard-y. Goats are sold as mature goat (mutton) or more mild-flavored kid goat, which may be labeled "chevon" (yearlings, seven to twelve months old) or "cabrito" (weanlings, three to six months old).

Bison and beefalo: Bison are native to North America and were nearly hunted to extinction until they were ranched and farm-raised. Bison meat is leaner, sweeter, and more complex-tasting than beef, and is not the least bit gamy. Bison meat is even leaner than some cuts of chicken. Beefalo are hybrid animals consisting of three-eighths bison and five-eighths domestic cattle, which gives the meat a flavor and composition closer to beef. Cuts of bison and beefalo are similar to those of beef.

Venison: Deer comprise a large family of antlered animals, including reindeer, moose, elk, caribou, gazelle, antelope, pronghorn, and white-tailed deer. To distinguish deer meat from other types of venison, the term "venison" usually refers exclusively to species of deer such as white-tailed deer, red deer, and fallow deer. Venison meat is somewhat similar to beef, but it is darker red; has shorter muscle fibers; less fat, cholesterol, and calories; and a more robust taste. Venison cuts are similar to those of beef.

Boar: An ancestor of the domesticated pig, boar may be wild or farm-raised and has lean, exceptionally flavorful meat, which is similar to pork but with a sweeter and nuttier flavor, and a tighter grain. Like other game, young boar less than one year old is preferred for its tenderness. Boar cuts are similar to those for pork.

Alligator: American alligators have pale pink meat with a pleasant firmness and a mild taste. Imagine the taste of chicken, pork, and rabbit all rolled together, with some marshy saltiness thrown in. The choicest cut is the tail, which contains the cylindrical tenderloin inside and is often sold pre-tenderized, meaning it has been pounded or marinated. Tail meat can be roasted or cut into medallions and grilled directly over the heat. The body and leg meat is darker and tougher—best for burgers and indirect grill-roasting.

Rabbit and hare: Rabbits have mild, finely grained, pinkish white meat with a texture somewhere between chicken and veal. Farm-raised rabbit is sold whole or in parts, typically the saddle, tender boneless loin, and slightly tougher legs. Hares (also called jackrabbits) are closely related to rabbits, but they have longer ears, bigger legs, and darker meat with a stronger flavor.

Squirrel and muskrat: As tree dwellers, squirrels feed on acorns and other nuts, which give their moist, pink meat a delicious nutty taste. Young squirrels are preferred for their tenderness and must be caught in the wild. Semiaquatic muskrats must also be trapped in the wild, near the salty marshes where they dwell. Muskrats have lean, tender, very flavorful meat with a fine grain and deep-pink color similar to hare.

In this chapter, you'll find recipes for most of the game mentioned above. Of course, hunters and trappers cook plenty of other game meat, such as bear, beaver, raccoon, and opossum. Even horse is enjoyed around the world in dishes like Japanese sakura nabe, horse loin marinated in soy and ginger, and then grilled on skewers. In Sweden, horse meat outsells lamb. But in the United Kingdom and North America, horses are too revered to be widely eaten, despite the fact that the U.S. horsemeat industry exports nearly as much meat as the beef and pork industries.

How to Grill Game

Game meat has been steadily increasing in popularity since the 1960s, in part because it is more richly flavored and lower in fat and calories than domestic meat. When considering how to grill game, think of domestic meat cuts like beef and pork. All four-legged animals have similar body parts. Where on the game animal the meat comes from and how thick the piece of meat is largely determine the best way to grill it. As the animal's muscles are exercised, they become more flavorful but also tougher. Cuts from well-exercised muscles like the shoulder tend to be thick and tough, requiring long, slow grilling with indirect heat and some form of moisture, such as a mop sauce, to dissolve tough connective tissue so the meat becomes fork-tender. Smaller cuts from the rack, loin, and upper leg tend to be thinner and more tender, and take well to direct grilling over medium or high heat.

In general, the meat of young game animals is preferred and, like domestic animals, farm-raised game animals are usually slaughtered before they reach sexual maturity to keep the meat tender and mild. But the lean composition of game meat makes it less forgiving on the grill than juicy, well-marbled domestic beef. It helps to soak game meat in brine (flavored salted water), which allows the meat to hang on to more moisture as it cooks over a dry fire. See the chapter How to Build Flavor into Anything Grilled for more details on brines, and use any of the brine recipes described there as "best with game meat."

It's also a good idea to add some fat to grilled game. Fat stimulates the flow of saliva in our mouths and increases the perception of juiciness in meats. It carries flavor, too. We only taste fat-soluble flavor compounds in the presence of fat. Rich sauces improve the taste of game meat by bringing more of its flavor compounds to our palates. A common technique is to bard (wrap) game meat in fatty ingredients like bacon or baste the meat with oil during grilling to add moisture and release the full flavor of the game.

When it comes to flavoring, think robust. Dark game meat like venison and boar takes well to bitter and tannic flavors such as cocoa, full-bodied red wine, cranberries, and red currants. Game also stands up to pungent flavors like chiles and horseradish and benefits from some sweet ingredients like fruit to round out the taste. Check out the marinades, brines, mops, rubs, and sauces beginning on page 26 to see some of the flavor possibilities.

Doneness is a matter of preference, but it pays to cook most game rarer than beef. Grilled venison chops and bison steaks can go from moist and tender to dry and tough in only a minute. For small, tender cuts, temperature is your best guide. Avoid cooking steaks and chops past 150°F; better yet, shoot for 135 to 140°F for supple, succulent meat. On the other hand, large tough roasts cooked by long, slow, indirect grilling should be cooked until they are fork-tender, no matter how long it takes. Follow the recipe and see the doneness chart on page 20 to make sure your grilled game reaches its full potential.

GAME IS NOT GAMY

Let's just dispense with the term "gaminess" to describe the taste of game meat. Gaminess is just a euphemism for strongly flavored, and is usually applied when someone doesn't like the taste. The meat of wild game is strongly flavored because the animals eat a much more varied, complex, and seasonally dependent diet than domesticated animals, which are given standardized feed. Plus, the flavor of game meat gets more robust as the animal ages. It's not as if all game meat has an identical composition with a particular flavor compound that can be identified as gamy.

Each type of game meat tastes different, even if it all tastes heartier than the mild, homogenous flavors of meat from domesticated animals such as milk-fed veal. The strong taste of wild animals is exactly what game lovers enjoy about game meat. Others might be shocked by the robust flavor at first, but it is the complexity of meat from a free-roaming animal feeding on an inconsistent diet of wild forage that makes wild game so compatible with the rich, dark flavors generated from a live fire.

GOAT SHOULDER

Jamaican Curry–Barbecued Goat Shoulder

MAKES 4 SERVINGS

The shoulder of a goat is no different than that of other four-legged animals. It supports and moves the animal, developing intricate musculature and tough fibers. Tenderizing the meat requires slow cooking with moisture to break down the connective tissue and dissolve it into delicious gelatin. In Jamaica, spit-roasting over an allspice wood fire gets the job done. Meat is usually jerked this way on the island, but curried goat is also ubiquitous in Jamaica, often served as a stew at celebrations. We barbecue the curried goat instead and serve it with a spicy sauce made with sour tamarind concentrate. This recipe tastes best with mature goat or yearlings rather than very young kid goat because the shoulder will have developed more flavor.

INGREDIENTS:

3 cups wood chips, such as allspice, cherry, or apple-wood, soaked in water for 30 minutes

Jamaican Barbecue Sauce:

2 cups chicken stock

¼ cup plus 1 tablespoon honey

3 tablespoons tomato paste

1 tablespoon tamarind paste concentrate

2 tablespoons dark rum

⅛ cup coarsely grated fresh ginger

2 tablespoons Jamaican Curry Powder (page 31)

½ small fresh Scotch bonnet or habanero chile, seeded and minced

2 tablespoons fresh thyme leaves

3 scallions (green and white parts), coarsely chopped

4 large garlic cloves, coarsely chopped

⅛ cup coarsely grated fresh ginger

½ small fresh Scotch bonnet or habanero chile, seeded and minced

2 teaspoons coarse salt

½ cup canola oil

⅓ cup Jamaican Curry Powder (page 31)

1 bone-in goat shoulder (3 to 4 pounds)

½ cup apple cider vinegar

½ cup water

DIRECTIONS:

For the barbecue sauce: combine the stock, honey, tomato paste, tamarind, rum, ginger, curry powder, and chile in a small saucepan and bring to boil over high heat. Reduce the heat to medium and boil until reduced by about a third, 10 to 15 minutes. When done, the sauce should coat the back of a spoon; it will thicken further upon standing.

Combine the thyme, scallions, garlic, ginger, chile, salt, oil, and 1 tablespoon of the curry powder in a food processor. Puree to a loose paste. Rinse the goat and pat dry, then smear the paste all over it. Cover and refrigerate for 8 to 24 hours.

Remove the goat from the refrigerator and scrape the marinade off the goat into a small saucepan. For a mop sauce, stir the vinegar, water, and ½ cup of the barbecue sauce into the pan. Bring to a boil over high heat and boil for 5 minutes. Remove and let both the mop sauce and goat stand at room temperature for about 1 hour.

Light a grill for indirect medium-low heat, about 300°F, with smoke (see pages 14 and 16). Drain about 1 cup of the wood chips and add to the grill. When you see smoke, brush the grill grate and coat with oil. Put the goat on the grill away from the heat over a drip pan filled with ¼ inch of water. Cover the grill and cook for 1 hour. Drizzle the goat generously with the mop sauce. Cover the grill and continue cooking until the goat is tender (155°F on an instant-read thermometer), about 1½ hours more, mopping the goat every 20 minutes and replenishing the wood chips as necessary to maintain smoke in the grill. If using charcoal, you will need to replenish the coals about halfway through cooking.

Remove the goat to a platter and let stand for 20 minutes. Slice or shred the meat and serve with the remaining barbecue sauce.

GOAT LOIN

Cocoa-Crusted Goat Loin Flecked with Orange and Rosemary

MAKES 4 TO 6 SERVINGS

Goat meat tastes somewhat strong and earthy, with the aromas of a trampled barnyard in autumn. The bitterness of cocoa tames those powerful flavors, and a combination of orange zest and rosemary bring out the best of the meat's bouquet. The rub here features a very special ingredient, cocoa nibs—roasted cocoa beans broken into bits. They embody everything we love about chocolate: dark, toasty bitterness and sensually rich cocoa butter. As a crust on goat loin, cocoa nibs are positively orgasmic. The loin is the lower back of the animal and, with the bone, includes a section of spine. When cut crosswise, the loin creates T-bone steaks, which from a goat are much smaller than beef T-bones. If the goat was very young, the T-bones may be smaller than a cell phone, like tiny triangular meat snacks. Even if they're larger, it's a treat to bite and lick the meat from the tiny bones as the aromas of chocolate, orange, and rosemary blossom in your nostrils.

INGREDIENTS:

2 tablespoons cocoa nibs	1½ cups ruby port
1 teaspoon black peppercorns	¼ cup balsamic vinegar
½ teaspoon coriander seeds	¼ cup chicken stock
½ teaspoon allspice berries	2 tablespoons minced shallots
1½ tablespoons coarse salt	Pinch of cayenne pepper
1 tablespoon dark brown sugar	½ cup dried tart cherries
Zest of 1 orange, chopped	2 tablespoons cold unsalted butter, cut into pieces
1½ tablespoons chopped fresh rosemary, plus 1 rosemary sprig	Pinch of coarse sea salt
2 bone-in goat loins (about 1 pound each)	Freshly coarsely ground black pepper
1 tablespoon olive oil	

DIRECTIONS:

Grind the cocoa nibs, peppercorns, coriander seeds, and allspice berries in a coffee grinder or with a mortar and pestle until coarsely cracked. Combine with the salt and brown sugar. Add the orange zest, and 1 tablespoon of the chopped rosemary. Rinse the goat, pat dry, coat with the oil, and sprinkle all over with the rub. Cover and refrigerate for 8 to 16 hours.

Remove the goat from the refrigerator and let stand at room temperature for 1 hour.

Light a grill for bilevel medium-high/medium-low heat, about 425/325°F (see page 13).

As the grill heats, combine the port, vinegar, stock, shallots, and cayenne in a small saucepan. Bring to a boil over high heat. Add the cherries, return to a boil, and then reduce the heat to medium-low. Simmer until the cherries are plumped and the liquid has reduced to about ½ cup, 25 to 30 minutes. Keep warm.

Brush the grill grate and coat with oil. Grill the goat directly over medium-high heat until nicely grill-marked, 3 to 4 minutes per side. Reduce the heat to medium-low on a gas grill or move the meat to the medium-low area on a charcoal or wood grill. Cover the grill and cook to an internal temperature of 135 to 140°F for medium-rare to medium-done, 10 to 15 minutes.

Remove to a platter and let rest for 15 minutes.

When ready to serve, whisk the butter into the sauce along with some juices from the platter. Cut the goat crosswise into tiny T-bone steaks with a cleaver or heavy chef's knife, season with salt and pepper, and serve with the sauce.

WHOLE KID

Spit-Roasted Whole Kid Spanish-Style

MAKES 6 TO 8 SERVINGS

The Spanish palate is nuanced and complex, born from a rich variety of native ingredients—bitter Valencia oranges, sweet smoked paprika, honeyed vinegar from Jerez, and an afterglow of saffron. Here those flavors infuse a whole baby goat cooked on a spit. Don't be intimidated by the prospect of cooking the whole animal. A kid goat only weighs about 15 pounds, and will fit nicely on any grill that's at least 36 inches wide. Once it's secured to the spit and turning steadily over the fire, it's really no bother at all. Carve the roasted goat into manageable pieces and serve.

INGREDIENTS:

2 quarts wood chunks or chips, such as oak or hickory, soaked in water for 30 minutes

1 small kid goat (10 to 12 pounds), trimmed of excess fat

½ cup olive oil

Zest of 1 orange

⅔ cup Smoked Paprika–Saffron Rub (page 28)

1 cup water and/or sherry, plus more as needed

Sherry Orange Mop:

3 cups dry sherry

½ cup olive oil

Zest and juice of 1 large orange

⅓ cup Worcestershire sauce

3 tablespoons smoked paprika

1 tablespoon red pepper flakes

3 garlic cloves, minced

¼ cup chopped onions

¼ cup chopped fresh flat-leaf parsley

1 teaspoon salt, preferably smoked

1 teaspoon ground black pepper, preferably smoked

½ cup honey, preferably orange blossom

Juice of 1 orange

DIRECTIONS:

Light a large grill for indirect medium heat, about 325°F (see page 14), with a rotisserie in place.

Rub the goat all over with ¼ cup of the olive oil. Rub the orange zest over the inside of the goat, then sprinkle the paprika-saffron rub evenly over the inside and outside. Secure the goat to the spit rod so that it will not spin loose on the spit. If your spit has skewers, slide the rod's skewers over the front and rear of the spit and push them deep into the shoulders and hips before tightening.

Set a large disposable aluminum drip pan beneath the goat and fill with 1 cup water (and/or additional sherry if you can spare it). If using wood chunks or chips, add a couple of handfuls to the grill and wait until you begin to see smoke. Put the spitted goat on the grill, cover, and cook until the rub has set, about 30 minutes.

For the mop: Mix the ingredients in a bowl and baste the goat with a generous coat of it. Cover and continue cooking until the meat registers 155°F on an instant-read thermometer inserted in a thigh, about 40 to 50 minutes more, replacing the coals, wood chunks or chips, and water (or sherry) in the drip pan, as necessary. Baste with the sherry-orange mop every 15 minutes. If your grill has a temperature gauge, it should stay at about 325°F.

Combine the remaining ¼ cup olive oil, the honey, and orange juice. During the last 15 minutes of cooking, brush the honey mixture over the goat and continue cooking to form a glaze.

Transfer the goat to a large work surface, remove the spit rod, and let rest for 15 minutes. Carve into pieces and serve.

GROUND BISON

Bison Cheeseburgers with Horseradish Mustard

MAKES 6 SERVINGS

If you didn't know they were bison, you'd swear these were all-American cheeseburgers. To ramp up the flavor of the mild meat, we mix a little steak sauce into the meat and spoon some mayonnaise flavored with horseradish and mustard over the burgers. The addition of toppings like ripe slices of beefsteak tomatoes and torn pieces of crisp lettuce are entirely up to you, but resist the urge to cook these past medium doneness. Grilled bison burgers go from juicy to leathery in minutes.

INGREDIENTS:

⅓ cup whole-grain Dijon mustard

2 tablespoons prepared mayonnaise

1 tablespoon prepared horseradish

2 pounds ground bison chuck

¼ cup bottled steak sauce, such as A1

1 tablespoon olive oil

3 scallions (green and white parts), sliced

¾ teaspoon coarse salt

¼ teaspoon freshly ground black pepper

6 slices sharp cheddar cheese

6 hamburger buns, split

DIRECTIONS:

Mix the mustard, mayonnaise, and horseradish in a small bowl.

Heat a grill for direct medium heat, about 375°F (see page 12). Using your hands, mix together the bison, steak sauce, oil, scallions, salt, and pepper in a bowl until well blended; avoid overmixing. Using a light touch, form into 6 patties no more than 1 inch thick (see page 62).

Brush the grill grate and coat with oil. Grill the burgers directly over the heat for 6 to 7 minutes for medium-done (about 150°F on an instant-read thermometer, and slightly pink in the center), flipping once. Put the cheese on the burgers 1 minute before they will be done. To toast the buns, grill them, cut-side down, directly over the heat for 1 to 2 minutes.

If serving the burgers directly from the grill, serve on the buns. If the burgers will sit, even for a few minutes, keep the burgers and buns separate until just before serving.

BISON RIBS

Fire-Roasted Bison Ribs with Anise Molasses Glaze

MAKES 4 SERVINGS

Although they conjure up images of the untamed Wild West, bison are now domesticated animals raised in every U.S. state. As bovines, their meat tastes similar to beef but lighter because it contains less fat, cholesterol, and calories. The leanness of bison means it can easily dry out on the grill. Brining the meat helps tremendously by allowing the muscle fibers to hang onto more moisture throughout cooking, which keeps the meat juicy. Bison ribs are big, similar to beef back ribs (dinosaur ribs). But they're more delicate in flavor, so we've shown some restraint here, some Asian self-control, by soaking the ribs in orange juice and pairing them with an aromatic rub featuring fizzy Szechuan peppercorns, star anise, and cloves. A buttery molasses glaze lacquers the ribs as they come off the grill.

INGREDIENTS:

2 racks bison ribs (about 4 pounds)

2 cups Orange-Anise Brine (page 35)

5 tablespoons Szechuan Anise Rub (page 31)

¼ cup molasses

¼ cup ketchup

1 tablespoon apple cider vinegar

¼ teaspoon ground black pepper

3 tablespoons unsalted butter

DIRECTIONS:

Combine the ribs and brine in a jumbo (2-gallon) zipper-lock bag and press out the air. Seal and refrigerate for 6 to 8 hours.

Remove the ribs from the brine and pat dry with paper towels. Discard the brine. Sprinkle the ribs with ¼ cup of the rub and let stand at room temperature for 1 hour.

Light a grill for indirect medium-low heat, about 300°F (see page 14). Brush and oil the grill rack. Put the ribs on the grill away from the heat over a drip pan filled with ½ inch of hot water. Cover the grill and cook until the ribs are browned, tender, and have shrunken away from the ends of the bones, about 1 to 1½ hours.

While the ribs are grilling combine the molasses, ketchup, vinegar, remaining tablespoon of rub, and pepper in a small saucepan and bring to a boil over medium heat. Remove from the heat and stir in the butter. During the last 10 minutes of cooking, brush all over with the molasses glaze.

Remove the ribs to a platter and let stand for 10 minutes. Cut into 1- or 2-rib sections and serve with any remaining glaze.

Beefalo Rib-Eye Steak with Wild Mushroom Butter

MAKES 4 SERVINGS

A beefalo is a cross of domestic cattle and bison, which was developed in the 1960s. Although a hybrid species, beefalo are not sterile like mules. They typically inherit the bison's production advantages—they can forage for feed and produce meat with little or no available grain—and the cattle's docile nature and manageability. Buy beefalo direct from farmers at farmers' markets or through farmers' Web sites (such as www.jcfarms.com and www.blackcanyonfoods.com). Beefalo is quite lean, so cook these rib-eyes rarer than you would a beef steak. If you go past medium-rare, you risk having a dry, tough steak. For added flavor and moisture, we add a dollop of softened butter infused with meaty mushrooms, shallots, and fresh thyme.

INGREDIENTS:

½ cup Fresh Herb Rub (page 32)

⅓ cup olive oil

4 beefalo rib-eye steaks, 1 to 1½ inches thick

4 tablespoons unsalted butter, softened

2 teaspoons minced shallots

2 ounces wild mushrooms, such as morels, porcini, cremini, and chanterelles, finely chopped

1 tablespoon dry white wine

½ teaspoon chopped fresh thyme leaves

½ teaspoon coarse sea salt

¼ teaspoon ground black pepper

DIRECTIONS:

Combine the herb rub and oil. Pat the steaks dry and coat all over with the herb mixture. Let stand at room temperature for 1½ hours.

Light a grill for bilevel high/low heat, about 500+/275°F (see page 13).

Melt 1 teaspoon of the butter in a small skillet over medium heat. When the butter foams, add the shallots and cook until soft, about 1 minutes. Add the mushrooms and cook until lightly browned and mostly dry, 6 to 8 minutes. Stir in the white wine and thyme and simmer until the mixture is dry, 2 minutes. Remove from the heat and let cool almost to room temperature. When cool, stir in the remaining butter, and season with salt and pepper. Keep warm.

Brush the grill grate and coat with oil. Grill the steaks directly over high heat until nicely grill-marked, about 3 minutes per side. Reduce the heat to low on a gas grill or move the steaks to the low heat on a charcoal or wood grill. Cover and cook to an internal temperature of 125 to 135°F for rare to medium-rare, about 3 minutes more.

Transfer to plates and let rest 5 minutes. Top each steak with about a tablespoon of the mushroom butter.

Grilled Fillet Steak of Elk with Spicy Green Tea Pesto

MAKES 4 SERVINGS

Roasted green tea (*hojicha* in Japanese) has deep umami and savory flavors that pair well with big game like elk. It's also much lower in caffeine than raw green tea, so in Japan it's preferred for consumption with evening meals. Look for roasted green tea in health food stores and well-stocked supermarkets. Here we use it to enhance the flavor of cilantro and basil pesto, which makes an unusually satisfying sauce for grilled elk steaks.

INGREDIENTS:

2 cups Green Tea Brine (page 35)

8 elk or deer tenderloin steaks, about ½ to ¾ inch thick

Spicy Green Tea Pesto:

2 tablespoons roasted green tea (hojicha)

1 large garlic clove, coarsely chopped

3 cups loosely packed fresh cilantro leaves and small stems

2 cups loosely packed fresh basil leaves and small stems, preferably cinnamon basil

1 cup grated Parmesan cheese

⅓ cup pumpkin seeds or pine nuts

½ teaspoon coarse salt

1 to 2 teaspoons wasabi paste

1 to 2 teaspoons green hot pepper sauce, such as Tabasco jalapeño

⅓ cup walnut oil or extra-virgin olive oil

¼ cup toasted sesame oil

Oil for coating steaks

DIRECTIONS:

Combine the brine and elk in a 1-gallon zipper-lock bag. Press out the air, seal, and refrigerate for 4 to 6 hours.

For the pesto: Grind the roasted green tea with a mortar and pestle or spice grinder until powdered. In a food processor or blender, combine the powdered roasted green tea, garlic, cilantro, basil, cheese, pine nuts, salt, wasabi paste, and hot sauce. Blend until finely chopped, about 30 seconds. Scrape down the sides, add the oil, and blend until fairly smooth. If too thick, thin the pesto with a little more oil or added water.

Light a grill for direct medium-high heat, about 450°F (see page 12). Brush the grill grate and coat with oil. Remove the elk from the brine, and discard the brine. Pat the meat dry, and coat with oil. Grill directly over the heat for 2 to 4 minutes per side for rare to medium-rare (about 130 to 135°F on an instant-read thermometer). Remove from the heat and let rest for 5 minutes. Serve with the pesto.

KEEP IT SIMPLE:

Instead of grinding the tea leaves, use roasted-green-tea bags. Open the tea bags and measure out 1½ tablespoons.

GROUND VENISON

Venison Burgers with Caramelized Onions and Bourbon BBQ Sauce

MAKES 6 SERVINGS

As with other ground meats, it pays to use tough cuts like shoulder when making venison burgers. The shoulder (chuck) has the richest taste, and grinding the meat negates its toughness but keeps the flavor. Deer is fairly lean, so we add bacon for richness and barbecue sauce for moisture and flavor. Avoid cooking these burgers past medium-done, or you'll be serving hockey pucks instead.

INGREDIENTS:

Caramelized Onions:

1½ pounds large onions

Olive oil for drizzling

1 teaspoon coarse salt

½ teaspoon sugar

4 slices bacon, preferably applewood-smoked

2 pounds ground venison, preferably chuck

1 cup Bourbon Barbecue Sauce (page 39)

¼ teaspoon ground black pepper

6 hamburger buns, split

DIRECTIONS:

For the carmelized onions: Light a grill for bilevel medium-high heat and medium-low heat, about 425/325°F (see page 13). Slice the onions into rounds about ¼ inch thick and coat generously with oil. Brush the grill grate and coat with oil. Put the onion rounds on the grill directly over medium-high heat until nicely grill-marked, 2 to 4 minutes per side. Rotate the onions 45 degrees halfway through the cooking on each side for more even browning. Put the browned onion rounds on one side of a large piece of foil. Cut each round in half lengthwise, and then separate into rings with tongs and arrange in a single layer. Sprinkle all over with ½ teaspoon of the salt and the sugar, and drizzle with a bit more oil. Fold the foil over the onions and crimp to seal. Reduce the heat to medium-low on a gas grill or put the foil over the medium-low-heat area on a charcoal or wood grill. Cover and grill until the onions are very soft, 10 to 15 minutes, turning the sealed packet once or twice. Let rest, wrapped in foil, for 5 minutes before using.

Meanwhile, cook the bacon in a medium skillet over medium heat until crisp, about 5 minutes. Remove the bacon to paper towels and let drain and cool. Let the bacon fat cool in the pan until warm but not solidified. Mince the bacon (a miniprocessor makes it easy) and transfer to a bowl. Add the cooled bacon fat, venison, ⅓ cup of the barbecue sauce, the remaining ½ teaspoon salt, and the pepper. Using your hands, mix just until blended; avoid overmixing. Using a light touch, form into 6 patties no more than 1 inch thick (see page 62).

Brush the grill grate and coat it with oil. Put the burgers on the grill, cover, and cook to an internal temperature of 150°F (slightly pink) for medium-done or 160°F for well-done, about 6 to 8 minutes, turning halfway through cooking. Put the buns, cut-side down, directly over the fire until lightly toasted, about 1 minute. If serving the burgers directly from the grill, serve on the buns. If the burgers will sit, even for a few minutes, keep the buns and burgers separate until just before eating.

Serve with the remaining ⅔ cup barbecue sauce and the caramelized onions.

VENISON RIB ROAST

Smoked Rib Roast of White-Tailed Deer with Hunter's Sauce

MAKES 4 TO 6 SERVINGS

Among hunters, venison rib roast is known as backstrap. Chefs call it the rack. When it comes from beef cattle, it goes by the name prime rib. This is a standing rib roast, a regal cut fit for a special meal. The easiest way to get a venison rib roast is to shoot a deer or befriend a neighbor who hunts. You could also see the sources on page 400. The loin end is preferred, as it is the most tender. Ask your butcher to cut the meat from the bone along the ribs but leave it attached at the wide end, so the seasonings can penetrate all areas of the meat. With a woodsy mushroom sauce and plenty of wood smoke, this venison will make you proud to be at the top of the food chain.

INGREDIENTS:

2 cups wood chips, such as hickory or oak, soaked in water for 30 minutes

Deer:

3 cups Smokin' Brine (page 33)

½ cup apple cider vinegar

1 white-tailed deer rib roast (4 to 6 pounds), preferably frenched (see Know-How, page 139)

1 tablespoon olive oil

¼ cup Smokin' Rub (page 26)

Hunter's Sauce:

4 tablespoons unsalted butter

2 tablespoons all-purpose flour

2½ cups beef stock, preferably homemade

1 pound wild mushrooms, such as morel, chanterelle, cremini, and oyster, sliced

2 shallots, minced

½ teaspoon fennel seeds

½ cup dry white wine

2 tablespoons brandy

1 tablespoon chopped fresh rosemary

2 tablespoons tomato paste

1 tablespoon chopped fresh flat-leaf parsley

½ teaspoon coarse salt

¼ teaspoon ground black pepper

DIRECTIONS:

For the deer: Put the brine and vinegar in a jumbo (2-gallon) zipper-lock bag. Add the roast, press out the air, seal, and refrigerate for 4 to 6 hours. Remove the roast and discard the brine. Pat the roast dry, and then coat all over with the olive oil and the spice rub. Let rest at room temperature for 1 hour.

Light a grill for indirect medium heat, about 325°F, with smoke (see pages 14 and 16). Brush and oil the grill grate. Put the roast on the grill, rib-side down, away from the heat. Put the wood chips in the grill. Cover and grill-roast to an internal temperature of 130 to 140°F for rare to medium-rare, about 1¼ to 1½ hours. Remove to a platter and let rest for 10 to 15 minutes.

For the hunter's sauce: Meanwhile, in a small saucepan over medium-low heat, melt 2 tablespoons of the butter. Stir in the flour and keep stirring until the mixture (or roux) turns caramel brown, about 5 minutes. Stir in 2 cups of the stock and bring to a boil over high heat; boil for 4 to 5 minutes. Reduce the heat to low and simmer for about 30 minutes, stirring now and then.

Melt the remaining 2 tablespoons butter in a deep skillet over medium-high heat. Add the mushrooms and cook until they brown lightly and begin to lose their liquid, about 5 minutes. Add the shallots and fennel seeds and cook for 2 minutes. Add the wine, brandy, and rosemary and simmer until the liquid reduces in volume by about one-third. Stir in the tomato paste and the brown sauce that's been simmering. Stir in the parsley, salt, and pepper. If the sauce is too thick, add more stock.

Carve the roast and serve with the sauce.

Venison Shoulder Roast with Forest Rub and Applejack Mop

MAKES 4 SERVINGS

The robust taste of deer pairs perfectly with woodsy flavors like rosemary and juniper. Add some wafting smoke from a nearby fire, and you've got the makings of a memorable meal. We keep the flavors all-American here with applejack, New Jersey's mouth-watering legacy to the world of distilled spirits. Its caramel-y aromas meld with the juniper-rosemary rub and the molasses in the barbecue sauce to balance the venison's assertive earthiness.

INGREDIENTS:

4 cups wood chips, preferably apple, cherry, oak, or hickory, soaked in water for 1 hour

1 bone-in deer shoulder roast (2 to 4 pounds)

¼ cup Forest Rub (page 32)

2⅓ cups Applejack Mop (page 38)

½ cup apple cider

2 cups Applejack Barbecue Sauce (page 39)

DIRECTIONS:

Sprinkle the roast with the spice rub and refrigerate in a 1-gallon zipper-lock bag for 6 hours or overnight. Remove and let stand at room temperature for 1 hour.

Light a grill for indirect low heat, about 225°F, with smoke (see pages 14 and 16). Brush the grill grate and coat with oil. Drain 1 cup of the wood chips and add to the grill. When you see smoke, put the roast, fatty side up, on the grill away from the heat over a drip pan half-filled with water. Cover and cook for 1 hour, replacing the wood chips (and charcoal or wood) as necessary to maintain smoke in the grill. After 1 hour, drizzle the mop generously over the roast and continue mopping once every 30 minutes. After 2 hours of cooking, place the roast on a large square of foil and drizzle once more. Wrap tightly in the foil and continue cooking to an internal temperature of 135 to 140°F for medium-rare to medium-done, about 3 to 4 hours total, depending on the size of your roast. Remove to a platter and unwrap, reserving any juices in the platter. Let stand for 15 minutes.

Mix the apple cider and juices from the platter into the barbecue sauce and keep warm. Slice the roast thinly and serve with the sauce.

WHOLE RABBIT

Rabbit Grilled Tuscan-Style with Rosemary, Fennel, and Parmesan

MAKES 4 SERVINGS

In the United Kingdom, Italy, and other parts of Europe, most butchers and farmers' markets carry rabbit. But bunnies haven't caught on as well in the United States. Maybe Americans are still charmed by the image of Bugs Bunny cleverly outwitting his would-be captors in the classic Warner Bros. cartoons. All joking aside, if you've never tried rabbit, you owe it to yourself to give it a whirl. It is quite mild, finely grained, and consists mostly of white meat—similar to chicken and veal. Most rabbit sold in the United States is farm-raised, and is more plump and tender than wild rabbit. Farmed or wild will do here. The bone-in rabbit is soaked in lemon brine for juiciness, and then rubbed with fresh rosemary and slowly grilled, whole. It is served accompanied by grilled fennel slices.

INGREDIENTS:

1 whole rabbit (about 3 pounds), skinned and cleaned

4 cups Lemon-Rosemary Brine (page 35)

½ cup olive oil

¼ cup Rosemary-Anise Rub (page 32)

2 fennel bulbs

¼ cup freshly grated Parmesan

DIRECTIONS:

Open up the rabbit by cutting through its rib bones near the breast bone. Remove any organs if still attached and reserve for another use. Remove any large bits of fat, but leave some fat to add moisture. Put the rabbit on a work surface, cavity side down, and flatten it by pressing down on its back.

Combine the brine and rabbit in a 1-gallon zipper-lock bag, folding the rabbit gently if necessary to fit. Press out the air, seal, and refrigerate for 2 to 3 hours.

Combine the oil and spice rub in a small bowl. Reserve 3 tablespoons of the mixture for the fennel.

Remove the rabbit from the bag, pat dry, then brush all over with the remaining olive oil mixture.

Heat a grill for indirect medium-low heat, about 300°F (see page 14). Brush the grill grate and coat with oil. Put the rabbit, bone-side down, on the grill away from the heat. Cover and cook until the juices run clear (they will still be slightly pink at the bone) and the thigh meat registers about 140°F on an instant-read thermometer, about 40 to 45 minutes, basting with the oil mixture every 15 minutes or so, and flipping over the rabbit after about 30 minutes. During the last 10 minutes of cooking, move the rabbit directly over the heat and sear the back until nicely grill-marked.

While the rabbit cooks, trim the fennel stems and reserve the fronds. Slice the bulb lengthwise about ¼ inch thick. Brush the fennel pieces all over with the reserved 3 tablespoons of the oil mixture. Grill directly over medium heat until tender, about 5 to 6 minutes per side. Remove to a platter.

Remove the rabbit to a cutting board and let rest for 5 minutes. Carve into 8 pieces and serve with the fennel. Sprinkle the rabbit with the Parmesan and garnish with the fennel fronds. Drizzle with any remaining oil mixture.

8

CHICKEN &TURKEY

Chicken is the most widely eaten animal protein in the United States, and yet there is probably no meat that is abused more frequently by grilling it. The problem seems to be a lack of understanding. Unlike steaks and chops, chicken needs time to cook through. Not only is rare chicken unappetizing, it's dangerous (all mass-produced chicken harbors harmful bacteria). Because chicken has a layer of fat right under the skin, it burns easily when exposed directly to a flame (especially when doused with a sweet barbecue sauce).

And because chickens are harvested while fairly young, their meat is tender and dries out quickly, especially breast meat, which is a favorite for grilling. All of which means grilling chicken takes extra care. Is it any wonder that when we innocently throw chicken pieces drenched in barbecue sauce over a roaring blaze, we're headed for disaster?

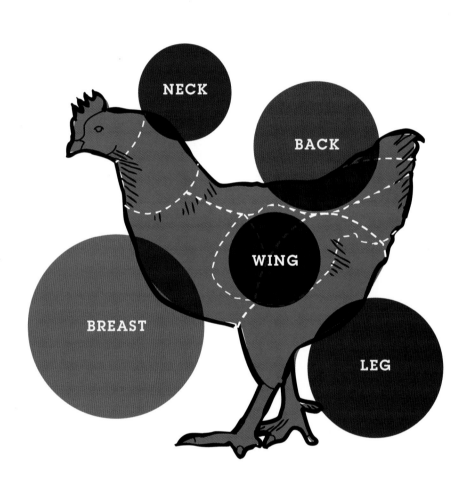

CHICKEN AND TURKEY

INGREDIENT / PRIMAL CUT	HOW TO GRILL	SUBSTITUTIONS
WHOLE CHICKEN	Indirect medium heat either horizontally or vertically Direct medium for butterflied broiler/fryer	Game Hen Capon
HALVED CHICKEN	Direct medium	Game Hen, Chicken Pieces, or Spatchcocked Chicken
SPATCHCOCKED (BUTTERFLIED) CHICKEN	Direct medium	Game Hen
CHICKEN, 8-CUT	Indirect medium	---
CHICKEN BREAST, BONE-IN	Direct medium	Half turkey breast
CHICKEN BREAST, BONELESS	Direct medium-high	Boneless turkey breast cutlets
CHICKEN LEGS	Indirect medium	Chicken drumsticks and/or thighs
CHICKEN DRUMSTICKS	Indirect medium	Chicken legs or thighs
CHICKEN THIGHS, BONELESS	Indirect medium	Boned chicken drumsticks
CHICKEN WINGS	Direct medium	Small drumsticks
CHICKEN LIVER	Direct medium-high	---
GAME HEN (Cornish Game Hen, Rock Cornish Game Hen, Poussin)	Indirect medium-high	Poussin Small broiler/fryer
CAPON	Indirect medium-low or rotisserie medium	Roaster chicken
TURKEY	Indirect medium or medium-low depending on size	Large roaster chicken for small turkey
TURKEY BREAST, BONE-IN	Indirect medium	Large chicken breast
TURKEY BREAST, BONELESS	Direct medium	Large full chicken breast, boneless
TURKEY TENDERS (TENDERLOINS)	Direct medium-high	Boneless chicken breast
TURKEY LEGS	Indirect medium	Large chicken thighs
TURKEY DRUMSTICKS	Indirect medium	Large chicken thighs
TURKEY THIGHS	Indirect medium	Large chicken thighs
GROUND TURKEY	Direct medium-high	Ground chicken, veal, or pork

The challenge of grilling chicken and turkey is cooking it evenly while keeping the meat moist and the skin crisp. Breast meat is lower in moisture than the dark-meat parts, containing only about 58 percent water compared to 72 percent for dark meat. Soaking poultry in brine before grilling increases its moisture content up to 10 percent. Vertical grill-roasting (or propping a chicken on a can of beer) keeps the tender breasts farther away from the fire and evens out the heat. For the most even doneness, it's easiest to grill poultry in parts rather than as a whole bird.

Poultry parts cook at different rates, depending on the amount of exercise each part gets. As grazing birds move around, their legs and thighs (dark meat) develop, causing the meat in these parts to become flavorful but tough. As the meat heats during cooking, the tough connective tissue between the muscle fibers melts. So when fully cooked, the legs and thighs of a whole roasted bird will move easily when wiggled, and they will release clear juices when cut or pierced. Dark-meat poultry is done at 165°F. The breasts (white meat) of poultry get less exercise, which makes them more tender, and more prone to overcooking. Chicken breasts are fully cooked when they reach about 155°F.

The type of exercise a muscle gets determines if it will have predominantly white muscle fibers or red ones. Poultry breasts are white because these muscles, which function in short bursts (fluttering the wings when a bird is excited) followed by long periods of rest, are fueled mainly by glycogen (a sugar stored in the muscle cells). The glycogen can be rapidly converted into energy and leaves the breast meat pale in color. By contrast, drumstick and thigh meat is dark because these muscles, which are used to support the weight of chickens and turkey as they stand and move around, work slowly and steadily and burn fat for energy, rather than sugar. To do that, they require a constant flow of oxygen, which is supplied by oxygen-binding red pigment in red muscle, called myoglobin. The more exercise these muscles get, the more oxygen (and myoglobin) they need, and the darker they become. Pastured poultry, which walk more than caged birds, tend to have darker meat.

Types of Chicken and Turkeys

The most widely bred chicken in the United States, the American Cobb, is a crossbreed of Britain's Cornish and America's White Plymouth Rock chickens. At around 5 weeks old, Cornish Rock game hens weigh 1 to 2 pounds and have tender, mild-tasting meat. Broiler-fryer chickens are less than 10 weeks old, and weigh 3 to 4 pounds. Roaster chickens weigh over 4 pounds, and can be as old as 16 weeks, although most are harvested closer to 3 months. They have well-developed, flavorful meat.

Capons (castrated roosters) are usually harvested at around 8 months and typically weigh around 8 pounds, although they can range from 6 to 10 pounds. Capons develop large, thickly muscled breast meat and have a pronounced layer of fat under the skin, which helps to keep them moist during roasting. Stewing chickens are harvested at 18 months and develop rich, flavorful meat that is great for soups and stews. But as their name implies, they are too tough for grilling.

Turkeys are members of the pheasant family of birds (*Meleagris gallopavo*). The most common commercial North American breed is the Broad Breasted White turkey, which is bred to have short, very plump breasts and legs. Their shorter skeleton has made the meat-to-bone ratio of these birds higher than most other land animals, but it has made it impossible for the birds to reproduce without assistance. Most of these turkeys reproduce through artificial insemination. An older breed, the Standard Bronze, is the most common heritage breed of turkey.

Turkeys are sold by age. Fryer-roasters of either sex are sold at less than 16 weeks of age; young turkeys, at between 5 and 6 months of age; and yearlings, at less than 15 months of age. Mature hens and toms are more than 15 months old.

In the United States, most chickens and turkeys are plucked, eviscerated, and water-chilled, causing them to absorb up to 10 percent of their weight in water, which dilutes the flavor of the meat, but increases the producer's profit per pound. In Europe, most birds are air-chilled. The meat of air-chilled birds is more flavorful, and the skin is drier and thinner, allowing it to crisp and brown better during grilling. Air-chilled birds are becoming increasingly available in America, and are worth seeking out.

Poultry Classification

In the decades after World War II, the mass farming of chickens reduced their cost, and thereby increased their popularity. In 1960 the per capita consumption of chicken in the United States was 28 pounds. In 2005 it was 87.4 pounds. Currently it takes less than 2 pounds of feed to produce 1 pound of industrially raised chicken. Even without growth hormones, broiler-fryer chickens can be made ready for market in less than 10 weeks.

Less industrialized agricultural methods have led to various alternative labels on poultry, including:

free-range: Unlike mass-produced chickens, these birds have access to the outdoors. Unfortunately, the birds may not avail themselves of the opportunity to exit the access door and may spend very little time outside. Credible producers of free-range chickens raise their flocks outdoors for a specified time each day. The meat of this type of free-range chicken may be slightly firmer and more flavorful than that of cage-raised chickens, depending upon how much exercise the birds get.

pastured: A more precise form of free-range production, pastured chickens live in outdoor pens that are moved from field to field, providing them with a diet containing a high percentage of natural forage. The meat is firmer and much more flavorful than that of mass-produced chickens.

organic: In the United States, organic chickens and their feed must be produced without the use of antibiotics, genetic engineering, chemical fertilizers, sewage, or synthetic pesticides. An organic label can be given to mass-produced chickens that meet these criteria. Organic chickens are not necessarily raised free-range or pastured.

kosher: In accordance with Jewish religious law, kosher chickens are raised and harvested humanely with tight bacterial controls. They are salted for up to an hour after being hand-slaughtered to draw out their blood, and are then rinsed, making them slightly saltier than other chickens. Don't brine them. Kosher chickens must be butchered by a certified kosher butcher.

Handling Chicken and Turkey

When preparing raw poultry, clean the birds and your working area thoroughly. Commercially raised poultry in North America live in crowded conditions and bacteria are easily spread between birds. For that reason, industrially produced chickens are regularly given antibiotics in their feed to combat bacteria like *Escherichia coli* (*E. coli*) and salmonella. U.S. Department of Agriculture studies show that the majority of mass-produced chicken sold in supermarkets is contaminated with these bacteria. To reduce the risk of food-borne illness, avoid storing or preparing chicken near foods that will be eaten raw. Use hot soapy water to wash all knives, boards, hands, and other surfaces that have come in contact with raw poultry.

Bacteria in poultry skin makes them spoil quickly so fresh, skin-on poultry is best refrigerated at less than 35°F for only 1 to 2 days, or frozen for no more than 2 months.

Since poultry spoils more easily than other meats, it's often sold frozen. Frozen chicken can be safely thawed in its packaging on a plate in the refrigerator or in cold water. Allow plenty of time to thaw a frozen bird, especially a large one. In the refrigerator, a 4-pound bird will thaw in about 1 day, whereas a 20-pound bird can take up to 4 days. In cold water, a 4-pounder will thaw in just 1 to 2 hours and a 20-pound turkey will take about 8 hours. When thawing in cold water, change the water every hour or so to maintain cool, safe temperatures (below 40°F).

When storing fresh poultry in the refrigerator, keep it in the coldest part (32 to 36°F). Store the giblets separately to help extend the bird's shelf life.

BLOODY BONES

Even when fully cooked, the meat of young birds (Cornish hens, broiler-fryers, fryer-roasters) may still appear red near the bone. Don't worry; the meat is done—it's just that the young animals have built up so little calcium in their bones that the bones leak hemoglobin.

WHOLE CHICKEN

Roasted Chicken with Garlic

MAKES 4 SERVINGS

We have gotten so used to roasting poultry in an oven that our first taste of fire-roasted chicken is often a palate-bending experience. The skin cracks between the teeth like a layer of lacquer, the flesh is soaked with juice, and the aromas of spices permeate every bite of meat. It is enough to make you chain up the oven and throw away the key. This recipe is basic and straightforward, and can be used as a standard template for grill-roasting chicken or any poultry (the timing will change, depending on the size of the bird).

Although chickens come in several sizes, if you don't have a rotisserie, choose a young bird (no more than 4 pounds). This will ensure that the flesh will cook through evenly in the time it takes the skin to brown and crisp. It is best to rub any seasoning under the skin of the bird, right on the meat, where it does the most good. The layer of skin protects it from scorching.

INGREDIENTS:

2 tablespoons Poultry Rub (page 29)

3 tablespoons salted butter

2 tablespoons minced garlic

2 tablespoons minced fresh flat-leaf parsley

1 chicken (about 4 pounds), washed and patted dry

1 tablespoon olive oil

KNOW-HOW: TYING UP A BIRD FOR GRILL-ROASTING

Cut off a 24-inch length of twine.

Put the bird on a clean work surface so that the ends of the legs are facing you. Tuck the wing tips behind the shoulders, locking them in place.

Slide the middle of the string under the chicken at the wing end and bring the ends of the string up through the wing (arm) pits. Slide the string to make sure the lengths on either side of the bird are relatively even.

Bring the string towards the legs, letting each length drape into the crevice where the thigh meets the body. Cross the two lengths in front of the pointed end of the breast and wrap around the ends of the drumsticks.

Draw the two ends of the string together, which will cause the ends of drumsticks to come together and cross. Bring the ends of the string toward the wings around the outside of the bird and pull the string taut, which will cause the legs of the bird to move toward the wings, giving the bird a compact, plump shape. Tie in place and cut off excess string.

If the bird is stuffed, you will want to take one more step. Don't cut off the excess string (if you already have, just get another piece of string and proceed). Wrap the string around the tail (the floppy piece right in front of you, directly below the ends of the drumsticks) and pull upward, so that it mostly covers the interior cavity of the bird, helping to hold the stuffing inside.

DIRECTIONS:

Light a grill for indirect medium heat, about 325°F (see page 14).

Mash together 1 tablespoon of the rub, the butter, garlic, and parsley until well blended.

Rub half the herb butter under the skin of the chicken all over the meat (see the Know-How, below); set aside the rest. Sprinkle the cavity with the remaining tablespoon of the rub. Adjust the skin so that it covers all of the meat and rub the skin liberally with the oil. Tie the chicken so that it holds its shape (see the Know-How, facing page).

Brush the grill grate and coat with oil. Put the chicken on the grill away from the heat, cover the grill, and cook until an instant-read thermometer inserted into the thickest part of the inside of the thigh registers 165°F, about 1 hour and 20 minutes. Brush twice with the remaining garlic-herb butter during the last 20 minutes of cooking. If you are using charcoal, you will probably have to replenish the coals after the first hour.

Remove chicken to a large serving platter. Let rest for 8 to 10 minutes, carve, and serve.

WHOLE CHICKEN

Rotisserie Chicken for Everyone

MAKES 6 SERVINGS

Similar to the preceding recipe, the following method can be used for any large chicken, even a small turkey.

INGREDIENTS:

¼ cup Smokin' Rub (page 26)

1 roaster chicken (about 5 pounds), washed and patted dry

2 tablespoons canola oil

DIRECTIONS:

Remove the grate from the grill. Light a grill for indirect medium-high heat, about 375°F (see page 14). Set up the rotisserie motor on the grill.

Rub 2 tablespoons of the rub under the skin of the chicken all over the meat (see the Know-How, right). Sprinkle the cavity with the remaining 2 tablespoons rub. Adjust the skin so that it covers all of the meat and rub the skin liberally with the oil. Tie the chicken so that it holds its shape and then secure on the rotisserie spit.

Insert the spit into the motor assembly and turn on the rotisserie motor. Make sure the chicken turns smoothly and does not come too close to the fire or lid. Cover the grill and cook until the skin is golden brown and an instant-read thermometer inserted into the inside of the thigh registers 165°F, about 1 hour and 20 minutes.

Remove the chicken from the spit and place on a cutting board. Snip the string and discard. Allow the chicken to rest on the board for 5 to 10 minutes. Cut into pieces and serve.

KNOW-HOW: SEASONING A WHOLE BIRD FOR THE GRILL

To keep seasoning from scorching during grilling and to get the flavor of a rub right on the meat, it's best to season whole poultry under its skin.

To separate the skin from the breast and legs of the chicken, gently but firmly insert your index finger under the skin at the neck end of the chicken. Move it around, separating the skin from the meat underneath. Use a small knife or scissors to cut any stubborn membrane holding the skin to the flesh. Be careful that you don't cut through the skin.

Gradually ease your whole hand under the skin, loosening the skin from the breast, legs, and drumsticks. Rub seasoning on top of the meat under the skin, and adjust the skin so that it covers the exposed flesh.

WHOLE CHICKEN

Black Pepper Beer Can Chicken

MAKES 4 SERVINGS

Anyone who has grilled a chicken in the last decade is familiar with the beer can trick. The sight of a humble chicken stoically roasting with a beer can stuck in its butt has become an icon of the backyard cookout. The technique is not just comical—it's brilliant. The juices from the beer steam the interior, keeping the meat moist and cooking it through faster, while the skin crisps. The breast meat stays juicy, the leg meat cooks through, and the resulting cooking liquid of beer inundated with pepper and chicken drippings makes a tasty jus for dipping.

INGREDIENTS:

1 tablespoon coarsely ground black pepper

1½ teaspoons ground allspice

1½ teaspoons grated nutmeg

1½ teaspoons ground ginger

1½ teaspoons coarse salt

1 chicken (about 4 pounds), washed and patted dry

1 tablespoon canola oil

1 can (about 12 ounces) lager beer

DIRECTIONS:

Light a grill for indirect medium heat, about 325°F (see page 14).

Mix the spices together. Rub the chicken inside and out with 2 tablespoons of the spice mixture, and rub the outside of the chicken with 2 teaspoons of the oil.

Open the can of beer, and pour off ¼ cup (toss if you don't want to drink it). Stir the remaining spice mixture into the beer in the can. Coat the outside of the can with the remaining oil. Lower the chicken onto the can, inserting the can into the cavity of the bird. Position the chicken so that the legs and the can form a tripod, which holds the chicken upright.

Put the chicken and can on the grill away from the heat, cover the grill, and cook until an instant-read thermometer inserted into the inside of a thigh registers about 165°F, about 1 hour and 10 minutes.

Transfer the chicken, still on the can, to a sturdy surface. Holding the can with tongs and gripping the chicken with a towel, twist and lift the chicken off the can. Transfer to a carving board. Let rest for 8 to 10 minutes, carve, and serve.

KNOW-HOW: VERTICALLY GRILL-ROASTING POULTRY

Poultry has a temperature problem; the white meat is done 10 degrees before the dark meat, resulting in roasted chickens with either dry breasts or undercooked thighs. The trick is to get the leg sections cooking faster or the breasts cooking slower, which is exactly what standing a chicken upright on a grill does. By perching a chicken on a can (or a vertical roaster), you lift the breasts away from the fire and place the legs (especially the pesky hip joint, which is always the last part to get done) right next to the flame. The outcome is miraculous: no parts are dry, and no parts are raw—perfect chicken every time.

Vertically Roasted Molasses-Mustard Chicken

MAKES 4 SERVINGS

A vertical roaster, a heavy wire armature that looks like a candlestick without the candle, does the same thing as a can of beer (see Black Pepper Beer Can Chicken, facing page), only without the beer. It has the added advantage of being able to support chickens of various sizes, from 1 to 5 pounds, and it is easier to remove from the hot bird when it comes off the grill. Other than that, everything we've said about grill-roasting poultry on a beer can applies to this method.

INGREDIENTS:

1 chicken (about 4 pounds), washed and patted dry

1 tablespoon canola oil

2 tablespoons Mustard-Wasabi Rub (page 26)

2 tablespoons spicy brown mustard

¼ cup dark molasses

2 tablespoon apple cider vinegar

1 tablespoon prepared wasabi

DIRECTIONS:

Rub the chicken with 2 teaspoons of the oil and dust all over with the rub. Coat a vertical roaster (see the Know-How, facing page) with the remaining teaspoon oil, and set on a sheet pan. Set the chicken on the roaster and set aside for 20 minutes.

Light a grill for indirect medium-high heat, about 350°F (see page 14).

Brush the grill grate and coat with oil. Place the chicken on the vertical roaster on the grill away from the heat. Close the lid and cook until an instant-read thermometer inserted into the inside of a thigh registers 165°F, about 1 hour and 10 minutes.

Meanwhile mix together the mustard, molasses, vinegar, and wasabi. Baste the chicken with this sauce 3 or 4 times, grilling for about 10 more minutes.

Remove to a cutting board and let the chicken rest on the roaster for 5 minutes. Carefully remove the chicken from the roaster and let rest for another 5 minutes. Cut into serving pieces and serve immediately.

BUTTERFLIED WHOLE CHICKEN

Lemon-Espresso Spatchcocked Chicken

MAKES 4 SERVINGS

"Spatchcock" is an old word (dating from the 1700s), which is derived from an earlier term, *spitchchock*, which means to split an eel lengthwise and grill it. The same technique is now applied to birds, specifically young chickens. All you do is cut along either side of the chicken's backbone (poultry shears work the best), remove it, and pull the chicken open like a book. Spatchcocking allows you to grill with direct heat and gives a whole chicken the same dimensions as a large steak. The technique is also called "butterflying," which sounds a little more polite, but it's not nearly as fun as saying "spatchcocking."

INGREDIENTS:

1 chicken (about 4 pounds), washed and patted dry and spatchcocked (see Know-How, below)

1 tablespoon olive oil

¼ cup Espresso Rub (page 26)

1½ cups Espresso Grilling Sauce (page 39), made with lemon juice

1 lemon, cut into 4 wedges

DIRECTIONS:

Light a grill for direct medium heat, about 375°F (see page 12).

Rub the chicken all over with oil and rub, concentrating on the skinless side.

Brush and oil the grill grate and place the chicken, skin-side down, on the grate. Grill for about 15 minutes and turn with a spatula and/or tongs. Grill for about 15 minutes more, until an instant-read thermometer inserted into the inside of a thigh registers 165°F.

Baste the chicken with ¼ cup of the grilling sauce, cook for a few minutes to brown, turn the chicken, and repeat, basting with another ¼ cup sauce.

If you like, coat the lemon wedges with oil and grill briefly. Serve the chicken with the lemon and the remaining 1 cup sauce on the side.

KNOW-HOW: SPATCHCOCKING A CHICKEN

To spatchcock the chicken place it, breast side down, on a cutting board. Cut along either side of the backbone with poultry shears or a knife with a thin, sharp blade. Remove the backbone. Open the chicken like a book. Run a small knife on either side of the breastbone and slide your thumb in the slit to loosen the sternum (the center of the breastbone) and the white cartilage attached to it. Remove the loosened bone and cartilage. Flatten the chicken gently with your hands. Fold the wing tips back until they are tucked behind the shoulders, which will lock them flat. With a small knife, make a slit (about 1 inch long) through one side of the apron of skin at the rear of the chicken. Reach under the bird and slide the end of the drumstick through the slit. Repeat on the other side.

Halved Grilled Coriander Chicken with Margarita Butter

MAKES 4 SERVINGS

Want to cut the time it takes to roast chicken in half? That's easy—cut it in half! By splitting a chicken down the middle you can change your cooking method from indirect to direct grilling, and since the heat only has to travel half the distance, the results are twice as fast. In this recipe the chicken is brined in a spicy coriander-cilantro liquid for added juiciness and flavor, and basted at the finish with a boozy margarita butter.

INGREDIENTS:

1 whole chicken (about 4 pounds), washed and patted dry and split in half lengthwise (see Know-How, below)

2½ cups Coriander Brine (page 36)

1 tablespoon olive oil

½ cup warm Margarita Butter (page 45)

DIRECTIONS:

Combine the chicken halves and brine in a 1-gallon zipper-lock bag, press out the air, and seal. Refrigerate for at least 6 hours or overnight.

Light a grill for direct medium heat, about 375°F (see page 12).

Remove the chicken from the brine and discard the brine. Pat the chicken dry with paper towels and coat with the olive oil.

Brush a grill grate and coat with oil. Put the chicken, bone-side down, on the grill. Cover the grill and cook until deeply browned on the bone side, about 15 minutes. Turn the chicken and brown lightly on the skin side, about 10 minutes.

Turn the chicken skin-side up and baste with margarita butter. Grill until an instant-read thermometer inserted into the inside of a thigh registers 165°F, about 10 minutes more, basting with the butter twice more.

Set the chicken aside to rest for 5 minutes, cut into pieces, and serve. If there is any margarita butter left, drizzle it over the chicken.

KNOW-HOW: HALVING POULTRY

To halve a whole chicken or any other bird, put the chicken, breast-side down, on a cutting board. Cut along either side of the backbone with poultry shears or a knife. Remove the backbone. Cut the chicken lengthwise down the center of the breast bone, to separate the bird in two halves. Trim visible deposits of fat and loose flaps of skin.

CHICKEN PARTS

Basic Barbecued Chicken

MAKES 4 SERVINGS

What we call barbecued chicken is actually grilled. For one thing, the temperature in a grill simply can't get low enough for barbecuing, and for another, chicken is better grilled than barbecued. Start by putting the chicken on the grill as far away from direct fire as possible in order to cook it through with a minimum of browning. Move it directly over the fire to brown, and then, only in the last minutes of cooking, glaze it with barbecue sauce to develop a sheen and a few charred marks.

The most common mistake is to sauce the bird too early, thinking that time spent in sauce will inundate the meat with flavor. Not so. Instead it's better to take the spicy, smoky flavors of the sauce and put them into a brine. The salt in the brine bonds both water (for juiciness) and spices (for flavor) with the fibers of the meat, and since brines are low in sugar, they do not cause the scorching problems of barbecue sauce.

INGREDIENTS:

3½ to 4 pounds bone-in chicken breasts, thighs, and drumsticks, washed and patted dry

4 cups Smokin' Brine (page 33)

1 tablespoon canola oil

Ground black pepper to taste

2 cups Easy Barbecue Sauce (page 39)

DIRECTIONS:

Trim any excess fat from the chicken parts and combine with the brine in a 1-gallon zipper-lock bag. Squeeze out the air, seal the bag, and refrigerate for 2 to 3 hours.

Light a grill for indirect medium heat, about 350°F (see page 14).

Remove the chicken from the brine and discard the brine.

Pat the chicken dry, coat with oil, and sprinkle all over with the pepper. Set aside for 10 minutes.

Brush the grill grate and coat with oil. Put the chicken over the unheated part of the grill, cover, and cook, turning once or twice, until the chicken is no longer pink and the juices run clear (about 155°F for breasts and 165°F for thighs on an instant-read thermometer inserted into thickest part), 30 to 40 minutes total. During the last 10 to 15 minutes of grilling, move the chicken over to the heated part of the grill to brown all over. Brush with half the barbecue sauce during the last 5 minutes.

Remove the chicken to a serving platter and serve with the remaining barbecue sauce for dipping.

KNOW-HOW: CUTTING A CHICKEN INTO PARTS

Put the chicken breast-side up, pull one of the legs away from the body, and cut through the skin and meat where the leg attaches to the body. Bend the leg away from the body until the ball of the thigh bone pops out of the socket. Cut between the ball and socket to remove the leg from the body. Repeat with the other leg.

Separate the drumstick from the thigh on each leg by cutting down firmly between the joints.

Pull a wing away from the body and cut near the joint at the base of the wing to remove it from the body. Repeat with the other wing.

Pry the back away from the breast with your hands and cut the back from the breast. Save the backbone for stock if you like.

Cut the breast lengthwise in half through the middle through the breastbone. If you like, cut each breast crosswise in half to make smaller pieces.

BONE-IN CHICKEN BREAST

Tandoori Chicken with Fresh Mint Salad

MAKES 4 SERVINGS

Tandoori is a technique for roasting ingredients in a wood-fired, bell-shaped ceramic oven, called a tandoor. Used throughout Central Asia, tandoori has also come to mean the spicy yogurt marinade typically used when preparing tandoori chicken, a classic dish in the cuisine of the Punjab region, which is part of present-day Pakistan and India. If you have a ceramic grill oven (such as Primo or Big Green Egg), you can get a fairly authentic tandoor effect. But with a good tandoori marinade, you can come close to the original with nothing more than a charcoal or gas grill and a medium-hot fire. The marinating spices permeating the chicken are calmed with a balm of melted butter and a cooling accompaniment of fresh mint salad.

INGREDIENTS:

4 bone-in chicken breast halves (about 12 ounces each), washed and patted dry

1 cup Tandoori Yogurt Marinade (page 37)

1 red onion, quartered lengthwise and sliced paper thin

1 bunch mint leaves, finely chopped (about ½ cup)

¼ habanero chile pepper, stemmed, seeded, and minced

Juice of ½ lemon

1 tablespoon extra-virgin olive oil

½ teaspoon coarse salt

2 tablespoons unsalted butter, melted

DIRECTIONS:

Combine the chicken breasts and marinade in a 1-gallon zipper-lock bag, press out the air, and seal. Refrigerate for at least 6 hours or overnight.

Combine the onion, mint, habanero, lemon juice, 1 teaspoon of the olive oil, and the salt in a small bowl and set aside.

Light a grill for direct medium heat, about 375°F (see page 12).

Remove the chicken from the marinade, discard the marinade, and pat the chicken dry. Coat with the remaining 2 teaspoons olive oil.

Brush the grill grate and coat with oil. Put the chicken, bone-side down, on the grill, cover the grill, and cook until the underside is dark brown and the top loses its raw look, about 15 minutes. Turn the chicken over, cover, and grill until the skin is browned, about 10 minutes. Turn again, cover, and grill until an instant-read thermometer inserted into the thickest part of the largest breast registers 155°F, about 5 more minutes.

Serve the chicken drizzled with butter.

BONE-IN CHICKEN BREAST

Hot Hot Grilled Chicken Breast with Fire-Quenching Cucumber Balm

MAKES 4 SERVINGS

Brines, especially those containing some alcohol, have the near magical ability to drench meat with flavor. In this recipe we use that phenomenon to achieve truly incendiary results. The heat in the brine is kicked up with a double punch of habanero (only the Naga Jolokia chile from India is hotter), which makes each bite of chicken radiate throughout the mouth. Alone the chicken can be quite intense, but served with a coolant of minty cucumber yogurt, it sets up a titillating tension between pain and relief, which takes dinner to a whole other level.

INGREDIENTS:

3 cups Chile Brine (page 34), made with double the quantity of habanero chile pepper

4 bone-in chicken breast halves (about 12 ounces each), washed and patted dry

1 tablespoon olive oil

1 ¾ cups Cucumber-Mint Yogurt (page 40)

DIRECTIONS:

Combine the brine and chicken breasts in a 1-gallon zipper-lock bag, press out the air, and seal. Refrigerate for 6 to 8 hours.

Light a grill for direct medium heat, about 375°F (see page 12).

Remove the chicken from the brine, discard the brine, and pat the chicken dry. Coat with the olive oil.

Brush the grill grate and coat with oil. Put the chicken on the grill, bone-side down, cover the grill, and cook until the underside is dark brown and the top has lost its raw look,

about 15 minutes. Turn the chicken over, cover, and grill until the skin is browned, about 10 minutes. Turn again, cover, and grill until an instant-read thermometer inserted into the thickest part of the largest breast registers 155°F, about 5 more minutes.

Serve the chicken with the yogurt on the side.

BONELESS CHICKEN BREAST

Quick Grilled Chicken Breast with Artichoke Rouille

MAKES 4 SERVINGS

This is a simple recipe: simply prepared, simply grilled, and simply elegant. It is destined to become one of your quick meal standbys. Usually we brine chicken breasts to keep them moist, but to save time, we've skipped that step. Feel free to brine, of course. The Poultry Brine (page 36) would be delicious (an hour or two is plenty).

INGREDIENTS:

4 boneless, skinless chicken breasts (about 8 ounces each), washed and patted dry

1 small jar (6 ounces) marinated artichoke hearts

1 jarred roasted red pepper, finely diced

2 garlic cloves, minced

2 tablespoons fresh lemon juice

1 tablespoon chopped fresh flat-leaf parsley

2 tablespoons chopped fresh basil

2 tablespoons seasoned breadcrumbs

2 tablespoons finely crumbled feta cheese

2 tablespoons olive oil

Coarse salt and ground black pepper

DIRECTIONS:

To keep the chicken breast from shrinking during cooking, cut out the tough white tendon that runs along its length (see Know-How, page 208).

Drain the marinade from the artichoke hearts and toss the chicken in the marinade on a plate. Set aside.

Light a grill for direct medium-high heat, about 425°F (see page 12).

Chop the artichoke hearts finely and transfer to a medium bowl. Mix in the red pepper, garlic, lemon juice, parsley, basil, breadcrumbs, feta, and 1 tablespoon of the olive oil. Season with salt and pepper and set aside.

Pat the chicken dry with paper towels and coat with the remaining tablespoon olive oil. Season liberally with salt and pepper.

Brush the grill grate and coat with oil. Put the chicken on the grill, cover the grill, and cook until the chicken is browned and an instant-read thermometer inserted into the thickest part registers 155°F, 5 to 6 minutes per side.

Serve the chicken topped with dollops of artichoke rouille.

KEEP IT SIMPLE:

Substitute 1½ cups salsa for the artichoke rouille.

BONELESS CHICKEN BREAST

Sesame-Crusted Chicken Paillards with Seaweed Salad

MAKES 4 SERVINGS

Most folks overcook grilled chicken breast, but it's not really their fault. The cut is too lean to stand up to lengthy cooking and too thick to cook through quickly—paillard to the rescue. A paillard (which means "ribald" or "bawdy" in French) is a boneless slice of meat pounded thin enough and wide enough to practically cover the surface of a large dinner plate. Because they are so thin, paillards grill through in seconds, so they are one of the quickest grilled meals one can imagine. They also look striking, flopping across a plate like an edible doily. In this recipe the lightness of the paillards is reinforced by a spare seaweed and cucumber salad with a Japanese-style vinaigrette.

INGREDIENTS:

1 cup rice vinegar (not seasoned)

2 tablespoons sugar

1 dried red chile pepper

¼ cup soy sauce

¾ ounce dried cut wakame seaweed

2 small Asian cucumbers, peeled and halved lengthwise

1 tablespoon coarse salt

4 red radishes, trimmed and cut into fine strips

2 tablespoons chopped fresh cilantro

2 scallions (green and white parts), thinly sliced

½ cup sesame seeds

4 boneless, skinless chicken breast halves (about 8 ounces each), washed and patted dry and trimmed of fat

1 tablespoon plus 1 teaspoon toasted sesame oil

Fine sea salt and ground black pepper

DIRECTIONS:

Combine the rice vinegar, sugar, and chile in a small saucepan and cook over medium heat until the sugar is dissolved, about 3 minutes. Remove the chile and discard. Stir in soy sauce and set aside to cool.

Cover the dried wakame with warm water in a medium bowl and soak for 5 minutes. Drain, squeeze dry, and set aside in a medium serving bowl.

Scoop out the seeds from each cucumber half with a small spoon and slice each cucumber half thinly. Sprinkle the salt over the sliced cucumbers and gently knead with your hands until the cucumber slices release their water, about 3 minutes. Transfer the to a clean kitchen towel, wrap the towel around the cucumbers, and squeeze out as much water as possible. Add to the bowl with the wakame.

Add the radishes, cilantro, and scallions to the wakame and cucumbers. Add half the rice vinegar mixture and 2 tablespoons of the sesame seeds. Toss to combine, and refrigerate until serving.

Light a grill for direct high heat, about 500°F (see page 12).

Coat the chicken breast halves with the sesame oil and the remaining 6 tablespoons sesame seeds. Place one of the breast halves on a large sheet of plastic wrap, season it with salt and pepper, top with another sheet of plastic wrap, and pound until uniformly ¹⁄₁₆ inch thick and the approximate diameter of a dinner plate. Set aside. Repeat with the remaining breast halves, using fresh sheets of plastic for each one.

Brush the grill grate and coat liberally with oil. Remove the plastic wrap from one side of two of the flattened breasts and place them on the grill so that they are spread out flat. The easiest way to do this is to support it from the plastic-wrapped side with your open hand and flip it onto the grill. Immediately lift off the sheets of plastic wrap. Grill until the chicken looks opaque at the edge, about 30 seconds. Flip with a spatula and grill 15 seconds on the other side. Remove to a platter, cover to keep warm, and repeat with the other two chicken breast halves.

Serve each paillard spread out flat on a dinner plate; it should nearly cover the entire serving surface of the plate. Drizzle the remaining rice vinegar mixture over the paillards, and place a large mound of seaweed salad in the center of each one.

WHOLE CHICKEN LEGS

....

Spicy Maple Sugar Chicken Legs

MAKES 4 SERVINGS

....

There's something surprisingly sexy about the clandestine meeting of hot spice and sweet sugar—the peppers burn and the sugar soothes, igniting the palate and caressing it all at once. The spice in this recipe comes from the brine, which puts all of the burn inside the meat. The sweet balm is brushed on at the end in the form of a roasted maple glaze. So the two elements are kept separate until they bump into one another in your mouth. Very hot. Very cool.

....

INGREDIENTS:

3 cups Chile Brine (page 34)

4 chicken legs (about 3 pounds total),
  washed and patted dry

1 tablespoon canola oil

Coarsely ground black pepper

½ cup Maple Lacquer (page 49)

....

DIRECTIONS:

Combine the brine and chicken legs in a 1-gallon zipper-lock bag, press out the air, and seal the bag. Refrigerate for 2 to 3 hours.

Light a grill for indirect medium heat, about 325°F (see page 14).

Remove the chicken from the brine and discard the brine. Pat the chicken dry, coat with the oil, and sprinkle all over with the pepper. Set aside for 20 minutes.

Brush the grill grate and coat with oil. Put the chicken over the unheated part of the grill, cover, and cook, turning once or twice, until the chicken is no longer pink and the juices run clear or an instant-read thermometer inserted into the thickest part (without touching bone) registers 165°F, about 40 minutes total. During the last 10 to 15 minutes of grilling, move the chicken over to the heated part of the grill to brown all over. Brush with the glaze during the last 5 minutes.

Serve immediately.

CHICKEN LEG DRUMSTICKS

....

Chicken Drumsticks Bathed in Riesling, Tarragon, and Garlic

MAKES 4 TO 6 SERVINGS

....

Rieslings can be dry or sweet, but they are always brightly acidic and full of fruit. And those are the elements we're playing with in this light and sultry herb-infused pick-up food. Because Rieslings tend to be low in alcohol (about 8 percent, compared to 13 percent for most chardonnays), it is possible to use a high percentage of wine in the brine without developing a strong alcoholic aftertaste. For that reason we are able to use this brine both as a way to infuse moisture into the chicken before grilling and as a mop to baste on the meat while it cooks, resulting in a finished dish that just about falls from the bone.

....

INGREDIENTS:

3 cups Riesling Brine (page 34), made
with tarragon instead of rosemary,
and garlic instead of shallots

12 chicken drumsticks (about 4 ounces
each), washed and patted dry

1 tablespoon olive oil

Coarsely ground black pepper

3 or 4 sprigs fresh tarragon for garnish

DIRECTIONS:

Combine 2 cups of the brine and the chicken in a 1-gallon zipper-lock bag, press out the air, and seal the bag. Refrigerate for 2 to 3 hours.

Light a grill for indirect medium heat, about 325°F (see page 14).

Remove the chicken from the brine and discard the brine in the bag. Pat the chicken dry, coat with the oil, and sprinkle all over with the pepper.

Brush the grill grate and coat with oil. Put the chicken over the unheated part of the grill. Cover and cook, turning once or twice and mopping with the remaining 1 cup brine every 10 minutes, until the chicken is no longer pink and the juices run clear, or until an instant-read thermometer inserted into the thickest part of a large drumstick (without touching bone) registers about 165°F, about 40 minutes total.

Garnish with fresh tarragon and serve.

BONELESS CHICKEN THIGHS

Grilled Chicken Thighs Stuffed with Fontina and Wrapped in Pancetta

MAKES 4 SERVINGS

Boneless, skinless chicken thighs are one of the best (and most economical) cuts for grilling. They cook through quickly, retain moisture even when heated to well-done, are versatile enough to blend with subtle seasonings, and full-flavored enough to stand up to strong marinades or a scorch of hot chiles. They also are the perfect size for stuffing into pretty, individually portioned packets. In this recipe the thighs are stuffed with Italian fontina cheese, not to be confused with Danish fontina, which is more commonly available in the United States. Italian fontina is semisoft and creamy and has a thin brown rind with a stamp of the Matterhorn on the outside. The stuffed thighs are wrapped in a few slices of pancetta. As the thighs grill, the pancetta shrinks and crisps, causing the packets to plump and delivering a deliciously crackled skin with every bite.

INGREDIENTS:

2 teaspoons minced garlic

1 teaspoon coarse salt

½ teaspoon ground black pepper

2 tablespoons olive oil

8 boneless, skinless chicken thighs (about 4 ounces each), washed and patted dry

8 ounces pancetta, cut into 16 slices

12 ounces Italian fontina cheese, cut into 8 strips

1 tablespoon olive oil

DIRECTIONS:

Light a grill for indirect medium heat, about 325°F (see page 14).

Mix together the garlic, salt, pepper, and olive oil in a small bowl. Rub the chicken all over with this mixture.

Place 2 pancetta slices on a clean work surface so they are slightly overlapping. Place a chicken thigh in the center, and a strip of cheese in the center of each chicken thigh. Fold the chicken around the cheese, and wrap the pancetta around the chicken thigh. Repeat with the remaining chicken, pancetta, and cheese.

Coat the outside of each "package" with some of the oil.

Brush the grill grate and coat with oil. Put the chicken over the unheated part of the grill, cover, and cook, turning once, until the chicken is no longer pink and the juices run clear (about 165°F on an instant-read thermometer), about 20 minutes total.

Serve 2 thighs to each person.

BONELESS CHICKEN THIGHS

Epazote Grilled Chicken Chili

MAKES 4 MAIN-DISH SERVINGS,
OR 6 APPETIZER SERVINGS

Chilis are usually long-simmered stews, but not this one. The fresh ingredients—the chicken and onions—are grilled ahead, and the fire-roasted tomatoes and cannellini beans are canned (which means they're precooked), so everything comes together in about 10 minutes. It couldn't be easier or quicker, and it reheats well, so feel free to make an extra big batch. Dried epazote is sold with other Mexican seasonings and is available through several spice markets on the Internet (see Sources on page 400). Fresh epazote grows wild all over the temperate world and is sold in Hispanic markets.

INGREDIENTS:

2 onions, sliced ½ inch thick

1½ pounds boneless, skinless chicken thighs, washed and patted dry

3 tablespoons canola oil

3 tablespoons Smokin' Rub (page 26)

2 garlic cloves, minced

2 tablespoons dried epazote, or ¼ cup fresh epazote, finely chopped

One 14.5-ounce can crushed fire-roasted tomatoes

2 cups chicken broth

One 15.5-ounce can cannellini beans, rinsed and drained

2 tablespoons chopped fresh cilantro

Kosher salt and ground black pepper

DIRECTIONS:

Light a grill for direct medium-high heat, about 400°F (see page 12).

Coat the onion and chicken with 2 tablespoons of the oil and season the chicken with 2 tablespoons of the rub.

Brush the grill grate and coat with oil. Put the onions and chicken on the grill and cook until browned on both sides, the onions are tender, and the chicken is resilient to the touch, 4 to 5 minutes per side for the chicken, and 5 to 6 minutes per side for the onions. Transfer to a cutting board. Cut the onions into ¼-inch pieces and the chicken into ½-inch pieces.

Put a heavy saucepan on the grill or on a burner turned to medium-high. Add the remaining oil and heat briefly. Add the onion and garlic and sauté until aromatic, about 1 minute. Add the epazote, the remaining tablespoon rub, and the chicken, and stir to coat. Add the tomatoes and chicken broth and heat to boiling.

Meanwhile, mash ½ cup of the beans with a fork in a small bowl. Add the whole beans and mashed beans to the pan and simmer until the chili is thickened and the flavors have blended, about 10 minutes. Stir in the cilantro and adjust the seasoning with salt and pepper.

CHICKEN WINGS

Teriyaki Star Anise Chicken Drumettes

MAKES 6 SERVINGS

In Japan, *teriyaki* refers to a sweet, soy sauce–based glaze that is brushed on grilled food in the final stages of cooking. *Teri* literally means "gloss" or "luster," which builds up on grilled (*yaki*) ingredients when they are basted with a sweet sauce. The unfortunate habit of marinating ingredients in teriyaki sauce has created an epidemic of soy-saturated skewers burnt

to a crisp from too much sugar coming in contact with fire. In this recipe, we infuse the chicken with moisture and flavor via brining and then add the glaze during the last half of grilling. Star anise, which flavors the brine, is the dried slice of a small, star-shaped fruit that tastes similar to anise seed. It is available in most supermarkets in the spice section, and can be ordered online (see Sources on page 400).

INGREDIENTS:

3 pounds chicken drumettes (wing drumsticks; about 24), washed and patted dry

2 cups Orange-Anise Brine (page 35)

⅔ cup Sweet Soy Glaze (page 49)

DIRECTIONS:

Put the wings in a 1-gallon zipper-lock bag. Add 1⅔ cups of the brine, press the air out of the bag, and seal. Refrigerate for 2 to 8 hours. Remove the wings from the refrigerator about 20 minutes before grilling.

Mix the remaining ⅓ cup brine with the glaze and refrigerate.

Light a grill for direct medium heat, about 350°F (see page 12).

Brush the grill grate and coat with oil. Put the wings on the grill and cook until well browned all over and no longer pink in the center near the bones, 10 to 12 minutes per side, turning every 5 minutes and basting with sauce before the last two turns. Serve immediately.

KEEP IT SIMPLE:

Substitute bottled teriyaki sauce for the sweet soy glaze.

CHICKEN LIVERS

Chicken Livers on Rosemary Branches with Balsamic Chocolate Drizzle

MAKES 4 SERVINGS

We know that liver is not the most popular chicken part, and rightly so. It's a strong, acquired taste. But if you have any sense of culinary adventure, this is a recipe for you. Livers have very little fiber and lots of protein, which means they overcook easily and can become unpleasantly grainy and bitter tasting if you're not careful. The trick is to stop cooking while the livers are ever so slightly soft in the center. At that point the texture is moist and creamy and the flavor is mild. After grilling, the finished livers are coated with balsamic chocolate drizzle (balsamic vinegar simmered into a syrup, enriched with bittersweet chocolate), a magical elixir equally good on grilled fillet steak, charred chicken liver, and fresh, ripe strawberries.

INGREDIENTS:

8 ounces chicken livers, separated into 16 lobes and washed and patted dry

1 tablespoon olive oil

2 tablespoons Mole Rub (page 27)

8 fresh rosemary branches, about 6 inches long, leaves removed

Cooking spray

⅓ cup Balsamic Chocolate Drizzle (page 48)

continued ➔

DIRECTIONS:

Light a grill for direct medium-high heat, 350 to 400°F (see page 12).

Toss the chicken livers and oil in a small bowl and season the livers liberally with the rub. Thread 2 liver pieces on each rosemary branch and coat liberally with cooking spray.

Brush the grill grate and coat well with oil. Put the chicken livers on the grill, cover the grill, and cook until firm, about 3 minutes, turning the livers halfway through.

Serve on the rosemary branches, drizzled with the balsamic chocolate glaze.

GAME HEN

Barely Burnt Honey-Lacquered Hens and Pears

MAKES 4 SERVINGS

We have often warned you against marinating in sweet liquids, not because they taste bad (on the contrary, they can be delicious), but because they cause meat to burn before it is cooked through. Well, if every rule needs an exception to prove it, this recipe is unequivocal proof that we have been telling you the truth. The fire is kept low to keep scorching to a minimum. Still, it is bound to happen in spots, which is part of the appeal of caramelized char-speckled grilled birds.

INGREDIENTS:

2 long metal skewers

½ cup Honey Marinade (page 36)

1 teaspoon dried lavender

2 large game hens (about 2 pounds each), washed and patted dry

2 barely ripe Bartlett pears, cored

2 tablespoons olive oil

¼ cup honey

1 teaspoon vanilla extract

¼ teaspoon Asian hot pepper sauce, such as Sriracha

Lavender blossoms for garnish (optional)

DIRECTIONS:

Combine the marinade, dried lavender, and game hens in a 1-gallon zipper-lock bag, press out the air, and seal. Refrigerate for 6 hours or overnight.

Light a grill for direct low heat, about 250°F (see page 12).

Remove the game hens from the marinade and pat dry, discarding the marinade.

Tie the ends of the drumsticks together. Coat the game hens and the pears with the oil. Arrange on the skewers so the skewers pierce each hen from the shoulder through the leg and hold a pear at each end. This arrangement allows you to turn all of the food easily at once.

Brush the grill grate and coat with oil. Grill until the game hens are lightly charred all the way around and an instant-read thermometer inserted into the interior of a thigh registers 165°F, 45 to 50 minutes, turning the skewers every 12 minutes or so.

While the game hens and pears are grilling, mix together the honey, vanilla, and hot pepper sauce.

Cut the game hens in half. Arrange a game hen half and a pear half on each plate and drizzle with some of the honey-vanilla mixture. Garnish with the lavender blossoms.

GAME HEN

Lemon-Bathed Game Hen with Toasted Almonds, Oregano, and Green Olives   MAKES 4 SERVINGS

Game hens (a.k.a. Cornish game hens or Rock Cornish game hens) are immature chickens. They range from 1 to 2 pounds, which means a small game hen is a good portion for one person and a large one could serve two people. They are mild tasting and easy to cook, and are considered elegant because of their diminutive size, which makes them look like an exotic game bird. Game hens are easy to grill-roast and benefit from an herb rub or a flavorful glaze, both of which help to keep the breast meat moist and crisp the skin.

INGREDIENTS:

¼ cup olive oil

30 whole almonds, skins on

12 large green olives, pitted and finely chopped

3 garlic cloves, minced

¼ cup chopped fresh oregano

½ teaspoon kosher salt

¼ teaspoon ground black pepper

4 game hens (1 pound each), washed and patted dry

Finely grated zest and juice of 2 lemons

2 tablespoons vodka

DIRECTIONS:

Light a grill for indirect medium-high heat, about 375°F (see page 14).

Heat 1 tablespoon of the olive oil in a small heavy skillet over high heat until very hot, about 3 minutes. Add the almonds and stir until lightly toasted, about 1 minute. Remove from the heat and continue stirring until fully toasted and aromatic, about 2 minutes more.

Remove the almonds with a slotted spoon to a cutting board and chop coarsely. In a small bowl, combine the almonds with the olives, garlic, oregano, salt, pepper, and 1 tablespoon of the remaining olive oil. Mix well.

Rub half the mixture under the skin of the game hens all over the meat (see page 183). Adjust the skin so that it covers all of the meat and rub the skin liberally with oil. Tie the hens so that they hold their shape (see page 182).

Mix the lemon zest, lemon juice, and remaining olive oil in a small bowl and coat the hens with 2 tablespoons of this mixture. Add the vodka to the remaining lemon juice mixture.

Brush the grill grate and coat with oil. Put the game hens on the grill away from the heat, cover the grill, and cook until golden brown and an instant-read thermometer inserted into the breast registers 155°F, about 40 minutes. Baste with some of the lemon juice mixture every 5 minutes after the first 15 minutes of cooking.

Transfer the hens to a serving platter. Remove the string and let rest for 5 minutes before serving.

WHOLE TURKEY

Maple-Glazed Smoked Turkey

MAKES 12 SERVINGS

Although it is possible to grill-roast a turkey in a few hours, when the objective is smoke, you want to slow the cooking down, drawing it out as long as possible. In this recipe we soak the bird in smoky flavored brine, and then grill the turkey as far away as we can get from the fire and still remain under the grill hood. As long as the meat cooks at a languid pace, it will have plenty of time to absorb the aromatic properties of the smoke. Smoke produced from a medium-hot fire is more aromatic than smoke from a roaring blaze, because the elements that give wood smoke its fragrant, caramel-like character are destroyed at high temperatures. Wood chips are soaked before smoking to prolong the period during which they produce the most aromatic smoke.

INGREDIENTS:

4 to 6 cups hardwood chips, preferably maple, soaked in water for 30 minutes

1 fresh turkey (12 to 14 pounds), washed and patted dry

3 cups Smokin' Brine, made with vodka (page 33)

1 tablespoon canola oil

2⅓ cups Bourbon-Cider Mop (page 38)

1 cup Maple Lacquer (page 49)

DIRECTIONS:

Put the turkey in a jumbo (2-gallon) zipper-lock bag. Add the brine to the bag, press out the air, and seal. Refrigerate for about 24 hours.

Light a grill for indirect medium heat, about 250°F, with smoke (see pages 14 and 16).

Drain 1 cup of the soaked wood chips and add to the grill.

Remove the turkey from the brine and pat dry with paper towels. Coat with the oil.

Put the turkey on a rack in a disposable or metal roasting pan large enough to hold it comfortably, and put on the grill away from the fire. Close the lid and cook for 1 hour. Replenish the wood chips, and if using charcoal, replenish the coals.

Brush one-third of the mop over the turkey. Cover the grill and cook until an instant-read thermometer inserted into the inside of a thigh registers 165°F, about 5 hours, basting with the mop every 30 minutes up until the last hour. You will need to replace the wood chips every hour or so, and if using charcoal, replenish the coals at the same time. During the last hour, baste with the maple lacquer instead of the mop.

Transfer the turkey to a carving board and let rest for 15 minutes. Carve and serve.

Sage-Brined Roast Turkey Stuffed with Chestnuts and Sausages

MAKES 12 TO 14 SERVINGS

Grill-roasted turkey takes on a golden patina that oven roasting can't match. This one is swollen with grilled chestnuts, apples, and mild sausage and napped with a sweet and tangy apple cider basting jus—perfect for Thanksgiving or any holiday feast. Most poultry benefits from brining, but for turkey (especially the breast) it is essential. Brining can add up to 10 percent moisture to turkey meat, which can be the difference between succulent and desiccated. A word of warning: to help heat circulate freely around and through the bird it is important to spoon the stuffing into the internal cavity loosely.

INGREDIENTS:

1 fresh turkey (12 to 14 pounds), washed and patted dry

4 cups Apple-Sage Brine (page 35)

Stuffing:

6 dozen chestnuts

2 pounds sweet Italian sausage

2 large onions, cut into ½-inch-thick rounds

2 large tart apples, peeled, cored, and each cut into 6 wedges

2 tablespoons olive oil

2 tablespoons unsalted butter

3 garlic cloves, minced

2 teaspoons rubbed dried sage

1 tablespoon chopped fresh rosemary

3 cups chicken broth

Coarse salt and ground black pepper

4 tablespoons unsalted butter, slightly softened

1 tablespoon minced garlic

2 teaspoons Poultry Rub (page 29)

18 fresh sage leaves

Pan Sauce:

1½ cups apple cider or apple juice

1½ cups chicken or turkey broth

1 teaspoon Poultry Rub (page 29)

2 tablespoons unsalted butter (optional)

Coarse salt and ground black pepper

DIRECTIONS:

The day before grilling the turkey, put the turkey and brine in a jumbo (2-gallon) zipper-lock bag. Press out the air and seal. Refrigerate for at least 12 hours.

For the stuffing: The day, or several hours, before grilling the turkey, prepare the stuffing. Light a grill for indirect medium-high heat, about 350°F (see page 14).

Using a serrated knife, cut a small X just through the shell of the rounded side of each chestnut. Put the grill screen on the grill, away from the fire. Arrange the chestnuts, cut-side up, on the screen, close the lid, and cook until the cuts in the shells open wide, the chestnut meat is tender, and the bottoms of the shells have browned, about 20 minutes. Allow to cool until comfortable to touch, but still warm, about 15 minutes. Peel away the shells and the hairy skin underneath. Chop the chestnut meat finely. While the chestnuts are cooling, coat the sausage, onion rounds, and apple wedges

with the oil and grill directly over the heat until the sausage is browned and firm to the touch, and the onions and apples are grill-marked and tender, 10 to 15 minutes, turning once or twice. Cool briefly and chop finely.

Melt the 2 tablespoons butter in a large, deep skillet over medium-high heat. Add the minced garlic and cook for 30 seconds. Add the grilled ingredients, the sage, rosemary, and chicken broth and boil until the liquid is almost all gone, stirring often. Season with salt and pepper. Cool to room temperature. Refrigerate if storing overnight, and return to room temperature before stuffing the turkey.

In a small bowl, mash the 4 tablespoons butter, 1 tablespoon garlic, and poultry rub together with a small fork until well blended; set aside. Remove the turkey from the brine and discard the brine. Pat the turkey dry.

continued ➔

Separate the skin from the breast and legs of the turkey by gently but firmly inserting your index finger under the skin at the neck end of the bird (you might need a small knife to slit some of the tougher sections of membrane attaching the skin to the meat). Move your finger around, separating the skin from the meat underneath. Gradually ease your whole hand under the skin, loosening the skin from the breast, the legs, and the drumsticks.

Spoon the seasoned butter under the skin and push it evenly over the breast and legs of the chicken by rubbing the skin to spread the butter. Lay the sage leaves all over the breast and leg meat under the skin.

Fill the cavity of the turkey with the stuffing. Do not pack tightly. If you have extra (you probably won't), you can warm it in a skillet and mix it with the stuffing in the turkey just before serving. Tie the drumsticks together to secure the stuffing inside the bird.

Put the turkey on a roasting rack in a roasting pan. Put the roasting pan on the grill away from the heat, cover the grill, and cook until an instant-read thermometer inserted into the inner thigh registers about 165°F, about 3 hours. If you are using charcoal, you will probably have to replenish the coals every hour.

When the turkey is done, use grill mitts to remove it to a carving board, and cover it with foil to keep warm.

For the pan sauce: Remove the rack from the roasting pan and put the roasting pan over medium heat. Add the apple juice, broth, and poultry rub. Bring to a boil, scraping any browned bits clinging to the bottom of the pan into the liquid. Boil until slightly thickened, about 5 minutes. Remove from the heat and swirl in the butter, if desired. Adjust the seasoning with salt and pepper, and strain into a serving dish.

Spoon the stuffing into a serving bowl, carve the turkey, and serve with the pan juices.

TURKEY BREAST

Whole Turkey Breast Studded with Pistachios and Lime

MAKES 6 TO 8 SERVINGS

There are several ways of stuffing ingredients into a solid chunk of meat. You can cut a pocket in the center, butterfly it and roll it, or disperse the stuffing throughout the roast as we do here, which is known as larding. Larding is traditionally done to game meats to get fat deep into the interior of very lean meats. In this recipe, you make holes all over a turkey breast, then plug them up with a nutty paste of pistachios, parsley, and lime zest. Try to space the holes evenly so that when you slice the turkey, every slice will get its share of the flavor.

INGREDIENTS:

⅓ cup chopped pistachios

1 garlic clove, minced

¼ cup chopped fresh flat-leaf parsley

1 teaspoon coarse salt

½ teaspoon ground black pepper

Finely grated zest and juice of 1 lime

2 tablespoons olive oil

1 boneless turkey breast half (about 3½ pounds), washed and patted dry

¼ teaspoon dried thyme leaves

½ cup Preserved Lemon Relish (page 41, optional)

DIRECTIONS:

Light a grill for indirect medium heat, about 350°F (see page 14).

Mix together the pistachios, garlic, parsley, salt, pepper, lime zest, and 2 teaspoons of the olive oil in a bowl. Plunge a long knife with a thin blade into the turkey breast and twist to make a hole. Stuff the hole with some of the pistachio mixture. Continue until the turkey is uniformly punctuated with stuffing, about 12 holes in all.

Mix together the lime juice and 1 tablespoon of the olive oil. Season with salt and pepper and coat the outside of the turkey with this mixture.

Combine the remaining teaspoon olive oil and the thyme in a small bowl and season with salt and pepper. Set aside.

Brush the grill grate and coat with oil. Put the turkey on the grill away from the heat, cover the grill, and cook until an instant-read thermometer inserted into the thickest part of the breast registers about 155°F, about 1 hour. Baste twice with the olive oil–lime mixture during the last 40 minutes of cooking.

Remove to a large serving platter. Let rest for 8 to 10 minutes, carve, and serve with the lemon relish, if desired.

TURKEY BREAST

Grilled Turkey Breast Medallions with Gribiche Sauce

MAKES 4 SERVINGS

When sliced into thick medallions (called cutlets), turkey breast can be grilled over direct heat, just like boneless, skinless chicken breast. Because turkey breast is firmer than chicken, the results are meatier. And because turkey medallions are evenly cut, they cook through evenly, unlike a half chicken breast, which tends to dry out at its tapered end. The medallions are served with a quick and easy cold sauce that is typically served with poultry and fish in classic French cuisine. Gribiche is a pungent mayonnaise, chunky with pickles, herbs, and hard-cooked egg—sort of an extra-tangy tartar sauce.

INGREDIENTS:

3 cups Poultry Brine (page 36)

Four 1-inch-thick slices boneless, skinless turkey breast cutlets (about 5 ounces each), about 3 inches across

2 teaspoons olive oil

2 tablespoons Poultry Rub (page 29)

1 cup Gribiche Sauce (page 42)

DIRECTIONS:

Combine the brine and turkey slices in a 1-gallon zipper-lock bag, press out the air, and seal. Refrigerate for 2 to 4 hours.

Light a grill for direct medium heat, about 350°F (see page 12).

Remove the turkey from the brine and discard the brine. Pat the turkey dry. If the turkey pieces are strips or are irregular, form into a compact disk about 3 inches in diameter. Fold in the edges and if necessary, secure with string. Coat the turkey with the oil, season all over with the spice rub, and set aside for 10 minutes.

Brush the grill grate and coat with oil. Put the turkey medallions on the grill, close the cover, and grill until browned on both sides and an instant-read thermometer inserted into the side of the thickest medallion registers 155°F, about 5 minutes per side.

Serve with the gribiche sauce on the side.

Skewers of Turkey Tenders Basted with Sage Butter

MAKES 4 SERVINGS

Turkey breast tenders (also called tenderloins) are the oblong strips of meat that run along the underside of each breast half right where the rib bones curve to meet the center breast bone (sternum). The muscle is relatively unexercised compared with the leg and wing meat on a turkey, but it gets a bit more workout than the outside breast muscles, which keeps it very tender but also a bit more flavorful and moist than the bulk of the breast. It is a great cut for grilling. The only hitch is that you have to remove the tendon that runs down its center. In this recipe the tenders are brined and seasoned with poultry herbs (sage, thyme, rosemary, and garlic) and drizzled with sage butter spiked with a little sherry vinegar.

INGREDIENTS:

4 bamboo or
metal skewers

4 turkey tenders (about 8 ounces each), washed and patted dry and center tendon removed (see Know-How, below)

1½ cups Poultry Brine (page 36)

1 teaspoon Poultry Rub (page 29)

1½ teaspoons canola oil

2 garlic cloves, smashed

2 tablespoons unsalted butter

2 tablespoons chopped fresh sage leaves, or 2 teaspoons rubbed dried sage

1 teaspoon sherry vinegar or apple cider vinegar

DIRECTIONS:

Combine the turkey tenders and brine in a 1-gallon zipper-lock bag, squeeze out the air, and seal the bag. Refrigerate for 2 to 4 hours.

Light a grill for direct medium-high heat, about 425°F (see page 12).

If you are grilling with bamboo skewers, soak them in water for at least 30 minutes.

Remove the turkey from the brine and pat dry. Discard the brine. Thread each tender onto a skewer and season with rub on all sides. If using bamboo skewers, cover the exposed parts of the skewers with foil. Set aside.

Put the oil and garlic in a small skillet and cook over medium heat until the garlic browns slightly, about 4 minutes. Remove from the heat and mix in the butter, sage, and vinegar. Stir until the butter melts and set aside.

Brush the grill grate and coat with oil. Put the turkey on the grill, close the lid, and grill until the tenders are firm to the touch and browned on both sides, about 10 minutes, turning halfway through.

Transfer to a serving platter, drizzle with the sage butter, and serve.

> ### KNOW-HOW: REMOVING THE TENDON FROM A POULTRY BREAST
>
> Grasp the exposed wide end of the white tendon that runs through the center of the small under-muscle (tender) on the breast. Lift gently and scrape the sharp edge of a knife with a thin blade down the tendon (as if you were shaving it with a straight razor), freeing it from the meat.

TURKEY BREAST

Turkey Tenderloins with Silk Road Spices

MAKES 4 SERVINGS

The Silk Road, which traversed Europe into Asia from the eastern shore of the Mediterranean to China, was the principal trade and communication route for the world from the second century BCE almost to the fifteenth century, when it was superseded by sea routes. It originated to fulfill the ancient Roman passion for Chinese silk, but during its heyday it also became the culinary conduit that moved tropical spices grown along its path into the cuisines of Europe and North Africa. It is those spices—cinnamon, allspice, cumin, nutmeg, coriander, ginger, clove, peppers—that are the inspiration for this no-fuss grilled turkey recipe.

INGREDIENTS:

4 turkey tenders (about 8 ounces each), center tendon removed (see Know-How, facing page), washed and patted dry

1½ cups Ginger Sake Brine (page 34)

1½ teaspoons canola oil

2 tablespoons Silk Road Spice Rub (page 31)

⅓ cup warm Saffron Butter (page 51)

DIRECTIONS:

Combine turkey tenders and brine in a 1-gallon zipper-lock bag, squeeze out the air, and seal the bag. Refrigerate for 2 to 4 hours.

Light a grill for direct medium-high heat, about 425°F (see page 12).

Remove the turkey from the brine and pat dry. Discard the brine. Coat the tenders with oil and season with 5½ teaspoons of the rub. Mix the remaining ½ teaspoon rub into the saffron butter and keep warm.

Brush the grill grate and coat with oil. Put the turkey on the grill, close the lid, and grill until the tenders are firm to the touch and browned on both sides, about 10 minutes, turning halfway through.

Transfer to a serving platter, drizzle with the butter, and serve.

TURKEY THIGHS

Barbecued Turkey Poblano Nachos

MAKES 4 SERVINGS

Mole poblano, the best known Mexican mole, is traditionally made with turkey, which became the inspiration for this extravagant grilled nacho platter. Turkey thighs are brined with chiles and cocoa, rubbed with more chiles and cocoa, and then grilled until the meat falls from the bone. The turkey meat is pulled apart, seasoned further, and then layered with grilled chiles, onions and tomatoes, tortilla chips, lime, and lots of cheese. The pile is then returned to the grill for a few minutes to melt the cheese. Mexican heaven is at hand.

INGREDIENTS:

3 bone-in turkey thighs (about 3 pounds total), washed and patted dry and skin removed

4 cups Mole Brine (page 35)

2 tablespoons canola oil

3 tablespoons Mole Rub (page 27)

1 medium onion, thickly sliced

2 poblano chiles

1 medium red bell pepper

1 large tomato

Finely grated zest and juice of 1 lime

¼ cup chopped fresh cilantro

Coarse salt and ground black pepper

5 ounces corn tortilla chips (about 3 dozen large chips), preferably unsalted

6 ounces Manchego cheese, coarsely shredded

DIRECTIONS:

Put the turkey in a 1-gallon zipper-lock bag. Add the brine, press out the air, and seal. Massage the brine into the turkey and refrigerate for 3 to 6 hours.

Light a grill for indirect medium heat, about 350°F (see page 14).

Remove the turkey from the brine (save the brine) and pat dry with paper towels. Coat the turkey with 1 tablespoon of the oil and the mole rub. Bring the brine to a boil in a saucepan or in a large microwave-safe bowl in the microwave; set aside.

Brush the grill grate and coat with oil. Put the turkey on the grill away from the direct fire. Close the lid and cook until the thickest part of the largest thigh is fork-tender (about 180°F on an instant-read thermometer), about 1 hour, basting the meat four times with 1 cup of the boiled reserved brine.

While the turkey is cooking, coat the onion slices with the remaining tablespoon oil. Put the onion slices, poblano chiles, bell pepper, and tomato on the grill directly over the fire and grill until browned, 10 to 15 minutes, turning as needed to brown the surfaces evenly.

Dice the onion slices coarsely. Remove the stem and skin from the tomato and chop coarsely. Remove the stem and seeds from the peppers and cut into a medium dice. Combine all of the vegetables in a bowl with the lime zest and juice and half the cilantro. Season with salt and pepper.

When the turkey is done grilling, remove it from the grill, but do not shut the grill down. Set the turkey aside to rest for 5 minutes. Remove the meat from the bone and cut or pull into bite-size pieces. Moisten with ⅓ cup of the reserved boiled brine (toss the remainder).

Make a layer of corn tortilla chips in a grill wok, a grill skillet, a grilling sheet, a large cast-iron skillet, or a large metal pie or pizza pan. Top with the turkey mixture, the vegetables, and the cheese. Return to the grill, close the lid, and grill until the cheese melts, about 8 minutes. Garnish with the remaining cilantro and serve.

TURKEY THIGHS

Slow-Grilled Turkey Thighs Stuffed with Hot Pepper Polenta

MAKES 4 SERVINGS

Turkey thighs are cheap. They are frequently on sale, and because they have the highest ratio of meat to bone of all poultry cuts, they are one of the best buys for cooking protein. Chicken breasts are often sold with the bones removed, but unfortunately, turkey thighs are not. It's easy enough to cut the bone out, though, and once you do, you have a perfect pocket for stuffing. These are filled with a creamy, spicy mixture of polenta infused with hot peppers. Each thigh is sliced into several thick medallions, revealing a core of polenta surrounded by tender meat. One thigh serves two people—now that's economical.

INGREDIENTS:

2 turkey thighs (1 pound each), washed and patted dry

½ cup Honey Marinade (page 36)

½ recipe Grilled Hot Pepper Polenta (page 382), made with stone-ground grits (skip the tomato marmalade)

2 teaspoons canola oil

DIRECTIONS:

Light a grill for indirect medium heat, about 325°F (see page 14).

Remove the skin and bones from the turkey thighs (see Know-How, page 227). Make slits in the thicker parts and open as flat as possible. Dip the thighs in half the marinade and place on a clean cutting board.

Divide the polenta in half and form each half into a flat rectangle that fits on top of a flattened turkey thigh with a ½-inch border of meat all the way around. Roll up the meat so that the polenta is completely encased. Tie like a package with kitchen twine and coat the outside of each thigh with oil.

Brush the grill grate and coat with oil. Put the thighs on the grill away from the fire, close the lid, and grill until the top of the turkey has lost its raw look and the bottom is browned. Turn and baste with some of the marinade. Continue to turn and baste the turkey with marinade every 10 minutes until an instant-read thermometer inserted into the meat (not the filling) registers at least 165°F, about 40 minutes.

Transfer to a carving board and let rest for 10 minutes. Cut into ½-inch-thick slices and serve.

TURKEY LEGS

Garlic-Seared Turkey Legs with Port Wine Vinaigrette

MAKES 4 SERVINGS

Unlike the breast, the legs of a turkey are moist and rich enough to grill without brining. This makes them a good choice for a spur-of-the moment meal, though they take longer to cook. Season them with a favorite rub and grill them over indirect heat to give the connective tissue time to soften as the skin crisps and the meat cooks through. Although any turkey legs will do, legs from hen turkeys tend to be more tender than those from the toms.

INGREDIENTS:

6 garlic cloves, minced

3 tablespoons olive oil

1 teaspoon Poultry Rub (page 29) or Umami Rub (page 27)

Coarse salt and ground black pepper

2 whole turkey legs (about 1 pound each), washed and patted dry

¾ cup Port Wine Vinaigrette (page 41)

2 tablespoons finely chopped fresh flat-leaf parsley

DIRECTIONS:

Light a grill grate for indirect medium-high heat, about 325°F (see page 14).

Mix together the garlic, oil, rub, salt, and pepper in a small bowl. Coat the turkey legs with this mixture and set aside for 10 minutes.

Brush the grill grate and coat with oil. Put the turkey legs on the grill over the fire and brown on both sides, about 5 minutes per side. Move the turkey so that it is away from the fire, cover the grill, and cook until an instant-read thermometer inserted into the thickest part of a thigh registers 165°F, about 40 more minutes.

Cut the legs into drumsticks and thighs. Spoon the vinaigrette over the turkey, scatter parsley over the top, and serve.

KEEP IT SIMPLE:

If you prefer drumsticks or thighs to full legs those turkey parts can be substituted.

GROUND TURKEY

Perfectly Great Turkey Burgers

MAKES 4 SERVINGS

Lean ground turkey is a healthful alternative to fattier beef. The only problem is it tastes like it. Naturally dry and mild, turkey burgers just come off wimpy when your mouth's attuned to beef. But that won't stop the true grill master. Such deficiencies are nothing more than the next grilling challenge. These burgers are awesome—rich and moist and dripping with flavor.

INGREDIENTS:

1½ pounds ground turkey

2 tablespoons apple butter

2 tablespoons ketchup

3 tablespoons finely grated onion

1 teaspoon Poultry Rub (page 29) or jarred poultry seasoning

¼ cup dried or fresh breadcrumbs

Coarse salt and ground black pepper

4 hamburger buns, split and toasted

DIRECTIONS:

Light a grill for direct medium-high heat, about 425°F (see page 12).

Combine the turkey, apple butter, ketchup, onion, seasoning, and breadcrumbs in a small mixing bowl. Season with salt and pepper, then, using your hands, mix gently. Form into 4 patties, no more than ¾ inch thick.

Brush the grill grate and coat with oil. Put the burgers on the grill and cook for 9 minutes, flipping after 5 minutes for medium-done (slightly pink, 150°F on an instant-read thermometer). Add a minute per side for medium–well done (160°F).

When serving, if the burgers will sit, even for a few minutes, keep them and the buns separate until just before eating.

DUCK, GOOSE & GAME BIRDS

Birds with dark meat, like duck, goose, pheasant, partridge, and wild turkey, are the epitome of fire-roasting. Rich, succulent, fat bubbles up through the skin, basting every luscious morsel of flavorful meat as it browns and crisps to roasted perfection. It's a pretty picture. Ah, if only reality were the same.

The truth is that all of these birds are delicious grilled, but attaining perfection takes some manipulation. Migratory birds, like ducks and geese, have large deposits of fat to provide energy for long, sustained flights. Wild birds deplete their fat stores, but domestic ducks and geese that no longer migrate retain the fat, which can make their meat greasy and their skin flabby and unpleasant. Short-flight birds, like pheasant and wild turkey, have the opposite problem. They tend to be lean and muscular, qualities that can make their meat dry and tough.

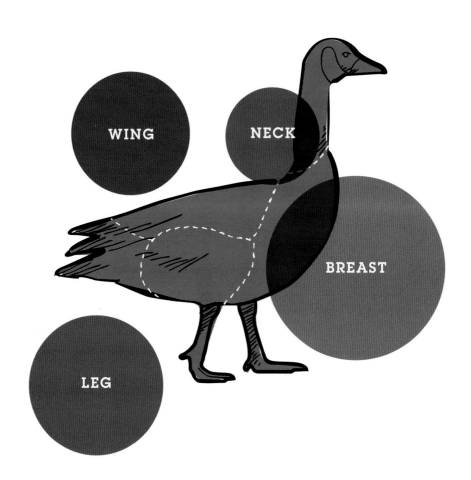

DUCK, GOOSE, AND GAME BIRDS

INGREDIENT	CLASSIFICATION	HOW TO GRILL	SUBSTITUTIONS
PEKIN DUCK (PEKING, LONG ISLAND)	Domestic	Drain fat, Indirect medium	Muscovy Duck Young Goose
MOULARD DUCK	Domestic	Drain fat, Indirect medium	Pekin Duck, Muscovy Duck
MUSCOVY DUCK (BARBARY DUCK)	Domestic	Drain fat, Indirect medium	---
DUCK BREAST, MUSCOVY OR MOULARD (MAGRET)	Domestic	Poke skin, Direct medium	---
DUCK LEGS	Domestic	Remove visible fat deposits, Indirect medium	---
DUCK LIVER	Domestic	Trim ducts and fat, halve, Direct medium-high	Chicken liver
FOIE GRAS	Domestic	Direct medium to brown, water bottle to douse flare ups, ignites easily	---
WHOLE GOOSE	Domestic	Indirect medium	Large Pekin duck
GOOSE BREAST	Domestic	Direct medium	Large duck breast
GOOSE PIECES	Domestic	Indirect medium-low	Large duck pieces
GUINEA FOWL, GUINEA HEN	Farm-raised	Indirect medium-high	Pheasant
OSTRICH BREAST	Farm-raised	Direct medium-high	Skinned duck or goose breast
PARTRIDGE OR CHUKAR	Farm-raised or wild game	Direct medium	Quail
PHEASANT (COMMON PHEASANT, RING-NECKED PHEASANT)	Farm-raised or wild game	Indirect medium-high	Guinea Fowl, Partridge
QUAIL	Farm-raised or wild game	Direct medium	Partridge
SQUAB	Farm-raised	Indirect medium-high	---
WILD TURKEY	Wild game	Indirect medium-low	---

Meeting these challenges on the grill takes ingenuity, which is why there are more unique techniques for grilling these birds than for any other class of ingredients. Take ducks, for example. The challenge of creating a crisp skin from the thick, flabby sheath surrounding a duck's legs and breast has spurred constant innovation. We inflate the skin with ball pumps, prick the skin to give the fat an escape route, douse the raw bird with boiling water to melt the fat, and then hang the animal on an armature in front of a fan to dry the doused skin—all for gustatory excellence. Grilling hamburgers is a lot easier. But ease is not the main attraction when grilling game birds; succulence is.

The Wild and the Tame

There are two main species of ducks that have been domesticated for food, mallard (*Anas platyrhynchos*) and Muscovy (*Cairina moschata*). Wild Mallard ducks have been bred to produce the domestic Pekin (Peking) or Long Island ducks, which have white feathers, large breasts, and dark rich meat. Muscovy ducks are a little larger than Pekin ducks and have stronger-tasting meat with about 30 percent less fat. Moulard ducks are a cross between a Pekin and a Muscovy that's raised primarily for foie gras. Because Moulards are continually fattened, they develop exceptionally rich breast meat (the magret), which is considered the best duck breast for grilling.

Most domesticated geese are descended from the European Graylag (*Anser anser*) or the Asian Swan goose (*Anser cygnoides*). Embden and Toulouse are the two most popular breeds, both of which yield dark, full-flavored meat. Farm-raised game birds are not bred to be different from their wild counterparts, but their life is substantially more controlled than an animal living in the wild. And therefore their meat is more consistent, more tender, and milder in flavor than their wild relatives. Like domestic animals, farm-raised game is usually slaughtered before it reaches sexual maturity to ensure mild flavor and tenderness.

How to Grill Duck, Goose, and Game Birds

When grilling migratory water birds like ducks and geese it is especially important to take steps to rid them of fat, both for the quality of the finished dish and to avoid flare-ups. These birds have evolved to store large amounts of fat under their skin as insulation in cold water and for fuel during long-distance flights. To keep the cooked skin from being flabby, it is important to render the excess fat by melting it before the meat is finished cooking.

For whole geese and ducks this means making a channel between the fat and the meat to give the fat an escape route as it melts. In Chinese cooking air is blown under the skin (usually with a bicycle or ball pump) to make such a channel. But you can also pierce the skin or make slits through the skin near the largest fat deposits at the sides of each breast and the undersides of the thighs. Then pour boiling water over the skin to soften the fat. When you start grilling, the fat will be ready to flow. Always grill these birds over a drip pan to keep the fat from dripping into the flames, where it can catch fire. Duck fat melts at a higher temperature than goose fat, and therefore is a little harder to get rid of during cooking.

Farm-raised game birds may be milder and more plump than their wild-living counterpart, but compared to the chicken and turkey that most people are used to, game birds are leaner, tougher, and more assertively flavored. There are several steps we take to overcome these limitations and turn them into assets. The low fat content of most game birds causes them to dry out during grilling. They cook faster and suffer from overcooking more readily. For that reason, most game birds are not cooked beyond medium-rare. Domestic commercially raised poultry needs to be thoroughly cooked, but because farm-raised game birds live in open space and are not confined to cages, they do not develop the bacterial infections common to mass produced poultry. Cooking them to an internal temperature of 150°F is sufficient to kill any bacteria on the surface and keep the breast meat moist.

Whole roasted game birds are either barded with a layer of fat or fatty bacon draped over the top, or are larded with plugs of fat inserted into their breast meat. Both of these practices add needed fat to the lean meat, but they also provide a vehicle for adding flavor. Frequently the fat is chopped finely and mixed with spices and herbs. The aromatic oils in the seasoning blend with the fat and flow into the meat as the bird cooks. Although barding and larding are traditionally used on game birds, you can take advantage of the same techniques when grilling poultry. Turkey breast is also lean and prone to dryness. Inserting lardoons of garlic and bacon, or chopped pistachio nuts and herbs can be a delicious addition to any grilled bird.

WHOLE DUCK

Duck Barbecued with Coffee-Cherry Sauce

MAKES 3 TO 4 SERVINGS

Here's an easy technique for roasting a crisp, fat-purged Pekin duck. Instead of blowing air under the duck skin as you do in a traditional Peking duck preparation you make slits through the skin on either side of the backbone. Because the back is not usually served, no one will see the escape route for the fat, and you can make the slits large enough to slip a finger up under the skin and dig out most of the fat before the duck starts cooking. Boiling water is poured over the skin to soften any remaining fat that can't be removed easily. The duck is seasoned with dark coffee and chiles, which intensify the rich flavors of Pekin duck meat, and it's served with a sweet and tangy barbecue sauce.

INGREDIENTS:

1 Pekin Duck (about 5 pounds), washed and patted dry

¼ cup Espresso Rub (Page 26)

1 cup brewed espresso or dark-roast coffee

½ cup jarred cherry preserves

DIRECTIONS:

Make slits through the skin of the duck on either side of the backbone from the wing to the leg. Work the knife into the slits as far as you can reach, separating the skin from the meat and removing as much visible fat from the sides of the breast and undersides of the thighs as possible. Place the duck in a sink. Bring at least 2 quarts of water to a boil and pour over the skin of the duck. Tie one end of a 1-foot string to the end of each drumstick and hang the duck over a sink or drip pan. Place an electric fan in front of the duck and turn to medium-high. Allow the duck skin to dry in front of the fan for 30 minutes to 1 hour.

Heat a grill for direct medium heat, about 375°F (see page 12). Place a large drip pan over the fire under the grill grate.

Rub 3 tablespoons of the espresso rub over the meat of the duck under the skin.

Brush and oil the grill grate and place the duck directly over the drip pan, breast-side up. Cover the grill and cook until the skin is browned and crisp and an instant-read thermometer

inserted in the inside of a thigh registers 165°F, about 1¼ hours. If using charcoal or wood, you might have to replenish the coals about three-quarters of the way through roasting.

While the duck is grilling, combine the espresso and remaining 1 tablespoon of rub in a small saucepan and bring to a boil. Stir in the cherry preserves and simmer until slightly thickened, about 3 minutes.

Remove the duck to a carving board and let rest for 10 minutes. Remove the drip pan from the grill. Heat the cherry sauce in a small saucepan and stir in 1 to 2 tablespoons of the drippings from the duck.

Carve the duck and serve with cherry sauce.

WHOLE DUCK

Quick-Grilled Duckling with Balsamic Syrup

MAKES 3 TO 4 SERVINGS

Moulard ducks are typically fattened for making foie gras, so they develop a very thick, uniform layer of fat all over their bodies. It makes their meat exquisitely rich, but requires some inventive cooking techniques to keep them from being greasy. One of the simplest ways to render duck fat during roasting is to cut the duck in half, which gives a channel all the way around the perimeter through which melting fat can flow. Because Moulard ducks have beautifully flavored meat, the seasoning in this recipe is kept to a minimum—rosemary, garlic, salt and pepper, and a little reduced balsamic vinegar drizzled over the top before serving.

INGREDIENTS:

1 Moulard or Pekin duckling (about 5 pounds), washed and patted dry

6 garlic cloves, minced

1 tablespoon minced fresh rosemary leaves

1 teaspoon coarse salt

½ teaspoon coarsely ground black pepper

2 teaspoons olive oil

⅓ cup Balsamic Syrup (page 50)

DIRECTIONS:

Split the duck in half lengthwise, removing the backbone and any visible fat. Place the duck halves, skin-side up, in a sink. Bring at least 2 quarts of water to a boil and pour over the skin of the duck. Tie an end of a 1-foot string to the end of the drumstick on each duck half and hang over a sink or drip pan. Place an electric fan in front of the skin side of the duck halves and turn to medium-high. Allow the duck skin to dry in front of the fan for 30 minutes to 1 hour.

Meanwhile mix together the garlic, rosemary, salt, pepper, and olive oil and set aside.

Light a grill for direct medium heat, around 375°F (see page 12). Place a large drip pan over the fire under the grill grate.

Using a small knife, make several slits (4 to 6) around the bones of the legs and fill with half the garlic-herb mixture. Make a small slit between the skin and meat over the breast section of each duck half. Insert a finger into the slit and move it back and forth, opening up a pocket between the skin and meat over the breast. Rub the remaining garlic-herb mixture in the pocket of each breast half.

Brush and oil the grill grate and place the duck halves directly over the drip pan, skin-side up. Cover the grill and cook until the bottom is browned and the skin is dry.

Turn the duck halves over and grill until an instant-read thermometer inserted in the inside of a thigh registers 165°F, about 20 more minutes.

Brush the bone side of the duck with some of the balsamic syrup and turn over. Brush the skin side with some of the syrup and grill until the underside is richly browned, about 4 minutes. Brush the skin side with another layer of balsamic syrup, turn, and grill until the skin side is browned and dry, about 4 more minutes.

Drizzle with the remaining balsamic syrup and serve.

WHOLE DUCK

Ginger Sake Muscovy Duck

MAKES 4 SERVINGS

Muscovy ducks have assertively flavored meat and about 30 percent less fat than Pekin birds, which means the fat-rendering techniques used for grilling Pekin duck are not needed for Muscovy. The downside of Muscovy is that its meat tends to taste a little gamy and when overcooked, it can have a bitter, liver-like edge. These tendencies are curtailed here by soaking the meat in a bright, clean-tasting ginger brine. The essential oil in ginger, zingiberene, has a mild floral sweetness, which is absorbed deeply into the meat because of the alcohol in the sake. The ginger counteracts any bitter notes that might develop as the duck roasts. In addition, the brine adds moisture to the lean breast, ensuring that it does not overcook before the legs are done roasting.

INGREDIENTS:

1½ cups Ginger Sake Brine (page 34)

1 Muscovy duck (about 4 pounds), washed and patted dry and visible fat removed

½ cup Sweet Ginger Glaze (page 50)

2 scallions (green and white parts), finely chopped

3 tablespoons finely chopped pickled (sushi) ginger

DIRECTIONS:

Combine the brine and duck in a jumbo (2-gallon) zipper-lock bag. Squeeze out the air and seal the bag. Massage the brine into the duck and refrigerate for about 12 hours.

Light a grill for indirect medium heat, 325°F (see page 14).

Put the duck, breast-side up, on a rack set in a disposable roasting pan. Put the pan on the grill away from the heat, cover the grill, and cook until an instant-read thermometer inserted into the inside of a thigh registers 165°F, about 1 hour, basting with the glaze halfway through. Remove the duck to a cutting board and let rest for 10 minutes. Carve it as you would a chicken.

Serve scattered with the scallions and ginger.

KEEP IT SIMPLE:

Replace the ginger glaze with equal parts of honey and prepared ginger teriyaki sauce (or teriyaki sauce with freshly grated ginger added).

DUCK BREASTS

Duck Breast Roulade

MAKES 3 TO 4 SERVINGS

Once the bones are removed from a whole duck breast, it spreads out nicely into a nearly flat, uniform rectangle. Cover the exposed meat with a colorful and flavorful stuffing, and you can roll it up into a log that reveals a striking spiral of filling in every slice. In this recipe the duck meat is sweetened with an apple brine, and rolled with a savory mixture of Italian sausage, spinach, feta cheese, and walnuts. When rolling up the roulade, try to avoid getting a lot of skin tucked inside the spiral because that skin will remain flabby after cooking.

INGREDIENTS:

1 whole Muscovy or Moulard duck breast (about 1 ¾ pounds), washed and patted dry and all bones removed (see Know-How, below)

2 cups Apple-Sage Brine or Apple-Thyme Brine (page 35)

1 microwaveable bag (6 ounces) baby spinach

1 tablespoon olive oil

2 ounces mild Italian sausage, casing removed

1 small onion, chopped

3 tablespoons chopped walnuts

1 garlic clove, minced

2 ounces crumbled feta cheese

2 teaspoons chopped fresh dill

Coarse salt and ground black pepper

DIRECTIONS:

Remove any visible fat from around the breast meat and discard. Combine the brine and duck breast in a 1-gallon zipper-lock bag. Press out the air and seal the bag. Refrigerate for at least 6 hours or overnight.

Puncture the bag of spinach with a small knife. Cook the spinach in the microwave oven at full power until wilted, about 3 minutes.

Heat the olive oil in a large skillet over medium-high heat. Add the sausage and onion and cook until the sausage is cooked through and the onion is tender, chopping the sausage into small pieces with the edge of a spatula as it cooks. Add the walnuts and sauté until toasted, about 2 minutes. Stir in the garlic and remove from the heat. Stir in the feta and dill. Season with salt and pepper and set aside to cool.

Light a grill for indirect medium-high heat, about 375°F (see page 14).

Remove the duck from the brine and pat dry. Discard the brine. Spread the duck breast out on a clean work surface, skin-side down. Trim off the excess skin from the narrow end (the neck end) of the meat, exposing about 1 inch of meat on the underside of the duck at the narrow end. Spread the spinach mixture over the duck meat. Roll up the breast and filling into a tight roll, starting with the narrow end. The skin should all be on the outside and completely surround the meat. Secure with several pieces of kitchen twine. It will look like a duck sausage.

Place on a roasting rack set in a disposable roasting pan and put on the grill away from the heat. Cover the grill and roast until an instant-read thermometer inserted in the middle of the meat registers 160°F, about 45 minutes.

Transfer to a carving board, remove the twine securing the roulade, and cut into ½-inch-thick slices. Serve immediately.

KNOW-HOW:
BONING A BREAST

To separate the breast from the bones, insert a knife with a thin blade, such as a boning knife, under the ribs on one side. Work your way around one side of the rib cage, using short strokes and making sure that you feel bone against one side of the knife. Eventually you will get to the sternum (a large flat bone that forms the arc of the breast). Scrape the meat from the sternum, stopping at its edge. Disengage the other side of the carcass in the same way, remove the bones, and discard.

DUCK LEGS

Hickory-Smoked Maple Duck Legs with Grilled Endive Slaw

MAKES 4 SERVINGS

The sweet-and-sour marinade in this recipe serves double duty. It permeates the duck meat and also acts as a dressing for a grilled slaw served on the side. The duck is hickory smoked over a bilevel fire so the chips smoke freely while the duck cooks gently over low heat. The resulting meat is very tender and permeated with smoke. The bittersweet radicchio and endive slaw that accompanies the duck delivers a bright, clean counterpoint to the richness of the meat.

INGREDIENTS:

3 cups hickory wood chips, soaked in water for 30 minutes

½ cup maple syrup

½ cup cider vinegar

1½ tablespoons coarse salt

2 teaspoons coarsely ground black pepper

4 duck legs, preferably Muscovy or Moulard (about 8 ounces each), washed and patted dry

4 Belgian endive, halved

1 radicchio, quartered

1 tablespoon olive oil

½ cup chopped fresh flat-leaf parsley

DIRECTIONS:

Mix together the maple syrup, vinegar, salt, and pepper in a 1-gallon zipper-lock bag until the salt dissolves. Remove ¼ cup and reserve.

Cut away all the visible fat and excess skin from the duck legs. (It's easiest to use kitchen shears.) Add the trimmed duck legs to the marinade remaining in the bag, press out the air, and seal. Refrigerate for 3 to 6 hours.

Light a grill for bilevel high/low heat, 500+/275°F, with smoke (see pages 13 and 16).

Remove the duck legs from the marinade and pat dry. Drain the wood chips and add to the grill.

Brush the grill grate and coat with oil. Arrange the duck legs, skin-side down, over the drip pan (away from the wood chips), over the low heat. Grill until an instant-read thermometer inserted into the thickest part of one of the thighs registers 165°F, about 1 hour, turning the legs halfway through.

While the duck is grilling, coat the endive and radicchio with the oil. Arrange on the grill directly over the high-heat fire and grill just until grill-marked, about 3 minutes per side. Don't cook through. Let cool.

Cut the vegetables into thin slices and toss with the reserved maple-cider mixture and the parsley. Adjust the salt and black pepper.

Serve the duck legs with slaw on the side.

DUCK LIVERS

Duck Liver Brochettes with Tangerines and Bacon

MAKES 4 SERVINGS

Duck livers are like chicken livers, only more so. They're slightly bigger, darker in color, and more pungent in both aroma and flavor. In this recipe their intensity is soothed and tempered with a wrap of smoky bacon and a counterpoint of moist, acidic, yet sweet tangerines (or clementines). On the grill the bacon fat bastes the livers and fruit, the livers become firmer and more compact, and the clementine sections plump with juice, ready to burst with the first bite.

INGREDIENTS:

4 bamboo or metal skewers at least 8 inches long

6 duck livers, washed and patted dry and trimmed of fat and tendon

2 tangerines or clementines, peeled and separated into sections (at least 12 sections total)

1 tablespoon bourbon

½ teaspoon dried thyme leaves

1 tablespoon olive oil

Coarse salt and coarsely ground black pepper

2 strips bacon, halved lengthwise

DIRECTIONS:

Toss the livers and tangerines with the bourbon, thyme, and olive oil in a small bowl. Season with salt and pepper and refrigerate for 20 to 30 minutes.

If using bamboo skewers, soak in water for at least 30 minutes. Light a grill for direct medium heat, around 375°F (see page 12).

Impale one end of a bacon strip on a skewer. Thread a duck liver half and a tangerine section onto the skewer. Fold the bacon around the liver and tangerine, securing it with the skewer to hold in place. Add another liver half and another tangerine section, fold the bacon over the top and secure in the same way. Add one more liver half and tangerine section and secure with the bacon. Trim away any floppy unsecured bacon ends. Repeat with the remaining 3 skewers.

Brush the grill grate and rub with oil. Put the skewers on the grill, and cover the grill. Cook until the bacon is cooked through and the livers are grill-marked and firm to the touch, 8 to 10 minutes, turning every 2 to 3 minutes.

WHOLE GOOSE

Grill-Roasted Young Goose Stuffed with Sauerkraut and Apples

MAKES 8 SERVINGS

The tendency of geese toward toughness and fattiness is moderated when the animal is young (less than 10 pounds). Unlike mass-produced poultry, geese are frequently grown on small farms, where farmers actually know the individual animals they raise. So even though geese are harder to come by than ducks, the birds are often of better quality. In this recipe the natural fattiness is countered by an acidic stuffing of cured sauerkraut, which in turn benefits from the infusion of the goose drippings it receives during roasting.

INGREDIENTS:

2½ cups Molasses Beer Brine (page 35)

1 young goose (about 8 pounds), washed and patted dry and carcass and thigh bones removed (see Know-How, below)

3 strips bacon, coarsely chopped

2 large onions, chopped

2 large apples, peeled, cored, and diced

1 pound refrigerated sauerkraut, drained and rinsed

2 teaspoons chopped fresh rosemary

1 tablespoon molasses

Coarse salt and ground black pepper

DIRECTIONS:

Combine the brine and goose in a jumbo (2-gallon) zipper-lock bag. Squeeze out the air and seal the bag. Refrigerate for about 12 hours.

Cook the bacon in a large skillet over medium heat until the bottom of the pan is covered with fat and the bacon is still soft. Add the onions and toss in the fat. Cover the pan and cook until the onions are tender, about 5 minutes. Add the apples and sauté until tender, about 5 minutes. Remove from the heat and stir in the sauerkraut, rosemary, molasses, salt, and pepper. Set aside to cool.

Light a grill for indirect medium-high heat, about 350°F (see page 14).

Remove the goose from the brine and pat dry. Fill the cavity of the goose with the sauerkraut. Skewer the cavity closed and tie the legs of the goose together with twine. Put on a roasting rack set in a disposable roasting pan.

Put the pan on the grill away from the direct heat. Cover the grill and cook until an instant-read thermometer inserted into the inside of a thigh registers 165°F, about 1¼ hours, basting the goose with drippings every 10 minutes after the first half hour.

Transfer to a carving board and let rest for 10 minutes. Remove the twine and scoop the sauerkraut into a serving bowl. Carve the goose as you would a turkey and serve with the sauerkraut.

KNOW-HOW: REMOVING THE BONES FROM A WHOLE BIRD

Place the bird, backbone up, on a work surface. Make a slit through the skin running straight down the center of the backbone. If you are right-handed, start boning the left side of the goose first. (Left-handed? Start on the right side.) Using short strokes, work your knife just under the skin, separating the meat from the bone all the way down the length of the backbone. As you are cutting, you should feel bone against one side of the knife at all times.

After the meat is disengaged from the backbone, move your knife over the outside of the rib cage. Continue to cut the meat from the rib cage in the same way that you disengaged it from the backbone. Stop when you reach the place where the leg joins the hip at one end of the goose, and where the wing joins the shoulder at the other end. If you pull the limbs up toward the backbone (in the opposite direction of the way they naturally move), the joints will pop out of their sockets. Cut through the tendons holding the joints in place, and the leg and wing will separate from the carcass.

In order to get the wing to disengage from the carcass, you will have to cut around the end of the wishbone and the thick bone that attaches the wing to the breast. In order to get the leg to disengage, cut around the hip bone and slit the membrane surrounding the internal cavity. The leg and wing will now fall away from the carcass.

To separate the breast from the carcass, continue to cut around the rib cage, still using short strokes and making sure that you feel bone against the knife. Eventually you will get to the sternum (a large, flat bone that forms the arc of the breast). Scrape the meat from the sternum, stopping at its edge.

Turn the bird around and bone the other side in the same way. The bird will now be attached only along the edge of the sternum. Holding the carcass with one hand, and with the sharp edge of the knife angled toward the bone, make small slits down the edge of sternum as you lift the carcass away from the meat. Be careful to avoid cutting through the skin, which lies right against bone along the sternum.

Gooschetta

MAKES 4 SERVINGS

We were inspired by porchetta—the classic Italian spit-roasted pig, which is gutted and massaged with garlic, rosemary and fennel, and turned over flaming coals for the better part of a day—but our version is at once simpler and more interesting. Goose breast, brined and stuffed with the same aromatics, is enhanced by the addition of fresh dates and Parmesan cheese. The combination of flavors and textures—crisp goose skin, silky and creamy date flesh, moist and succulent goose meat, pungent hints of garlic and fennel—is awe-inspiring. The dish is suitable for a grand dinner, and any leftovers become stellar cold cuts. If you can't find boneless goose breast, you can bone it yourself (see the Know-How, page 223).

INGREDIENTS:

2 cups Poultry Brine (page 36)

1 boneless goose breast half (1½ to 2 pounds), washed and patted dry

3 garlic cloves, minced

1 tablespoon fennel seeds, crushed

1 tablespoon finely chopped fresh rosemary

3 Medjool dates, pitted and finely chopped

⅓ cup freshly grated Parmigiano-Reggiano cheese

Coarse salt and freshly ground black pepper

1 tablespoon olive oil

DIRECTIONS:

Combine the brine and goose breast in a 1-gallon zipper-lock bag. Squeeze out the air and seal the bag. Refrigerate for 6 hours or overnight.

Light a grill for direct medium heat, about 375°F (see page 12). Set up a drip pan at least slightly larger than the goose breast under the grill grate.

Mix together the garlic, fennel seeds, rosemary, dates, and cheese in a small bowl and set aside.

Make a slit in the side of the goose breast large enough to allow you to open the thick part of the breast like a book.

Season the interior with salt and pepper and fill with the fennel mixture. Close the goose breast over the filling and secure the open edge with a toothpick or thin skewer. Coat the goose breast with the olive oil and poke the skin all over with the tines of a fork.

Brush the grill grate and coat with oil. Put the goose breast, skin-side down, over the drip pan. Close the lid and cook until the goose breast is resilient when pressed in its thickest part (about 140°F on an instant-read thermometer), about 20 minutes, turning halfway through.

Remove the goose breast to a cutting board and allow to rest for 10 minutes. Cut into 4 portions.

OSTRICH BREAST

Grilled Ostrich Breast with Worcestershire Teriyaki Sauce

MAKES 4 SERVINGS

Ostrich is often touted as a low-fat alternative to beef, and for a red meat it is very lean (2.8 percent fat, as opposed to beef, which is at 9.3 percent fat). The flavor is mild and the color deep red, with no marbling. Only the breast is tender enough for grilling, and it is sold as steaks, cutlets, or fillets. Legs and wings are usually used for making sausage or for ground meat. Ostrich does not have the same bacterial problems as chicken and turkeys and is safe to eat medium-rare (about 145°F).

INGREDIENTS:

¼ cup white wine

¼ cup Worcestershire sauce

1 tablespoon balsamic vinegar

2 tablespoons brown sugar, light or dark

3 ostrich fillets (boneless ostrich breast, 8 ounces each), washed and patted dry

2 tablespoons canola oil

¼ cup pickled (sushi) ginger, finely chopped

2 red radishes, trimmed and finely diced

1 scallion (green and white parts), finely chopped

DIRECTIONS:

Heat the white wine, Worcestershire, balsamic vinegar, and brown sugar in a small saucepan over medium heat until the sugar dissolves, stirring often. Cool.

Combine the ostrich fillets with ½ cup of this glaze in a 1-gallon zipper-lock bag, press out the air, and seal. Shake to coat the fillets with the glaze and refrigerate for 30 minutes.

Light a grill for direct medium-high heat, about 375°F (see page 12).

Remove the ostrich fillets from the bag and discard the glaze. Pat the ostrich fillets dry, and coat with the oil.

Mix the ginger, radishes, and scallion in a small bowl; set aside.

Brush the grill grate and coat with oil. Grill the ostrich fillets until grill-marked and an instant-read thermometer inserted into the center of the thickest piece registers 145°F, 4 to 6 minutes per side, depending on the thickness of the fillets.

Cut on the diagonal into ¼-inch-thick slices and arrange on a serving plate so the slices overlap. Drizzle with the remaining ¼ cup glaze. Scatter the ginger mixture over the top.

Whole Roast Pheasant with Seared Brandied Grapes

MAKES 4 TO 8 SERVINGS

Pheasants are the largest category of game birds and have been numerous in the wilds of North America since the turn of the last century. Wild pheasants vary greatly in quality, depending on habitat, sex, and age. As with most game birds, farmed specimens have more consistently good meat and usually give more tender and moist results. Male pheasants are slightly larger, and females are more tender. A farm-raised hen will feed 2 people generously, with some leftovers. This recipe requires some planning. The grapes need to marinate for about 3 days (otherwise they'll be harsh) and the pheasant does well with a day in brine before grilling.

INGREDIENTS:

2 cups large grapes, green or purple

2 tablespoons plus 1 teaspoon extra-virgin olive oil

¼ cup light maple sugar or brown sugar

¼ cup water

¼ cup brandy

1 tablespoon Poultry Rub (page 29)

4 cups Apple-Sage Brine (page 35)

2 whole female pheasants (about 2½ pounds each)

2 strips bacon, finely chopped

DIRECTIONS:

Three days before grilling the pheasants, light a grill for direct medium heat, about 375°F (see page 12).

Place a grill screen on the grill if the grapes will fall through the grill grate. Toss the grapes with 1 tablespoon of the olive oil. Pour onto the grill screen, cover the grill, and grill the grapes until flecked with brown, about 4 minutes.

Heat the maple or brown sugar and water in a small saucepan until the sugar dissolves, stirring occasionally. Stir in the brandy and ½ teaspoon of the poultry rub. Transfer to a pint-size container and add the grapes. Cover and set aside at room temperature for 3 days, shaking the container every day or so.

One day before grilling the pheasants, combine the brine and the pheasants in a 1-gallon zipper-lock bag, press out the air, and seal. Refrigerate for about 24 hours.

Light a grill for indirect medium-high heat, about 375°F (see page 14).

Combine the bacon and the remaining 2½ teaspoons poultry rub; chop and mash with the side of the knife into a fine paste. Mix in 2 teaspoons of the olive oil.

Remove the pheasants from the brine and pat dry. Discard the brine. Run a finger under the skin covering the breast, separating the skin from the meat, and spread the bacon mixture over the breast meat. Drain the brandy mixture from the grapes into a small skillet. Add the remaining 2 teaspoons olive oil to the skillet and boil until slightly thickened, 3 to 4 minutes over medium-high heat. Pour all but a tablespoon of the glaze into a bowl for basting the pheasant.

Fill the cavity of the pheasant with half of the grapes and tie to hold the bird in a compact shape and keep the grapes from rolling out (see Know-How on page 182). Secure the pheasant on the rod of a rotisserie or put on a rack set in a small roasting pan and put on the grill away from the heat. Close the cover and grill until the bird is browned, and an instant-read thermometer inserted into the thickest part of the breast registers 166°F, about 45 minutes. Baste with the glaze every 10 minutes for the last half hour.

Remove to a carving board and let rest for 10 minutes. Meanwhile add the remaining grapes to the reserved glaze in the skillet and stir to coat. Heat through. Carve the pheasant and serve with the brandied grapes.

Coconut Butter–Basted Quail with Grilled Tropical Fruits

MAKES 4 SERVINGS

Quail are fair game throughout North America, but they are also one of the most frequently farmed game birds, and all of the quail sold commercially are farm-raised. Quail are so small (about 6 ounces whole, and 3 ounces of meat per bird) that you need two, which is called a brace, for one serving. They are sometimes sold semi-boneless, meaning only the wing bones and drumsticks are left intact. One of the advantages of their small size is that they cook very quickly, grill-roasting in a mere 15 minutes. In this recipe the delicate quail meat is inundated with tropical flavors—fruit and rum and, most intriguingly, with coconut oil, which gives the meat a rich mouthfeel and permeates the dish with a subtle coconut fragrance.

INGREDIENTS:

8 quail, preferably whole, washed and patted dry

2 cups Pineapple Brine (page 34), made with rum

¼ cup coconut oil

1 teaspoon saffron, crumbled

¼ cup honey

1 teaspoon Asian hot pepper sauce, such as Sriracha

Coarse salt and ground black pepper

½ pineapple, peeled and cut into large chunks

1 mango, peeled, pitted, and cut into thick wedges (see Know-How, below)

2 bananas, peeled and cut on the diagonal into thick slices

Chopped fresh cilantro for garnish

DIRECTIONS:

Using kitchen scissors, cut the backbone from each quail and open the birds up flat (see Know-How, page 186). Put in a 1-gallon zipper-lock bag with the pineapple brine. Press out the air and seal the bag. Refrigerate for at least 1 hour or up to 6 hours.

Light a grill for direct medium heat, about 375°F (see page 12).

Melt the coconut oil in a skillet over medium heat. Remove from the heat and stir in the saffron, honey, and hot pepper sauce. Season with salt and pepper.

Remove the quail from the marinade and pat dry with paper towels. Brush on both sides with the coconut oil mixture. Brush the fruit with the coconut oil mixture. You will have used about a third of the mixture by this time. Brush the grill grate and coat with oil.

Place the quail flat on the grill grate, skin-side up, and grill until golden brown, grill-marked, and firm to the touch, about 16 minutes, turning and brushing with more of the coconut oil mixture three or four times.

Grill the pineapple and mango for 10 minutes, turning once, and grill the banana slices for 5 minutes, turning once. Serve the quail on a bed of the grilled fruit and garnish with chopped fresh cilantro, if desired.

KNOW-HOW: PITTING A MANGO

Hold the mango on end with the stem up and a narrow side facing you. Cut straight down the length of the mango, beginning about ¼ inch from the stem. Your knife will glide by the flat side of the pit. If you should hit the pit, adjust your cut accordingly. Repeat on the other side. The small amount of fruit clinging to the pit cannot be removed easily and must be discarded—or eaten in private!

Chapter 10

FISH

Fish is the most popular animal protein on the planet. It's no wonder why: Fish cooks quickly, adapts to an array of seasonings, and provides beneficial nutrients with relatively few calories. As worldwide demand for fish has increased, wild stocks have gradually become depleted, which has led to an increase in farmed or aquacultured fish. Both wild and farmed fish have pros and cons.

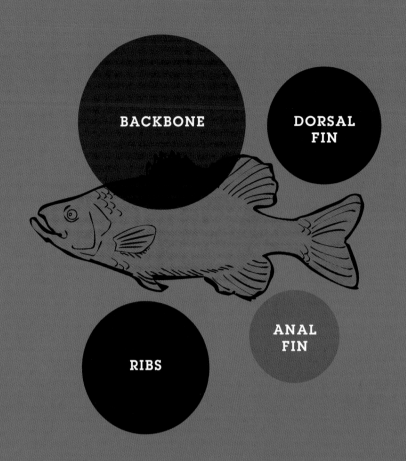

BACKBONE

DORSAL FIN

RIBS

ANAL FIN

FISH			
INGREDIENT	OTHER NAMES OR VARIETIES	HOW TO GRILL	SUBSTITUTIONS
RED SNAPPER (*Lutjanus campechanus*)	Onaga	Whole: indirect, medium-high heat Fillets: direct, medium-high heat	Other snapper (such as yellowtail), rockfish, striped bass, black bass
OPAKAPAKA (*Pristipomoides filamentosus*)	Hawaiian pink snapper, crimson snapper, crimson jobfish	Whole: indirect, medium-high heat Fillets: direct, medium-high heat	Other snapper (red, gray, yellowtail), rockfish, striped bass, black bass, grouper, halibut
TURBOT (*Psetta maxima*)	European turbot	Whole: direct, medium-high heat Fillets: direct, medium-high heat	Dover sole, halibut, brill, flounder
TILAPIA (*Oreochromis and Sarotherodon*)	St. Peter's fish, Hawaiian sunfish	Whole: direct, medium-high heat Fillets: direct, medium-high heat	Ocean perch, porgy, snapper, orange roughy, flounder
OCEAN PERCH (*Sebastes spp.*)	Norway haddock, redfish, rockfish, red bream, rose fish, sea perch	Whole: direct, medium to medium-high heat Fillets: direct, medium-high heat	Rockfish, porgy, red snapper, mullet
STRIPED BASS (*Morone saxatilis*)	Greenhead, linesider, rock, rockfish, roller, striper, sunshine bass	Whole large: indirect, medium-high heat Whole small: direct, medium-high heat Fillets: direct, medium-high heat	Black bass (sea bass), rockfish, grouper, red snapper, halibut
SEA BASS (*Centropristis striata*)	Black bass, blackfish	Whole: direct, medium-high heat Fillets: direct, medium-high heat	Striped bass, rockfish, red snapper, grouper, halibut
POLLOCK (*Theragra chalcogramma and Pollachius pollachius or P. virens*)	Alaska pollock, Atlantic pollock, Pacific pollock, Bigeye cod, Boston blue, coalfish, coley, Pacific Tomcod, lythe, saithe, walleye cod	Whole Alaska pollock: direct, medium-high heat Steaks and fillets: direct, medium-high heat	Cod, sole, plaice, flounder, halibut, haddock

FISH, continued

INGREDIENT	OTHER NAMES OR VARIETIES	HOW TO GRILL	SUBSTITUTIONS
CATFISH (*Ictalurus furcatus and I. punctatus*)	Mississippi catfish, channel catfish, Vietnamese catfish, Mekong catfish, Pacific dory, China sole, river cobbler	Whole small: direct, medium-high heat Fillets: direct, medium-high heat	Grouper, tilefish, monkfish, mahi-mahi
COD (*Gadus spp.*)	Atlantic cod (*Gadus morhua*), Pacific cod (*Gadus macrocephalus*), scrod (young cod)	Steaks and cheeks: indirect, medium-high heat Fillets: direct, medium-high heat	Pollock, haddock, cusk, hake, whiting, halibut, sole, flounder, orange roughy
GROUPER (*Epinephelus spp. and Mycteroperca spp.*)	California sea bass, jewfish, cabrilla	Whole: indirect, medium-high Fillets: direct, medium-high	Cod, mahi-mahi, striped bass, black sea bass, red snapper, catfish
MONKFISH (*Lophius spp.*)	Anglerfish, goosefish, frogfish, sea devil, lotte	Tail: indirect, medium-high heat Fillets: direct, medium-high heat	Black sea bass, mahi-mahi, red snapper, grouper
HALIBUT (*Hippoglossus spp.*)	Greenland turbot, California flounder	Roasts and loins: indirect, medium-high Steaks and fillets: direct, medium-high heat	Turbot, Dover sole, cod, haddock, black sea bass, tilefish
Skate (*Rajidae spp.*)	Thornback ray, thorny skate, starry ray, barndoor skate	Direct, medium-high heat	Sea scallops
MAHI-MAHI (*Coryphaena hippurus*)	Dolphinfish, dorado	Steaks and fillets: direct, medium heat	Pompano, swordfish, mako shark, tuna, monkfish
TUNA (*Thunnus spp.*)	Albacore, ahi, bigeye, bluefin, skipjack, yellowfin	Steaks or fillets (cut thick): direct, medium-high; cook only to rare	Mackerel, mahi-mahi, monkfish, salmon, swordfish
SWORDFISH (*Xiphias gladius*)	Billfish, marlin, spearfish	Steaks: direct, medium	Halibut, mahi-mahi, shark. monkfish, salmon, tuna
MAKO SHARK (*Isurus oxyrhynchus*)	Bonito shark, shark	Steaks, fillets, chunks: direct, medium	Dogfish, monkfish, swordfish, tuna
ANCHOVY (*Engrauls spp.*)	Pilchards	Whole or fillets: direct, medium-high	Sardines, smelts
ARCTIC CHAR (*Salvelinus alpinus*)	Alpine trout, salmon trout	---	Salmon, trout
TROUT (*Oncorhynchus spp.*)	Rainbow trout, brook trout	Direct, medium-high	Arctic char, salmon
BLUEFISH (*Pomatomus salatrix*)	Chopper, tailor	Whole: indirect, medium-high Fillets: direct, medium-high	Mackerel, salmon
SHAD (*Alosa sapidissima and other species*)	Atlantic shad, state-name shad	Whole: indirect, high Boneless fillet: direct, medium-high	Bluefish, mackerel, salmon, swordfish
WILD SALMON (*Salmonidae spp.*)	King salmon, Coho salmon, sockeye, Alaskan salmon	Whole: indirect, medium Fillet or steak: direct, medium-high	Arctic char, shad, trout
FARMED SALMON (*Salmonidae spp.*)	Atlantic salmon, Norwegian salmon	Whole: indirect, medium Fillet or steak: direct, medium-high	Bluefish, mackerel
CHILEAN SEA BASS (*Dissostichus eleginoides*)	Patagonian toothfish, Antarctic toothfish, Blake hake, icefish	Steaks and fillets: direct, medium-high	Mahi-mahi, monkfish, pompano, pollack
OPAH (*Lampris spp.*)	Moonfish, sunfish	Steaks, cubes, or fillets: direct, medium to medium-high	Mahi-mahi, monkfish, pompano, salmon, swordfish
POMPANO (*Trachinotus carolinus*)	Florida pompano, butterfish, dollarfish, sunfish	Whole or fillet: direct, medium-high	Flounder, mahi-mahi, red snapper, sea bass

Wild Fish and Farmed Fish

The quality of any fish is determined by its species, how and where it was raised, its diet, age, and how and when it was harvested. Wild fish feed on various forms of marine life, which flavor and color the meat in unique ways. They also swim far and wide from season to season, altering their diet and the composition of their meat. These variables cause the quality of the wild fish in your market to change from season to season and even day to day, which is why it's so important to talk to your fishmonger and ask what is especially fresh and good in your market.

Ocean management has come a long way to help ensure the long-term abundance of wild fish and the vitality of our oceans. Seafood watch groups like the Monterey Bay Aquarium, Environmental Defense Fund, and Blue Ocean Institute have helped save species like swordfish and Chilean sea bass from the endangered species list. Other species, like wild Atlantic salmon, have not been so fortunate.

To help meet market demands without endangering wild stocks, the fishing industry has turned to farming popular and adaptable varieties like salmon, sea bass, trout, and tilapia in enclosed ocean pens or freshwater ponds and tanks. Aquaculture is now used to supply more than 40 percent of the world's fish and shellfish, and fishing industry analysts predict that by 2020, fish farms will surpass capture fisheries in supplying the majority of the world's seafood.

Like domesticated land animals, bred and farmed fish are not the same as their wild counterparts. But the quality of aquacultured fish is far from standardized. It varies widely from farm to farm and country to country. To ward off disease, aquacultured fish are routinely given antibiotics in their feed. For fish farms with open water pens, excess waste, disease, and harmful organisms can migrate from the pens to wild fish and impact the health of the wild stocks. Farmed carnivorous fish like salmon also tend to be higher in contaminants such as polychlorinated biphenyls (PCBs) because they are fed fishmeal made from fish refuse, which is higher in such contaminants. You can minimize contaminants in farmed fish by removing the skin and trimming any visible fat.

Determining Quality

Animals that live in water need to be buoyant. To that end they tend to have delicate skeletons, slightly oily flesh (oil is lighter than water), and air bladders that keep them afloat. Because water supports their weight, their muscles don't need to be as dense as those of land animals. So even though fish move constantly, their muscles tend to be soft,

and their meat very tender. This means that all fish are tender enough to be grilled, but their soft flesh is also vulnerable to damage, which is why fish is the most perishable of animal proteins. It is easier to determine how fresh a fish is while it is whole. Once it is filleted or cut into steaks, most of the areas where deterioration shows up have been cut away.

Here's what to look for:

- Healthy-looking skin. Fish skin should be dry. If the skin is broken or bruised, it is a sign that the fish was roughly handled, and probably damaged beneath the skin as well.

- Firm flesh. When you poke the side of a fish (or the skin of a fish fillet or steak) the imprint of your finger should spring back.

- Clear, bulging eyes. Flat, sunken, or cloudy eyes indicate a fish that has been out of the water for a few days.

- Bright gills. The spongy, crescent-shaped gills lying under the gill-flaps on either side of the back of the head should be bright red, without hints of brown or gray.

- Shiny, tight scales. Most ocean fish have scales. If they are still on the fish when you buy it, they should be shiny and firmly attached.

- Little or no odor. Fresh fish has no odor, except possibly the faint aroma of seawater. A fishy odor is an indication of decay.

Grilling Fish: The Fat and the Lean

Unlike the muscle fibers of land animals, which are arranged in bundles, fish muscle fibers are structured in thin layers. The layers are separated from one another by connective tissue, which runs from the center skeleton out to the skin. When a fish cooks, the muscle fibers contract and the connective tissue softens, resulting in flaking (the separation of one layer of muscle fibers from another), which is the sign that the fish is done.

It is important to stop cooking fish as soon as the connective tissue softens, but before it breaks. As fish muscle fibers heat and contract, water held in the cells is forced out. The moisture stays in the meat as long as the connective tissue stays intact. But if the connective tissue breaks, all of the juices run out and the fish immediately becomes dry. Our grilling directions always say to stop cooking when a fish looks opaque on the surface but is still filmy and moist

in the center. At that point you are assured that the muscle fibers are cooked through, and the connective tissue has not yet broken.

In most cases fish should be cooked to an internal temperature of between 125 and 140°F. Some fish with a lot of connective tissue, like shark, needs to be cooked to the upper end of that range, because the collagen in the connective tissue will not gelatinize much before 140°F.

Fish skin is high in collagen. When fish is cooked with its skin on, that collagen melts into gelatin, giving the flesh a luscious mouthfeel. In addition the collagen, which is all protein, becomes brittle when exposed to direct flame. That's why grilled fish skin is so deliciously crispy. If you have the option of keeping the skin on a fillet or steak, the grilled results will be far superior to one that has had the skin removed.

Fish bones are delicate and tend to dissolve more quickly than the harder bones of land animals. During grilling the bones of most fish won't melt away, but they will dissolve slightly, releasing their flavor into the fish flesh. This is why fish grilled on the bone is much tastier than one that is boneless.

Compared to land animals most fish are low in fat, and the fat is far less saturated. The fat content of fish varies widely, ranging from practically none to about 25 percent. Fat content is somewhat dependent on the fish type, but it can be affected by diet and environment (deep-swimming and cold-water fish tend to have more fat).

Wild and Farmed Fish on the Grill

Farmed fish tend to be higher in fat and take longer to cook. Farmed salmon, for instance, will drip more fat into the fire, cause more flare-ups, and need a little more time over the heat than wild salmon. The farmed fish will also have a richer mouthfeel, if somewhat less complex taste overall. Wild fish, on the other hand, tends to have leaner, stronger muscles and may benefit from soaking in a brine or marinade before grilling to enhance juiciness. Either way, most fish species can be easily grilled if you use a hot grill grate and oil both the rack and the fish to prevent sticking. It also pays to pick up a wide fish spatula for easy turning or, better yet, a fish grilling basket so you can pick up the entire fish or fillet and flip it with a flick of the wrist.

WHOLE FISH, FILLETS, AND STEAKS

Once you have selected a fish, the fishmonger can butcher or dress it in several ways.

The standard ways of dressing fish are:

WHOLE DRESSED: Guts, scales, gills, and fins usually removed; head and tail still on. Good for stuffing. If the dressed fish is thicker than 2 inches, it is usually grilled over indirect heat; if thinner, direct heat usually works.

PAN DRESSED: Same thing as whole dressed except the head is removed. Grill the same way as whole dressed.

SPLIT: A whole dressed fish split lengthwise. The central skeleton can be removed or not. Unless the fish is very large, split fish are usually grilled over direct heat.

FILLETS: The large muscles running on either side of the central skeleton are lifted from the skeleton. Fish fillets are not necessarily boneless. Many fish have pin bones, a fine line of bones radiating at a right angle from the skeleton. When a fish is filleted, the pin bones remain and must be cut out or removed with pliers, usually by the cook. The pin bones on small fish (anchovies, sardines, herring) are so fine that they tend to dissolve during cooking.

STEAKS: Made by cutting across the body through the skeleton. If the cut is made across the middle part of the body, the steak will have a horseshoe shape. If it is taken from the tail end, it will be oval. Tail steaks are more flavorful than center-cut fish steaks. The steaks of very large fish, like tuna and swordfish, are crosscut from a fillet, so they do not contain bones.

LEAN, DELICATE WHITE FISH FILLETS

Soy-Marinated Opakapaka with Pineapple-Ginger Salsa

MAKES 4 SERVINGS

In Hawaii, the local crimson-skinned snapper goes by the name opakapaka. This elegant fish has a refined flavor enjoyed wherever people fish the Pacific waters, but Hawaiians treasure it the most. On the islands, it's sometimes served raw as sashimi, especially in winter when the fish's fat content increases for warmth. Raw or cooked, Hawaiian pink snapper has light pink, delicious flesh that marries beautifully with tropical fruit. A brief dip in lemon soy marinade and a topping of juicy, chunky pineapple salsa make this an ideal grilled summer dish. If opakapaka isn't available, use another snapper variety, such as red snapper (onaga) or gray snapper (uku).

INGREDIENTS:

4 opakapaka fillets (each at least 6 ounces), at least ½ inch thick

1 cup Lemon Soy Marinade (page 38)

Pineapple-Ginger Salsa:

¾ cup finely chopped fresh or canned pineapple

1½ teaspoons minced fresh ginger

½ tomato, cored, seeded, and chopped

¼ small red bell pepper, seeded and chopped

½ jalapeño chile pepper, stemmed, seeded, and minced

1 scallion (green and white parts), finely chopped

2 tablespoons chopped fresh Thai basil or cilantro

Juice of 1 lime

1 teaspoon brown sugar, light or dark

¼ teaspoon coarse salt

DIRECTIONS:

Rinse the opakapaka and put in a 1-gallon zipper-lock bag. Add the marinade, press out the air, and seal. Refrigerate for 1 to 2 hours. Remove the opakapaka from the refrigerator and let marinate at room temperature for another 30 minutes.

For the salsa: Mix all the ingredients in a serving bowl and set aside.

Light a grill for direct medium-high heat, about 425°F (see page 12). Preheat a fish basket on the grill. When hot, brush the grill basket and coat liberally with oil. Put the opakapaka in the hot basket, skin-side down, and put the basket directly over the heat. Grill until the fish looks opaque on the surface, but is still filmy and moist in the center (about 125°F on an instant-read thermometer), 3 to 4 minutes per side.

Remove to a platter or plates and serve with the salsa.

KNOW-HOW: SLASHING FISH SKIN

Slashing a fish through its thicker parts helps the fish cook more evenly. It also gets the seasoning deeper into the flesh and allows you to peek into the flesh to check for doneness. Use a sharp knife to make diagonal slashes through the skin and down to the bone on each side. Slash in 2-inch intervals along the thickest part of the fish.

LEAN, DELICATE WHITE FISH FILLETS

Grilled Tilapia Jalapeño Poppers

MAKES 4 SERVINGS

Along with catfish, tilapia is among the most extensively aquacultured fish in North America. It's also one of the leanest white fish fillets, with a honey-like sweetness and fine texture, which make it ideal as a stuffing. In a whimsical spin on a bar food classic, this recipe combines tilapia's somewhat creamy texture with melting Jack cheese, minced onions, and fresh cilantro inside bacon-wrapped jalapeños. Serve with Salsa Ranchero (page 46) or your favorite salsa.

INGREDIENTS:

12 toothpicks

1 small tilapia fillet (about 3 ounces)

3 tablespoons cream cheese, softened

3 tablespoons finely shredded Monterey Jack cheese

2 tablespoons grated onion (grate on a box grater on the medium holes)

1 tablespoon finely chopped fresh cilantro

12 large jalapeño chile peppers, with stems attached

6 thick strips bacon, halved crosswise

DIRECTIONS:

Soak the toothpicks in cold water for 20 minutes. Meanwhile, finely chop the tilapia, and then mix in a bowl with the cream cheese, Monterey Jack, onion, and cilantro. Set aside.

Hold a jalapeño by the stem and slit lengthwise from stem to tip. Gently squeeze the ends of the pepper toward the middle to open the center. Scrape out the seeds and ribs with a grapefruit spoon or the tip of a butter knife. Stuff with the tilapia mixture and wrap with a half-slice of bacon. Secure the bacons ends with a toothpick so they lay flat. Repeat with the remaining jalapeños, filling, and bacon.

Light a grill for direct medium-high heat, about 425°F (see page 12). Brush the grill grate and coat with oil. Grill the jalapeños directly over the heat until the bacon is almost crisp, the cheese oozes, and the stuffing registers about 125 to 130°F on an instant-read thermometer, 6 to 8 minutes total, turning a few times.

Remove to a platter, remove the toothpicks, and let stand for 10 minutes to cool down and firm up the cheese before serving.

LEAN, DELICATE WHOLE WHITE FISH

Whole Red Snapper Stuffed with Feta Pilaf and Wrapped in Vine Leaves

MAKES 4 SERVINGS

Red snapper is one of the world's great eating fish, and the most popular member of the large snapper family (some 250 members strong). Its fine texture and sweet, subtle flavor take to a wide range of seasonings. We love the fish with Greek bursts of salt-cured olives, feta cheese, lemon, and cinnamon. A wrapping of grape leaves also perfumes the fish with briny, vinous aromas. More important, it keeps the skin from sticking to the grill. Look for small snappers, as large ones can develop a somewhat coarse texture. A fish just under 2 pounds is perfect for grilling whole and provides two servings. Here we remove the central skeleton to make serving the whole fish a breeze. It makes a great presentation without the fuss of filleting the cooked fish. You can remove the central skeleton at home in about 5 minutes or have your fishmonger do it. Be sure to keep the bones for making the light fish broth that flavors the feta pilaf stuffing.

continued →

INGREDIENTS:

2 small whole red snappers (1¾ pounds each), gutted, scaled, fins removed, heads on

3 cups water

⅓ cup dry white wine

1 medium onion, coarsely chopped

1 small carrot, coarsely chopped

5 sprigs fresh flat-leaf parsley, plus 1 tablespoon chopped

8 black peppercorns

3 garlic cloves, minced

1 teaspoon coarse salt

⅓ cup olive oil

⅓ cup pine nuts

1½ cups long-grain white rice

1 whole lemon, plus 4 lemon wedges

1 cinnamon stick

2 scallions (green and white parts), chopped

¾ cup crumbed feta cheese

⅓ cup pitted and halved green Greek olives

1 tablespoon chopped fresh oregano

14 to 16 jarred grape vine leaves, preferably early harvest

¼ teaspoon ground black pepper

⅛ teaspoon grated nutmeg

DIRECTIONS:

Remove the central skeletons from the fish (see Know-How, right), and then cover and refrigerate the fish.

Put the fish skeletons in a medium saucepan along with the water, wine, onion, carrot, parsley sprigs, peppercorns, 1 clove of the garlic, and ¾ teaspoon of the salt. Bring to a gentle boil over medium heat, making sure the skeletons are submerged. Reduce the heat to medium-low and simmer for 30 minutes. Strain through a mesh sieve, pressing on the solids to extract as much liquid as possible. Measure out 2½ cups liquid and set aside. Discard the rest or save for another use, and wipe out the saucepan.

Heat 2 tablespoons of the oil in the saucepan over medium heat. Add the pine nuts and remaining 2 garlic cloves and cook until the garlic is soft but not brown, 2 to 3 minutes. Add the rice and cook until it absorbs some of the oil, 2 to 3 minutes. Meanwhile, cut the outer yellow zest from the lemon in one continuous strip. Add to the pan along with the cinnamon stick and reserved fish stock. Cover and bring to a boil over high heat. Reduce the heat to low and simmer until the liquid is absorbed, 12 to 15 minutes. Scatter the scallions on top of the rice, cover, and let stand for 5 minutes. Remove the lemon and cinnamon and fluff the rice with a fork. Mix in the feta, olives, oregano, and chopped parsley.

Light a grill for indirect medium-high heat, about 375°F (see page 14).

On a large work surface, lay out the vine leaves, overlapping them to create two rectangles, each a little longer than the fish and a little more than twice as wide. Place each fish at one edge of a rectangle. Cut the zested lemon in half and squeeze the juice into a cup. Mix in 2 tablespoons olive oil, the remaining ¼ teaspoon salt, the ground pepper, and nutmeg, and then drizzle the mixture all over the inside and outside of the fish. Stuff each fish with the rice pilaf, and then fold over the vine leaves, patting them smooth. Coat all over with the remaining olive oil.

Brush the grill grate and coat with oil. Put the fish on the grill away from the heat, cover, and cook until the fish looks opaque on the surface, but is still filmy and moist in the center (about 125°F on an instant-read thermometer), 8 to 10 minutes per side. Remove to a platter with a large spatula and let rest for 5 minutes. Slit open the vine leaves and serve with the lemon wedges.

KNOW-HOW: REMOVING THE CENTRAL SKELETON FROM WHOLE FISH

Lay the fish on its side on a cutting board with its back facing you. Insert the knife just above the central back ridge (skeleton) of the fish. Using short strokes, work your knife along the bones, lifting flesh from bone down the length of the backbone from head to tail. Keep the knife against bone at all times. When the entire backbone and rib bones are exposed on one side, lay the flat side of the knife against the backbone, near the tail. Hold the head of the fish steady and cut through the skin toward the tail, but stop before cutting all the way through the tail (leave the tail attached). One side of the skeleton will now be separated from the flesh from head to tail. Flip the fish over and fillet the other side in the same way. Using scissors, cut the backbone where it connects to the head and again where it connects to the tail. Remove the skeleton. Use the tip of your knife to remove any small bones along the inner belly.

Almond-Crusted Monkfish with Anchovy Sauce

MAKES 4 SERVINGS

Monkfish is often compared to lobster, but we don't taste the similarity. At best, monkfish picks up some briny flavor from its steady diet of shellfish. The one thing monkfish and lobster do have in common is looks: they're both hideous. Lobster would actually win this beauty contest because monkfish is positively revolting. This fish is all mouth, with a monstrously large but nearly flat, spiny head, dozens of widely spaced pinlike teeth, and one or two lanky antennae sprouting haphazardly from its upper lip, complete with a fleshy lure at the end of each one, which it uses to entice eels, cod, flounder, haddock, crabs, ducks, and other hapless prey before it ensnares them in its leviathan maw on the ocean floor. Not exactly the kind of girl you want to take home to dinner. Which is why monkfish are rarely sold with the head intact. All of the meat is in the tail anyway. And, truth be told, the meat is deliciously firm, sweet, and succulent. You can't judge a fish by its kisser. Marinated in buttermilk, grilled with a crust of toasted almonds, and laced with a simple sauce of oil, lemon, anchovy, and fresh oregano, this fish goes from beast to beauty.

INGREDIENTS:

2 pounds monkfish fillets, or 2¼ pounds monkfish tail, filleted, cleaned, and trimmed (see Know-How, below)

2 cups Buttermilk Marinade (page 37)

¾ cup all-purpose flour

1 teaspoon salt

¼ teaspoon ground black pepper

1 cup almonds

½ cup plain dry breadcrumbs

½ cup olive oil

Juice of 1 lemon

6 canned anchovy fillets

2 tablespoons fresh oregano leaves

Cooking spray

DIRECTIONS:

Put the monkfish fillets in a wide, shallow dish and pour on the marinade. Cover and refrigerate for 2 to 3 hours.

Light a grill for direct medium-high heat, about 400°F (see page 12).

Mix the flour, salt, and pepper in a shallow dish and set aside. Put the almonds and breadcrumbs in a food processor and process until finely ground. Pour into another shallow dish.

Remove a fillet from the marinade and dredge in the flour, shaking off the excess. Dip in the marinade again, then dredge in the almond mixture. Set on a rack and repeat with the remaining fillets. Combine the oil, lemon juice, anchovies, and oregano in the food processor. Process to a coarse puree and set aside.

Brush the grill grate and coat with oil. Coat the monkfish generously with cooking spray, and then grill directly over the heat until the coating browns, but the fish is still filmy and moist in the center (about 130°F on an instant-read thermometer), 5 to 6 minutes per side. Remove to a platter or plates and drizzle judiciously with the anchovy sauce.

KNOW-HOW: FILLETING A MONKFISH TAIL

If you're starting with whole monkfish tails instead of fillets, remove the skin. Then, to remove a fillet from the backbone, run your knife along its top side, moving toward the tail and always keeping the blade against the bone. Flip and remove the other fillet the same way. Remove any blue-gray membrane from the fillets to keep the fish from shrinking and toughening during cooking.

LEAN, FIRM WHITE FISH FILLETS

Grilled Cod Escabeche

MAKES 4 MAIN-DISH
OR 8 APPETIZER SERVINGS

Cod is a culinary chameleon. It can be as pedestrian as a fish-and-chip dinner or as cosmopolitan as escabeche, a marinated dish that is one of Spain's culinary gifts to the world. Instead of marinating the fish before cooking, the fish is marinated afterward, when the cod's cells have swelled from heat and become more receptive to absorbing a spicy lemon, lime, and orange marinade. What a great make-ahead dish for a party. Grill a few cumin-rubbed fillets, soak the cooked fish in marinade, then serve it up to 2 days later, after the cod's large flakes have absorbed as much marinade as they can possibly hold. Although completely unnecessary, a spoonful of creamy Caper Mayonnaise (page 42) makes this dish taste doubly great.

INGREDIENTS:

1½ cups Adobo Marinade (page 37)

½ cup sliced pimento-stuffed Spanish green olives

¼ cup finely chopped red onion

¼ cup finely chopped red bell pepper

1 large jalapeño chile pepper, seeded and finely chopped

2 tablespoons red wine vinegar

1 teaspoon sugar

¼ teaspoon red pepper flakes

4 cod fillets (about 6 ounces each)

1 tablespoon olive oil

¼ cup Orange-Cumin Rub (page 29)

DIRECTIONS:

Combine the marinade, olives, onion, bell pepper, jalapeño pepper, vinegar, sugar, and red pepper flakes in a small saucepan. Bring to a boil over high heat and boil for 1 minute. Remove from the heat and set aside.

Light a grill for direct medium-high heat, about 425°F (see page 12). Preheat a fish basket on the grill.

Coat the fish with olive oil, and then sprinkle the rub all over it. Brush the grill grate and coat the grate and the hot fish basket generously with oil. Put the fillets in the basket and the basket on the grill, directly over the heat. Cover and grill until the fish looks opaque on the surface, but is still filmy and moist in the center (an internal temperature of 130°F), 2 to

3 minutes per side. Transfer the fillets to a large, shallow, nonreactive dish such as a 13-by-9-inch baking dish. Pour the marinade mixture over the fish and let cool to room temperature. Cover and refrigerate for at least 6 hours or up to 2 days. Return to room temperature before serving.

KEEP IT SIMPLE:

Replace the orange-cumin rub with store-bought Mexican chili powder or Cajun seasoning.

LEAN, FIRM WHITE FISH FILLETS

Smokin' Catfish with Cayenne Praline Crumble

MAKES 4 SERVINGS

Catfish fillets consistently rank among the top five fish consumed in North America. Most catfish are farmed responsibly with little environmental impact. Wood smoke tastes particularly good with catfish, and in a tip of the tongs to Louisiana, crunch comes to this recipe from homemade praline spiked with cayenne, which is crumbled over the fillets. The praline can be made up to 2 weeks ahead and stored, covered, at room temperature.

INGREDIENTS:

¾ cup sugar

2 tablespoons water

½ cup pecans

¼ to ½ teaspoon cayenne pepper (more if you like it hot)

1½ teaspoons dried thyme leaves

4 catfish fillets (6 to 8 ounces each), rinsed and patted dry

¼ cup Smokin' Rub (page 26)

½ cup olive oil

4 lemon wedges

DIRECTIONS:

Grease a baking sheet and set aside. Combine the sugar and water in a 4-cup heat-proof glass bowl, stirring until the sugar is evenly moistened. Microwave on high until the mixture bubbles and appears light caramel in color, 4 to 8 minutes (ovens vary in wattage, so check every minute or so after 4 minutes). Remove and let cool just until the bubbling subsides. Using a wooden spoon, carefully stir in the pecans, cayenne, and ½ teaspoon of the thyme. Quickly spread out on the greased baking sheet in a thin layer. Let cool completely, then crack into pieces. Put the pieces in a food processor and grind until crumbly.

Put the catfish in a large baking dish. Mix the remaining 1 teaspoon thyme into the rub and sprinkle the rub all over the fish. Let stand at room temperature for 30 minutes.

Light a grill for direct medium-high heat, about 425°F (see page 12). Preheat a fish basket directly over the heat.

Brush the fish basket and coat with oil. Put the olive oil in a shallow dish and dip each fillet in the oil, letting the excess drip back into the dish. Put the oiled fillets in the hot fish basket and put the basket directly over the heat. Cover the grill and cook until the fish looks opaque on the surface, but is still filmy and moist in the center (130°F on an instant-read thermometer), 5 to 6 minutes per side.

Remove to a platter or plates and sprinkle with the praline crumble. Serve with the lemon wedges.

LEAN, FIRM WHITE FISH FILLETS

Grilled Grouper Fillets with Zhug

MAKES 4 SERVINGS

The country of Yemen borders the Red Sea, Arabian Sea, and Gulf of Aden. In coastal areas, Yemeni people eat a fair amount of fish like snapper and grouper. Topped with zhug, Yemen's signature chile paste, sweet fish like grouper take on a whole new taste. The chiles awaken your taste buds; the parsley and cilantro freshen your palate; and the aromas of caraway, cardamom, and cumin set your mind to dreaming. Look for skinless grouper fillets no more than ¾ inch thick.

INGREDIENTS:

4 skinless grouper fillets (6 to 8 ounces each), at least ½ inch thick

2 tablespoons olive oil

¼ teaspoon coarse salt

⅛ teaspoon ground black pepper

1 cup Zhug (page 33)

DIRECTIONS:

Light a grill for direct medium-high heat, about 425°F (see page 12).

Coat the grouper all over with the olive oil and season lightly with the salt and pepper.

Brush the grill grate and coat with oil. Grill the grouper directly over the heat until the fish looks opaque on the surface, but is still filmy and moist in the center (130°F on an instant-read thermometer), 4 to 6 minutes per side. After turning the fish on the grill, slather the top side (the just-grilled side) with half of the zhug.

Remove to a platter or plates and carefully invert so the uncoated side is up. Slather with the remaining zhug and let stand for a few minutes before serving.

LEAN, FIRM WHITE FISH FILLETS

Grilled Ocean Perch with Parsley-Walnut Sauce

MAKES 4 SERVINGS

Ocean perch is one of those fish given wildly conflicting names. When it comes from the North Atlantic Ocean, perch goes by the name redfish, but in the Southern states, it's known as ocean perch, to distinguish it from the South's beloved redfish (which is actually red drum). When perch is from the Pacific, it is commonly known as rockfish because it is a member of the rockfish family, but Pacific perch is sometimes mistakenly called red snapper. True, the skin is red or pink like red snapper, but the flesh of ocean perch is more delicate and the taste is milder. Just remember this: if it's called redfish or rockfish, it will still be good eating. For grilling, use ocean perch fillets at least ½ inch thick. Thinner ones tend to get sacrificed to the flame gods. You can also grill whole ocean perch, gutted and scaled with the fins removed, but the head left on. Here we serve fillets with a rich, toasty parsley-walnut sauce made with browned butter, garlic, white wine, and lemon juice; it would also be delicious drizzled over the crackling skin of whole grilled fish.

INGREDIENTS:

4 ocean perch fillets (at least 6 ounces each), at least ½ inch thick

2 tablespoons olive oil

½ teaspoon salt

¼ teaspoon ground black pepper

1½ cups Parsley-Walnut Sauce (page 44)

DIRECTIONS:

Light a grill for direct medium-high heat, about 425°F (see page 12). Preheat a fish basket on the grill.

Pat the perch dry, and then rub all over with the olive oil. Sprinkle with the salt and pepper and let stand until the grill is ready. Meanwhile, make the parsley-walnut sauce and keep warm.

Brush the fish basket and coat liberally with oil. Put the fish in the hot basket, skin-side down, and put the basket directly over the heat. Grill until the fish looks opaque on the surface, but is still filmy and moist in the center (about 125°F on an instant-read thermometer), 3 to 4 minutes per side.

Remove to a platter or plates and drizzle with the sauce.

LEAN, FIRM WHITE FISH STEAKS

Herb-Bathed Grilled Pollock Steaks with Gribiche

MAKES 4 SERVINGS

Pollock is the culinary world's most plentiful fish. In the Pacific, this small, sleek animal runs from the central California coast to Alaska's Bering Sea all the way to the Sea of Japan. It's used in everything from McDonald's Filet-O-Fish sandwich to Gorton's fish sticks to imitation crabmeat (a.k.a. surimi). Atlantic pollock is a larger, oilier fish with a stronger taste. A member of the cod family, pollock flakes up fairly large when cooked and holds its own with a range of mild and bold-flavored seasonings. To keep it simple, the usual seafood partners show up here—fresh dill, tarragon, lemon, and white wine—along with a creamy caper mayonnaise, which is given an acidic edge with the addition of sour cream.

INGREDIENTS:

Grated zest of 1 lemon

Juice of 2 lemons

½ cup dry white wine

¾ cup olive oil

⅓ cup Dill-Tarragon Rub (page 32)

4 pollock steaks (1½ to 2 pounds total), 1 to 1½ inches thick

1 cup Gribiche Sauce (page 42)

DIRECTIONS:

Combine the lemon zest and juice, white wine, olive oil, and 2 tablespoons of the herb rub in a 1-gallon zipper-lock bag. Add the pollock steaks and press out the air. Seal and refrigerate for 2 to 3 hours.

Remove the pollock from the marinade, reserving the marinade. Coat the fish all over with the remaining rub and let stand at room temperature for 30 minutes.

Light a grill for direct medium-high heat, about 425°F (see page 12). Preheat a fish basket directly over the heat. Brush the fish basket and coat with oil. Put the pollock in the hot basket and put the basket directly over the heat. Grill until the fish looks opaque on the surface, but is still filmy and moist in the center (about 130°F on an instant-read thermometer), drizzling often with the reserved marinade, 3 to 4 minutes per side.

Transfer to a platter or plates and serve with the gribiche.

LEAN, FIRM WHITE FISH

Grilled Skate with Brown Butter

MAKES 4 SERVINGS

Skate is a type of ray with huge pectoral fins, which constitute most of its body and flap like wings as the fish skates along the ocean floor. Like other members of the shark family, skate has no bones, only flexible cartilage. Cooking skate wings with the cartilage (unfilleted) helps it hold up on the grill and keeps the fish juicy and luscious. The cartilage is crunchy so enjoy it, or flake the cooked fish away from the cartilage, if you prefer. Either way, eat skate hot before the gelatin in the flesh firms up and gets sticky. Although we have some unusual flavor combinations in this book, we stayed true to a classic French preparation for this dish by drizzling it with a sauce of browned butter, white wine, lemon juice, and capers. Okay, we did take one or two liberties: The skate is grilled instead of sautéed, as it would normally be cooked in France. And to the browned butter sauce, we've added a little honey for sweetness and a few almonds for crunch.

INGREDIENTS:

2½ pounds skinless skate wing, unfilleted

¼ cup olive oil

¼ teaspoon sea salt

⅛ teaspoon ground black pepper

¾ cup Black Caper Butter (page 44)

1½ tablespoons honey

2 tablespoons slivered almonds

DIRECTIONS:

Set the skate in a large dish and coat all over with the oil. Sprinkle with the salt and pepper and let stand at room temperature for 30 minutes.

Light a grill for direct medium-high heat, about 425°F (see page 12). Preheat a fish large basket on the grill.

Make the caper butter and when adding the wine, also add the honey. Stir in the almonds along with the capers. Keep warm over low heat.

Brush the fish basket and coat with oil. Put the fish in the hot basket and put the basket directly over the heat. Grill until the fish looks opaque on the surface, but is still filmy and moist in the center (about 130°F on an instant-read thermometer), 4 to 5 minutes per side.

Remove to a platter or plates and pour on the butter sauce.

LEAN, FIRM WHOLE WHITE FISH

Whole Sea Bass Grilled in Wasabi Crust

MAKES 4 SERVINGS

Whole fish grilled over an open flame develops a crackled skin and concentrated moisture that is the essence of succulence. Unfortunately, the increasing popularity of fish has not translated into greater availability of whole fish. Almost everything you see is already filleted. This is a shame because the flesh of fish cooked whole on the bone has more flavor and stays moister during cooking. If you don't mind serving whole fish with the head on, shop around for a fish market that sells whole fish. And even if you don't want to bring a fish head to the table, you'll get better flavor by cooking the whole fish, and then removing the head just before serving. Slashing the flesh in its thicker parts helps the fish grill more evenly and gets any seasoning closer to the meat, where it does the most good. In this recipe, those slashes deliver the bracing flavors of wasabi, lemon zest, garlic, and ginger on luscious sea bass (black bass). This firm, lean white fish runs anywhere from 1 to 3 pounds. Most are sold at 1½ to 2 pounds, which is enough for two people. To serve four to six, we prefer grilling two to three fish of similar size, but if you are serving more people, you would do best to buy bigger fish.

INGREDIENTS:

3 tablespoons Mustard-Wasabi Rub (page 26)

1 teaspoon lemon zest

2 whole sea bass (about 1½ pounds each), scaled, fins removed, head left on

2 tablespoons canola oil

⅓ cup pickled (sushi) ginger, finely chopped

3 scallions (green and white parts), thinly sliced

1 teaspoon minced garlic

1 teaspoon soy sauce

DIRECTIONS:

Light a grill for direct medium heat, about 375°F (see page 12). Preheat a grill tray or fish basket directly over the heat.

Mix the wasabi rub and lemon zest in a small bowl and set aside.

Scrape the dull side of a knife against the skin of the fish, running from tail to head, to remove excess moisture and fine scales. Cut three or four diagonal slashes through the flesh of the fish on each side, down to the bone. Rub the fish inside and out with the oil, then season inside and out with the wasabi rub.

Combine the sushi ginger, scallions, garlic, and soy sauce and set aside.

Brush the grill grate and coat with oil. Oil the grill tray or fish basket liberally and put the fish on the tray or in the basket; put on the grill directly over the heat. Cover and cook until the fish is browned on both sides, but is still filmy and moist in the center (about 130°F internal temperature), about 15 minutes, turning once. If your grill has a temperature gauge, it should stay around 375°F.

Serve the fish with the pickled ginger mixture.

KNOW-HOW: CARVING A WHOLE FISH

A whole cooked fish makes an impressive presentation but it can be intimidating to carve. Here's the most elegant method: Remove the top fillet by inserting the side of a spatula just behind the head. When you feel bone, slide the spatula along the backbone toward the tail. Use the long side of the spatula to lift the entire fillet off the backbone; or for very long fish, cut into manageable pieces and lift them one by one. Next, grab the tail with one hand and insert the spatula beneath the tail to cut the fillet from the base of the tail. Lift the tail and backbone off the bottom fillet toward the head, cutting the fillet from the head. Discard the fish carcass—from head to tail—and serve the bottom fillet.

RICH, COLORED FISH STEAK

Chilean Sea Bass with Grilled Lemon "Tartar" Sauce

MAKES 6 SERVINGS

The marketing name for Patagonian toothfish is Chilean sea bass. It is a large, meaty, slow-growing fish that lives in the frigid waters around Antarctica. Because these fish breed late in life, they are naturally vulnerable to overfishing, which is what has happened to most of the world's supply. The fish is listed as one to avoid by the Monterey Bay Aquarium Seafood Watch, but there are a few fisheries that are harvesting Chilean sea bass sustainably. These carry the seal of the London-based Marine Stewardship Council (MSC), and reputable fish markets make a point of only carrying certified Chilean sea bass. The meat of Chilean sea bass is pristine white, and very firm. If you can't find the fish, monkfish is a good substitute. We grill the fish simply with a little olive oil, salt, and pepper to highlight its natural sweetness, and then serve it with a dynamite condiment, grilled lemon tartar sauce, made by grinding grilled lemon, peel and all, with oil and dill.

INGREDIENTS:

2 pounds Chilean sea bass fillets or steaks, about 1 inch thick

1 tablespoon olive oil

Coarse salt and ground black pepper

1¼ cups Grilled Lemon "Tartar" Sauce (page 42)

DIRECTIONS:

Light a grill for direct medium-high heat, about 425°F (see page 12).

Coat the sea bass with the oil and season with salt and pepper.

Brush the grill grate and coat with oil. Put the sea bass on the grill, cover the grill, and cook until the fish looks opaque on the surface, but is still filmy and moist in the center (130°F on an instant-read thermometer), about 4 minutes per side.

Serve the fish with the sauce.

RICH, COLORED FISH FILLET

Coriander-Crusted Char Fillet with Cilantro Pesto

MAKES 4 SERVINGS

Although wild Arctic char is caught throughout the North Atlantic, most of the Arctic char sold in fish stores is farmed in closed, nonpolluting systems. The fish is related to salmon and looks similar to a small one. When filleted, most consumers can't tell the difference, although a char fillet tends to be thinner. Char can be cooked in any recipe that calls for salmon, which means it is one of the most versatile fish. Moist and meaty, forgiving of slight overcooking, with an edible skin, and consistent, environmentally friendly production, it should be part of every grill master's repertoire.

INGREDIENTS:

⅓ cup Coriander Rub (page 28)

2 tablespoons breadcrumbs

2 skinless Arctic char fillets (about 12 ounces each)

Cooking spray

⅓ cup Cilantro Pesto (page 43)

DIRECTIONS:

Light a grill for direct medium heat, about 375°F (see page 12).

Mix the coriander rub and breadcrumbs together and pat into both sides of the fillets. Spray the fillets with oil and set on a sheet of plastic wrap for about 10 minutes.

Brush the grill grate and coat with oil. Put the char on the grill and cook until both sides are browned and the fish looks opaque on the surface, but is still filmy and moist in the center, about 4 minutes per side.

Transfer to a platter using an extra-wide spatula, top with the pesto, and serve immediately.

RICH, COLORED FISH FILLET

Alder-Planked Pacific Salmon Fillet with Black Mustard Butter Sauce

MAKES 4 SERVINGS

There are several varieties of sustainably caught wild Pacific salmon that are readily available. King salmon, also called chinook, is the most majestic, and the best tasting, but procuring a real king salmon is difficult. Most of the good quality king salmon goes directly to restaurants and rarely comes on the retail market. Coho salmon are slightly smaller, with flesh that is more deeply colored than king. The darkest and most assertive is sockeye, which is dark red. Lesser varieties include pink salmon (mostly used for canning), and chum salmon, whose quality varies greatly, depending where it was caught. All of the varieties grill well on a plank. Alder grilling planks have a sweeter flavor than cedar, and we prefer them for salmon. We also think you get a better flavor if you allow one side of the plank to char well before putting the fish on. Note that wild salmon and farm-raised salmon, even when of the same variety, are not completely interchangeable. Farm-raised fish are both fatter and more tender, so if you are substituting farmed fish for wild, you will need to extend the grilling time and maybe lower the heat level.

INGREDIENTS:

1 alder plank, about 15 by 6 by ¼ inches

1 wild Pacific salmon fillet (about 1¾ pounds)

2 teaspoons canola oil

1 tablespoon Garam Masala Rub (page 30)

½ cup Black Mustard Butter (page 45)

DIRECTIONS:

Soak the alder plank in water for at least 1 hour.

Light a grill for direct medium heat, about 375°F (see page 12).

Rub the flesh side of the salmon with the oil and season with the rub; set aside. Put the plank over the fire, cover the grill, and heat until the plank is charred on one side, about 10 minutes. If the wood should catch fire, douse with water. Place the fish, skin-side down, on the charred side of the plank.

Return the plank to the grill with the fish on it, cover, and grill until the fish looks opaque on the surface, but is still filmy and moist in the center (130°F on an instant-read thermometer), about 10 minutes.

Serve the salmon from the plank, drizzled with the mustard butter.

RICH, COLORED FISH FILLET

Hot Smoked Norwegian Salmon with Grilled Onions

MAKES 8 TO 10 SERVINGS

The populations of wild Atlantic salmon are so depleted that they are no longer commercially viable. So all Atlantic salmon are farm-raised, and since the largest farms are in Norway, Norwegian salmon is now the common name for Atlantic salmon. Although farm-raised Atlantic salmon has its problems (see page 238), it is the salmon that grill-smokes the best. We find Pacific salmon too lean to hold up to smoking on a grill. Look for a thick fillet with full (but not dark) color, which indicates a high enough fat content to keep the fish moist during smoking. To enhance its moisture, the fillet is brined for a few hours. Then it's rubbed with a smoke-flavored rub, and cooked gently beside a smoky fire.

INGREDIENTS:

2 cups hardwood chips, soaked in water for 30 minutes

1 large side farmed Norwegian salmon (about 3 pounds), pin bones removed

3 cups Smokin' Brine, made with vodka (page 33)

¼ cup Smokin' Rub (page 26)

1 tablespoon dried dill weed

1 teaspoon onion powder

2 large red onions, cut into ¼-inch-thick rounds

¼ cup extra-virgin olive oil

1 bunch fresh dill

Finely grated zest of 1 lemon

1 garlic clove, minced

Coarse salt and ground black pepper

DIRECTIONS:

Put the salmon in a jumbo (2-gallon) zipper-lock bag. If you only have 1-gallon bags, cut the fish in half and use two bags. Add the brine to the bag(s), press out the air, and seal. Refrigerate for 3 to 4 hours.

Mix all but 1 tablespoon of the rub with the dried dill and onion powder and set aside.

Soak the onion slices in ice water.

Heat a grill for indirect low heat, about 225°F, with smoke (see pages 14 and 16). Drain the wood chips and add them to the grill.

Remove the salmon from the brine and pat dry with paper towels. Discard the brine. Coat the fish with 1 tablespoon of the oil and sprinkle the meaty side with the rub that has dried dill in it.

Lift the onions from the ice water and pat dry. Coat with 1 tablespoon of the oil and sprinkle with the remaining 1 tablespoon rub. Set the fish and onions aside to rest for 15 minutes.

Brush the grill grate and rub well with oil. Place the salmon, flesh-side down, directly over the heat and grill for 5 minutes until the surface is golden brown. Using a large fish spatula or two regular spatulas, turn the fish skin-side down and position on the grill grate away from the fire. Put the onion slices directly over the fire. Close the grill and cook until the salmon is firm on the outside, but not dry, and resilient in the center, about 25 minutes. When done, moisture will bead through the surface when the fish is gently pressed. It should not fully flake under pressure. Turn the onions once during the cooking time.

While the salmon is cooking, remove the leaves from the fresh dill and chop coarsely. Mix with the lemon zest, garlic, salt, pepper, and remaining 2 tablespoons olive oil.

When the salmon is done, transfer to a platter using a fish spatula. Let rest for 5 minutes to finish cooking. Surround with grilled onion slices and scatter the fresh dill mixture over the top.

RICH, COLORED FISH STEAK

Whole Roasted Shad Stuffed with Onions and Buckwheat

MAKES 4 SERVINGS

Shad is very popular along the Atlantic Coast, where shad season is a reason for local festivals. But its baroque bone structure makes it difficult to prepare. A skilled fishmonger can remove all the bones easily, and we suggest you have him or her do it for you. In this recipe, the shad's thin, shingle-patterned skin becomes taut and crisp, the flesh softens, and the stuffing gets fluffier as it absorbs moisture from the fish during grilling.

INGREDIENTS:

¼ cup extra-virgin olive oil

1 onion, coarsely chopped

2 ounces mushrooms, sliced

1 garlic clove, minced

1 cup whole buckwheat groats (kasha)

2 cups chicken broth

½ teaspoon coarse salt

½ teaspoon ground black pepper

1 teaspoon chopped fresh rosemary

½ tablespoon chopped fresh parsley

1 large shad (about 4 pounds), boned, head and tail left on

¼ cup orange juice

DIRECTIONS:

Light a grill for indirect high heat, about 425°F (see page 14).

Heat 1 tablespoon of the olive oil in a large skillet over medium heat. Add the onion and mushrooms and sauté until browned, about 5 minutes. Add the garlic and buckwheat and stir to moisten with the oil. Stir in the broth, salt, pepper, and rosemary, cover, and bring to a simmer. Continue simmering until all of the liquid has been absorbed and the buckwheat is soft and fluffy, about 12 minutes. Stir in ¾ teaspoon of the parsley and adjust the salt and pepper to taste.

Open the shad like a book. Season with salt and pepper and drizzle 1 tablespoon of the olive oil and 2 tablespoons of the orange juice over the interior of the fish. Fill the cavity with the cooked buckwheat and close the fish around the filling.

Secure with 3 lengths of twine to keep the fish together. Coat the outside of the fish with 1 tablespoon of the olive oil.

Brush the grill grate and coat liberally with oil. Put the fish on the grill away from the heat. Close the lid and grill until the fish looks opaque on the surface, but is still filmy and moist in the center (135°F on an instant-read thermometer), about 35 minutes.

Transfer to a platter using an extra-wide spatula or two regular spatulas. Remove the twine. Drizzle with the remaining 1 tablespoon olive oil and 2 tablespoons orange juice and scatter the remaining ¾ teaspoon parsley over the top. To serve, cut the fish in 4 sections.

RICH, COLORED FISH FILLET OR STEAK

Garlic-Crusted Opah Squares with Sweet Soy Dipping Sauce

MAKES 4 SERVINGS

Opah is new to the continental U.S. fish market. Native to the waters around Hawaii, it is a delicious fish with sweet, firm flesh. The fish tend to be large (small specimens weigh about 50 pounds), so you will only able to purchase it as individual fillet steaks or chunks for kebabs. The meat is rich tasting and ranges from a deep coral color (taken from the back) to pale pink (from along the belly).

INGREDIENTS:

6 garlic cloves, minced

3 tablespoons mayonnaise

1½ teaspoons Asian hot pepper sauce, such as Sriracha

1 opah fillet (1½ pounds), 2 inches thick

⅓ cup Sweet Soy Glaze (page 49)

DIRECTIONS:

Light a grill for direct medium-high heat, about 425°F (see page 12).

Mix the garlic, mayonnaise, and pepper sauce.

If there is skin on the fish, remove it, and cut the fillet into 2-inch cubes. Coat with the garlic mixture.

Brush the grill grate and coat well with oil. Put the fish cubes on the grill, cover the grill, and cook until browned on all sides, about 20 minutes (about 3 minutes per side).

Serve immediately with the soy glaze for dipping.

RICH, COLORED FISH STEAK

Grilled Bluefish with Grilled Tomato Oil

MAKES 4 SERVINGS

Bluefish is a migratory, open-ocean fish of the North Atlantic, which can range in size from 1-pound snappers (young bluefish) to strapping 10-pounders. Most of the bluefish you find at the market weigh about 4 pounds (the size of a medium salmon), with fillets of 1½ to 2 pounds. Bluefish fillets have a rich flesh with a gray-blue cast and a soft, meaty consistency. Like many oily fish bluefish are perishable, so freshness is paramount. The best indication of quality is aroma. Bluefish develop a distinctly fishy aroma within a few days of being caught. So always ask to take a sniff before you buy.

INGREDIENTS:

1½ pounds bluefish fillet, about 1½ inches thick

1 tablespoon olive oil

Coarse salt and coarsely ground black pepper

¼ cup Grilled Tomato Oil (page 50)

DIRECTIONS:

Light a grill for direct medium-high heat, 425°F (see page 12).

Remove the pin bones from the bluefish (see Know-How, right) and coat with olive oil. Season with salt and pepper.

Brush the grill grate and rub with oil. Put the fish on the grill, flesh-side down. Close the lid and grill until browned, about 5 minutes. Flip the fish onto its skin side. Brush the flesh with the glaze, close the lid, and grill until the fish looks opaque on the surface, but is still filmy and moist in the center (135°F on an instant-read thermometer), 8 to 10 minutes more.

Slide a wide spatula between the fish and the skin and lift the fish onto a serving platter and serve. (Leave the skin on the grill and discard later, before cleaning the grill.)

> ### KNOW-HOW: REMOVING PIN BONES FROM FISH FILLETS
>
> Filleted fish contains a line of small bones, called pin bones, running lengthwise down the center of each fillet. Pin bones are easily removed either by pulling them out with needle-nose pliers (pull toward the wide end of the fillet), or by making a slit on either side of the line of bones with a small boning knife and then pulling the bones out in a single strip.

Whole Trout Stuffed with Pickled Ginger and Chives

MAKES 4 SERVINGS

We brine this trout in green tea because scientists in Japan have found that green tea counteracts strong fishy aromas.

INGREDIENTS:

4 boneless brook trout or rainbow trout (about 6 ounces each)

2 cups Green Tea Brine (page 35)

¼ cup pickled (sushi) ginger, chopped

8 fresh chives, finely chopped

2 tablespoons canola oil

1 tablespoon soy sauce

1 teaspoon fresh lemon juice

1 teaspoon toasted sesame oil

DIRECTIONS:

The trout will be split down their bellies; open them up like a book to expose the interior to the brine. Combine the fish and brine in a 1-gallon zipper-lock bag, press out the air, and seal. Refrigerate for 1 hour.

Mix together the pickled ginger and chives in a small bowl.

Light a grill for direct medium-high heat, about 425°F (see page 12).

Remove the fish from the brine and discard the brine. Fill the fish cavities with the ginger mixture, and close the fish. Pat the fish skin with paper towels until dry, and rub with the oil.

Brush the grill grate and coat with oil. Put the fish on the grill, close the lid, and grill until the skin is crisp and the fish looks opaque on the surface, but is still filmy and moist in the center (130°F on an instant-read thermometer), 4 to 5 minutes per side.

Mix the soy sauce, lemon juice, and sesame oil in a small bowl. Put the fish on a serving platter and drizzle with the soy mixture. Serve immediately.

Cracked Black Pepper–Crusted Swordfish with Lime

MAKES 4 SERVINGS

The overfishing of swordfish during the 1990s sparked the first widespread public ban on harvesting or consuming a particular fish. It was the starting point in raising consumer consciousness about the sustainability of wild fishing. Since then swordfish populations have increased, and the Monterey Aquarium Seafood Watch now lists most varieties of swordfish as a best or good choice. Swordfish meat is very firm and pale beige in color. Virtually all of it is cut into steaks and skinned (the skin is tough and inedible). It is one of the easiest fish to grill because it doesn't stick, and it is difficult to overcook. Look for fish with glistening flesh and tight swirls. An open muscle structure is an indication that the fish is starting to dry out.

INGREDIENTS:

2½ cups Lemon–Black Pepper Brine (page 35)

1½ pounds swordfish steaks, ¾ to 1 inch thick

1 tablespoon olive oil

2 tablespoons cracked black pepper

1 tablespoon finely grated lime zest

½ teaspoon coarse sea salt

2 tablespoons unsalted butter

2 tablespoons fresh lime juice

DIRECTIONS:

Combine the brine and fish in a 1-gallon zipper-lock bag, squeeze out the air, and seal. Refrigerate for 3 to 6 hours.

Light a grill for direct medium-high heat, 400 to 450°F (see page 12).

Remove the fish from the brine and pat dry with paper towels. Discard the brine. Coat the fish liberally with the olive oil.

Mix together the cracked pepper, lime zest, and sea salt, and season both sides of the fish with this mixture.

Brush the grill grate and coat with oil. Put the fish on the grill, close the lid, and grill until the fish looks opaque on the surface, but is still filmy and moist in the center (130°F on an instant-read thermometer), about 15 minutes, flipping halfway through.

Melt the butter in a small saucepan over medium heat. Remove from the heat and stir in the lime juice.

Using an extra-wide spatula, or two regular spatulas, transfer the fish to a serving platter. Drizzle with lime butter and serve.

RICH, COLORED FISH STEAK

Grilled Mako Shark Steaks with White Steak Sauce

MAKES 4 SERVINGS

Properly handled, shark steak has a firm meaty texture and an ivory-pink pearlesence. It is also one of the mildest tasting fish around. But mishandled or over-the-hill shark meat is repulsive. Sharks build up urea (a protein waste product) to balance the sodium their flesh absorbs from seawater. Once a shark is out of water, the urea starts to break down and forms ammonia compounds, which accounts for the noxiously bad smell of old shark. Look for shark meat that is glistening and odorless. Even a whiff of ammonia is unacceptable.

INGREDIENTS:

2 garlic cloves, minced

2 tablespoons fresh lemon juice

2 tablespoons olive oil

1 teaspoon dried oregano leaves

4 mako shark steaks (about 6 to 7 ounces each), about ¾ inch thick

Coarse salt and coarsely ground black pepper

2 tablespoons chopped fresh flat-leaf parsley

¾ cup White Steak Sauce (page 42)

continued

DIRECTIONS:

Light a grill for direct medium-high heat, 425°F (see page 12).

Mix the garlic, lemon juice, olive oil, and oregano in a small bowl. Season the shark steaks with salt and pepper and coat with the garlic-lemon mixture. Set aside for 20 minutes.

Brush the grill grate and coat with oil. Grill until the fish looks opaque on the surface, but is still filmy and moist in the center (140°F on an instant-read thermometer), 4 to 5 minutes per side.

Scatter the parsley over the steaks and serve with sauce on the side.

KEEP IT SIMPLE:

Replace the steak sauce with jarred tartar sauce or ½ cup mayonnaise mixed with ¼ cup jarred steak sauce, such as A1.

RICH, MEDIUM COLORED FISH FILLETS

Mahi-Mahi Skewers with Seafood Butter

MAKES 4 SERVINGS

Mahi-mahi is rich and meaty, but it dries out mercilessly when overcooked. One of the best ways to ensure temperature control is to cut the fish into cubes, which cook through as they brown. The cubes are marinated in aromatic sesame oil and lemon, skewered with bite-size tomatoes, and basted with seafood-flavored butter before they hit the grill. The added oil and butter lubricate the fish from the outside as it cooks, guaranteeing that the each grilled morsel remains moist. We suggest serving these skewers on a bed of brown rice or whole-wheat couscous.

INGREDIENTS:

4 bamboo or metal skewers

¼ cup olive oil

1 tablespoon toasted sesame oil

Zest and juice of ½ lemon

1 tablespoon chopped fresh flat-leaf parsley

¼ teaspoon coarse salt

⅛ teaspoon ground black pepper

2 pounds skinless mahi-mahi steaks or thick fillets, cut into 1½-inch cubes

1 lemon, cut into 8 wedges

16 cherry or grape tomatoes

6 strips bacon, preferably applewood-smoked, cut into 3-inch lengths

⅓ cup Seafood Butter (page 44)

DIRECTIONS:

Combine the olive oil, sesame oil, lemon zest, lemon juice, parsley, salt, and black pepper in a 1-gallon zipper-lock bag. Add the mahi-mahi, press out the air, and seal the bag. Refrigerate for up to 12 hours.

If you are grilling with bamboo skewers, soak them in water for at least 30 minutes. Light a grill for direct medium heat, about 400°F (see page 12). Thread the lemon wedges, tomatoes, and mahi-mahi cubes alternately on the skewers, using about 2 pieces of each per skewer. For the mahi-mahi, wrap each cube on three sides with a piece of bacon, and skewer

through the ends of the bacon to secure it. Set aside some of the seafood butter for serving and brush the skewers with the rest.

Brush the grill grate and coat with oil. Grill the skewers directly over the heat until the fish looks opaque on the surface, but is still filmy and moist in the center (130°F on an instant-read thermometer). Drizzle with the reserved seafood butter and serve with the grilled lemon wedges for squeezing.

RICH, DARK BONELESS FISH STEAK

Raw Charred Tuna with Green Tea Ponzu Sauce

MAKES 4 SERVINGS

Like prime rib of beef, tuna is red, tender, meaty, and better cooked rare than well done. But tuna flesh is more porous than beef and it cooks quickly, so it is a challenge to get a great crust while maintaining a rare interior. We have found a simple solution— stick the fish right in the fire. We had grilled steaks directly on coals and the results were always spectacular, but doing the same thing with tuna was a revelation. Not only did we get an amazing crispy crust and a completely luscious raw tuna core, but the flesh soaked up wood flavor like a sponge. Every bite was moist, crisp, sumptuously rare, and saturated with the aroma of wood smoke. You will need either a wood fire or one made from hardwood (lump) charcoal for this preparation. Charcoal briquettes, which are made from sawdust, produce a powdery ash that soils the surface of the fish. Wood charcoal, made from solid pieces of wood, doesn't create the same problem. All you need to do is blow the film of ash off the coals before laying on the fish. We use a leaf blower because it's fast and fun, but anything that creates a breeze (a hair dryer, folded newspaper, or sheet of cardboard) will work. It is also important to make the coal bed as even as possible. Air spaces can cause flare-ups, which will burn the surface of the fish rather than brown it.

INGREDIENTS:

2 tablespoons pickled (sushi) ginger, finely chopped

2 thin scallions (green and white parts), finely chopped

1 garlic clove, minced

1 ¾ pounds tuna steaks, 2 inches thick

1 tablespoon toasted sesame oil

1 tablespoon Mustard Wasabi Rub (page 26)

1 tablespoon sesame seeds

1 ¼ cups Green Tea Ponzu Sauce (page 46)

DIRECTIONS:

Light a hardwood charcoal fire for direct high heat, about 475°F (see page 12).

Combine the pickled ginger, scallions, and garlic in a small dish. Insert a knife with a thin blade horizontally into the tuna steaks three or four times, creating slits that go directly toward the center of the tuna steaks. Stuff the slits with the ginger mixture. Coat the tuna steaks all over with sesame oil.

Combine the rub and sesame seeds on a sheet of foil or plastic wrap and coat the edges of the tuna steaks (not the tops and bottoms) with the mixture.

Make the charcoal bed as even as possible and blow off excess ash with a hair dryer, leaf blower, or fan. Put the steaks directly on the hot coals and grill until the bottoms are lightly charred, about 1½ minutes. Turn with long-handled tongs, picking off any coals clinging to the surface, and grill 1½ minutes on the other side. The center should remain raw. Remove to a cutting board.

Slice against the grain into ¼- to ½-inch-thick slices and serve with the ponzu sauce.

Spanish Mackerel Grilled with Apples and Beets

MAKES 4 SERVINGS

Mackerel are not just about bling, although their ostentatious turquoise-blue-black-silver skin might lead you to believe otherwise. (The French word for mackerel, *macquereau*, also means "pimp"). The proof is on the plate. Mackerel flesh is sweet, and so rich in omega-3 fatty acids that it is difficult to ruin by overcooking. The skin is sleek and completely edible once scaled. So why is mackerel so cheap? For one thing, it is highly perishable, and it is important to buy mackerel as fresh as possible. More then two days out of the sea, and it becomes decidedly stinky, so only purchase mackerel that smells clean and fresh. And then cook it right away. Spanish mackerels run in size from about 7 ounces (mackerel pike) to 2 pounds or so. This recipe is designed for bigger fish, which are easier to stuff. The heartiness of the beet and apple stuffing stands up well to the richness of mackerel, and the contrast of magenta beets and blue-black fish skin is stunning.

INGREDIENTS:

2 Spanish mackerel (about 2 pounds each), scaled and cleaned, with gills removed

2¼ cups Fennel Brine (page 34)

1 tablespoon olive oil

1 medium onion, finely chopped

2 medium beets, roasted, boiled, grilled (see page 304), or canned; finely chopped

1 tart apple, peeled, cored, and finely chopped

1 garlic clove, minced

1 tablespoon finely chopped fresh dill or fennel fronds

3 tablespoons fresh goat cheese

1 lime, cut into 8 wedges

DIRECTIONS:

Rinse the fish and put in a 1-gallon zipper-lock bag with the brine, press out the air, and seal the bag. Refrigerate for 2 to 6 hours.

Heat the oil in a large skillet over medium heat. Add the onions and sauté until tender, about 3 minutes. Add the beets and apple and sauté until the apple is tender, about 4 minutes. Stir in the garlic and dill and heat through, about 1 minute. Cool the mixture to room temperature and stir in the goat cheese.

Meanwhile light a grill for direct medium heat, about 375°F (see page 12).

Remove the fish from the brine and pat dry. Discard the brine. Stuff the cavities of the fish with the cooled beet and apple mixture and secure with string, if needed.

Brush the grill grate and coat with oil. Grill the fish until the skin is crisp and the fish looks opaque on the surface, but is still filmy and moist in the middle (130°F on an instant-read thermometer), 5 to 7 minutes per side. Remove the fish to a serving platter and serve with the lime wedges.

SMALL RICH, COLORED WHOLE FISH

Grilled Anchovies Stuffed with Dukkah and Drenched in Olive Oil

MAKES 4 SERVINGS

Anchovies have an image problem, largely because most people have never tasted them fresh. Canned anchovies are as much like fresh anchovies as canned tuna is like a slice of tuna sashimi—in other words, there is no comparison. Fresh anchovies have a delicate texture and pleasant, sweet rich flavor. The overt saltiness and pungent aroma associated with anchovies happens during the preservation process and is not characteristic of the fresh fish in any way. Anchovy populations are abundant, so there is no danger of overfishing, and they are high in omega-3 fatty acids (three times higher than salmon). The one problem you might have is finding them. Their season is usually in the spring, but availability has more to do with demand than supply. If you ask for them at your local fish market, the store probably can get them. You can also make this recipe with any small oily fish—sardines, herring, mackerel, or sprats. Anchovies are tiny with feathery rib bones that are edible. We like to fill the body cavities with spicy, nutty Egyptian dukkah. They are great right off the grill, but also make a perfect pick-up food, served at room temperature the next day.

INGREDIENTS:

34 large anchovies (about 1½ ounces each), cleaned and heads removed

½ cup Dukkah (page 28)

¼ cup plus 1 tablespoon olive oil

Juice of 2 limes

Coarse sea salt

DIRECTIONS:

Light a grill for direct medium-high heat, 400 to 450°F (see page 12)

Remove the backbones from the fish: make a slit down one side of the spine along the cavity of the fish, and then just lift it out with your fingers. Don't worry about removing the small rib bones—they are edible.

Mix the dukkah with 2 tablespoons of the olive oil. Drizzle the inside of the fish with half the lime juice and put a scant tablespoon of dukkah down the center of each fish; close the fish to enclose the dukkah. Coat with 1 tablespoon of the oil.

Brush the grill grate and coat liberally with oil. Put the fish on the grill, close the lid, and cook until the fish looks opaque on the surface, but is still filmy and moist in the center (130°F internal temperature), about 4 minutes, turning halfway through. Don't worry if the fish open up during grilling; you can reassemble them on the platter.

Remove to a platter. Drizzle with the remaining 2 tablespoons olive oil and lime juice and season with sea salt. Serve immediately.

LEAN, DELICATE WHOLE FLAT FISH

Whole Flounder Grilled with Lemon and Marjoram

MAKES 4 SERVINGS

The large flounder family includes sole, plaice, fluke, and a variety of fish that go by the name "flounder." In North America, the most common flounder are lemon sole and black back in winter, and fluke in summer. These bottom feeders have both eyes on one side of their flat bodies so they can easily catch small prey while resting on and blending into the ocean floor. Flounder has an easygoing, adaptable taste with fine textured flakes. Cleaned, scaled, and cooked whole with lemon and fresh herbs, the fish makes an unfussy meal. If flounder isn't available, use another whole flatfish like sole or turbot.

INGREDIENTS:

2 whole flounder (about 2 pounds each), gutted and scaled, fins removed, heads left on (see Know-How, page 242)

½ cup olive oil

Grated zest and juice of 1 lemon

¼ cup chopped fresh marjoram

2 garlic cloves, minced

½ teaspoon coarse salt

¼ teaspoon ground black pepper

1 cup Grilled Lemon "Tartar" Sauce (page 42), made with marjoram

DIRECTIONS:

Cut four or five diagonal slices through the flesh of the fish on each side down to the bone (see Know-How on page 240). Set the fish in a shallow baking dish.

Combine the oil, lemon zest and juice, marjoram, garlic, salt, and pepper in a measuring cup. Pour over the fillets, lifting them to coat completely. Cover and refrigerate for 1 hour.

Remove the fish from the refrigerator and let stand in the marinade for 20 minutes.

Light a grill for direct medium-high heat, about 400°F (see page 12). Preheat a fish basket directly over the heat (use a basket large enough to hold both fish at once or grill in batches). When hot, brush the grill basket and coat with oil. Put the fish in the hot basket (reserve the marinade) and put the basket directly over the heat with the dark side of the fish down. Grill until the fish looks opaque on the surface, but is still filmy and moist in the center (about 125°F on an instant-read thermometer), basting with the remaining marinade a few times, 3 to 4 minutes per side.

Remove to a large platter. Serve with the "tartar" sauce.

> ### KNOW-HOW: BUYING FLOUNDER FILLETS
>
> Some flounder and sole fillets are "brined," meaning they are soaked in sodium tripolyphosphate (STP), which plumps up their total weight (and price) and helps the fish last a bit longer. It also gives the fillets an off-putting aroma that masks their simple sweet flavors. For the best quality and taste, ask for fillets that have not been brined or soaked.

LEAN, FIRM FLAT FISH FILLETS

Coconut Halibut with Red Curry Sauce

MAKES 4 SERVINGS

Cooked halibut has snow-white flesh with extra-large satiny smooth flakes. This fish is so big it can be cut into roasts and loins in addition to steaks and fillets. If you can't find it, try lingcod, another sweet, firm white fish that will complement the creamy Thai coconut curry sauce featured here as both marinade and sauce. Toasted coconut lovers will enjoy the crunchy crust, made with shards of unsweetened shredded coconut.

INGREDIENTS:

2 cups Coconut Red Curry Sauce (page 45), cooled

4 halibut fillets (6 to 8 ounces each), less than 1 inch thick (see Know-How, page 268)

1¼ cups Smoky Coconut Rub (page 31)

1 large egg white

Cooking spray

4 lime wedges

continued ➔

DIRECTIONS:

Pour 1 cup of the sauce in a 1-gallon zipper-lock bag. Add the halibut and press out the air. Seal and refrigerate for 2 to 3 hours.

Light a grill for direct medium-high heat, about 450°F (see page 12). Put the spice rub in a wide shallow bowl. Beat the egg white in another wide shallow bowl until frothy. Remove the halibut from the marinade and dredge in the egg white, and then in the spice rub. Sprinkle any remaining rub over the fish, press in gently, and spray liberally with oil. Let stand for 15 minutes.

Brush the grill grate and coat with oil. Grill the halibut directly over the heat for 4 to 5 minutes. Carefully flip and grill until the coconut is darkened around the edges and the fish looks opaque on the surface, but is still filmy and moist in the center (about 130°F on an instant-read thermometer), 3 to 5 minutes. At the same time, grill the lime wedges until nicely grill-marked, 2 to 3 minutes per side. Remove to a platter or plates and serve with the remaining 1 cup sauce and the lime wedges for squeezing.

> ### KNOW-HOW: BUYING HALIBUT
>
> The largest flatfish in the sea, halibut has been known to live for more than forty years and weigh upward of 700 pounds. Fishermen call the biggest ones barn doors. But bigger means tougher. Pacific halibut, especially those from Alaska, tend to be firmer and chewier than Atlantic halibut, which have all but disappeared because of overfishing. When buying halibut fillets, look for pieces less than 1 inch thick for the most tender and delicate texture.

LEAN, FIRM FLAT FISH STEAKS

Lemon-Brined Halibut with Guajillo-Blueberry Salsa

MAKES 4 SERVINGS

The largest flatfish in the sea, halibut has been known to live for more than forty years and weigh upwards of 700 pounds. Fishermen call the biggest ones barn doors, which a halibut resembles as its huge flat body rests on the ocean floor, waiting to close in on small fish, squid, and octopus. Cooked halibut has snow-white flesh with extra-large, satiny smooth flakes. This fish is so big that it can be cut into roasts and loins in addition to steaks and fillets. You may also find halibut cheeks from time to time. Brining the fish keeps it extra-moist on the grill, and pairing it with a puree of rehydrated guajillo chiles and fresh blueberries brings depth to its slightly sweet flavor, adding a little earthiness, a little smoke, and a touch of tartness. If you like, put the lemon wedges directly on the grill to char them a bit before serving.

INGREDIENTS:

1¼ cups Lemon-Oregano Brine (page 34)

4 halibut steaks (6 to 8 ounces each)

Guajillo-Blueberry Salsa:

2 ounces dried guajillo chiles (8 to 10), stemmed, split open, and seeded

3 garlic cloves, unpeeled

½ teaspoon dried oregano leaves

⅛ teaspoon ground cumin

⅛ teaspoon ground black pepper

Pinch of ground cinnamon

1¾ cups fish broth or chicken broth

1 tablespoon olive oil

½ to 1 teaspoon sugar

½ teaspoon kosher salt

¾ cup blueberries

1 tablespoon olive oil

2 teaspoons chopped fresh oregano

4 lemon wedges

DIRECTIONS:

Put the brine and halibut in a 1-gallon zipper-lock bag. Press out the air, seal, and refrigerate for 1 to 2 hours.

For the salsa: Light a grill for direct medium heat, about 400°F (see page 12). Open the seeded chiles and put them flat on the grill. Press down with a spatula and toast until fragrant and nicely grill-marked, about 30 seconds to 1 minute per side. Transfer the toasted chiles to a bowl and cover with hot water. Let soak until soft and pliable, about 30 minutes.

While the chiles are toasting, add the unpeeled garlic cloves to the grill and cook until the skins are blackened all over, 10 to 15 minutes. Remove and let cool, and then peel.

Drain the soaked chiles and discard the water. Transfer to a blender along with the garlic, oregano, cumin, black pepper, cinnamon, and ¾ cup of the broth. Blend until smooth, and then press the mixture through a medium-mesh strainer into a bowl.

Heat the oil in a medium saucepan over medium-high heat. Add the chile mixture and simmer until reduced by about one-third, 6 to 7 minutes. Add the remaining 1 cup broth and reduce the heat to low. Partially cover and simmer, stirring now and then, until the flavors blend and the salsa thickens slightly yet remains pourable, about 40 minutes. Stir in ½ teaspoon of the sugar, the salt, and blueberries and reduce heat to keep warm. Taste and stir in additional sugar if necessary.

Heat the grill for direct medium-high heat, about 450°F (see page 12). Pat the halibut dry and let rest for 15 minutes. Rub the olive oil all over the halibut.

Brush the grill grate and coat with oil. Grill the halibut directly over the heat for 4 to 5 minutes. Carefully flip and grill until the fish looks opaque on the surface, but is still filmy and moist in the center (about 130°F on an instant-read thermometer), 3 to 5 minutes. Remove to a platter or plates and garnish with the oregano. Serve with the salsa and lemon wedges for squeezing.

11

CRUSTACEANS & MOLLUSKS

Crab, lobster, shrimp, clams, mussels, oysters, scallops, squid, octopus, and cuttlefish rank among the world's favorite seafood. They're so popular that the continual harvest of wild seafood like shrimp has endangered the survival of other marine life for a variety of reasons, including habitat destruction. The aquaculture industry has blossomed in the last century in response to the ever-increasing global demand for shellfish. But not all farmed shellfish gets an eco-friendly OK from seafood watch groups. Both wild and farmed shellfish have their advantages and disadvantages.

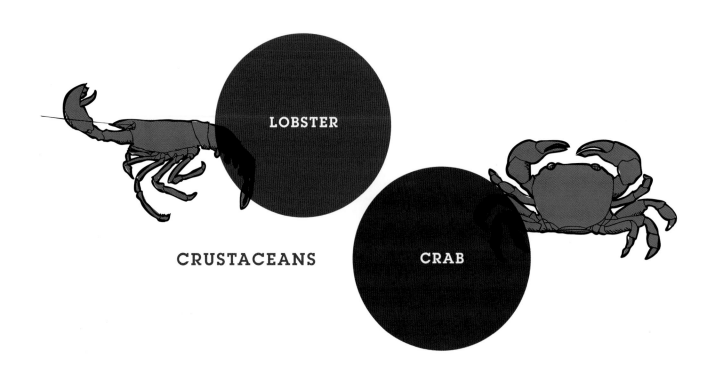

CRUSTACEANS

LOBSTER

CRAB

MOLLUSKS

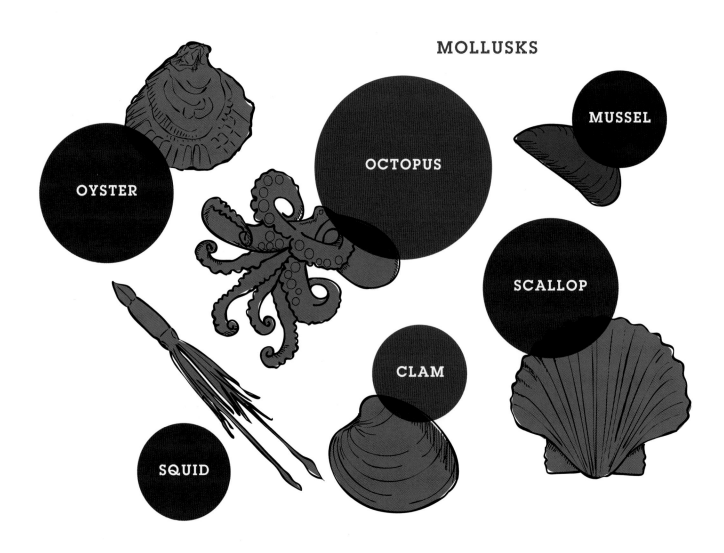

OYSTER

OCTOPUS

MUSSEL

SCALLOP

CLAM

SQUID

CRUSTACEANS AND MOLLUSKS

INGREDIENT	CLASSIFICATION	HOW TO GRILL	SUBSTITUTIONS
SOFT-SHELL CRAB	Crustacean	Direct, medium-high heat	---
WHOLE BLUE CRAB	Crustacean	Direct, medium-high heat	Dungeness crab
WHOLE DUNGENESS CRAB	Crustacean	Indirect, medium-high heat	Blue crab
KING CRAB LEGS	Crustacean	Direct, medium heat	Snow crab
SNOW CRAB (QUEEN CRAB)	Crustacean	Direct, medium-high heat	King crab
CRABMEAT	Crustacean	Direct, medium heat	---
CRAYFISH TAIL (CRAWFISH; CRAWDAD)	Crustacean	Direct, medium-high to high heat	Prawns, shrimp, small lobster tail
LOBSTER TAIL	Crustacean	Direct, medium heat	Crayfish tails, prawns
WHOLE LOBSTER	Crustacean	Direct, medium heat	Whole crayfish
SHRIMP (PRAWN)	Crustacean	Direct, medium-high heat	Crayfish tails
LITTLENECK CLAMS (SMALL HARD CLAMS)	Bivalve mollusk	Direct, medium-low to medium heat	Mussels
MUSSELS	Bivalve mollusk	Direct, medium-low to medium heat	Littleneck clams
OYSTERS	Bivalve mollusk	Direct, medium-low to medium heat	Cherrystone clams
SCALLOPS	Bivalve mollusk	Direct, high heat	Shrimp, crayfish tails
ABALONE STEAK	Gastropod mollusk	Direct, high heat	Conch
CONCH STEAK	Gastropod mollusk	Bilevel, medium-high/ medium-low heat	Abalone
OCTOPUS	Cephalopod mollusk	Direct, medium-high heat	Squid, cuttlefish
SQUID (CALAMARI)	Cephalopod mollusk	Direct, medium-high heat	Octopus, cuttlefish

Wild vs. Farmed

Managing the vitality of our oceans is complicated. Every country and region has different levels of regulation. Some countries harvest wild shellfish indiscriminately, destroying coral reefs and endangering marine life. Others strictly regulate harvest months and limit total catch to ensure the continued abundance of seafood from our oceans. For instance, in the 1980s, sea scallops fished from North American waters were endangered from overfishing, but careful management has replenished wild stocks and U.S. sea scallops are now considered abundant.

Similar concerns about other shellfish have been a boon to the aquaculture industry. Farmed seafood now accounts for more than 40 percent of the world's supply. Although it accounts for a small amount of the current U.S. supply of all shrimp, shrimp farmed in the United States come from well-managed aquaculture operations with minimal environmental impacts such as water pollution. Farmed bivalves like clams, mussels, and oysters make a low environmental impact and can even improve water quality since filter feeders help to clean the water.

With all these variables, trying to make wise shellfish choices can be confusing. The United States Department of Agriculture (USDA) has stepped in and now requires that all seafood carry a label stating whether it is wild-caught or farm-raised and identifying its country of origin.

Crustaceans

Crustaceans and mollusks are the two major families of edible shellfish. Crustaceans include crab, lobster, crayfish, and shrimp. They have a hard shell, which they periodically outgrow, a process called molting, during which the animal forms a tough outer cuticle over its body, crawls from its shell, and pumps itself up with water equaling nearly twice its original body weight. The cuticle slowly mineralizes and hardens, forming a new shell with enough room for growth. During molting the flesh of wild crustaceans becomes inedible, except for soft-shell crabs, which are removed from the water as soon as they are about to shed their shells. Crustaceans are also highly perishable, spoiling within hours of death. That's why they are mostly sold alive or cooked. Most shrimp are frozen at sea, and then thawed for sale at markets. When buying live lobsters and crabs, make sure they are active with a clean, fresh scent and no ammonia odor.

Mollusks—Bivalves, Gastropods, and Cephalopods

Clams, mussels, oysters, and scallops are bivalves enclosed in a pair of calcified shells. The part we eat differs slightly in each bivalve. All bivalves consist of a "foot" to secure them and adductor muscles to open and close their shell.

The foot is the main edible part of clams, as it is for mussels, but mussels attach their feet to rocks or ropes, with the help of fibrous hairs called the beard, which must be removed before cooking. Oysters also attach themselves to rocks, but their edible part is called a mantle instead of a foot.

Scallops neither burrow nor attach themselves to rocks. They rest on the ocean floor, using their adductor muscles to rapidly open and close their fan-shaped shells, which propels them away from predators. The large, tender portion of the scallop's adductor muscle is the part that we eat.

Gastropod mollusks like abalone and conch have a single shell, called the univalve, and a wide, very muscular foot, which is the part that we eat. Abalone muscles are so strong that the meat is usually pounded to tenderize it before it is sold. Squid, octopus, and cuttlefish are cephalopod mollusks. "Cephalopod" literally means "head-foot"; the heads of these animals are attached to their feet, which take the form of tentacles. Instead of an outer shell, cephalopods have a softer, internal shell remnant called a pen, quill, cuttlebone, or beak. Strong muscles in their heads and tentacles contract and expand to propel themselves through the water. The head and tentacles of squid, octopus, and cuttlefish are entirely edible after the eyes, mouth, and inner organs are removed.

Shellfish Safety

Bivalve mollusks filter large volumes of water in search of food. For this reason, water quality affects bivalve quality. Clams, oysters, mussels, and scallops may be unsafe to eat if they have fed on toxic marine plankton and algae. To minimize health risks, many countries vigilantly monitor water quality for algae bloom such as red tide and test bivalves to ensure their safety, particularly if they will be eaten raw. Grilling offers additional protection, as most bacteria and parasites are killed at 140°F. Among bivalves, scallops are the safest to eat raw because their filtration mechanism is discarded during processing. We only eat the scallop's adductor muscles, where few toxins accumulate.

How to Grill Shellfish

With no internal skeleton, crustaceans and mollusks rely on their muscles for movement. As a result, their meat contains more of the connective tissue called collagen than finfish. The extra collagen makes clams, mussels, oysters, scallops, crab, crayfish, lobster, shrimp, squid, and octopus taste richer and more succulent than flounder, snapper, and other finfish. It also makes them trickier to grill because the connective tissue can shrink and toughen, giving the meat a rubbery texture.

For crustaceans, quick grilling is best. When held for too long at temperatures between 130 and 140°F, shrimp, crab, lobster, and crayfish can go from mouth-watering to mushy because of protein-digesting enzymes in the muscles. Whenever possible, grill them in the shell. Basting the shells with fat helps release fat-soluble compounds from the shell to the meat. The shell also helps protect the delicate meat from drying out over the fire. The main reason for removing the shell before grilling is to add a rub or other seasoning directly to the meat of the crustacean.

Clams, oysters, and other bivalve mollusks also taste best grilled in the shell to help retain their briny liquor and keep the meat moist and tender. Cook bivalves just until the shells open, removing each one from the heat as it's done. Older, tougher clams and mussels may take longer to cook than younger ones. Discard any bivalves that don't open because they have probably expired before cooking. When buying oysters and clams, keep in mind that they tend to have richer flavor in the cold winter months because they use up some of their energy to spawn in the summer months. But bivalves are more tender in the summer months, when they are growing. To rid clams of sand, scrub the shells and soak them for 1 hour in salty water, about ⅓ cup salt per gallon of water, along with 2 tablespoons cornmeal. They'll feed on the cornmeal and eject sand. For mussels, use scissors to snip the black hairs or beard from the shell.

As for abalone and conch, don't turn up your nose at the frozen product. These mollusks have very tough meat, and starting with a frozen product naturally tenderizes the meat because expanding ice crystals stretch and soften the tough cell walls.

Shell-less cephalopods like octopus, squid, and cuttlefish contain even more connective tissue than crustaceans and mollusks. They are best when quickly grilled over high, dry heat or slowly grill-braised with indirect, low heat. Anywhere in between and cephalopods will become tough and rubbery. As with all other foods, youth equals tenderness among cephalopods. Baby octopus can be grilled with no pre-tenderizing, but mature octopus is so tough that it's often tenderized by pounding or blanching in salted water several times. Starting with a frozen product will make mature octopus more tender due to the stretching effect of the freeze-thaw process.

Shrimp Counts

Shrimp are sized for sale according to the number of them in a pound. The higher the count, the smaller the shrimp. Since consumers judge by size, shrimp are also given market names like small and jumbo. Jumbo shrimp and larger are best for the grill.

Count Per Pound	Retail Name
Under 10 (U10)	Extra-colossal
10–15 (U15)	Colossal
16–20 (U20)	Extra-jumbo
21–25 (U25)	Jumbo
26–30 (U30)	Extra-large
36–40 (U40)	Medium-large
41–50 (U50)	Medium
51–60 (U60)	Small
61–70 (U70)	Extra-small (titi)

SOFT-SHELL CRAB

Grilled Lemon Soft-Shell Crabs with Herbed Tzatziki

MAKES 4 SERVINGS

Soft-shell crabs have just molted, or shed their shells, in order to grow new ones, which renders the outside of the crab soft enough to eat. Fresh soft-shells are only available from late spring through early fall, and demand is high. (They are also available frozen, but freezing can render the meat somewhat stringy in texture.) Unlike hard-shell blue crabs, soft-shells can be eaten whole and grilled directly over the heat from start to finish. Soaking them in briny lemon juice helps keep the crabmeat moist. A creamy Greek sauce provides some contrast with the crunch of the blistered surface.

INGREDIENTS:

8 live soft-shell crabs (about 5 ounces each), cleaned (see Know-How, below)

5 cups Lemon-Oregano Brine (page 34)

½ teaspoon red pepper flakes

¾ cup Herbed Tzatziki (page 40)

Cooking spray

4 lemon wedges

DIRECTIONS:

Put the cleaned crabs in a roasting pan just large enough to hold them. Add the brine and red pepper flakes, and then cover and refrigerate for 2 to 3 hours. Make the tzatziki and let stand as you fire up the grill.

Light a grill for direct medium-high heat, about 425°F (see page 12).

Pluck the crabs from the brine with tongs and stash them in a big bowl. Discard the brine. Coat the crabs generously all over with cooking spray. Brush the grill grate and coat with oil. Grill the crabs, upside down, directly over the heat until nicely grill-marked, 3 minutes. Flip and grill, right-side up, until nicely grill-marked, another 2 minutes.

Serve with the tzatziki and lemon wedges.

KNOW-HOW: CLEANING SOFT-SHELL CRABS

Store soft-shell crabs in the refrigerator, which will render them listless enough to clean. Put a crab on a plate or platter to catch the juices and use kitchen scissors to cut the eyes from the top shell, removing as little of the top shell as possible. Cut off the stiff part of the mouth on the beige underside, removing as little as possible of the more tender shell.

Lift and twist or cut off the apron on the underside. Male crabs have a T-shaped apron; females have more rounded aprons. Flip the crab right-side up, curl back one of the pointed sides of the top shell, and snip off the spongy, finger-shaped gills underneath. Repeat on the other side.

WHOLE BLUE CRABS

Coriander-Brined Blue Crabs on the Grill

MAKES 3 TO 4 SERVINGS

Live blue crab season runs from April through November, giving you plenty of time to enjoy these ocean beauties. We prefer to grill crabs in the shell, but the meat of small blue crabs can stick to the shells so much that picking them clean becomes a huge bother. If you want to cook them outside, grill-steaming makes a great alternative. Basically you just set a roasting pan on the grill, pour your brine or another flavored liquid into the pan, and add the crabs. The liquid will infuse the crabs with enticing aromas. Cumin and lime are some of our favorite flavors with blue crab.

INGREDIENTS:

12 live blue crabs

5 cups Coriander Brine (page 36)

2 tablespoons Shellfish Seasoning (page 32)

DIRECTIONS:

Put the crabs in a roasting pan just large enough to hold them. Add the brine, cover, and refrigerate for 2 to 3 hours.

Light a grill for direct high heat, about 500°F (see page 12).

Pluck the crabs from the brine with tongs and stash them in a big bowl in the refrigerator. Set a roasting rack in the roasting pan, or, if your pan is too nice for the grill, set the rack in a disposable aluminum pan. Pour in the brine. Put the pan directly over the heat, cover the grill if possible, and heat until the brine is steaming hot. Using tongs, place the crabs on the roasting rack; they should be well sedated from the chilling, but work quickly before any escape. Sprinkle with the seasoning, and then cover the pan tightly with heavy-duty aluminum foil (use grill mitts). Cover the grill and cook until the crabs turn bright orange, 25 to 30 minutes. Remove from the heat and pick the meat from the shells (see Know-How, at right).

KEEP IT SIMPLE:

Replace the shellfish seasoning with a purchased crab boil seasoning, such as Old Bay.

> ### KNOW-HOW: EATING BLUE CRABS
>
> Eating crab is wonderfully messy. Set the crabs out on newspapers or scrap paper, so when you're done, you can simply fold up the paper and toss the mess. To begin, unfold, twist off, and remove the flap, or apron, on the underside of the crab. Pull off the top shell and pull away the gills attached to the bottom shell. Pick the crabmeat from the body, discarding any bits of shell. Twist off the legs and claws, crack them with a small hammer or nutcracker, and suck or pick out the meat.

WHOLE DUNGENESS CRAB

Vine-Smoked Dungeness Crabs with Preserved Lemon Relish

MAKES 4 SERVINGS

Here's a technique used by grillers in the wine-growing regions of California: smoking shellfish over vine cuttings. The grape vines impart a gentle smoke, which perfectly matches the sweetness of the fish. If you don't live near any vineyards or wineries, buy some grapevine chips from a gourmet store such as Kalamazoo Gourmet (www.kalamazoogourmet.com). We use Dungeness crabs, the Pacific species first harvested near the small fishing village of Dungeness in Washington state. They're in season from December to August all along the West Coast and are widely available cooked, so that's what we call for here. If you're lucky enough to have fresh crabs, boil them first in salted water for 15 to 20 minutes. Grilling Dungeness crab in the shell makes for more flavor. We brush them with butter during grilling to help release fat-soluble flavor compounds from the shell.

INGREDIENTS:

A big handful of dried grapevine cuttings or grapevine chips, soaked in water for 1 hour

⅔ cup unsalted butter

⅓ cup olive oil

1 large garlic clove, minced

Grated zest and juice of 2 lemons

2 tablespoons chopped fresh flat-leaf parsley

4 cooked Dungeness crabs (1½ to 2 pounds each), cleaned and cracked (see Know-How, below)

2 cups Preserved Lemon Relish (page 41)

DIRECTIONS:

Light a grill for indirect medium-high heat, about 375°F, with smoke (see pages 14 and 16).

Melt the butter with the olive oil in a small saucepan over medium heat. Add the garlic and cook for 1 minute. Remove from the heat and stir in the lemon zest and juice and parsley. Keep warm. Drain the cuttings or chips and add them to the grill. When you see smoke, brush the grill grate and coat with oil. Put the cracked crabs on the grill, right-side up, away from the heat and brush all over with the butter mixture. Cover and cook for 3 to 4 minutes. Baste again with the butter mixture, flip the crabs, cover, and cook until the crabs are heated through, another 8 to 10 minutes, brushing often with the butter mixture.

Remove to a platter and serve with the remaining butter mixture and the relish.

> **KNOW-HOW:**
> **CLEANING AND CRACKING DUNGENESS CRABS**
>
> Unfold, twist off, and remove the flap, or apron, on the underside of the crab. Pull off the top shell and pull away the spongy gills attached to the bottom shell. Crack off and discard the front mouth parts of the crab and then rinse the crab clean. Hold the crab upside down in both hands and crack in half along the center line.

KING CRAB LEGS

Grilled King Crab Legs with Ginger-Lime Butter

MAKES 4 SERVINGS

King crab legs come precooked, so a brief reheating is all they need. Steaming them makes the crab taste rather waterlogged, so we prefer to toss the legs over dry grill heat for a few minutes. We like to cut the legs in half lengthwise clear through the shell, and then grill them, meat-side up. This method simplifies the crab picking and allows you to flavor the meat. We serve these kings with salmon roe salsa for briny crunch between bites of the succulent crabmeat.

INGREDIENTS:

¾ cup unsalted butter

1 small garlic clove, minced

1 tablespoon grated fresh ginger

Grated zest and juice of ½ lime

3½ to 4 pounds Alaskan king crab legs, thawed in the refrigerator if frozen

10 to 12 fresh lime leaves (optional)

DIRECTIONS:

Light a grill for direct medium heat, about 375°F (see page 12).

Melt the butter in a small saucepan over medium heat. Add the garlic and ginger and cook for 1 minute. Remove from the heat and stir in the lime zest and juice.

Using a sharp, heavy knife or kitchen scissors, cut each crab leg in half lengthwise through the shell. If using the lime leaves, tear any large ones in half and tuck the pieces inside the shells under the meat in several places. Brush the meat with some of the ginger-lime butter.

Brush the grill grate and coat with oil. Grill the crab legs, meat-side up, directly over the heat just until warm to the touch, 2 to 3 minutes. Avoid overcooking, or the meat will dry out.

Remove to a platter and serve with the remaining ginger-lime butter.

CRAWFISH TAIL

Crawfish and Foie Gras Brochettes with Creole Butter

MAKES 6 SERVINGS

In Louisiana, steamed or boiled whole crawfish are as popular as blue crabs in Maryland. When you can't get them whole, frozen crawfish tails are the next best thing. They come peeled and need only to be thawed and briefly grill-marked. They also benefit from rich accompaniments, and we've found that foie gras is just the thing. For this recipe, it's imperative to use cold, firm grade A foie gras; otherwise, the foie will melt into the fire. The crawfish tails should be at room temperature.

INGREDIENTS:

8 large bamboo or metal skewers

1 pound cold duck foie gras

⅔ cup unsalted butter, melted

4 teaspoons Creole Rub (page 27)

8 ounces peeled crawfish tails, thawed if frozen, and brought to room temperature

continued

DIRECTIONS:

If you are grilling with bamboo skewers, soak them in water for at least 30 minutes. Light a grill for direct high heat, about 475°F (see page 12).

Cut the foie gras into 1-inch cubes and refrigerate for 30 minutes. Combine ¼ cup of the melted butter and 1 teaspoon of the rub in a medium bowl. Add the thawed crawfish tails, toss to coat, and let stand at room temperature for 30 minutes. Combine the remaining melted butter with another 1 teaspoon of the rub and keep warm over low heat.

Sprinkle the remaining 2 teaspoons rub over the cold foie gras cubes and thread the foie gras and crawfish on skewers, alternating between them.

Brush the grill grate and coat with oil. Grill the brochettes directly over the heat just until nicely grill-marked, about 30 to 45 seconds.

Remove to plates and serve with the warm Creole butter.

LOBSTER TAIL

Sweet Soy Lobster Tail with Grilled Tropical Fruit

MAKES 4 SERVINGS

You'd be hard pressed to find a simpler and better looking grilled meal than lobster tail. When you split the tails lengthwise, you see both bright red shell and snow white meat. We glaze the meat with a combination of soy sauce, molasses, toasted sesame oil, rice vinegar, and Chinese five-spice powder. The same sweet mixture tastes fabulous on grilled pineapple, bananas, and mango, which relax alongside the lobster like a Hawaiian sunset.

INGREDIENTS:

4 bamboo or
metal skewers

½ golden pineapple, peeled, cored and cut into 1½-inch wedges

2 bananas, peeled and cut crosswise into eight 1½-inch pieces

1 mango, peeled, pitted, and cut into 1½-inch cubes

4 rock lobster or large Maine lobster tails (8 to 10 ounces each), thawed if frozen

⅓ cup Sweet Soy Glaze (page 49)

½ cup butter, melted

4 lime wedges

DIRECTIONS:

If you are grilling with bamboo skewers, soak them in water for at least 30 minutes. Light a grill for direct medium heat, about 350°F (see page 12).

Alternately thread the pineapple, banana, and mango pieces on the skewers, using about 2 pieces of each fruit per skewer (skewer the banana pieces through the rounded edge so that the flat sides will be grilled). Reserve any remaining fruit for another use.

Butterfly the lobster tails by splitting each tail lengthwise through the rounded top shell and through the meat, leaving the flat bottom shell intact. If the shell is very hard, use kitchen shears to cut through the rounded shell and a knife to cut through the meat.

Gently open the tail to expose the meat.

Brush the soy glaze lightly over the fruit skewers and the lobster meat. Brush the grill grate and coat with oil. Put the lobster tails, meat-side down, directly over the heat and grill until nicely grill-marked, 3 to 4 minutes. Press the tails onto the grill grate with a spatula or tongs to help sear the meat. Flip and grill until the meat is just firm and white, basting with the soy glaze, 5 to 7 minutes more. Meanwhile grill the fruit skewers alongside the lobster until nicely grill-marked, about 3 to 4 minutes per side.

Serve with the melted butter and lime wedges for squeezing.

Wood-Grilled Creole Lobster

MAKES 4 SERVINGS

Shellfish decompose quickly after dying, so whole lobster must be cooked within minutes of killing them. You can either buy them cooked or do the deed yourself. It's easiest to boil live lobsters, but that steams them and negates the flavor of the grill. Instead, follow the directions below for cooking a split lobster completely on the grill. Or, if you really want to avoid cutting the live lobster with a knife, boil the lobsters in a large pot of salted water just until they are bright red, split them in half lengthwise, then proceed with the rest of the recipe. We sprinkle spicy Cajun seasonings on the meat and serve it alongside a butter dip scented with fresh garlic, lemon, parsley, and thyme. The flavors combine perfectly with the subtle smoke of hardwood charcoal. We use a charcoal grill for this recipe, but if you must use a gas grill, soak some wood chips, add them to the grill (see page 16), and then start grilling when you begin to see smoke

INGREDIENTS:

4 live lobsters (about 1 pound each)

⅓ cup Creole Rub (page 27)

⅓ cup Seafood Butter (page 44), warmed if made in advance

3 tablespoons olive oil

Grated zest and juice of ½ lemon

DIRECTIONS:

Light a charcoal grill for indirect medium heat, about 350°F, using hardwood charcoal (see page 14).

Split the lobsters (see Know-How, right), saving the tomalley and roe (if present) in a saucepan. Drain any liquid that has collected on the lobster plate into the pan holding the tomalley. Cook over medium-low heat just until the lobster drippings turn white and the tomalley brightens, about 1 minute. Let cool.

Mix 2 tablespoons of the rub and all of the seafood butter into the cooled tomalley mixture. Mix the olive oil with the remaining rub and spoon the mixture over the exposed lobster meat (and into the claws as much as possible).

Brush the grill grate and coat with oil. Put the lobsters, cut-sides down, on the grill directly over the heat. Cover and grill for about 4 minutes, until the edges start to brown.

Flip the lobsters over and move them away from the heat, cover, and grill until the meat just turns opaque (140°F on an instant-read thermometer), about 10 minutes.

Remove the lobsters to a large serving platter. Sprinkle the lemon zest and juice over the lobster meat, and place a spoonful of the seafood butter in the cavity of each lobster half for dipping.

KNOW-HOW: SPLITTING A LOBSTER

Refrigerate the lobster for 30 minutes to help sedate it. Hold the lobster by its back shell and place it on its belly on a rimmed sheet pan. Uncurl the tail and lay it out flat. Insert a sharp knife just behind the head and cut the shell of the thorax (its back) in half lengthwise, killing the lobster. Turn the lobster onto its back and insert the knife into the abdomen right where the tail meets the thorax, with the edge of the blade facing the head.

In one motion, bring the knife down the center line of the body, splitting the front end of the lobster in half. Now reverse directions and split the back end the same way. Separate the two halves by pressing lightly on them. Remove and discard the sand sac from behind the head. Remove the light green tomalley from the body cavity and, if present, the long sac of dark green roe that runs down the back of the lobster. Put them in a small skillet or saucepan to flavor a sauce (or discard). Crack the claws by whacking them across the crest of their bulge with the back of a heavy knife. Put the lobster halves on a plate to catch their juices.

PRAWNS

Pesto-Stuffed Prawns with Guacamole Vinaigrette

MAKES 4 SERVINGS

If you happen to need an emerald-green appetizer for St. Patrick's Day, look no further. It's not very Irish, but it is magically delicious. Prawns (essentially big shrimp—how's that for an oxymoron!) are slit along the backs and stuffed with cilantro pesto and then grilled and drizzled with a saucy guacamole. You shouldn't need skewers or a grill tray for this dish, but if your prawns are on the small side, either one will keep the crustaceans from falling into the flames.

INGREDIENTS:

12 prawns or colossal (10–15 count) shrimp (about 1 pound), peeled and deveined

⅓ cup Cilantro Pesto (page 43)

3 tablespoons olive oil

Guacamole Vinaigrette:

2 Hass avocados, pitted and peeled

Juice of 1 large lime

1 tomato, seeded and finely chopped

1 jalapeño chile pepper, seeded and finely chopped

3 tablespoons chopped shallot

1 small garlic clove, minced

3 tablespoons chopped fresh cilantro

¾ teaspoon coarse salt

Pinch of ground black pepper

½ cup extra-virgin olive oil

DIRECTIONS:

Light a grill for direct medium-high heat, about 425°F (see page 12).

Slit the prawns along their backs to open up the center crevice slightly. Fill the opening in each prawn with about ½ to 1 teaspoon pesto. Coat the stuffed prawns all over with the olive oil.

For the guacamole vinaigrette: Mash the avocado in a medium bowl with a fork. Stir in the remaining ingredients. Set aside.

Brush the grill grate and coat with oil. Grill the prawns directly over the heat until firm and nicely grill-marked, about 4 minutes per side.

Remove to plates and drizzle with the guacamole vinaigrette.

SHRIMP

Grilled Paella with Hazelnut Picada

MAKES 6 SERVINGS

We have more recipes for shrimp than for any other shellfish in this book. But grilled paella is just too cool to pass up. Shrimp, chicken, and smoky chorizo are briefly charred and then tossed in a paella pan or a skillet right on the grill with the usual paella partners: onions, garlic, saffron, tomatoes, peas, and rice. After everything gets acquainted, we introduce some Spanish olives and a crumble of lemon-scented hazelnuts and parsley.

INGREDIENTS:

1 pound boneless, skinless chicken (thighs and/or breasts)

1 pound jumbo (21–25 count) shrimp, peeled and deveined

2 tablespoons olive oil

Coarse salt and ground black pepper

4 ounces Spanish chorizo sausage

1 cup diced red onion (small dice)

1 tablespoon finely chopped garlic

1 tablespoon tomato paste

1 bay leaf

1 teaspoon dried rubbed sage

2 cups medium-grain or short-grain rice

1 teaspoon saffron threads

¼ teaspoon red pepper flakes

4 cups chicken, seafood, or vegetable broth

2 cups drained canned diced tomatoes

¾ cup green peas, fresh or thawed

½ cup finely chopped fresh flat-leaf parsley

⅔ cup Hazelnut Picada (page 47)

2 lemons, each cut into 6 wedges

24 medium green olives, preferably manzanilla

DIRECTIONS:

Light a grill for indirect medium-high heat, 350 to 375°F (see page 14).

Coat the chicken and shrimp with a thin film of olive oil and season with salt and pepper. Brush the grill grate and coat with oil. Grill the chicken, shrimp, and chorizo directly over the fire just long enough to brown their surfaces, 2 to 3 minutes per side. Set the shrimp aside. Cool the chicken and chorizo slightly and cut into bite-size pieces; set aside.

Place a large paella pan, deep skillet, or brazier directly over the heat. Add the remaining olive oil and heat until smoking. Add the onion and stir until tender and barely browned (about 2 minutes). Add the garlic and cook 10 seconds. Stir in the tomato paste, bay leaf, and sage and cook 20 seconds. Move the pan so that it is not directly over the fire.

Stir in the rice, saffron, ½ teaspoon ground black pepper, and the red pepper flakes. Season with salt. Cook until aromatic, stirring constantly for about 2 minutes. Add the broth, tomatoes, and reserved chorizo and chicken. Cover the grill and cook, undisturbed, until most of the liquid has been absorbed, about 25 minutes. The rice will still be a little chewy.

Add the shrimp and peas on top of the rice; do not stir. Cover with foil, cover the grill, and cook until the rice is tender and all of the liquid has been absorbed, 4 to 5 minutes.

Remove from the grill and let rest for 5 to 10 minutes. Remove the bay leaf, sprinkle with the parsley, and fluff with a fork. Drizzle half the hazelnut picada over the top and garnish with the lemon wedges and olives. Serve the remaining picada on the side.

SHRIMP

Charred Lemon-Garlic Shrimp with Dukkah

MAKES 4 SERVINGS

Dukkah is an enchanting spice mix from Egypt, featuring toasted and ground sesame seeds, coriander, cumin, and hazelnuts. It makes a fantastic crust for grilled shrimp, especially after the shrimp soak in a bath of lemon juice, garlic, olive oil, and fresh herbs, such as dill, tarragon, and parsley. The marinade includes enough lemon juice to start coagulating and whitening the protein near the surface of the shrimp. Not to worry; just keep the marinating time under 2 hours. Any longer than that, and you may end up with ceviche! Couscous makes a nice side dish here.

INGREDIENTS:

4 garlic cloves, crushed or pressed with a garlic press

Grated zest of 1 lemon

Juice of 2 lemons

½ cup dry white wine

¾ cup olive oil

2 tablespoons chopped fresh herbs

½ teaspoon coarse salt

1 pound extra-large (26–30 count) shrimp, peeled and deveined

½ cup Dukkah (page 28)

1 cup Preserved Lemon Yogurt (page 40)

DIRECTIONS:

Combine the garlic, lemon zest and juice, white wine, olive oil, herbs, and salt in a 1-gallon zipper-lock bag. Add the shrimp, press out the air, seal, and refrigerate for 1 to 2 hours.

Remove the shrimp from the marinade and thread on skewers. Discard the marinade. Sprinkle all over with the dukkah and let stand at room temperature for 30 minutes.

Light a grill for direct medium-high heat, about 450°F (see page 12). Brush the grill grate and coat with oil. Grill the shrimp directly over the heat until firm and charred in a few places, 1 to 2 minutes per side.

Remove to a platter or plates and serve with the preserved lemon yogurt.

SHRIMP

Smoky Coconut Shrimp with Tamarind–Peanut Butter Sauce

MAKES 4 SERVINGS

If you love coconut, you'll find it here in the marinade, spice rub, and sauce for grilled shrimp. Coconut milk spiked with rum, lime, garlic, ginger, and cilantro bathes the shrimp in tropical flavors. Then a coarse mixture of shredded coconut, smoked paprika, ground chipotle chile, coriander, and cinnamon create a shaggy crust. The sauce lends some richness by combining coconut milk with creamy peanut butter.

INGREDIENTS:

4 long bamboo or metal skewers

1½ cups Smoky Coconut Marinade (page 38)

1 pound extra-large (26–30 count) shrimp, peeled and deveined

1¼ cups Smoky Coconut Rub (page 31)

1 large egg white

Cooking spray

1 cup Tamarind–Peanut Butter Sauce (page 40)

DIRECTIONS:

Combine the marinade and shrimp in a 1-gallon zipper-lock bag. Press out the air, seal, and refrigerate for 2 hours.

If you are grilling with bamboo skewers, soak them in water for at least 30 minutes. Light a grill for direct medium-high heat, about 425°F (see page 12).

Put the spice rub in a wide shallow bowl. Beat the egg white in another wide shallow bowl until frothy. Remove the shrimp from the marinade and toss in the egg white. Press the shrimp into the spice rub to coat all over, and then thread onto skewers. Sprinkle any remaining rub over the shrimp and coat liberally with cooking spray.

Brush the grill grate and coat with oil. Grill the shrimp directly over the heat until the shrimp are just firm and opaque, 2 to 3 minutes per side. It's okay if the coconut rub chars slightly on the edges (and some of the rub may fall into the fire). Put the peanut sauce in a microwaveable bowl and heat briefly until warm, about 30 to 90 seconds. Serve with the shrimp.

LITTLENECK CLAMS

Smoked Clams Marinara

MAKES 4 SERVINGS

In this fired-up version of the classic, smoky aromas come from fire-roasted tomatoes, liquid smoke, and the fragrance of burning wood chips.

INGREDIENTS:

2 cups wood chips, such as oak, alder, apple, or cherry, soaked in water for 30 minutes

¼ cup olive oil

1 small onion, finely chopped

3 large garlic cloves, minced

Two 15-ounce cans diced fire-roasted tomatoes, 1 drained and 1 with juice

2 canned anchovy fillets (optional)

5 teaspoons liquid smoke

¼ teaspoon sugar

3 tablespoons chopped fresh basil

Coarse salt and ground black pepper

¾ cup dry white wine

3 dozen littleneck clams, scrubbed

1 tablespoon liquid smoke

12 ounces dried linguine

DIRECTIONS:

Heat the oil in a large skillet over medium heat. Add the onion and garlic and cook until soft and lightly browned, 4 minutes. Add the can of tomatoes with the juice and the one without juice. Add the anchovies, 2 teaspoons of the liquid smoke, the sugar, and 2 tablespoons of the herbs and bring to a boil. Reduce the heat to medium-low and cook until the tomatoes begin to break down, 10 to 15 minutes, crushing the tomatoes with a wooden spoon. Season with salt and pepper and the remaining 1 tablespoon herbs.

Light a grill for direct medium-low heat, about 325°F, with smoke (see pages 12 and 16). Puree the marinara and wine in a blender, then heat in a large saucepan over medium heat for 5 minutes. Pour half the mixture into a disposable aluminum pan just large enough to hold the clams in a single layer. Add the clams.

Add the wood chips to the grill. When you see smoke, put the pan on the grill and close the lid. Cook until the clams open, spooning some of the sauce over the clams as they cook, about 30 minutes, which is about when the clams should open. Discard any clams that do not open.

Meanwhile, bring a large pot of salted water to a boil. Add the remaining tablespoon of liquid smoke and linguine and cook until the linguine is just tender, 8 to 10 minutes. Drain and toss with the marinara while still in the saucepan. Divide among 4 plates and top with the opened clams and marinara from the clam pan.

MUSSELS

Wasabi-Drizzled Mussels Grilled with Green Tea Fumes

MAKES 4 SERVINGS

Mussels, especially New Zealand green mussels, pair remarkably well with pungent wasabi and softly bitter green tea. To infuse the mussels with green tea aromas, we grill them over soaked green tea leaves, and then serve them with soy sauce and green tea ponzu. A drizzle of wasabi vinaigrette opens up the flavor profile. Most mussels available today are farmed on ropes, but some are harvested from sand. If yours are sandy, purge them of sand by soaking them in salted water for 1 to 2 hours.

INGREDIENTS:

½ cup loose green tea leaves, such as bancha or hojicha

1¼ cups Green Tea Ponzu Sauce (page 46)

¼ cup tamari or soy sauce

3 scallions (green and white parts), finely chopped

1 tablespoon grated fresh ginger

Grated zest and juice of 1 large lemon

Grated zest and juice of 1 small lime

½ ounce kombu (dried kelp), torn into pieces

4 pounds mussels, debearded and scrubbed

2 teaspoons wasabi paste

DIRECTIONS:

Soak the tea leaves in cold water for 30 minutes.

Light a grill for direct medium heat, about 350°F, with smoke (see pages 12 and 16). Combine the ponzu sauce, tamari, scallions, ginger, lemon zest and juice, lime zest and juice, and kombu in a disposable aluminum pan large enough to hold the mussels in a single layer (or nearly single). Add the mussels to the pan.

Add the soaked tea leaves to the grill as you would wood chips. Put the pan of mussels directly over the heat, close the lid, and cook until the mussels open, 15 to 20 minutes, spooning the liquid over the mussels a few times.

Pluck the mussels from the liquid and transfer them to shallow bowls, discarding any mussels that do not open. Strain the liquid through cheesecloth into another bowl. Pour 1 cup of the strained liquid into a bowl and stir in the wasabi paste. Pour the remaining strained liquid over the mussels. Drizzle with the wasabi mixture and serve.

KNOW-HOW: DEBEARDING MUSSELS

Grasp the tuft of "hair" protruding from the opening in the mussel shell between your thumb and first finger. Gently pull until you see a little of the mussel flesh ease from the shell. Give a quick tug and snap the beard off where it attaches to the mussel meat.

Oysters Grilled with Roasted Garlic Butter and Romano

MAKES 6 SERVINGS

The International Association of Culinary Professionals holds an annual conference, and New Orleans was the site of the 2008 meeting. On Iberville Street, the Acme Oyster House is something of a tourist trap, but it's justly famous for its char-grilled oysters. After devouring several bar trays full, we went home and started experimenting. Grill-roasted garlic, parsley, and Romano cheese give the oysters some Italian aromas, but the Creole rub is pure New Orleans. Serve the oysters with lemon wedges for squeezing and French bread for sopping up the extra sauce. When shucking the oysters, make sure the shell edges are clean, with no bits of broken shell. Even a bit of crunch would ruin the creamy luxury of the warm oysters oozing with butter and cheese.

INGREDIENTS:

1 cup (2 sticks) unsalted butter, cut into pieces

2 teaspoons Creole Rub (page 27)

1 tablespoon fresh lemon juice

2 tablespoons chopped fresh flat-leaf parsley

¼ cup Grill-Roasted Garlic (page 33), mashed

2 dozen large oysters, shucked

1½ cups grated Romano cheese

4 lemon wedges

DIRECTIONS:

Combine the butter, Creole rub, lemon juice, parsley, and mashed roasted garlic in a small saucepan. Cook over medium heat until the butter is no longer foaming and has started to brown slightly, about 5 minutes.

Light the grill for direct medium heat, about 375°F (see page 12). Brush and oil the grill grate. Place the oysters directly on the grate and top each with about 2 teaspoons of the sauce and 1 tablespoon of the cheese. Grill until the oyster shells char and the cheese melts and browns around the edges, about 8 to 10 minutes.

Remove the oysters to a heat-proof platter or tray. Drizzle another teaspoon of the sauce over each oyster and serve hot with the lemon wedges for squeezing.

KNOW-HOW: SHUCKING OYSTERS

To make shucking easier, freeze the oysters for 20 minutes to numb their muscles. Press a strong, dull knife between the hinged ends of the shells to pop the shells apart. Run the knife along the inside of the top shell to cut the meat from the shell, and then remove the top shell. Run the knife under the oyster to detach it from the bottom shell, but leave the oyster nestled in the shell. The liquor from fresh oysters should be clear. Cloudiness indicates an older bivalve whose tissues have begun to break down.

Scallop and Bacon Brochettes with Pineapple-Rum Glaze

MAKES 4 SERVINGS

Cut-rate scallops are soaked in sodium tripolyphosphate (STP), which whitens them and causes them to absorb water. As they cook, soaked scallops shed their excess water and steam, which makes it impossible to sear them or develop a rich browned crust. On the grill, "dry" scallops that have not been soaked work best. They may be pink, gray, or beige in color. (Avoid pure white scallops that clump together, indicating they've been soaked.) Marinated in coconut milk, wrapped in bacon, and glazed with rum and pineapple juice, these scallops will take you to the islands. Put a piña colada in one hand and some bacon-wrapped scallops in the other. Sip. Eat. Repeat.

INGREDIENTS:

4 bamboo or
metal skewers

1¼ pounds large, wild-caught sea scallops
(about 16 scallops)

1½ cups Coconut-Thyme Marinade
(page 38)

8 strips bacon, preferably applewood-
smoked

⅔ cup Pineapple-Rum Glaze (page 51)

DIRECTIONS:

Pull off each scallop's white gristly tendon, if not already removed, and rinse. Combine the scallops with the marinade in a 1-gallon zipper-lock bag. Press out the air, seal, and refrigerate for 1 hour.

If you are grilling with bamboo skewers, soak them in water for at least 30 minutes. Cut the bacon in half crosswise. Remove the scallops from the marinade, pat dry, and wrap a half-slice of bacon around each one so that it looks like a little drum. Thread onto skewers through the bacon ends to secure, allowing about 4 scallops per skewer. Let stand while you heat the grill and make the glaze.

Light a grill for direct high heat, about 500°F (see page 12). Brush the grill grate and coat with oil.

Grill the brochettes directly over the heat until nicely grill-marked and springy to the touch but still a bit soft in the center, about 3 minutes per side. Brush the cooked sides often with the glaze during grilling and serve with any remaining glaze.

SCALLOPS

Pepper and Salt Block Scallops with Grapefruit Mojo

MAKES 4 SERVINGS

Mojo (MO-ho) is ubiquitous in Cuba. The garlicky citrus sauce shows up on all kinds of foods. It's traditionally made with sour orange juice, which is hard to come by. We use grapefruit juice and lime juice for a slightly different flavor, and we sear the scallops on a block of salt right on the grill. Salt blocks are the coolest thing to happen to grills since cedar planks. And they work in a similar way. Heat up the salt block directly over the grill, then sear your food right on the hot block. It cooks and seasons in one step! Our favorite is a Himalayan pink salt block, which we like to get from The Meadow, owned by salt fanatic and self-described "selmelier" Mark Bitterman (see Sources on page 400 and the Know-How, below, for more tips on salt blocks).

INGREDIENTS:

1 large salt block, at least 1½ inches thick

½ cup extra-virgin olive oil

6 garlic cloves, minced

½ teaspoon ground cumin

¾ cup fresh red or pink grapefruit juice

Juice of 1 lime

½ teaspoon dried oregano leaves

1 teaspoon coarse salt

¾ teaspoon ground black pepper

2 tablespoons chopped fresh cilantro

1¼ pounds large wild-caught sea scallops (about 16 scallops)

2 tablespoons olive oil

DIRECTIONS:

Light a grill for bilevel high/low heat, about 500+/275°F (see page 13). Brush the grill grate and coat with oil. Heat the salt block directly on the grill grate over low heat for 15 minutes. Raise the heat to medium on a gas grill. On a charcoal or wood grill move the block halfway between the high- and low-heat areas and heat for another 15 minutes. Raise the heat to high on a gas grill or move the salt block over to the high-heat area on a charcoal or wood grill and heat for 15 to 20 minutes more.

Meanwhile, heat the extra-virgin olive oil in a small saucepan over medium heat. Add the garlic and cumin and cook until the garlic begins to color, 1 to 2 minutes. Stir in the grapefruit juice, lime juice, oregano, salt, and pepper. Simmer for 1 minute, then remove from the heat and let cool to room temperature. Stir in the cilantro. Pull the white gristly tendons from the scallops if not already removed. Rinse the scallops and pat dry. Coat the scallops with the olive oil and let stand at room temperature until the salt block is hot.

When the salt block is very hot (you should only be able to hold your hand above it for a few seconds), place the scallops on the hot block and sear until browned and springy to the touch, but still a little soft in the center, about 3 minutes per side. Work in batches if your salt block cannot comfortably fit all the scallops at once.

Remove to a platter or plates and serve with the mojo.

KNOW-HOW: CARING FOR SALT BLOCKS

Salt blocks will last for about a dozen grillings if heated carefully and cleaned well after each use. Heat the blocks gradually to prevent cracking. Start over low heat and, over a 30-minute period, move the block in two steps to high heat. After each use wipe the block clean of any debris with a plastic scrubbing pad, using warm water and gentle pressure. Blot the stone on a flat-weave towel to dry the surface. Each time the salt block is used and cleaned a thin film of salt will be washed away. As long as the block is at least 1½ inches thick, it can still be used for grilling.

Sicilian Grilled Baby Octopus

MAKES 4 SERVINGS

Among the ocean's most intelligent creatures, octopuses demonstrate problem-solving skills during scientific tests. It's a gifted animal that evades even our most concerted efforts to cook it. Often, the octopus ends up being as tough and inscrutable on the plate as it is in the ocean. The risk of toughening the meat is doubly great on the grill. We've found that best way to grill an octopus is to simmer it first until tender. You can simmer it up to 2 days ahead of grilling time and keep it refrigerated. It also helps to use young octopus, which has more tender meat than mature octopus. You can grill the cephalopod, head and all, but many prefer to serve only the tentacles. Either way, separate the head from the tentacles, then serve what you like. Both parts will marry well with the flavors of orange, lemon, mint, olives, and arugula in this Sicilian-style recipe. Most octopuses are sold cleaned and frozen, but if you have fresh octopus (lucky you!), see the Know-How below.

INGREDIENTS:

2½ pounds cleaned and frozen baby octopus

2 cups full-bodied red wine, such as Pinot Noir or Cabernet Sauvignon

1 small onion, sliced

1 teaspoon black peppercorns

½ teaspoon whole cloves

1 bay leaf

1 cup Sicilian Citrus Marinade (page 38)

¼ cup pitted and coarsely chopped Sicilian or Cerignola green olives

3 ounces baby arugula leaves

1 tablespoon chopped fresh mint

Coarse sea salt and freshly ground black pepper

DIRECTIONS:

Rinse the octopus, and then put in a soup pot with the wine and enough water to cover. Add the onion, peppercorns, cloves, and bay leaf. Bring to a boil over high heat, and then reduce the heat to medium-low, cover, and simmer gently until the octopus is tender enough for a knife to enter easily, 45 minutes to 1 hour. Drain the octopus and discard the liquid or strain and reserve for seafood stock or risotto. When the octopus is cool enough to handle, cut the tentacles away at the head.

Combine the octopus and marinade in a 1-gallon zipper-lock bag. Press out the air, seal the bag, and refrigerate for 2 to 3 hours.

Light a grill for direct medium-high heat, about 450°F (see page 12).

Remove the octopus from the marinade, pat dry, and let stand at room temperature for 20 minutes. Strain the marinade into a saucepan and bring to a simmer over medium heat. Add the olives and remove from the heat.

Brush the grill grate and coat with oil. Grill the octopus directly over the heat until nicely grill-marked, 3 to 4 minutes per side, pressing gently on the octopus to get a good sear.

Arrange the arugula on a platter or plates and top with the octopus. Spoon some of the warm sauce, including a good amount of olives, on each serving. Sprinkle with the mint, salt, and black pepper.

KNOW-HOW: CLEANING FRESH OCTOPUS

Insert your fingers into the body (the head), and turn inside out. Scrape away and discard the ink sac and other innards, and then rinse the body well. Turn the body right-side out, and remove the eyes and black mouth (beak), located at the center, where the tentacles meet the body. Scrub the tentacles very well with coarse salt, rinse, and repeat until the tentacles are very clean. The salt and scrubbing also helps to tenderize the octopus a little.

SQUID

Grilled Squid Salad

MAKES 4 SERVINGS

Salads are best made with your mind wide open. Almost anything can go in, and they're a good opportunity to try new flavor combinations. Squid makes a great salad; its relatively mild taste becomes amiably acquainted with all manner of ingredients. Here it pairs up with oranges, olives, and pine nuts for a Mediterranean flavor, and we toss in some avocado for richness. Orange vinaigrette made with walnut oil adds to the salad's sunny disposition.

INGREDIENTS:

1½ pounds cleaned small squid, bodies intact

2 tablespoons extra-virgin olive oil

¼ teaspoon salt

⅛ teaspoon ground black pepper

6 cups mesclun greens

2 shallots, thinly sliced

½ cup Orange Vinaigrette (page 41)

1 seedless orange, cut into supremes (see Know-How, below)

1 ripe avocado, pitted and cut into ½-inch cubes

⅓ cup pitted black Gaeta or kalamata olives, halved lengthwise

1 tablespoon pine nuts, toasted

Juice of 1 lemon

DIRECTIONS:

Cut the tips off the squid bodies to allow steam to escape. Toss the squid in a bowl with the oil, salt, and pepper and let stand for 15 minutes.

Light a grill for direct medium-high heat, about 425°F (see page 12). Brush the grill grate and coat with oil. Grill the squid directly over the heat until nicely grill-marked, about 2 to 3 minutes per side. For great grill marks, put a heavy weight, such as a cast-iron pan, on the squid as it grills. You can also use the pan for toasting the pine nuts right on the grill. Cut the grilled squid bodies into rings and leave the tentacles whole.

Toss the greens with the shallots and vinaigrette and arrange on plates. Scatter the orange supremes, avocado, olives, toasted pine nuts, and grilled squid over the greens.

Drizzle with the lemon juice.

KNOW-HOW: MAKING ORANGE SUPREMES

To cut an orange into supremes (membrane-free segments), trim off about ½ inch from the top and bottom of the orange—just enough to reveal the inner fruit. Stand the orange on a flat end and make several cuts from top to bottom all around the fruit, running your knife blade just beneath the white pith but not through the flesh. Remove the entire rind in strips and discard. Next remove one orange segment at a time by running the knife close to the membrane to release it (it's like sectioning a grapefruit). Discard the membrane.

Chapter **12**

VEGETABLES

Among all the foods that can be grilled, vegetables undergo the most delicious transformation. We're so used to eating them boiled, steamed, or sautéed, that tasting grilled vegetables can be a revelation. Beets, sliced thin and grilled directly over the heat, develop an almost candylike sweetness. Corn, grilled right in the husk, remains juicy, but with a more concentrated flavor, and the caramelized kernels pick up a hint of smoke.

Asparagus grills in less than 3 minutes; the spears char in spots and intensify in sweetness, balancing out their green, grassy aromas. While other cooking methods might express only the obvious character of a particular vegetable, the high and dry heat of the grill amplifies a vegetable's most subtle flavors, making grilled vegetables unlike any you've ever tasted.

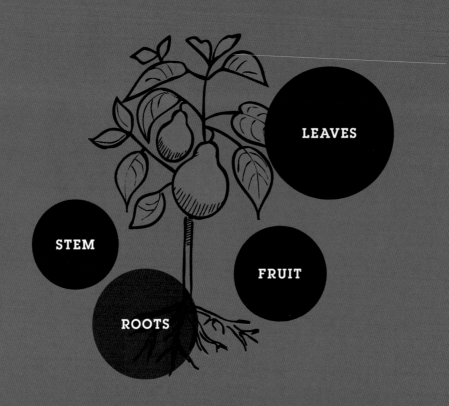

STEM

LEAVES

FRUIT

ROOTS

VEGETABLES

INGREDIENT	CLASSIFICATION	HOW TO GRILL	SUBSTITUTIONS
BEETS	Roots/Tubers	Whole: indirect medium-heat or in the embers Sliced: direct, medium heat	Sweet potatoes
CARROTS	Roots/Tubers	Large, cut lengthwise or small whole: direct, medium to medium-low heat	Parsnips, turnips
SUNCHOKES AND JICAMA	Roots/Tubers	Sliced: direct, high heat	Water chestnuts, Asian radishes
RADISHES	Roots/Tubers	Sliced: direct, medium-high heat	Turnips, parnsips, carrots, jicama
POTATOES	Roots/Tubers	Whole: indirect, medium heat or in the embers Sliced: direct, medium heat	Sweet potatoes
SWEET POTATOES	Roots/Tubers	Whole: indirect, medium heat or in the embers Sliced: direct, medium heat	Beets
CELERY	Stems	Whole: direct, medium-high heat	Cardoons, fennel
CARDOONS	Stems	Whole: direct, medium-high heat	Celery, fennel
FENNEL	Stems	Whole or halved: indirect, medium heat Sliced: direct, medium heat	Cardoons, celery
HEARTS OF PALM	Stems	Whole: direct, medium-high heat	Asparagus, halved baby artichokes
ASPARAGUS	Stem-Blossoms	Whole: direct, medium heat	Hearts of palm
CAULIFLOWER	Stem-Blossoms	Whole or florets: indirect, medium to medium-high heat	Broccoli, romanesco, broccoflower
ROMANESCO	Stem-Blossoms	Whole or florets: indirect, medium to medium-high heat	Broccoli, cauliflower, broccoflower
ARTICHOKES	Blossoms	Whole mature: indirect, medium heat Halved baby: direct, medium heat	Asparagus, hearts of palm

VEGETABLES, continued

INGREDIENT	CLASSIFICATION	HOW TO GRILL	SUBSTITUTIONS
BROCCOLINI	Stems and Leaves	Whole: direct, medium-high heat	Asparagus, blanched broccoli rabe, hearts of palm
BROCCOLI RABE	Stems and Leaves	Whole: direct, medium-high heat	Broccolini, mature asparagus
FIDDLEHEADS	Stems and Leaves	Whole: direct, medium-high heat	Asparagus, Broccolini, blanched broccoli rabe
RADICCHIO	Leaves	Wedges: direct, medium-high heat	Belgian endive
BELGIAN ENDIVE	Leaves	Halved: direct, medium-high heat	Radicchio
BOK CHOY	Leaves	Halved baby or sliced mature: direct, medium-high heat	Napa or green cabbage wedges
NAPA CABBAGE	Leaves	Wedges: direct, medium-high heat	Baby bok choy, green cabbage wedges
GREEN CABBAGE	Leaves	Wedges: direct, medium-high heat	Baby bok choy, Napa cabbage wedges
BRUSSELS SPROUTS	Leaves	Whole: indirect, medium heat Halved: bilevel medium/low heat	Baby bok choy
NOPALES (CACTUS PADS)	Leaves	Whole: direct, medium-high heat	Okra
LEEKS	Leaves	Halved lengthwise: direct, medium-high heat	Ramps, large scallion, onion wedges
SWEET ONIONS	Bulbous Leaves	Whole: indirect, medium heat Wedges or sliced: direct, medium-high heat	For stuffing: cored whole bell peppers For grilling: leeks, large scallions
CHESTNUTS	Fruit/Nuts	Whole: direct, medium heat	None
CHICKPEAS	Fruit/Beans	Cooked or canned: direct, medium-high heat	Green beans, large fresh peas
EDAMAME (GREEN SOYBEANS)	Fruit/Beans	Whole in pods: direct, high heat	Green beans
GREEN BEANS	Fruit/Beans	Whole: direct, high heat	Edamame
FAVA/BROAD BEANS	Fruit/Beans	Whole in pods: direct, high heat	Edamame
CORN ON THE COB	Fruit	In husk: direct, medium-high heat Husk removed: direct, medium heat	None
ZUCCHINI	Fruit	Sliced: direct, medium-high heat	Yellow or pattypan squash
CUCUMBER	Fruit	Sliced: direct, medium-high heat	Small zucchini
OKRA	Fruit	Whole: direct, medium-high heat	Nopales
TOMATOES	Fruit	Cored: direct, medium heat	None
BELL PEPPERS	Fruit	Whole for grill-roasted peppers: direct, medium-high heat Quartered for grilling: direct, medium heat	Mild chile peppers
CHILE PEPPERS	Fruit	Whole for grill-roasted peppers: direct, medium-high heat Quartered for grilling: direct, medium heat	Bell peppers
EGGPLANT	Fruit	Whole: indirect, medium-low heat Sliced: direct, medium-high heat	Portobello mushrooms
DELICATA SQUASH	Fruit	Halved: indirect, medium-high to high heat Sliced: direct, medium-high heat	Sweet dumpling or small butternut squash
WILD MUSHROOMS	Fungus	Whole or sliced: direct, medium-high heat	Cultivated mushrooms

Classes of Vegetables

We grill all manner of vegetables, from celery and potatoes to hearts of palm and cardoons. They all have different characteristics, so it helps to classify them into plant parts to discover the best grilling method for each one. In broad terms, vegetables are the edible parts of a plant. Some are leaves, some are roots, some are stems, and some are fruits (botanically speaking). The part of a plant that a vegetable comes from, its color, age, and density, determine its quality.

Roots

Beets, carrots, radishes, and other roots anchor the plant to the ground. A root absorbs moisture and nutrients from the soil and makes them available to the aboveground parts of the plant. Most plant roots are spindly, fibrous, and inedible, but some are engorged with storage cells that are loaded with carbohydrates and other nutrients, and these are the ones that have been cultivated as vegetables. To support the plant and store nutrients, roots need strong walls and rigid fibers. As a plant matures, the roots pack in more sugar and get bigger; the walls thicken and get harder. The quality of a root vegetable becomes a balance between toughness and sweetness. Harvested too young, root vegetables will lack flavor; too late and the tough fibers will turn wooden. As with other food, small roots will be tender and mild. Medium-size roots are more crunchy and sweet. Large ones are tough and flavorful. Some roots are actually underground stems, for example, potatoes and sunchokes. They have a different botanical name, tubers, but they store starch the same way other roots do and are grilled much like other roots.

Stems

Continuing up the plant, stems like celery help to stabilize a plant's structure and also conduct nutrients between its various parts. They transport sugars produced in the leaves down to the roots for storage as starch and move sugars back up from the roots to other parts of the plant for energy. For this reason, stems are rigid, fibrous, and veined with vascular channels. They also support a steady flow of liquid from the bottom to the top of the plant, a characteristic that helps us judge their quality. Stems like celery and the bulbous part of fennel should be snappingly crisp. This plant part also includes vegetables located further up the plant, such as cauliflower and broccoli. These vegetables are known as stem-blossoms because they include a flowering portion of the plant. An artichoke, on the other hand, is a true blossom, the flowering part of a thistle plant. The plant category of stems also includes some vegetables that combine stem and leaf, such as broccoli rabe, Broccolini, and fiddlehead ferns, all of which can be grilled. Because stems are thruways for liquid, flaccid stems can be restored to their former turgidity. Cut the bottom of the limp stalks, submerge them in ice water, and they will draw up moisture and become rigid again.

Leaves

Vegetables like cabbage, Brussels sprouts, and Belgian endive are actually the plant's leaves. They produce energy for the plant through photosynthesis, which transforms sunshine and the carbon dioxide in the air into sugar. To soak up as much sunshine and carbon dioxide as possible, leaves are broad and flat and consist of a large network of air pockets. They are mostly air, in fact, which is why leaves such as cabbage and spinach can shrink by up to 75 percent in volume when cooked. The air pockets make leaf vegetables highly susceptible to dehydration and wilting, which is why tender mesclun greens quickly go from tender-crisp to limp in your refrigerator. But on the grill fresh, crisp leaf vegetables like radicchio, bok choy, and even cactus pads (nopales) concentrate in flavor with only minimal shrinkage.

Fruits

Savory or sweet, the part of the plant known botanically as the fruit guarantees the plant's regeneration. The fruit produces the seed. Whether savory or sweet, fruits tend to be brightly colored to entice creatures to eat the fruit and spread the seed, ensuring the plant's survival. Vegetables in this category take many forms, such as tomatoes, peppers, okra, eggplant, corn, zucchini, winter squash, and green beans. They all have seeds and come in various colors and degrees of sweetness. As its seed matures, a fruiting vegetable ripens and fills up with sugar and juices, all of which make these vegetables the most popular type that we eat. In general, choose vegetables in this category by how plump and colorful they look and how fragrant they smell.

How to Grill Vegetables

Vegetables come in all shapes and sizes. Each one requires slightly different preparation, and many vegetables can be grilled in more ways than one. Almost all benefit from generous oiling to help prevent the vegetables from sticking to the grill. Beyond that, size, thickness, and density are your best criteria for choosing how to grill a vegetable.

Roots

The fibrous density of roots and tubers means they grill fastest when sliced. Beets, carrots, potatoes, sweet potatoes, and radishes can be sliced about ¼ inch thick, oiled and seasoned, and grilled directly over medium-high heat until tender. Roots can also be grilled whole using indirect medium heat. Tough roots with thick skins, such as beets, potatoes, and sweet potatoes, can also be wrapped in foil and nestled in the embers of a hot charcoal fire. The skins will char and the flesh inside will absorb some smoke flavor as it softens from the heat. Scoop the flesh right from the jacket.

Stems and Stem-Blossoms

Stems and stem-blossoms like celery, cardoons, fennel, asparagus, and hearts of palm are best grilled whole over direct medium-high heat. To grill large or bulbous stem vegetables like fennel, slice them first. Very large stem-blossoms such as cauliflower can be grill-roasted whole or cut into florets over indirect medium heat.

Leaves and Stem-Leaves

Leaf vegetables like radicchio, bok choy, Brussels sprouts, cabbage, and leeks grill best when halved (if small) or cut into wedges (if large). Leaves are quite tender, so grill them very briefly over direct medium-high heat just until grill-marked. The same goes for tender stem-leaves like fiddleheads and Broccolini. Vegetables that are fruiting bodies vary widely in size and shape, requiring different preparations and grilling methods. Most, like zucchini, peppers, and eggplant, do best when cut into slabs, oiled, seasoned, and grilled directly over medium-high heat.

Fruits

Vegetables in this category are particularly tender, so avoid overcooking or they will quickly turn mushy. In fact, most vegetables can be eaten raw, so grilling them is merely a matter of marking the surface and developing some flavor by caramelizing their inherent sugars. While most vegetables can be grilled directly on a hot, oiled grill grate, some like chickpeas are so small that you'll need a vegetable grill tray, grill wok, or grill skillet. Grill woks and skillets expand the possibilities of your grill because you can "stir-grill" and "grill-sauté" small tender vegetables over the fire without any danger of sacrificing them to the flames.

BEETS

Mixed Grilled Beets with Orange-Hazelnut Gremolata

MAKES 4 SERVINGS

Beets contain about 6 percent sugar. When the beets are boiled, the sugar dissolves in the cooking liquid and you're left with earthy-tasting tubers. But grill them and the sugars concentrate and caramelize, transforming the beets into a sort of vegetable candy. In this recipe, their sweetness gets a complement of pungent herb relish. Gremolata is a classic Italian garnish for osso buco. Usually it's made with garlic, pine nuts, lemon zest, and parsley. Ours is more fragrant; we swap tarragon for some of the parsley and hazelnuts for the pine nuts.

INGREDIENTS:

4 multicolored beets, such as red, golden, and Chioggia (about 18 ounces total)

1 tablespoon olive oil

¼ teaspoon salt, preferably smoked

⅛ teaspoon ground black pepper, preferably smoked

Orange-Hazelnut Gremolata:

1 garlic clove, peeled

1 tablespoon packed fresh flat-leaf parsley leaves

1 tablespoon packed fresh tarragon or mint leaves

1 tablespoon grated orange zest

1 tablespoon blanched hazelnuts

¼ teaspoon salt

⅛ teaspoon ground black pepper

Pinch of sugar

DIRECTIONS:

Light a grill for direct medium heat, about 400°F (see page 12). Scrub the beets well, then slice about ¼ inch thick. Combine the oil, salt, and pepper in a shallow dish. Add the beets and coat well.

For the orange-hazelnut gremolata: Combine the garlic, parsley, mint, orange zest, hazelnuts, salt, pepper, and sugar in a minichopper or a small food processor. Pulse until finely chopped and granular in texture, but not pureed.

Brush the grill grate and coat with oil. Grill the beet slices directly over the heat until tender, about 4 to 5 minutes per side. Arrange on a platter and top with the gremolata.

CARROTS

Grilled Carrot Planks Persillade

MAKES 4 SERVINGS

Like beets, carrots are little sugar factories packing in as much as 5 percent of their weight in sucrose. They're also the best vegetable source of beta-carotene, a potent antioxidant that gives carrots their orange hue. Because beta-carotene is concentrated right under the skin of carrots, it's helpful not to peel them. A good scrub is sufficient to remove surface dirt. Purple carrots, which are also great grilled, contain anthocyanin pigments, another antioxidant, rather than carotene. The effect of the pigments and sugar in carrots increases as they grill, making grilled carrots higher in many nutrients than raw ones. We dress up these colorful roots with chopped parsley and garlic, known in France as *persillade*.

continued ⊕

INGREDIENTS:

3 large carrots, ends trimmed

1 tablespoon olive oil

¼ teaspoon coarse salt

⅛ teaspoon ground black pepper

Pinch of nutmeg

¼ cup chopped fresh flat-leaf parsley

2 tablespoons minced garlic

DIRECTIONS:

Cut the carrots lengthwise into planks about ⅜ inch thick, and then toss with the oil, salt, pepper, and nutmeg. Light a grill for direct medium heat, about 350°F (see page 12). If using a grill tray, preheat the tray on the grill. Brush the grill grate and coat with oil or oil the grill tray. Grill the carrot planks directly over the heat until just tender, turning once or twice, about 10 minutes total. Combine the parsley and garlic. Transfer the grilled carrots to a platter and immediately scatter the parsley and garlic on top.

RADISHES

Grilled Sweet and Sour Asian Radishes

MAKES 4 SERVINGS

Asian radishes are sweetest in winter, when they store up sugar for survival, which makes them a great winter grilling dish. Look for jade green Korean radishes (called *mu*). The green fades to white at the tips. They have a short, squat shape that slices into large disks, perfect for showing off a wide expanse of grill marks. Korean radishes are thick-skinned, so they generally need to be peeled (unless very young). You can also use slender white Japanese daikon, which are easier to come by but less sweet. You could even try the familiar red or pink European radishes, but they are generally smaller and won't yield as much surface area for grilling.

INGREDIENTS:

1 minced garlic clove

1 teaspoon minced fresh ginger

¾ cup store-bought sweet and sour sauce

1 pound large green Korean radishes (mu) or white Japanese radishes (daikon)

1 tablespoon canola oil

1 tablespoon toasted sesame oil

1 scallion (green and white parts), chopped

DIRECTIONS:

Light a grill for direct medium-high heat, about 425°F (see page 12).

Add the garlic and ginger to the sweet and sour sauce. Warm gently. If using small radishes, preheat a grill-wok or perforated grill pan on the grill.

Scrub the radishes and peel if thick-skinned. Cut on a sharp diagonal into oval slices about ¼ inch thick. Toss in a medium bowl with the canola oil and sesame oil. Brush the grill grate and coat with oil. If using a grill-wok, coat the hot grill-wok generously with oil. Grill the radishes directly over the heat (in the grill-wok, if using) until nicely grill-marked, about 2 minutes per side.

Remove and cut into bite-size pieces. Toss with the sweet and sour sauce. Drizzle with any oil left in the bowl. Scatter the scallion on top.

POTATOES

Grilled Potato Cakes

MAKES 4 SERVINGS

Briefly cooking and then chilling potatoes softens and gelatinizes some of the starch, so that when shredded, the shreds cling to each other and easily form into cakes. It's easiest to chill the potatoes the night before, but you could chill them in the morning if you plan to cook them that night. The addition of potato flakes helps to bind the mixture and adds more potato flavor. If you like, add some chopped fresh parsley, dill, or rosemary to the cakes along with the salt and pepper. Serve with applesauce or sour cream, or as a side dish for beef, veal, or poultry.

INGREDIENTS:

2 pounds russet potatoes, skins left on

1 large onion

1 cup potato flakes

2 large eggs, beaten

1 tablespoon chopped fresh flat-leaf parsley

1½ teaspoons sea salt

¾ teaspoon ground black pepper

Cooking spray

DIRECTIONS:

Put the potatoes in a large saucepan and cover with salted water by about 1 inch. Bring to a boil over high heat and continue boiling until the potatoes begin to soften (just under the skin), 7 to 10 minutes. Drain the potatoes, cover, and refrigerate for 8 to 16 hours.

Peel the potatoes and onion and grate them both, using the large holes of a box grater or the grating disk of a food processor. Transfer to cheesecloth and wring out as much liquid as possible over a bowl (there may only be a few tablespoons). Let the liquid stand for 5 minutes so that the potato starch settles to the bottom. Carefully pour off the water, leaving the starch in the bottom of the bowl. Add the potatoes

and onions, ⅓ cup of the potato flakes, the parsley, eggs, salt, and pepper. Mix thoroughly.

Put the remaining ⅔ cup potato flakes in a shallow bowl. Form the potato mixture into 8 patties no more than ¼ inch thick and dredge in the potato flakes. Let the cakes stand at room temperature as the grill heats up.

Light a grill for direct medium-high heat, about 400°F (see page 12). When it's hot, brush the grill grate and coat with oil. Coat all the surfaces of the potato cakes generously with cooking spray and grill them directly over the heat until well browned, about 5 minutes per side.

SWEET POTATOES

Fire-Roasted Sweet Potatoes with Root Beer–Rum Butter

MAKES 4 SERVINGS

If you like sticky-sweet sweet potatoes with marshmallows or maple syrup, try this combo. You'll need a charcoal grill or campfire with burned-down embers. Burying the sweet potatoes in hot coals is cool as hell and guaranteed to make you a grill master.

INGREDIENTS:

4 orange-fleshed sweet potatoes (3 to 3½ pounds total), pricked several times with a fork

½ cup Root Beer–Rum Butter (page 48)

1 teaspoon grated orange zest

continued

DIRECTIONS:

Light a charcoal grill or campfire grill. Leave the grill grate off so the coals are accessible. When they glow bright reddish-orange, rake them to make a coal bed at least 2 inches deep. Bury the sweet potatoes directly in the coals, raking the coals to nearly cover the potatoes. Cook until a skewer slides in and out of the center of each potato easily, about 45 minutes, turning once or twice. Using tongs, brush off any loose ash, and then remove the sweet potatoes to a platter or plates. Let cool for a few minutes, and then cut each sweet potato in half lengthwise and mash the flesh of each half with a fork. Drizzle with the root beer–rum butter and sprinkle with the orange zest.

CELERY

Grilled Celery, Apple, and Sour Cherry Slaw

MAKES 4 SERVINGS

Slaws are such a common accompaniment to grilled food, it only seems fitting that they experience fire on their own. Here, we briefly grill celery stalks and carrots then toss them with crisp raw apple, sweet and sour cherries, chopped walnuts, and a creamy blue cheese dressing. Just the side dish to make a cookout of grilled burgers and dogs a whole new kind of meal.

INGREDIENTS:

Dressing:

¼ cup apple cider vinegar

2 tablespoons sour cream

2 tablespoons mayonnaise

1 very small shallot, minced

¼ teaspoon coarse salt

⅛ teaspoon ground black pepper

¼ cup crumbled blue cheese

Salad:

8 ounces celery (about 8 ribs), trimmed

1 small carrot, trimmed and scrubbed

1 tablespoon canola oil

1 small apple, cored and cut into matchsticks about 1½ inches long

½ cup dried sour cherries

¼ cup finely chopped walnuts

DIRECTIONS:

For the dressing: Combine the vinegar, sour cream, mayonnaise, shallot, salt, pepper, and blue cheese in a serving bowl.

For the salad: Light a grill for direct medium-high heat, about 400°F (see page 12). Cut the celery ribs and carrot in half lengthwise and toss with the oil until well coated. Brush the grill grate and coat with oil. Grill the celery and carrot so they are perpendicular to the bars of the grate, directly over the heat, until nicely grill-marked yet quite firm, about 2 minutes per side. Remove to a cutting board and cut the celery and carrot into matchsticks about 1½ inches long. Add to the dressing along with the apple, cherries, and walnuts. Toss to coat. Serve immediately or refrigerate for up to 1 day.

FENNEL

Grilled Fennel, Orange, and Olive Antipasto

MAKES 4 SERVINGS

Fennel's heady scent of anise is frequently paired with oranges in the cuisines of the French and Italian Riviera. The combination breathes bright aromas into this light antipasto, in which sliced fennel is slowly grilled and basted continuously with a mop of white wine. Fennel bulb is the vegetable form of fennel weed, which is an herb. Buy bulbs that are round and heavy for their size, and avoid specimens with lots of stalk, which is fibrous and unusable here. The feathery fronds aren't terribly aromatic, but they make an attractive garnish, so save them when you trim the stalks.

INGREDIENTS:

¼ cup extra-virgin olive oil

2 garlic cloves, minced

¼ teaspoon salt

⅛ teaspoon ground black pepper

2 fennel bulbs, trimmed and sliced lengthwise ½ inch thick

½ cup crisp, fruity white wine such as ribolla gialla or pinot grigio

2 seedless oranges, cut into supremes (see Know-How, page 296)

½ cup grill-roasted red bell pepper (see Know-How, page 47) or jarred roasted pepper

4 ounces prosciutto, salami, and/or coppa, thinly sliced

4 ounces provolone, thinly sliced

½ cup Gaeta and/or Cerignola olives

DIRECTIONS:

Light a grill for direct medium heat, about 350°F (see page 12).

Combine 2 tablespoons of the oil, the garlic, salt, and pepper in a shallow dish. Add the fennel slices, turning to coat. Brush the grill grate and coat with oil. Grill the fennel slices directly over the heat until tender and nicely grill-marked, about 5 minutes per side, basting frequently with the wine. Arrange the fennel, orange supremes, roasted peppers, prosciutto, provolone, and olives on a platter. Drizzle with the remaining 2 tablespoons oil before serving.

Grilled Leeks with Pomegranate Vinaigrette

MAKES 4 SERVINGS

Leeks are cousins to onion and garlic. Like their relatives they have a sweet, sulfurous pungency. But unlike other alliums, leeks do not form a bulb, so they remain sweeter, less pungent, and more leafy. To maintain their mild flavor, leeks are grown under soil so they do not develop chlorophyll from exposure to sunlight. This cultivation practice means that leeks are often dirty and need to be well washed before cooking. In this recipe, the leeks are split lengthwise, making it a cinch to rinse between the leaf layers. The grilled leeks are then drizzled with a gorgeous, ruby-red pomegranate vinaigrette. If you can find wild leeks (ramps), they can be substituted for cultivated leeks. Just double the quantity.

INGREDIENTS:

Pomegranate Vinaigrette:

1 pomegranate

1 tablespoon raspberry vinegar

⅓ cup walnut oil or extra-virgin olive oil

½ teaspoon Dijon mustard

1 shallot, minced

¼ teaspoon coarse salt

⅛ teaspoon freshly ground black pepper

Leeks:

4 leeks, trimmed

2 tablespoons olive oil

¼ teaspoon coarse salt

⅛ teaspoon ground black pepper

1 tablespoon pine nuts, lightly toasted

1 tablespoon chopped fresh mint or flat-leaf parsley

DIRECTIONS:

For the pomegranate vinaigrette: Cut the pomegranate in half from stem to blossom end. Reserve half of the pomegranate for another use. Cut the other half in half again from stem to blossom end. Remove all of the seeds and transfer half of the seeds to a minichopper or food processor, reserving the remaining seeds. Process until the juice and seeds separate, and then strain the juice into a cup or bowl. Measure out 3 tablespoons pomegranate juice and transfer to a small bowl. Add the vinegar and then whisk in the oil in a steady stream until blended. Whisk in the mustard, shallot, salt, and pepper.

For the leeks: Light a grill for direct medium-high heat, about 400°F (see page 12).

Trim off the tough green tops and the roots of the leeks, and then halve the leeks lengthwise. Rinse the cut sides under cold running water to remove any grit from between the layers. Pat dry and rub all over with the oil. Season all over with the salt and pepper. Brush the grill grate and coat with oil. Grill the leeks, cut side down, until nicely grill-marked, 3 to 4 minutes. Flip and grill until just tender, about 3 minutes more.

Transfer to a platter and top with the vinaigrette, pine nuts, reserved pomegranate seeds, and mint.

CAULIFLOWER

Tandoori Cauliflower with Mint Chutney

MAKES 4 SERVINGS

Cauliflower is a member of the cabbage family. The plant's flower stalks are forced to grow in on themselves, forming a dense mass or curd. Because the stalks never fully mature, they do not become very fibrous. But they are rich in pectin, which is why grilled cauliflower is so creamy, and why overcooked boiled cauliflower turns into mush. To keep the curd pale white, the outer leaves are tied around the cauliflower head, which shields the curd from sunlight and limits the development of green chlorophyll through photosynthesis. We like to grill-roast cauliflower and jolt its mild flavor profile with Indian spices and a refreshing splash of mint chutney. Serve it as a side dish for fish or chicken or as the centerpiece of a vegetarian meal.

INGREDIENTS:

1 head cauliflower, cut into large florets (about 4 cups)

2 cups Tandoori Yogurt Marinade (page 37)

Mint Chutney:

½ cup fresh mint leaves and small stems

⅓ cup fresh cilantro leaves and small stems

½ small onion, coarsely chopped (about ¼ cup)

1 clove garlic, coarsely chopped

1 small serrano chile pepper, stemmed and coarsely chopped (remove seeds for less heat)

Juice of 1 lime

2 tablespoons water

½ teaspoon coarse salt

DIRECTIONS:

Combine the cauliflower and marinade in a 1-gallon zipper-lock bag. Press out the air, seal the bag, and refrigerate for 3 to 4 hours.

For the mint chutney: Combine the mint leaves, cilantro leaves, onion, garlic, chile pepper, lime juice, water, and salt in a small food processor or blender. Blend until relatively smooth. Scrape into a small serving bowl and set aside.

Light a grill for indirect medium-high heat, about 400°F (see page 14). Put a disposable aluminum pan beneath the grill grate over the unheated area of the grill. Fill the pan with ½ inch of hot water. Set the grill grate in place, brush it, and coat with oil.

Remove the cauliflower from the marinade, reserving the marinade. Put the cauliflower florets on the grill so they are over the pan of water. Close the lid and cook until fork-tender, 20 to 30 minutes. Dab the florets with some of the remaining marinade just before removing from the heat.

Serve hot with the chutney.

ROMANESCO

Grill-Roasted Romanesco with Caper Mayonnaise

MAKES 4 SERVINGS

Romanesco's chartreuse head of conical florets spirals outward and upward in a dizzying display of natural beauty. It's just too gorgeous to cut up for cooking, so we like to cook and present this vegetable whole, and then carve it into servings at the table.

INGREDIENTS:

1 head broccoli Romanesco (1 to 1½ pounds)

¼ cup olive oil

½ teaspoon coarse salt

1¼ cups Caper Mayonnaise (page 42)

DIRECTIONS:

Light a grill for indirect medium-high heat, about 400°F (see page 14).

Trim the base and leaves from the Romanesco so it will stand on its base. Mix together the oil and salt and brush generously over the florets. Fill an 8-inch square pan with ½ inch of hot water and nest the head of Romanesco in the pan. Brush the grill grate and coat with oil. Put the Romanesco pan on the grill away from the heat, close the lid, and cook until fork-tender, 25 to 30 minutes, basting several times with the salted oil.

Remove the head of Romanesco to a platter. Carve into florets and serve hot with the caper mayonnaise.

BROCCOLINI

Quick Charred Broccolini with Spiced Cider Syrup

MAKES 4 SERVINGS

The trademark name for baby broccoli, Broccolini is a hybrid of broccoli and Chinese kale. Its slender, juicy stems and small, delicate, broccoli-like flowers are tender enough to grill directly. Sweet apple syrup balances the sharp flavor.

INGREDIENTS:

1 pound Broccolini, stems trimmed if thick

2 tablespoons canola oil

¼ teaspoon coarse salt

½ cup Spiced Cider Syrup (page 49)

2 teaspoons grated orange zest

DIRECTIONS:

Light a grill for direct medium-high heat, about 425°F (see page 12).

Toss the Broccolini, oil, and salt in a bowl. Brush the grill grate and coat with oil. Grill the Broccolini directly over the heat until crisp-tender and charred in spots, 3 to 4 minutes, turning once. Remove to a platter or plates and pour on the syrup. Sprinkle with the orange zest before serving.

ARTICHOKES

Grilled Baby Artichokes with Garlic–White Wine Butter Sauce

MAKES 4 TO 6 SERVINGS

An artichoke is the flower bud of a thistle. It consists of a cluster of leaves surrounding a spiky flower (the choke), which nestles in a tender flower base (the heart). Baby artichokes are the secondary buds, which grow up the stalk. They are small and tender enough to grill directly over the heat. Check the center when halving them. If the choke is purple, remove it. If not, it's fine to eat.

INGREDIENTS:

Juice of ½ lemon

12 baby artichokes (about 2 pounds total)

6 tablespoons unsalted butter

2 garlic cloves, minced

1 cup dry white wine

2 tablespoons white balsamic vinegar

1 teaspoon chopped fresh flat-leaf parsley

½ teaspoon coarse salt

⅛ teaspoon ground black pepper

DIRECTIONS:

Squeeze the lemon juice into a bowl of cold water. Trim each artichoke by snapping off and discarding the tough outer green leaves until you are left with a small, bullet-shaped artichoke with pale yellow leaves that are green at the tips. Cut off the green tips crosswise. Cut the stem flush with the bottom of the artichoke, so that no green remains. Cut the artichokes in half lengthwise and scoop out and discard any purple choke. Drop the halved artichokes into the bowl of lemon water as you cook.

Bring a large pot of salted water to a boil. Add the artichokes and boil until crisp-tender, 5 to 6 minutes. Drain and pat dry.

Meanwhile, melt 1 tablespoon of the butter in a small saucepan over medium-low heat. Add the garlic and cook until soft but not browned, about 4 minutes. Add the wine and

vinegar, raise the heat to medium-high, and cook until the liquid is reduced by half, 5 to 7 minutes. Melt the remaining 5 tablespoons butter in a medium skillet over medium-low heat. Cook slowly until the butter turns golden brown and smells toasty, 6 to 8 minutes, stirring now and then. Remove from the heat and stir in the wine mixture. Season with the parsley, salt, and pepper.

Brush the artichokes with some of the butter sauce. Light a grill for direct medium heat, about 375°F (see page 12). Brush the grill grate and coat with oil. Grill the artichokes directly over the heat until tender and nicely grill-marked, about 5 minutes per side.

Serve with the butter sauce.

ASPARAGUS

Charred Pencil Asparagus in Vinaigrette

MAKES 6 SERVINGS

Asparagus are the above-ground shoots of a rhizome, consisting of a stalk topped with a pointed tip. The tip is a cluster of leaf-like bracts. If the tips are not harvested, they eventually sprout long, feathery fronds. The stalks can be green, purple, or white, and run from pencil-thin to jumbo. To test the freshness of a bunch of asparagus, squeeze the stalks—they should squeak.

INGREDIENTS:

2 pounds thin asparagus (30 to 35 spears)

¼ cup plus 2 tablespoons extra-virgin olive oil

3 tablespoons white wine vinegar

1 teaspoon minced shallots

½ teaspoon Dijon mustard

½ teaspoon lemon zest

¼ teaspoon coarse salt

¼ teaspoon ground black pepper

Pinch of sugar

DIRECTIONS:

Light a grill for direct medium heat, about 375°F (see page 12).

Trim the asparagus, one at a time. Take a stalk and hold one end in each hand. Gradually bend the stalk and it will naturally snap where the stalk becomes tough. Discard the tough end. Place the asparagus in a shallow glass baking dish just large enough to hold them in a single layer. Combine the oil, vinegar, shallots, mustard, lemon zest, salt, pepper, and sugar in a jar with a tight-fitting lid. Shake vigorously to combine, and then pour over the asparagus.

Brush the grill grate and coat with oil. Remove the asparagus from the vinaigrette, reserving the oil. Grill directly over the heat, perpendicular to the bars of the grill grate. Grill until just tender but not limp, 3 to 4 minutes, rolling the asparagus once or twice with tongs. Return the grilled asparagus to the baking dish and shake to coat with the vinaigrette. Let cool to room temperature and serve. (Or cover and refrigerate for up to 1 day. Remove from the refrigerator 15 minutes before serving.)

BELGIAN ENDIVE

Grilled Belgian Endive with Persimmon and Speck

MAKES 4 SERVINGS

Belgian endives are the bullet-shaped shoots of chicory, grown to control their bitterness and increase their juiciness. Grilled wedges of sweet persimmon and salty speck make an intriguing counterpoint.

INGREDIENTS:

4 medium heads Belgian endive (about 1½ pounds total)

2 tablespoons olive oil

8 thin slices speck or regular smoked bacon, halved lengthwise into 16 strips

16 fresh basil leaves

2 Fuyu persimmons, each cut into 8 wedges

½ cup Brandied Ginger Glaze (page 50)

DIRECTIONS:

Light a grill for direct medium-high heat, about 400°F (see page 12).

Cut the Belgian endive in half lengthwise and brush all over with the oil. Lay a strip of speck on a work surface, put a basil leaf at one end then top the basil with a wedge of persimmon positioned crosswise. Roll up to enrobe the persimmon, and then skewer with toothpicks to secure. Repeat with the remaining speck, basil, and persimmon wedges.

Brush the grill grate and coat with oil. Grill the speck-wrapped persimmon and the Belgian endive, cut-side down, directly over the heat until the endive is crisp-tender and all are lightly grill-marked, 3 to 4 minutes per side. Brush all over with the glaze toward the end of cooking.

BOK CHOY

Grilled Baby Bok Choy and Shiitakes with Sesame-Ginger Dressing

MAKES 4 SERVINGS

More than twenty varieties of bok choy are available in Asia, varying in size, shape, and color. Baby bok choy is a miniaturized version of Shanghai choy, which has a mild, cabbage-like flavor, apple-green leaves, and pale green stems. It grills in about the same time as shiitake mushrooms, and the pair are a natural match for a pungent, Asian-style dressing.

INGREDIENTS:

Sesame-Ginger Dressing:

2 tablespoons soy sauce

1 tablespoon oyster sauce

1 teaspoon rice vinegar

½ to 1 teaspoon chile-garlic paste

1 teaspoon toasted sesame oil

2 teaspoons minced fresh ginger

4 baby bok choy, halved lengthwise (about 1 pound)

4 ounces fresh large-cap shiitake mushrooms, stems removed

½ teaspoon toasted sesame seeds

DIRECTIONS:

For the sesame-ginger dressing: Combine the soy sauce, oyster sauce, rice vinegar, chile-garlic paste, sesame oil, and ginger in a small bowl.

Brush the dressing over the bok choy and mushrooms.

Light a grill for direct medium-high heat, about 400°F (see page 12). Brush the grill grate and coat with oil.

Put the bok choy on the grill with the cut side down and the tender leaves away from the heat. Put the mushrooms, gill-side down, on the grill. Cover and grill until nicely grill-marked and tender, 1 to 2 minutes per side for the mushrooms and 3 to 4 minutes per side for the bok choy. After flipping, brush the vegetables with some of the dressing so it runs into the crevices.

Serve drizzled with the remaining dressing and sprinkled with the sesame seeds.

GREEN CABBAGE

Grilled Coleslaw

MAKES 8 TO 10 SERVINGS

If you're grilling anyway, why not grill the slaw, too? Heat brings out some sweetness in the cabbage and allows it to soak up more of the dressing. We cut the mayonnaise with sour cream for extra tang and mix in some vinegar to brighten the flavors.

INGREDIENTS:

½ head green cabbage (about 1 pound)

2 tablespoons peanut oil or canola oil

¼ cup mayonnaise

¼ cup sour cream

¼ cup cider vinegar

2 tablespoons sugar

1 teaspoon salt

¼ teaspoon ground black pepper

⅛ teaspoon dill seeds

1½ cups carrot matchsticks

continued ⮕

DIRECTIONS:

Light a grill for direct medium-high heat, about 400°F (see page 12).

Cut the cabbage lengthwise through the core into four wedges. Brush all over with the oil. Whisk together the mayonnaise, sour cream, vinegar, sugar, salt, black pepper, and dill seeds in a large serving bowl. Set aside.

Brush the grill grate and coat with oil. Grill the cabbage wedges directly over the heat until nicely grill-marked, about 2 minutes per side. Remove to a cutting board and cut out the core from each wedge. Slice the wedges crosswise into shreds about ¼ inch wide. Add to the bowl along with the carrots and stir to combine. Let stand for 15 minutes before serving. Or refrigerate for up to 1 day.

BRUSSELS SPROUTS

Skewers of Sprouts, Pancetta, and Grilled Garlic

MAKES 4 SERVINGS

Philadelphia chef Marc Vetri makes great pan-fried Brussels sprouts with pancetta at his eponymous restaurant in Center City. We thought it would be fun to try the combination on the grill. It worked like a charm, with the sprouts picking up a bit of char, the pancetta crisping on the surface, and the garlic mellowing into golden roasted goodness. For the pancetta, you'll need a chunk instead of slices. It all looks great presented on skewers, but tastes better when the pieces, especially the pancetta and garlic, are cut a bit smaller after grilling. Best to let your guests do that.

INGREDIENTS:

8 skewers, preferably flat metal ones

16 Brussels sprouts, halved lengthwise through the core

8 garlic cloves, skins left on

2 tablespoons olive oil

2 ounces pancetta, cut into ½-inch cubes

1 tablespoon balsamic vinegar

3 tablespoons unsalted butter, melted

Coarse sea salt and ground black pepper

DIRECTIONS:

Light a grill for bilevel medium/low heat, about 375/275°F (see page 13).

Toss the sprouts and unpeeled garlic with the oil in a bowl until well coated. Arrange the sprouts, garlic, and pancetta on the skewers, using about 4 sprout pieces, 2 pancetta pieces, and 1 garlic clove per skewer. Skewer the sprouts through or just above the core, so the flat, cut sides can rest on the grill. Stir the vinegar and butter into the remaining oil in the bowl.

Brush the grill grate and coat with oil. Grill the skewers, with the cut sides of the sprouts down, over medium heat until the sprouts are nicely grill-marked, about 5 minutes. Brush with the balsamic mixture, and then flip and brush the cut sides

generously. Cook for 1 more minute. Reduce the heat to low on a gas grill, or move the skewers to the low-heat area on a charcoal or wood grill. Brush the cut sides of the sprouts again to saturate the leaves. Cover the grill and cook until the sprouts are just tender (a knife should slide in and out of the leaves easily).

Remove to a platter or plates and season with the salt and pepper. Serve with any remaining balsamic mixture. Allow guests to pop the roasted garlic from its skin, cut the pancetta, and eat small amounts with the sprouts.

CHICKPEAS

Seared Chickpeas Glazed with Harissa

MAKES 6 TO 8 SERVINGS
(2 CUPS)

Grilled chickpeas? Absolutely. Here's one recipe where you definitely need a grill skillet, grill tray, or grill wok. Otherwise, the chickpeas will just fall into the fire. But these gadgets make it a snap to stir-fry ingredients as small as chickpeas directly on the grill (most have ¼-inch holes). Chickpeas are eaten throughout the Middle East in the form of hummus, falafel, and other popular dishes. We like to glaze them with harissa, the caraway-scented hot sauce from Tunisia. They make an eye-opening nosh before a spicy meal.

INGREDIENTS:

2 cups cooked or canned chickpeas, drained

2 teaspoons olive oil

¼ cup Harissa (page 46)

DIRECTIONS:

Light a grill for direct medium-high heat, about 400°F (see page 12). Preheat a grill skillet on the grill.

Rinse the chickpeas well to remove most of the loose skins. Pat dry on paper towels, and then toss in a bowl with 1 teaspoon of the oil.

Brush the grill grate and grill skillet and coat both with oil. Pour the chickpeas into the hot, oiled skillet and shake them into a single layer. Cook, undisturbed, for 1 minute. Shake the pan, and continue cooking until the chickpeas are crisp and browned on the outside and tender inside, 5 to 7 minutes, shaking a few times and drizzling with the remaining teaspoon oil. Scrape the pan with a spatula if necessary to loosen the chickpeas. During the last minute of cooking, drizzle with the harissa while shaking to coat completely. Cook until the chickpeas are glazed, about 1 minute.

Remove to a bowl and serve warm.

Grilled Edamame with Black Sesame Smoked Salt

MAKES 6 SERVINGS

Edamame (ee-dah-MAH-may) are immature soybeans harvested while the beans are still green and have grown to between 80 and 90 percent of their full size. At harvest, edamame have less indigestible ogliosaccharides (the sugars that cause flatulence) and more vitamins than mature soybeans. They are also slightly higher in oils and sugars and slightly lower in protein, which accounts for their sweet flavor, creamy texture, and fresh green vegetable aroma. Although edamame are available fresh, they are very perishable and are more commonly sold frozen in their pods or already shelled. We've found that grilling edamame in their pods complements their sweet greenness in an extraordinary way. On the grill, the pods become speckled with char as the beans inside whistle and steam. At the last minute, we scatter them with black sesame seeds and smoked salt. To eat them, pop the warm beans from the rounded side of the pod directly into your mouth. Unavoidably, bits of sesame salt will graze your lips and stick to your fingertips. That's how the seasoning is delivered to your palate. As you lap up the errant smoky salt, dual sensations fight for your attention: steamy, sugary edamame in the mouth and smoky salt flecking the tip of your tongue.

INGREDIENTS:

1 pound frozen edamame in their pods, thawed

1 teaspoon toasted sesame oil

1 tablespoon black sesame seeds

1 tablespoon white sesame seeds

1 teaspoon smoked salt

DIRECTIONS:

Heat a grill for direct high heat, about 500°F (see page 12).

Blot the edamame with paper towels until they are completely dry. Toss with the sesame oil.

Mix together the black and white sesame seeds and smoked salt and set aside.

Coat a grill skillet or grill wok with oil and place on the grill; wait a few minutes for the pan to get very hot. Add the edamame in two batches; do not crowd the pan. Grill for 2 minutes without moving the pan, or until the edamame are blistered and begin to whistle (the sound of steam escaping from the pods). Shake the pan vigorously, flipping the edamame, and grill for 2 minutes more, flipping the edamame two more times. Transfer to a serving bowl, and toss with half the sesame salt. Grill the remaining edamame in the same way and toss with the first batch and the remaining sesame salt. Serve immediately.

KNOW-HOW: BUYING AND MAKING SMOKED SALT

There are several varieties of smoked sea salt. Cherry smoked Iburi Jio from Japan is available at The Meadow (www.atthemeadow.com), and Salt Traders (www.salttraders.com) sells darker and smokier Viking smoked salt from Denmark. Both are quite expensive and powerful enough to be mixed in equal parts with regular sea salt or coarse salt; they will still give quite a smoky kick. If you don't want to order smoked salt, you can make a reasonable (though less assertive) facsimile. Mix 2 tablespoons coarse sea salt and 6 drops liquid smoke until thoroughly combined. Heat a cast-iron skillet over high heat until smoking, and then add the salt and stir until it turns golden brown, about 30 seconds. Smoked salt can be stored at room temperature for several months.

FAVA BEANS

Grilled Fava Bean and Shrimp Salad with Avocado and Grapefruit

MAKES 4 TO 6 SERVINGS

Let's face it: peeling fava beans is a pain. Unless they're very young and very fresh, the pods have to be split, and then the waxy-looking hull must be removed to uncover the glossy beans. Grilling makes the process much easier. The high heat splits open the pods and loosens the hulls, so you can just squeeze out the tender green beans.

INGREDIENTS:

Bamboo or metal skewers

1 pound whole fresh fava beans in the pods

6 ounces medium (41–50 count) shrimp, peeled and deveined

2 tablespoons Cumin-Oregano Rub (page 29)

1 tablespoon olive oil

1 red grapefruit, cut into supremes (see Know-How on page 296)

1 avocado, cut into ¾-inch cubes (see Know-How, below)

2 scallions (green and white parts), finely chopped

1 large garlic clove, minced

2 jalapeño chiles, seeded and finely chopped

1 medium tomato, cored, seeded, and finely chopped

¼ cup Jalapeño-Lime Vinaigrette (page 41)

6 ounces mâche or baby oak leaf lettuce

1 tablespoon chopped fresh cilantro

DIRECTIONS:

If you are grilling with bamboo skewers, soak them in water for at least 30 minutes. Light a grill for direct medium-high heat, about 425°F (see page 12).

Toss the fava bean pods and shrimp with the rub and oil in a shallow dish until well coated. Arrange the shrimp on skewers.

Brush the grill grate and coat with oil. Grill the favas directly over the heat until the pods speckle with char and start to burst at the seams, 4 to 5 minutes per side. Grill the shrimp skewers directly over the heat until firm and nicely grill-marked, about 2 minutes per side. Remove from the heat and cool for 10 minutes. Scrape the beans from the pods, and then split the hulls and squeeze out the glossy green beans. Put the beans in a serving bowl along with any residual char. Add the shrimp, grapefruit, avocado, scallions, garlic, chile, tomato, and vinaigrette to the bowl. Toss gently to coat.

Divide the mâche among plates and top with the fava salad. Scatter the cilantro on top.

KNOW-HOW: PREPARING AVOCADO

Cut the avocado in half lengthwise around and down to the pit. Twist the halves to separate them, and then whack your knife into the pit, which will be embedded in one half. Twist the pit free of the avocado, then knock off and discard the pit, using your knuckles or another utensil. To mash the avocado, scoop it from the peel with a spoon, and then mash. To slice it, slice down to but not through the peel, then carefully scoop the slices from the peel. To cut cubes, make a tic-tac-toe pattern of cuts down to but not through the peel, and then carefully scoop the cubes from the peel.

EGGPLANT

Sweet Mirin Grilled Eggplant with Wasabi Ginger Drizzle

MAKES 4 SERVINGS

Asian eggplants have creamy sweet flesh, which chars deliciously on the grill and pairs well with a pungent marinade.

INGREDIENTS:

4 medium Japanese eggplants or 1 large globe eggplant (about 1¼ pounds total)

1 cup Sweet Mirin Marinade (page 38)

2 tablespoons peanut oil or canola oil

½ to 1 teaspoon wasabi paste

1 teaspoon pickled (sushi) ginger, minced

1 teaspoon toasted sesame seeds

DIRECTIONS:

Light a grill for direct medium-high heat, about 400°F (see page 12).

Cut the eggplant lengthwise into ⅜-inch-thick slices all the way to, but not through, the stem end so the eggplant can be fanned out. Fan out the slices, put in a shallow dish, and pour on the marinade. Let stand at room temperature for 20 to 30 minutes.

Remove the eggplant from the marinade and reserve the marinade. Pat the eggplant dry with paper towels and brush with 1 tablespoon of the oil.

Brush the grill grate and coat with oil. Fan out the eggplant slices on the grate directly over the heat and grill until tender and nicely grill-marked, 3 to 4 minutes per side.

Spoon ¼ cup of the marinade into a cup and whisk in the wasabi, minced pickled ginger, and remaining 1 tablespoon oil. Drizzle over the eggplant and scatter with the sesame seeds.

OKRA

Grilled Okra with Muhammara

MAKES 4 SERVINGS

Okra is one of the most popular vegetables in the Middle East. We like to grill it in that tradition with a crusty glaze of spicy muhammara, the walnut and pomegranate paste popular all over Syria, Turkey, and Egypt.

INGREDIENTS:

1 pound fresh okra, stems trimmed but otherwise left whole

1 cup Muhammara (page 47)

continued

DIRECTIONS:

Light a grill for direct medium-high heat, about 450°F (see page 12).

Toss the trimmed okra with ¼ cup of the muhammara in a bowl. Let stand for 20 minutes at room temperature.

Brush the grill grate and coat with oil. Put the okra on the grill directly over the heat perpendicular to the bars of the grate. If the okra is at risk of falling into the fire, double-skewer it crosswise and put the skewers directly over the heat. Grill until nicely grill-marked, 4 to 6 minutes, turning once or twice.

Serve hot with the remaining muhammara.

CORN

Charred Corn on the Cob with Grilled Tomato Oil

MAKES 4 SERVINGS

A grill is the best vessel you have for cooking corn. You don't need to husk, soak, boil, or foil-wrap the corn. Just start the fire and throw the cobs on, husks and all. Close the lid and sit back. It will take about 15 minutes, and you will have to turn the cobs every 5 minutes or so, but that's it. During that time the husks will char and send a sweet vegetal smoke through the corn. When they're done, the husks will be burnt and you will hear steam hissing inside. You can let them sit for a minute or two and then peel and enjoy; or get some extra grill flavor by peeling back the husks and charring the corn briefly over the fire. Here, we serve the grilled corn with glistening, rose-colored oil, flavored and tinted with grilled tomato.

INGREDIENTS:

4 ears corn, husks left on

½ cup Grilled Tomato Oil (page 50)

DIRECTIONS:

Light a grill for direct medium-high heat, about 425°F (see page 12).

Grill the corn in their husks directly over the heat, turning every 5 minutes, until the husks are blackened all over, 15 to 18 minutes total. During the last 5 to 8 minutes, put on grill mitts and peel back the outer blackened husks to expose some of the corn kernels. Continue grilling until some of the corn kernels are browned and lightly charred.

Remove from the grill and let cool slightly. Remove the husks and brush generously with the tomato oil.

KEEP IT SIMPLE:

Of course, you can slather your grilled corn with other sauces like pesto or good ol' butter and salt.

Grilled Tomatoes Stuffed with Gorgonzola, Poblanos, and Pine Nuts

MAKES 4 SERVINGS

The Poblano-Gorgonzola Butter that we developed to go with lamb noisettes was so good that we had to use it again with tomatoes. It's hard to know which combination tastes best. Usually we don't seed tomatoes because you lose too much of the flavorful gel that surrounds the seeds. But when grilling tomatoes, you have to get rid of some of the liquid. If you don't, it steams the fruit and the concentration of flavor that is the hallmark of great grilled vegetables never happens. When tomatoes are at their peak of ripeness in the summer, pull out this recipe. It makes a great late-summer first course.

INGREDIENTS:

4 medium-size ripe tomatoes

¼ teaspoon coarse salt

⅛ teaspoon ground black pepper

¾ cup Poblano-Gorgonzola Butter (page 45)

¼ cup grated Parmesan cheese

1 large scallion (green and white parts), finely chopped

3 tablespoons finely chopped fresh flat-leaf parsley

¼ cup pine nuts, toasted

DIRECTIONS:

Light a grill for direct medium heat, about 350°F (see page 12).

Remove the tomato cores by cutting a cone shape around the core that's about 2 inches in diameter at the top. Scoop out the seeds. Lightly season the insides with the salt and pepper.

Stir together the butter, Parmesan, scallion, parsley, and 3 tablespoons of the pine nuts. Stuff the mixture loosely into the tomatoes, mounding it well above the top (it will shrink some when cooked). Top with the remaining 1 tablespoon pine nuts.

Brush the grill grate and coat with oil. Put the stuffed tomatoes directly over the heat and close the lid. Grill until the stuffing is warm and the tomatoes juices begin to run, 6 to 8 minutes.

Remove to plates and serve warm.

Grilled Chiles Rellenos with Corn

MAKES 3 TO 4 SERVINGS

Stuffed peppers are great on the grill, and these will satisfy both carnivores and vegetarians. Traditionally, chiles rellenos are made by stuffing poblano chiles with copious amounts of cheese, rolling them in thick egg batter, and deep-frying them. We always thought there was room for a grilled version filled with grilled vegetables and a bit less cheese. Here it is—the lighter relleno, with grilled corn and scallions in the stuffing and a grilled ranchero salsa on the side. If you can't find poblanos, you can use the slender, longer Anaheims.

INGREDIENTS:

4 large poblano chiles

2 medium ears corn, husks and silks removed

2 scallions (green and white parts), trimmed

1 tablespoon olive oil

¾ teaspoon sea salt

½ cup finely crumbled queso fresco or feta cheese

½ cup crumbled or shredded Chihuahua or Monterey Jack cheese

1 garlic clove, minced

2 tablespoons chopped fresh cilantro

¾ cup all-purpose flour

2 large eggs, lightly beaten

¾ cup plain dry breadcrumbs

¼ cup yellow cornmeal, preferably stone-ground

½ teaspoon ground ancho chile

Cooking spray

1 cup Salsa Ranchero (page 46)

DIRECTIONS:

Light a grill for bilevel medium-high/medium heat, about 425/325°F (see page 13). Brush the grill grate and coat with oil.

Grill the chiles directly over medium-high heat until soft and blackened all over, 8 to 10 minutes, turning once or twice. Remove the chiles to a paper bag or shallow baking dish. Seal the bag or cover the dish and let rest for 15 to 20 minutes. When cool enough to handle, peel and discard the skin with your fingers or the edge of a paring knife (wear plastic gloves if you're very sensitive to the heat-producing capsaicin in chiles). Cut a 2-inch-long slit through the flat side of each chile and use a melon baller or grapefruit spoon to scrape out the seeds and core, leaving the stem intact.

While the chiles are grilling, coat the corn and scallions with the oil, season with ¼ teaspoon of the salt, and grill directly over medium-high heat until tender and charred in spots, turning often. The scallions will take 4 to 6 minutes; the corn 8 to 10 minutes. Remove to a cutting board. Stand the corn on the stem end and cut the kernels from the cobs. Scrape the cobs with the back of the knife to release some of the corn "milk." Scrape half of the kernels and all of the milky bits into a small food processor. Coarsely chop the scallions and add to the processor. Process until the corn is pureed and the scallions are finely chopped. Scrape into a bowl and stir in the remaining corn kernels, cheeses, garlic, and cilantro.

Carefully spoon the stuffing into the chiles, plumping up each one.

Put the flour in one shallow dish, the eggs in another, and mix the breadcrumbs, cornmeal, ancho, and remaining ½ teaspoon salt in a third. Carefully dredge each chile first in the flour to coat, shaking of the excess, then in the egg, then in the crumbs.

Generously coat the breaded chiles all over with cooking spray. Brush the grill grate and coat with oil. Reduce a gas grill to medium or place the chiles over the medium-heat area on a charcoal or wood grill. Grill the breaded chiles, slit-side down, directly over the heat until nicely browned and grill-marked, 3 to 4 minutes. Turn and grill until nicely browned and grill-marked on the other side, 3 to 4 minutes.

Remove to plates and serve with the salsa.

Grilled Zucchini with Brown Butter and Oranges

MAKES 4 SERVINGS

If zucchini isn't your favorite vegetable, try it grilled. When exposed to a hot fire, its subtle green sweetness concentrates and its meaty pulp gets firmer. Any flavorful ingredients rubbed on the surface sink easily into the flesh. In this recipe, that means a rich nutty mixture of browned butter and orange juice. It's really delicious. Just be sure not to overcook the zucchini, or it will turn mushy.

INGREDIENTS:

2 medium zucchini (about 6 ounces each)

1 tablespoon olive oil

Coarse salt and ground black pepper

½ cup Orange Brown Butter (page 44)

1 orange, cut into supremes (see Know-How, page 296)

DIRECTIONS:

Light a grill for direct medium-high heat, about 400°F (see page 12).

Cut the zucchini lengthwise into slabs about ⅜ inch thick. Coat the slabs all over with the oil, then season with salt and pepper.

Brush the grill grate and coat with oil. Grill the zucchini directly over the heat until nicely grill-marked yet somewhat firm, 2 to 3 minutes per side. Remove to a platter, spoon on the brown butter, and top with the orange supremes.

DELICATA SQUASH

Grill-Roasted Delicata Squash with Cardamom and Thyme

MAKES 4 SERVINGS

Delicata squash is, well, delicate. Its soft and tender flesh spoons up easily when grill-roasted. Its flavor is savory, sweet, and scented with musk—an alluring combination. This makes a delicious side dish, but you can make it a main dish by stuffing the cavities with bits of grilled lamb and/or rice. If delicatas aren't available, use this simple grill-roasting technique for other orange-fleshed squash, like acorn and butternut; they'll just take a little longer to become tender.

INGREDIENTS:

2 medium delicata squash

4 tablespoons unsalted butter, melted

1 tablespoon fresh thyme leaves

½ teaspoon ground cardamom

½ teaspoon coarse salt

⅛ teaspoon ground black pepper

DIRECTIONS:

Light a grill for indirect high heat, about 425°F (see page 14).

Cut the squash in half lengthwise and scoop out the seeds and strings. Prick the flesh with a fork in a few spots without going all the way down to the skin (this helps the squash absorb the seasonings).

Combine the melted butter, thyme, cardamom, salt, and pepper in a bowl. Brush all over the cut sides of the squash, and then divide the remainder among the cavities.

Brush the grill grate and coat with oil. Put the squash on the grill away from the heat over a drip pan filled with ½ inch of hot water. Cover the grill and cook until the squash is tender (a fork should slide in and out of the flesh easily), about 20 to 30 minutes.

Allow guests to scoop the flesh from the squash.

Chapter 13

FRUIT

Humans have an intimate relationship with fruit. After succumbing to the forbidden fruit, the story goes, we lost our innocence and were consigned to an agrarian future of raising plants for our survival. The Biblical trope makes sense because, botanically speaking, fruit is the ripened ovary of a plant containing the plant's seed. The bright colors and tempting aromas of fruit are designed to entice creatures to eat the fruit and spread the seed to ensure the plant's survival. We eat the fruit. The plant regenerates. We regenerate. A happy ecology is born.

FRUIT

FRUIT

INGREDIENT	CLASSIFICATION	HOW TO GRILL	SUBSTITUTIONS
APPLES	Pome fruit	Whole, cored: indirect, medium heat Halved or sliced: direct, medium-high heat	Pears
QUINCE (MARMELO)	Pome fruit	Whole, cored: indirect, medium heat Halved or sliced: direct, medium-high heat	Tart apples, Asian or bosc pears
PEARS	Pome fruit	Whole, cored: indirect, medium heat Halved or sliced: direct, medium-high heat	Apples, Asian pears, quince
ASIAN PEARS (APPLE PEAR, CHINESE PEAR)	Pome fruit	Whole, cored: indirect, medium heat Halved or sliced: direct, medium-high heat Chips: indirect, medium-low heat	Apples, pears
APRICOTS	Stone fruit	Pitted whole, halved, or sliced: direct, medium to medium-high heat	Apriums, pluots, plums, peaches, nectarines
PLUMS (PRUNE)	Stone fruit	Pitted whole, halved, or sliced: direct, medium to medium-high heat	Pluots, apriums, apricots, peaches, nectarines
PEACHES	Stone fruit	Pitted whole, halved, or sliced: direct, medium to medium-high heat	Nectarines, apricots, plums
NECTARINES	Stone fruit	Pitted whole, halved, or sliced: direct, medium to medium-high heat	Peaches, apricots, plums
WATERMELON	Melon	Sliced 1 to 2 inches thick: direct, medium- high heat or indirect, medium heat	Honeydew melon, Galia melon
STAR FRUIT (CARAMBOLA)	Tropical fruit	Sliced: direct, medium-high heat	Kiwi fruit, navel oranges
CHERIMOYA (CUSTARD APPLE)	Tropical fruit	Whole: indirect, medium heat Sliced: direct, medium-high heat	Atemoya
PINEAPPLE (ANANA)	Tropical fruit	Sliced: direct, medium-high heat	Papaya, mango
BANANAS	Tropical fruit	Unpeeled and halved lengthwise or peeled and cut into 2-inch lengths: direct, medium-high heat	Ripe black plantains
DRAGON FRUIT (PITAYA)	Tropical fruit	Sliced: direct, medium-high heat	Kiwi
GRAPEFRUIT	Citrus	Halved, sliced 1-inch thick, or segmented: direct, medium to medium-high heat	Oro blanco, pomelo
PERSIMMONS (KAKI)	Subtropical fruit	Sliced: direct, medium-high heat	Peaches, nectarines, plums
FIGS	Flower	Whole or halved: direct, medium-high heat	Peaches, nectarines, plums

Classes of Fruit

Fruits are among the most nutritious foods on the planet. They contain virtually no fat, and they're loaded with fiber, vitamins, minerals, and health-protecting antioxidants. Most are sweet, juicy, and bursting with delicious aromas. The high sugar content of fruits makes them ideal for the grill. The sugars melt, brown, and caramelize, creating hundreds of new flavor compounds, which make the fruit taste even better.

To get a handle on grilling fruit, it helps to observe where the fruit grows and to learn about its family. Temperate-climate fruits grow on trees, bushes, and vines. These plants needs a period of cold before they will flower and bear fruit. Temperate-climate fruits include pome fruits like apples, stone fruits like peaches, and other fruits such as berries, grapes, and kiwis. Subtropical fruits are similar but not hardy to extreme cold. Most can tolerate a mild frost but also withstand tropical climates, depending upon their location. Subtropical fruits include citrus fruits, figs, avocados, dates, persimmons, and pomegranates. Tropical fruits grow in any frost-free environment, and many can tolerate the coolest temperatures of subtropical climates. Here are more details on the most popular fruit families for grilling.

Pome Fruit

This family includes apples (*pomum* in Latin), pears, quince, loquats, and medlars. All pome fruits develop from the plant's flower base rather than its ovary, which makes pome fruits more fibrous than other fruits. Fiber gives apples and pears their crisp texture. When pomes are overripe, though, they become mushy or grainy, which is why most of them are picked underripe. The fibrous structure allows pome fruits to withstand long cooking, as in grill-baked apples and grill-poached pears. These fruits also contain enough pectin to thicken into sauces like applesauce. Quince contain so much pectin that they are too firm to be eaten raw and must be cooked. For the best quality, choose firm, unblemished pome fruits. To prevent enzymatic browning, coat apples and pears with citrus juice or another acid once they are cut.

Stone Fruit

Peaches, nectarines, apricots, plums, and cherries all have a hard stone or pit at the center. The family also includes mangoes, dates, and olives. There are two subcategories of stone fruits: Clingstone fruit ripen early and contain pits that cling tightly to the flesh. Freestone fruit ripen later in the season and release the flesh from the pit easily. The soft, sweet, juicy flesh of freestone peaches, nectarines, apricots, and plums take extremely well to the grill. When ripe, stone fruits will yield to gentle pressure and emit a fragrant aroma.

Melons

As members of the gourd family, melons come in a staggering variety of shapes and sizes. Most melons, like honeydew and cantaloupe, belong to the *Cucumis* genus, which is characterized by seeds, gel, and/or strings at the center of the fruit. But watermelons belong to the *Citrullus* genus and their seeds are scattered throughout the fruit. Melons have thick rinds and firm, sweet, very juicy flesh, which is typically eaten fresh. We've found that watermelons, despite being 92 percent water, make a delicious grilled steak. Choose firm melons that feel heavy for their size, indicating maximum water content. Watermelons with a pale patch on one side (where the melon sat on the ground) have been ripened on the vine, rather than picked when immature and ripened during shipping. If the melon still has a bit of stem attached, look for a sweet-smelling ooze at that spot.

Tropical Fruit

A diverse group, no single fruit family dominates in this category, but most tropical fruits display brilliant colors on their skins and emit a rich perfume of aromas in their flesh. The best tropical fruits for grilling include bananas, cherimoyas, mangoes, papayas, pineapples, plantains, and star fruit (carambola). See the chart on page 335 for details about how to grill specific tropical fruits.

Citrus

These fruits are the third-most commonly cultivated fruit in the world (just behind pome fruits and the banana/plantain family), not least because citrus trees yield large quantities of fruit. There are hundreds of varieties, but all have a similar anatomy. The outer colored peel or zest is known as the flavedo, a good name because that's where the intensely flavorful essential oils and vitamin C tend to concentrate. Just beneath the flavedo lies the inner white peel or albedo (white pith), which tastes bitter yet is rich in pectin. The entire peel encases the pulp with segments consisting of delicate juice sacs (vesicles) held together by a fibrous membrane. Citrus fruits do not continue to ripen after harvest, so they must develop sweetness on the tree. The ripest citrus will feel plump, firm, and heavy for its size.

How to Grill Fruit

Most fruit can be eaten fresh, so there's really no need to grill it to a certain degree of doneness (except for quince, which must be softened to be edible). You simply want to grill-mark it to caramelize some sugars and develop flavor. Direct, medium-high heat usually gets the job done quickly without turning the fruit to mush. Fruits are generally halved or sliced before grilling, but pome fruits like apples and pears can be cored and grill-baked or grill-poached whole over indirect heat. Stone fruits like peaches and plums only need to be pitted. Then the fleshy fruit can be grilled whole, halved, or sliced over direct medium-high heat. Citrus fruit like grapefruit is often halved and grilled cut-side down just until lightly browned. To expose more of the fruit to flame, slice the citrus crosswise into rings and grill the rings. When serving lemon or lime wedges for squeezing alongside fish or another dish, consider tossing the wedges on the grill for a smoky finish in the squeezed juice.

Eaten raw, most fruit tastes best at the peak of ripeness. But for grilling, sometimes you want slightly underripe fruit so it won't fall apart or get mushy. Choose just-ripe pears, peaches, nectarines, and bananas for the grill. The sky's the limit when it comes to flavoring. Sweet is the defining flavor of most fruit, so try to round out the taste by adding pungency (chiles or mustard), saltiness (soy sauce), or richness (butter, yogurt, cream, or other dairy products). The flavor of some fruits, like tart apples and lemons, is naturally balanced with sour notes. As with meats and vegetables, you can flavor grilled fruit with all manner of marinades, glazes, syrups, spice rubs, and sauces (see the recipes beginning on page 26 for some possibilities). You can also core pome fruits or halve and pit stone fruits, and then stuff them with something delicious like cheese or nuts. You can grill whole stone fruits. Slit them along the seam, remove the stone, then replace it with a flavorful filling.

Grilled fruit is typically served alongside dessert, but grilled apples, peaches, and other fruit pair well with savory dishes, too. When grilling pork, poultry, or fish, consider tossing some fruit on the side of the grill as an accompaniment.

APPLES

Grill-Baked Apples with Sweet Sausage Stuffing

MAKES 4 SERVINGS

Baked apples are usually stuffed with nuts and sticky-sweet brown sugar or maple syrup. But apples are also delicious with pork, so we've gone savory here and stuffed them with toasted walnuts, grilled cipollini onions, sweet sausage, and sage. On the grill, the apples pick up a hint of smoke, which enhances the taste of the sausage. There's a bit of chopping and mixing, so bring a cutting board to the grill for this one.

INGREDIENTS:

4 small cipollini onions, peeled

3 large garlic cloves, skins left on

1 tablespoon olive oil

½ cup walnuts

6 ounces loose sweet Italian sausage

¼ cup finely chopped celery

4 teaspoons Poultry Rub (page 29)

4 large Gala, Rome, or other large baking apples

1 cup apple cider

2 tablespoons Nocello (walnut liqueur) or another nut liqueur

1 tablespoon cider vinegar

1 tablespoon chopped fresh sage

DIRECTIONS:

Light a grill for indirect medium heat, about 350°F (see page 14).

Cut the onions in half through their equators, and then toss with the unpeeled garlic and oil in a bowl. Brush the grill grate and coat with oil. Grill the onions, cut-side down, and the unpeeled garlic directly over the heat until the onions are tender and the garlic is charred in spots, about 5 minutes, turning once or twice. Squeeze the garlic from its skins, and then chop along with the onions.

Put a large cast-iron skillet or heavy-duty roasting pan directly over the heat. Add the walnuts and toast until fragrant, about 5 minutes, shaking occasionally. Remove the walnuts from the pan and chop.

Add the sausage to the pan and cook until lightly browned all over, 5 to 8 minutes, stirring occasionally. Remove and set aside. Add the celery to the drippings in the pan and cook for 4 minutes, stirring now and then. Add the onions, garlic, sausage, and the poultry rub and cook for 1 minute. Scrape the stuffing into a bowl.

Cut the apples in half crosswise and remove the core from each half with a melon baller. Put the apples, cut-side up, in the skillet or in a roasting pan. Fill the center of each half with the sausage mixture. Mix together the apple cider, liqueur, vinegar, and sage and pour around and over the apples. Cover the pan with foil and put the pan on the grill away from the heat. Cover the grill and cook for 20 minutes. Remove the foil and cook until the apples are tender, 15 to 20 minutes more.

Let cool for 10 minutes before serving. Drizzle the apples with the cider syrup from the pan and serve.

Grilled Quince and Cranberry Compote

MAKES 4 TO 6 SERVINGS

Quince is too firm to eat out of hand. But when cooked, the fruit softens and the abundant pectin is released from the cell walls, helping to thicken any liquid mixture in which it is simmered. Historically, quince has been cooked down to preserves and jams, explaining why the word "marmalade" stems from the Portuguese name for quince, *marmelo*. Here the fruit thickens the juices in a simple compote. Quince has a floral aroma reminiscent of pineapple, which pairs remarkably well with tart cranberries. This garnet-colored compote would make a great side dish for an autumn meal of grilled poultry.

INGREDIENTS:

2 medium quince, peeled, cored, and quartered lengthwise

2 teaspoons canola oil

1½ cups fresh or frozen cranberries, thawed if frozen

¾ cup sugar

4 large slices fresh ginger, about ¼ inch thick

1 strip orange zest, about 4 inches long and 1 inch wide, with no white pith

1 cinnamon stick, about 3 inches long

1 teaspoon raspberry vinegar

DIRECTIONS:

Light a grill for direct medium-high heat, about 425°F (see page 12).

Toss the quince quarters with the oil. Brush the grill grate and coat with oil. Grill the quince directly over the heat until grill-marked and beginning to soften, 8 to 10 minutes, turning a few times. Remove to a cutting board and chop into bite-size pieces.

Meanwhile, combine the cranberries, sugar, ginger, orange zest, and cinnamon stick in a medium saucepan. Cook over medium heat until the cranberries start to pop and release their juice, 5 to 6 minutes. Add the chopped grilled quince (and any accumulated juices) and cook until the quince is soft and the liquid thickens slightly, 3 to 4 minutes. Remove from the heat and let cool to room temperature.

Pluck out the ginger, orange zest, and cinnamon stick and stir in the vinegar. Serve at room temperature or cover and refrigerate for up to 1 week.

PEARS

Grilled Pear Soup with Porcini and Gorgonzola

MAKES 4 SERVINGS

Pear varieties differ in aroma and in the firmness of their flesh. Boscs smell like sweet spices and hold their shape well, which makes them great for poaching. But in this recipe, we recommend creamy-fleshed pears like Comice or Bartlett. Their smooth texture purees into a luscious, velvety soup. The combination of pears and mushrooms may seem odd at first, but Italians have been pairing mushrooms with peaches, apples, plums, and other fruits for centuries. The woodsy taste of porcinis is perfect with pears but if you can't find them, use large cremini mushrooms. For the Gorgonzola, try mild and creamy Gorgonzola dolce, aged only about three months. Stronger aged Gorgonzolas will also work.

INGREDIENTS:

2 cups boiling water

½ ounce dried porcini mushrooms

4 just-ripe pears, such as Comice or Bartlett

1 tablespoon olive oil

4 ounces fresh porcini mushrooms

4 tablespoons unsalted butter

1 large sprig fresh rosemary

¼ cup dry sherry

2 cups chicken broth

1 tablespoon honey

3 ounces mascarpone or cream cheese

Kosher salt

½ cup crumbled Gorgonzola cheese, preferably Gorgonzola dolce

DIRECTIONS:

Light a grill for direct medium-high heat, about 400°F (see page 12). If the bars of your grill grate are widely spaced, preheat a grill tray on the grill.

Pour the boiling water over the dried porcini in a heat-proof bowl and soak for 20 minutes. When reconstituted, pluck the mushrooms from the liquid with a slotted spoon, reserving the soaking liquid, and finely chop the mushrooms.

Peel and core the pears, and then slice lengthwise about ½ inch thick. Toss immediately with the oil in a shallow dish. Slice the fresh porcinis about ⅜ inch thick with some stem attached to each slice; if they are too small, just halve them lengthwise. Toss gently with the pears and oil to coat.

Brush the grill grate and coat with oil (oil the grill tray if using). Grill the pears and porcini directly over the heat until nicely grill-marked, 3 to 4 minutes per side.

Melt the butter in a medium soup pot over medium heat. Add the grilled pears to the pot along with the rosemary sprig. (Reserve the grilled porcini for garnish.) Cook the pears for 2 minutes, and then add the sherry. Cook until most of the liquid evaporates, about 5 minutes. If the mushroom soaking liquid is very gritty, strain it through cheesecloth or a wet coffee filter. Pour the liquid into the pot, leaving behind any grit. Add the chopped reconstituted mushrooms, chicken broth, and honey. Simmer gently until the flavors blend, about 10 minutes. Reduce the heat to low and remove the rosemary sprig. Stir in the mascarpone or cream cheese and puree the soup with a stick blender or in an upright blender. Season with salt.

Ladle the soup into bowls and top with the reserved grilled porcini and the Gorgonzola.

APRICOTS

Amaretto-Seared Apricots with Almond Praline

MAKES 4 SERVINGS

Stone fruits like apricots grill beautifully. Just halve them, remove the stone, and sear, cut-side down, until grill-marked. You can glaze them, stuff them, or flavor them almost any which way. Almonds and apricots share similar flavor compounds, making them a natural match. Serve these with almond-scented whipped cream.

INGREDIENTS:

Almond Praline:

¾ cup sugar

2 teaspoons water

½ cup almonds with skins

8 ripe apricots

2 tablespoons unsalted butter

2 tablespoons honey

1 tablespoon amaretto liqueur

½ teaspoon ground allspice

¼ teaspoon pure vanilla extract

DIRECTIONS:

For the almond praline: Combine the sugar, water, and almonds in a small heavy saucepan over low heat. Cook without stirring until the sugar is deep amber (about 300°F). Pour the mixture onto a greased baking sheet, spreading it quickly with a wooden spoon. Let cool completely, and then crack into small pieces. Chop the praline to the size of large crumbs in a minichopper or put the praline in a plastic bag and crush with a heavy rolling pin or pan.

Light a grill for direct medium heat, about 375°F (see page 12). Brush the grill grate and coat with oil. Halve and pit the apricots.

In a small microwaveable bowl, combine the butter, honey, amaretto, allspice, and vanilla. Microwave on high power just until the butter melts, about 30 seconds. Stir until smooth.

Brush the apricots all over with the amaretto mixture. Grill the apricots, cut-side down, until nicely grilled-marked, 2 to 3 minutes. Flip, brush the cut side generously with more amaretto mixture, and grill until the apricots are just tender, about 2 minutes more.

Top the apricots with the crushed almond praline before serving. Reserve any remaining praline for another use.

PLUMS

Grilled Plums Stuffed with Feta and Pistachios

MAKES 4 SERVINGS

Although widely cultivated in California, pistachios are underappreciated in North America. So we turn to the Mediterranean region for this flavor profile. There, pistachios are widely used in both savory and sweet dishes. The rich, distinctive taste of pistachios marries perfectly with the juicy, sweet-tart flesh of fresh plums. A tinge of purple and green colors in both ingredients further unites them. A crumble of salty feta cheese provides contrast. If the plums in your market aren't ripe, use a hybrid such as pluots or apriums. Or use apricots.

continued

INGREDIENTS:

2 ounces feta cheese, crumbled
(about ½ cup)

1½ tablespoons honey

2 tablespoons ground roasted pistachios

¼ teaspoon finely chopped fresh rosemary

8 ripe plums

Cooking spray

1 tablespoon unsalted butter, melted

Finely grated zest of ½ lime

⅛ teaspoon pure vanilla extract

DIRECTIONS:

Light a grill for direct medium heat, about 325°F (see page 12).

Combine the feta, 1 tablespoon of the honey, pistachios, and rosemary. Slice the plums down one side along their "seam" and lift out the pit. Stuff each plum with some of the feta mixture and gently press closed. Coat all over with cooking spray.

Combine the melted butter, remaining ½ tablespoon honey, lime zest, and vanilla in a small bowl and set aside.

Brush the grill grate and coat with oil. Grill the plums directly over the heat until nicely grill-marked and warm, about 2 minutes per side. Serve drizzled with the vanilla-lime butter.

PEACHES

Grilled Peaches Agrodolce

MAKES 4 SERVINGS

Peaches love the grill. These take on a garnet hue from the agrodolce or "sour-sweet" syrup made with honey, red wine, and red wine vinegar. We serve them with a dollop of crème fraîche, but a good fresh sheep's or cow's milk ricotta would also be delicious. Or skip the dairy products and serve these as is with grilled chicken or pork.

INGREDIENTS:

1¼ cups dry red wine

⅔ cup red wine vinegar

⅔ cup honey

1 vanilla bean, split

3 whole cloves

4 just-ripe peaches, pitted and quartered lengthwise

3 tablespoons unsalted butter, melted

Pinch of salt

¼ cup crème fraîche (optional)

DIRECTIONS:

Light a grill for direct medium-high heat, about 400°F (see page 12). If the bars of your grill grate are widely spaced, preheat a grill tray on the grill.

As the grill heats, combine the wine, vinegar, honey, vanilla bean, and cloves in a medium saucepan. Bring to a boil over high heat and continue boiling until reduced to a medium-thin syrup, 5 to 6 minutes. Keep hot.

Brush the grill grate and coat with oil; oil the tray if using. Toss the peaches with the melted butter and salt to coat.

Grill the peaches directly over the heat, perpendicular to the bars of the grill grate, until nicely grill-marked, 2 to 3 minutes per side. Immediately add the grilled peaches to the wine syrup and remove from the heat. Let cool until lukewarm or room temperature, about 30 minutes. Fish out the cloves and vanilla bean pod halves.

Serve the peaches warm or at room temperature, drizzled with some of the syrup and a dollop of the crème fraîche, if desired.

Marinated Watermelon Steak with Pink Peppercorn Rub

MAKES 4 SERVINGS

What would happen if you cut a watermelon into manageable slabs, marinated the slabs in rum (just as you would marinate a beefsteak in wine), and then grilled them over a low and slow fire? As we discovered, the watermelon cells open, moisture evaporates, and the melon's flavor and texture concentrate, becoming succulently compact yet tender and juicy. Kind of like a fillet steak. We were charmed. This recipe may be a bit of grill frippery, but it's utterly delicious. We experimented with a few flavoring options and decided pink peppercorns were the best. Not a true peppercorn, this dried berry (*Schinus terebinthifolius*) is the fruit of a Baies rose, a Brazilian rose bush. The berries have a sweet, peppery flavor, which sparks the taste of the rum-, mint-, and lime-soaked grilled watermelon.

INGREDIENTS:

1 crosswise center-cut slice of a large watermelon, about 1½ inches thick

¾ cup light rum

5 tablespoons unsalted butter, melted

1 tablespoon chopped fresh mint

1 lime

Coarse salt

2 tablespoons pink peppercorns, crushed

2 teaspoons sugar

2 tablespoons honey

DIRECTIONS:

Remove the green and white rind from the watermelon, and then cut crosswise into quarters to make four wedge-shaped steaks.

Combine the rum, butter, and mint in a 1-gallon zipper-lock bag. Grate the zest from half of the lime into the bag, then squeeze in all of the juice. Add a pinch of salt and the watermelon steaks. Press out the air, seal, and shake gently to blend. Let stand at warm room temperature (at least 72°F) for 1 to 2 hours.

Light a grill for indirect medium heat, about 350°F (see page 14).

Combine the crushed pink peppercorns, sugar, and ¼ teaspoon salt in a small dish. Remove the watermelon from the marinade and pat dry with paper towels; reserve the marinade. Sprinkle the rub all over the steaks.

Brush the grill grate and coat with oil. Grill the watermelon directly over the heat until nicely grill-marked, 3 to 4 minutes per side. Move the watermelon away from the heat, close the lid, and cook until very tender and slightly shrunken, 30 to 40 minutes.

Boil the marinade in a small saucepan until reduced to ⅓ cup, about 10 minutes. Stir in the honey and drizzle over the steaks.

Star Fruit Glazed with Sweet Mustard

MAKES 4 SERVINGS

There are two types of star fruit: sweet and sour. Look for sweet yellow ones for this recipe. They will exude an aromatic perfume of plum, apple, grape, and lemon. Their thin skin needs no peeling, but trim any dark skin from the ridges, which can be tough. Sliced crosswise, grilled and glazed, the fruit makes a stunning partner for salmon or chicken.

INGREDIENTS:

1½ tablespoons spicy brown mustard

1 tablespoon orange marmalade

Juice of 1 lime

Pinch of ground cloves

1 tablespoon unsalted butter, melted

1 tablespoon chopped fresh basil leaves

2 sweet star fruit

DIRECTIONS:

Light a grill for direct medium-high heat, about 400°F (see page 12). If the bars of your grill grate are widely spaced, preheat a grill tray on the grill.

Mix together the mustard, marmalade, lime juice, cloves, butter, and basil.

Trim the ends of the star fruit and trim off any dark skin from the long ridges. Cut the fruit crosswise into slices about ¼ inch thick. Toss the slices with the glaze in a shallow dish until coated all over.

Brush the grill grate and coat with oil; oil the grill tray if using. Grill the star fruit directly over the heat until nicely grill-marked, 2 to 3 minutes per side. Brush any remaining glaze over the fruit near the end of cooking.

Molasses-Seared Pineapple with Pineapple-Rum Glaze

MAKES 4 TO 8 SERVINGS

You won't know what hit you when you taste this fruit. Grilled pineapple tastes wonderful enough on its own. Glaze it with lime, cardamom, molasses, coconut rum, and habanero hot sauce, and your taste buds start swaying to a reggae beat while your mind wanders off to the farthest reaches of the island.

INGREDIENTS:

1 medium pineapple, peeled and cored (see Know-How, below)

3 tablespoons molasses

⅓ cup Pineapple-Rum Glaze (page 51)

DIRECTIONS:

Light a grill for direct medium-high heat, about 425°F (see page 12).

Cut the pineapple crosswise into rings about 1 inch thick. Brush the rings all over with the molasses.

Brush the grill grate and coat with oil. Grill the pineapple rings directly over the heat until nicely grill-marked, 3 to 5 minutes per side. Brush both sides with the glaze during the last 2 minutes of cooking.

Remove to plates and brush with the remaining glaze before serving.

KEEP IT SIMPLE

Replace the whole pineapple with a peeled, cored golden pineapple from the refrigerated produce section of your market. Cut into rings as directed.

KNOW-HOW: PEELING AND CORING PINEAPPLE

Cut off the spiky top and ½ inch from the base of the pineapple. Stand it upright and cut repeatedly from top to bottom around the fruit to remove the peel and eyes. For rings, cut the pineapple crosswise into slices. Lay the slices on the cutting board and use the large side of a melon baller or a sharp paring knife to remove the tough core from each slice. For quarters or wedges, cut the pineapple lengthwise into quarters. Stand each quarter upright and slice off the core. Cut crosswise into wedges.

BANANAS

Grilled Banana Satay

MAKES 4 SERVINGS

Beef makes good satay, so why not banana? After all, it's meaty and rich. Enrobed in sweet peanut sauce and shaggy shredded coconut, these banana medallions are delicious with grilled pound cake. They'd be even better with grill-toasted pandan cake (a light, fluffy Southeast Asian cake traditionally made from the juice of a pandan plant) and coconut whipped cream.

INGREDIENTS:

4 bamboo skewers, soaked in water for 30 minutes

4 fat, barely ripe bananas, peeled

¼ cup peanut butter

½ cup coconut milk

2 tablespoons dark brown sugar

1 teaspoon ground ginger

¼ teaspoon ground cinnamon

Pinch of salt

Pinch of cayenne pepper

⅔ cup sweetened shredded coconut

DIRECTIONS:

Light a grill for direct medium-high heat, about 400°F (see page 12).

Slice the bananas crosswise into medallions 1 to 2 inches thick. Skewer the banana pieces through the edges so that the flat sides can be grilled, threading 6 to 8 pieces on each skewer.

Whisk together the peanut butter, coconut milk, brown sugar, ginger, cinnamon, salt, and cayenne pepper in a bowl. Pour half of the peanut sauce into a wide shallow dish.

Brush the grill grate and coat with oil. Grill the banana skewers directly over the heat until nicely grill-marked, 2 to 3 minutes per side. Dip the flat sides of the bananas in the peanut sauce. Sprinkle with the coconut to coat. Return to the grill and cook until lightly browned, 1 to 2 minutes per side.

Serve with the remaining sauce for dipping.

DRAGON FRUIT

Charred Red Dragon Fruit Pizza

MAKES 4 SERVINGS

Dragon fruit (also called pitaya) comes in several shades and both sweet and sour versions. For this recipe, choose the most common red-skinned, white-fleshed dragon fruit. It's one of the most striking fruits you'll ever see, resembling a fuchsia-colored hand grenade with flame-like yellowed leaves. When cut, its white flesh, riddled with tiny black seeds, contrasts beautifully with the outer ring of red skin. Dragon fruit has a somewhat mild flavor—with hints of strawberry, kiwi, and watermelon—that's delicious on a fruit pizza. To echo the colors, we mix strawberry puree into mascarpone cheese, creating a pink spread for the pizza, which is topped with chunks of the white fruit and grilled until crisp.

continued ➔

INGREDIENTS:

8 ounces fresh or frozen strawberries (about 20 medium), thawed if frozen

8 ounces mascarpone cheese or cream cheese

⅓ cup sugar

¼ teaspoon ground cinnamon

Cooking spray

1 recipe Pizza Dough (page 381), or 1 pound store-bought pizza dough

2 sweet red dragon fruit (pitaya)

1 tablespoon chopped fresh mint

DIRECTIONS:

Light a grill for bilevel medium-high/medium heat, about 425/325°F (see page 13).

Put the strawberries in a small food processor and puree. Add the mascarpone, 3 tablespoons of the sugar, and the cinnamon; process until well blended and set aside.

Cut four pieces of aluminum foil, each about 12 inches square. Coat one of the pieces with cooking spray. Divide the dough into four pieces and put a piece on the prepared foil. Cover the other pieces to keep them from drying out. Press and stretch the dough on the foil into a circle 8 to 10 inches in diameter and ⅛ to ¼ inch thick. Don't bother making a rim around the edge of the crust unless you like it for aesthetics. Coat the top of the dough round with cooking spray. Repeat with the remaining dough and foil, oiling each dough round well and stacking them up.

Quarter the dragon fruits lengthwise through the peels. Cut the peel from each quarter, then sprinkle 1 tablespoon sugar all over the quarters.

Brush the grill grate and coat with oil. Grill the dragon fruit directly over medium-high heat perpendicular to the bars of the grill grate until charred in spots, 3 to 4 minutes, turning once or twice. Remove to a cutting board, let cool slightly, then chop into bite-size pieces.

Oil the grill grate again. On a gas grill, reduce the heat to medium. Invert each round of dough onto the grill directly over the heat, placing the rounds over the medium-heat area of a charcoal or wood grill, and working in batches if necessary. Carefully remove the foil. Close the lid and grill until the dough is bubbly on top and nicely grill-marked on the bottom, 2 to 3 minutes, rotating the dough with tongs after about a minute for more even browning.

Remove the dough rounds and invert them onto a cutting board so that the grilled side is up. Spread about ⅓ to ½ cup of the mascarpone mixture over the surface of each dough round. Arrange the pieces of grilled dragon fruit over the mascarpone and sprinkle with the mint and remaining sugar.

Slide each pizza back onto the grill over medium heat and cook until the bottom is nicely grill-marked, about 3 to 4 minutes, rotating the dough after a minute or two for even browning.

Cut each pizza into 8 wedges and serve.

GRAPEFRUIT

Grilled Grapefruit with Pomegranate Molasses Glaze

MAKES 4 SERVINGS

Halved grapefruits taste delicious with a kiss of smoke from the grill. But they're even better sliced to expose more of the fruit to the caramelizing fire. Pomegranate molasses, with its sweet-tart flavor and syrupy texture, makes a tasty, ruby-hued glaze. Try this recipe with oro blanco (a white-fleshed pomelo), too. If you have fresh pomegranates, scatter the seeds over the top.

INGREDIENTS:

¼ cup pomegranate molasses

2 tablespoons dark brown sugar

1 tablespoon unsalted butter, melted

¼ teaspoon ground cardamom

¼ teaspoon ground cinnamon

⅛ teaspoon grated nutmeg

Pinch of coarse salt

2 ripe ruby grapefruits

DIRECTIONS:

Light a grill for direct medium-high heat, about 425°F (see page 12).

Mix the pomegranate molasses, brown sugar, butter, cardamom, cinnamon, nutmeg, and salt in a small bowl with a whisk until smooth.

Using a sharp paring knife, remove the peel and bitter white pith from the grapefruits. Cut the fruit crosswise into 1-inch-thick slices, and then brush all over with the pomegranate molasses glaze.

Brush the grill grate and coat with oil. Grill the grapefruit directly over the heat until nicely grill-marked, 2 to 3 minutes per side. Remove from the heat and brush with any remaining glaze.

PERSIMMONS

Grilled Persimmon Sorbet

MAKES ABOUT 3½ CUPS

Grilling the fruit for sorbet gives the dessert's iciness a warmer, friendlier tone. Persimmons taste delicious grilled and chilled. There are two main varieties: astringent and nonastringent. Fuyu persimmons are among the sweet, nonastringent types and resemble squat, orange-colored tomatoes. Slightly larger, flame-orange Hachiya persimmons are heart-shaped and higher in bitter tannins. They also have a luscious texture just shy of creamy, which makes them delicious for eating raw but difficult to grill. Hachiyas also become tougher and more astringent with cooking. Fuyus are much easier to grill because they are firmer. We recommend Fuyus here, but if you enjoy astringency and have Hachiyas that are not too soft, you can use them in this recipe. There is enough sugar to help tame the puckery effect. You'll need about 1½ cups pureed fruit for the sorbet, and three Fuyus should do it. If using Hachiyas, two to three large ones will give you enough puree.

INGREDIENTS:

Sugar Syrup:

1½ cups sugar

⅔ cup water

⅓ cup light corn syrup

1 cinnamon stick, about 3 inches long

2 tablespoons amaretto

Persimmons:

1¼ pounds Fuyu persimmons (about 3 medium)

1 tablespoon olive oil

¾ cup water

continued →

DIRECTIONS:

For the sugar syrup: Combine the sugar, water, corn syrup, and cinnamon stick in a small saucepan. Heat over low heat until the sugar dissolves, 5 to 6 minutes. Remove from the heat and let cool to room temperature. Remove the cinnamon stick and stir in the amaretto.

For the persimmons: Light a grill for direct medium-high heat, about 425°F (see page 12).

Remove the leaves, and then slice the persimmons crosswise about ⅜ inch thick. Coat the slices all over with the olive oil.

Brush the grill grate and coat with oil. Grill the persimmons directly over the heat until nicely grill-marked, 2 to 3 minutes per side. Remove to a food processor and puree. Strain the puree through a medium-mesh strainer, and then measure out 1½ cups puree. Discard the rest. Combine the strained persimmon puree, cooled sugar syrup, and water in a food processor and blend until smooth.

Transfer the mixture to an ice cream machine and freeze according to the manufacturer's directions. Or transfer to a shallow metal pan and freeze until slushy, about 2 hours, stirring every 30 minutes to keep large ice crystals from forming. Once frozen, transfer to an airtight container and press a piece of plastic wrap on the surface. Cover with a tight-fitting plastic lid and freeze until ready to serve, up to 3 days.

FIGS

Grilled Figs in Vin Santo Over Ricotta Ice Cream

**MAKES 4 SERVINGS
(4 CUPS OF ICE CREAM)**

There are hundreds of fig varieties, from green-skinned Smyrna and Calimyrna figs to purple-skinned Mission figs. All have a teardrop shape and an abundance of edible little crunchy seeds. When sliced, ripe figs ooze with nectar, which browns deliciously on the grill. A glaze of honey and vin santo, Tuscany's sweet holy wine, makes grilled figs even more divine. Serve with the ricotta ice cream and almond or hazelnut biscotti.

INGREDIENTS:

Vanilla-Honey Ricotta Ice Cream:

1 container (15 ounces) whole-milk ricotta cheese

1 cup honey

Pinch of salt

1 pint heavy cream

1½ teaspoons pure vanilla extract

Figs:

½ cup vin santo

¼ cup honey

12 large fresh figs, stemmed and halved lengthwise

DIRECTIONS:

For the ice cream: In a food processor, combine the ricotta, honey, and salt. Puree until completely smooth, about 2 minutes, scraping down the sides as necessary. Add the cream and vanilla and pulse until blended. Transfer to an ice-cream maker and freeze according to the manufacturer's directions. Once frozen, transfer to an airtight container and press a piece of plastic wrap on the surface. Cover with a tight-fitting plastic lid and freeze until ready to serve, up to 3 days.

For the figs: Light a grill for direct medium-high heat, about 400°F (see page 12). In a small bowl, whisk together the vin santo and honey. Add the halved figs and gently toss until coated all over. Brush the grill grate and coat with oil. Or, if the bars of your grate are spaced far apart, preheat and oil a grill screen to prevent the figs from falling into the fire. Grill the figs, cut-side down, directly over the heat until nicely grill-marked, 1 to 2 minutes. Flip, brush the cut sides of the figs again with the vin santo mixture, and grill until nicely marked on the rounded side, 1 to 2 minutes.

Scoop the ice cream into bowls, top with the grilled figs, and drizzle with the remaining vin santo mixture.

14

CHEESE, OTHER DAIRY FOODS & EGGS

Milk and eggs, and the products made from them, are the only forms of protein that are not commonly grilled. It's not hard to see why. Milk products are either liquid, or become fluid when exposed to heat (for example, cheese and ice cream), making it difficult to keep them on a grill grate. And eggs curdle when exposed to intense heat.

So why try? For one thing, grilling unlikely ingredients is one of the things this book is about; and for another, quiche baked over an open fire is mind-boggling and grilled ice cream sandwiches are a blast.

Milk has to be made solid in order to grill it, which means there are three options for grilled dairy products: cheese, ice cream, and custard.

CHEESE, DAIRY, AND EGGS

ITEM	DESCRIPTION	HOW TO GRILL
SEMIFIRM CHEESE	Fully ripened, mild to full flavored, thin rind or rindless, can be coated, around 40% moisture, includes Swiss, raclette, gruyere, cheddar	Indirect or direct medium
HARD CHEESE	Grainy, hard enugh to grate, pungent, thin rind, less than 38% moisture, any fat content, includes Parmesan, romano, sapsago	Cannot be grilled alone, used to flavor other preparations
BLUE CHEESE	Semisoft to semifirm depending on age, inundated with blue mold, any moisture or fat, includes Roquefort, stilton, Maytag blue	Indirect medium, usually used to flavor other preparations
SURFACE-RIPENED CHEESE	Soft-ripened, exposed to surface mold faster ripening, thin rind (white to red), mild to pungent, 45 to 50% moisture, 50 to 75% fat, includes Brie, Limburger, Camembert	Direct or indirect low to medium, wrapped to protect surface
SEMISOFT CHEESE	Fully ripened, mild to full flavored, thin rind or rindless, can be coated, semisoft (42 to 50% moisture) to semifirm (around 40% moisture), includes provolone, Gouda, edam, Monterey Jack, Swiss.	Direct or indirect low to medium
FRESH CHEESE	Unripened or only slightly ripened, soft, moist, flavor of fresh dairy, mild, more than 50% moisture, between 5% and 45% fat, includes cottage cheese, cream cheese, mozzarella	Indirect low to medium in mold to hold shape
GOAT AND SHEEP'S CHEESES	Strong tasting, slightly grainy, very white, does not melt when heated, variety of moisture and fat contents, includes chevre, feta, haloumi	Indirect or direct medium
ICE CREAM	Frozen sweetened fresh dairy dessert with fat content of at least 10%, Contains air (overrun), budget ice cream has high overrun and melts quickly, so only use premium ice cream for grilling	Brief direct high, protect by coating
MILK AND CREAM	Fresh dairy liquid, varies in fat content from 0% to 38%	Indirect in mold
EGGS	From poultry, contains albumen and yolk	Whole eggs, indirect low; Shelled egg, direct or indirect medium in container

Cheese

Milk is a matrix of protein, water, and fat. In order to turn it into cheese, bacteria are added to the milk. The bacteria feed on the sugar (lactose) in the milk and produce acids as part of their life process. The acids make the milk proteins coagulate, causing the proteins to squeeze out the water they were holding in suspension. Eventually the matrix breaks, and the milk separates into solid curds (consisting of large proteins, big globules of fat, and a little water) and liquid whey (small proteins, a little fat, and a lot of water). The curd is then salted, cooked, pressed, and/or ripened into various kinds of cheese.

Depending on the type of animal (usually cow, sheep, or goat), what the animal recently ate, and where it lived, the composition of the curd will be different. And, depending on how long and under what conditions the curd is aged, the resulting cheese may be hard or soft, pungent or mild, creamy or crumbly, surface-ripened or veined with blue mold.

Following are the principal types of cheese. They are categorized by the method of production with examples of each type.

Fresh: Uncooked and either unripened or only slightly ripened curd. Fresh cheeses are soft and mild, and sometimes slightly tart. Examples: cream cheese, feta.

String: Fresh curd dipped in a bath of hot whey (about 140°F) to soften it, and then kneaded, stretched, and pulled into strands, which are pliable enough to be shaped. These cheeses have a mild flavor and chewy, elastic texture. They do not become fluid when melted. Examples: mozzarella, provolone.

Surface-ripened or bloomy rind: Molded, drained curd is exposed to molds or bacteria so that they ripen from the outside in. They have a thin rind with a downy surface and are soft below the rind. They may be mild and buttery or slightly pungent. Examples: Brie, Camembert.

Washed-rind: Surface-ripened cheese that is washed or rubbed with brine or other liquids to create changes in the surface mold and produce various flavors. Washed-rind cheeses are usually strongly aromatic and have a red or orange rind. Examples: Taleggio, Limburger.

Natural rind: The rinds of these cheeses are not exposed to mold, bacteria, or liquids. The rinds are kept clean, and the cheeses are well aged. Depending on whether the curd was cooked or not, and how long the cheese was aged (both of which affect its moisture content), these cheeses can be semisoft, semifirm, or hard. Examples: Gouda, emmentaler, cheddar, havarti, Parmesan.

Blue-veined: Inoculated with *Penicillium* bacteria and deeply pierced to provide air circulation, help the mold develop throughout the cheese, and discourage the growth of anaerobic bacteria, which could destroy it. Veined with blue-green mold, these cheeses vary widely in tartness, intensity, and creaminess. Examples: Roquefort, Gorgonzola, Stilton.

Grilling Cheese

All cheese changes when exposed to fire. Dairy fat begins to melt at about 90°F, which causes most cheese to soften slightly. A little hotter, at about 120°F, the protein tightens, squeezing water out of suspension, which causes small beads of water to form on the surface of the cheese. As the cheese gets hotter, the fat continues to liquefy, increasing the cheese's fluidity. The protein continues to coagulate, causing the protein and water to separate from the fat. At a certain point, the protein can no longer hold onto the fat and water, and the cheese slumps. That's the time to get the cheese off the fire. Any further heating will cause the fat and water to separate and turn the cheese grainy.

Cooking times vary according to the proportions of protein, fat, and water, the kind of milk a cheese was made from, and how long it was aged. Cheeses that are higher in fat and water and lower in protein melt more easily. Creamy, moist cheese, like Brie, will melt when barely warm, at about 130°F; firm cheeses like Cheddar or Swiss start to flow at about 150°F; and hard, dry grating cheese such as Parmesan won't show any signs of softening until it's over 180°F. High-protein, low-fat cheeses like mozzarella melt into gooey strings, rather than become fluid. And some cheeses, like fresh goat cheese, haloumi, and paneer, don't melt at all, which means they will not lose their shape during grilling.

Grilling Ice Cream

Grilling ice cream is a bit of sleight of hand. The trick is getting a grilled flavor, or a crispy texture, or a charred appearance while keeping the ice cream frozen solid. This can mean protecting the ice cream inside a wrapper or crust, putting something on the outside of the ice cream that will brown quickly (before the ice cream gets hot enough to melt), or getting the ice cream so frigid that it keeps its shape while its surface melts. However you choose to achieve the feat you will need high quality ice cream to do it.

During ice-cream production, air is incorporated into the mix. The air inflates the volume of the ice cream, making it creamy rather than hard. In ice-cream manufacturing, all the volume in excess of the volume of the original mix is called overrun. In very fluffy ice creams, the overrun can be as much as 100 percent, which means the ice cream is half air. Budget ice creams, with the most overrun, have little substance per square inch of volume, so they melt easily. They cannot be grilled. Premium ice creams and denser gelati tend to have less overrun than budget ice cream, usually less than 25 percent. The denser the ice cream, the better it is for grilling.

Grilling Custard

Custards are suspensions of milk and eggs. As custard heats, the protein in both the milk and eggs becomes firm. At a certain temperature, usually about 190°F, the mixture turns solid and smooth. At that point the custard is set, and the cooking must stop. If it gets hotter, the protein will coagulate too much and the custard will separate. Because temperature is harder to control on a grill than it is in an oven or on a stove top, custards are not usually cooked over an open fire. We have found that not only is it possible to get custard to set smoothly on a grill, but also, if the heat is kept very low, you can achieve a delicate consistency infused with subtle, smoky aromas.

The trick is to build a fire small enough yet hot enough to generate a good amount of smoke while maintaining a gentle ambient temperature under the grill hood, around 200°F (one burner on a multiburner gas grill works). We have cooked some excellent baked custards and cheesecakes over a fire using this technique (a cheesecake is just custard in which cream cheese or ricotta cheese replaces the milk).

Grilling Eggs

Like milk, raw eggs are fluid. In order to grill them you have to contain them in some way. Fortunately, eggs come in their own natural containers, and it is easy to hard- or soft-cook eggs in their shells. You can also fry an egg in a frying pan set on a grill, or bake them in ramekins over a fire, but the pans keep the fire so far away from the food that we have found there is little to no difference between cooking eggs in a pan over an open fire and cooking them on a stove top. Unless you are cooking over fire out of necessity (you're camping or your electricity is out), the process seems more like a gimmick than a legitimate grilling technique.

We have found two ways of cooking eggs over fire that have a significant effect on texture and flavor—slow-smoking and grilling on a salt block.

"Hard-boiled egg" is really a misnomer if you've cooked them properly. Boiling is not a good way to cook eggs. An egg white begins to coagulate at 145°F and finishes at 180°F. Yolks set between 150 and 158°F. Boiling water, which occurs at 212°F, overcooks egg proteins, making them tough and rubbery. Which means that when cooking eggs in hot water, you don't want the water temperature to get much hotter than a simmer, about 190°F.

That got us thinking about smoke. The temperature for slow-smoking on a grill is around 200°F. By putting some eggs right in the smoking pan over very low indirect heat, we were able to get incredible smoke-laden, hard-cooked eggs with a gorgeous amber patina. In a smoking rig, where you can get temperatures around 170°F, you can cook smoked soft-cooked eggs with creamy yolks and gelatinous, barely set egg whites.

Fried eggs can be grilled in a heavy pan, but the results are indistinguishable from fried eggs cooked on a stove top. Grilling eggs on a salt block is a different story. Himalayan salt plates are cut from a salt deposit in Pakistan that formed about 600 million years ago. They are solid blocks of dense salt, which can be heated over a fire and then grilled on. The salt retains heat exceptionally well, and we have used them for grilling fish, seafood, eggs, and thinly sliced meat. You need to heat the block gradually over a bilevel fire to ensure that it doesn't crack. The preheating takes about 30 minutes, but once the salt is hot, eggs will cook in a few minutes.

SEMIFIRM CHEESE

Campfire Raclette with New Potatoes Cooked in the Coals

MAKES 4 SERVINGS

Raclette is both a Swiss cheese, similar to Gruyère, and a traditional alpine party food of the same name. The latter consists of a chunk of raclette cheese that is exposed to heat (traditionally an open fire) and scraped off, as it melts, onto a plate of garnishes, including potatoes, bread, ham, and pickles. Sounds like perfect campfire fare to us, so we created this extravagant raclette meal. Part of it, the potatoes and shallots, are cooked right in the coals of a charcoal or wood fire while more delicate vegetables grill on the grate above. The cheese is melted in a cast-iron skillet at the last minute.

INGREDIENTS:

24 small red-skin or gold potatoes, scrubbed

2 to 3 tablespoons canola oil

Coarse salt and ground black pepper

12 shallots, skins left on

2 small zucchini, thickly sliced lengthwise

1 bunch asparagus, trimmed

2 large plum tomatoes, thickly sliced in rounds

24 cornichons (small pickled gherkins), drained

4 ounces Black Forest ham, thinly sliced

1¾ pounds raclette cheese, rind removed, thickly sliced

Paprika

1 French baguette, sliced

DIRECTIONS:

Light a charcoal or wood fire for medium-high heat, about 400°F (see page 19). Leave the grill grate off the grill so the coals are accessible.

Coat the potatoes with a thin film of oil and season liberally with salt and pepper. Wrap individually in small squares of heavy-duty aluminum foil. Put the potatoes in the coals and cook until they can be easily pierced with a fork, about 20 minutes, turning once or twice.

About 5 minutes before the potatoes are done, scatter the shallots in the coals and cook until the skins are charred, turning several times, about 5 minutes. Using long-handled tongs or heavy grill gloves, remove the potatoes and shallots to a platter and cool for 5 minutes.

Put the grill grate over the fire.

Coat the zucchini, asparagus, and plum tomatoes with oil and season with salt and pepper.

Brush the grill grate and coat with oil. Grill the vegetables until grill-marked and barely cooked through, 3 to 5 minutes per side. Arrange on a serving platter. Unwrap the potatoes and peel the charred skins from the shallots. Arrange on the serving platter. Arrange the cornichons and ham on a separate platter.

Place a cast-iron skillet directly over the hottest part of the fire and heat for 5 minutes. Cover the bottom of the skillet with slices of cheese. It is preferable to cook the cheese in batches, as people want more. Cook until the cheese is melted and beginning to brown on the edges. Using a heavy pot holder or grill gloves, remove the skillet from the heat.

Sprinkle the cheese with paprika. Serve 6 potatoes and 3 shallots per person. Scrape some cheese over the top, making sure to include some of the browned edges. People should serve themselves grilled vegetables, cornichons, and ham to eat with the raclette. Serve with bread.

Stilton and Pear Quiche

MAKES 8 SERVINGS

One would think that a cheese and custard tart (a quiche, in other words) would be too delicate to bake over an open fire, but the custard filling absorbs fire flavors, especially wood smoke, spectacularly well. We bake the custard filling in a pie shell. Since the pastry is closest to the heat, it crisps and dries, protecting the custard from the flame. This custard is flavored with blue cheese and the subtle sweet-tart flavor of pears. It can be served as a not-too-sweet dessert, an elegant hors d'oeuvre, or an all-in-one fruit and cheese course.

INGREDIENTS:

1 recipe Flaky Pie Pastry (page 364)

2 tablespoons canola oil

3 Bosc pears, peeled, cored, and cut into 6 wedges

1 medium onion, peeled and cut into ½-inch slices

2 eggs, large or extra-large

1 egg yolk, large or extra-large

1 cup half-and-half

¼ teaspoon ground black pepper

½ teaspoon coarse salt, preferably smoked salt

1 small garlic clove, minced

1 ounce Parmesan cheese, grated

4 ounces Stilton cheese, finely chopped

DIRECTIONS:

Light a grill for indirect medium heat, about 325°F (see page 14).

Pour the canola oil in a large mixing bowl, and toss the pears in the oil as soon as they are peeled and cut to keep them from browning. Add the onion and coat with oil.

Brush a grill grate and coat with oil. Put the pear wedges and onion slices directly over the heat, cover the grill, and cook until browned and tender, about 12 minutes, turning the pear wedges two times, and the onion slices once. Remove to a cutting board and cool for 10 minutes. Chop the onion finely and the pear coarsely.

Roll out the pastry on a lightly floured board into a 12-inch circle, about ¼ inch thick. Transfer the pastry to a 10-inch heavy skillet with a metal handle. A cast-iron one works well. Make sure the pastry sinks into the corners of the pan. Trim the edges of the pastry, allowing a 1-inch overhang. Fold the edges to create a thick edge. Crimp the edges (see the Know-How, page 364), and put in the refrigerator.

Whisk the whole eggs and yolk in a small mixing bowl. Mix in the half-and-half, pepper, salt, and garlic.

Remove the pastry shell from the refrigerator. Pack the Parmesan in an even layer over the bottom of the pastry. This will help to keep it crisp as it cooks.

Mix together the Stilton and chopped pears and onions, and pat into an even layer in the pastry shell. The pastry should be almost full. Pour the custard evenly over the top.

Carefully carry the pan out to the grill and put on the grill away from the heat. Cover the grill and bake until the custard is just set in the middle, and the pastry and the top of the custard are browned, 45 to 50 minutes.

Allow the quiche to cool for at least 30 minutes before cutting. Cut into 8 wedges.

continued ➔

Flaky Pie Pastry

MAKES 1 PASTRY CRUST

INGREDIENTS:

1½ cups all-purpose flour

¼ teaspoon salt

4 ounces cold unsalted butter, cut into pieces

¼ cup ice water

DIRECTIONS:

Combine the flour and salt in the work bowl of a food processor with the metal blade in place. Process until combined, scatter the butter pieces evenly over the flour, and process in pulses until the mixture resembles coarse meal. Add half the water, pulse to distribute, and add the remaining water a bit at a time, until the dough begins to climb the walls of the work bowl but is still rough and unformed. Gather the dough into a ball, flatten it into a disk, wrap in plastic wrap, and refrigerate for at least 30 minutes (and no more than 2 days) before using in a recipe. Let the dough sit at room temperature for 10 minutes before rolling.

> ### KNOW-HOW: CRIMPING PASTRY EDGES
>
> After you have rolled under the edge of the piecrust, press your thumb and index finger together to create a small V shape at your fingertips. Put these fingers behind the edge of the pastry, and with the index finger of your other hand push the pastry into the V. Move your finger over and make another crimp right next to the first. Continue all the way around the edge of the pastry.

SURFACE-RIPENED CHEESE

Camembert Wrapped in Grape Leaves and Served with Sweet Cranberry Mustard Vinaigrette

MAKES 8 TO 10 SERVINGS

Baked Brie has become a dinner party cliché. This Camembert undermines the stereotype by wrapping the cheese in fragrant grape leaves, moving it out to the grill, and later serving it with sweet-tart cranberry vinaigrette. One of the reasons that surface-ripened cheeses are frequent candidates for warming whole is that the outside rind helps to keep the cheese's shape while the interior turns molten, allowing you to serve the cheese intact and cut it open to reveal its melted center.

INGREDIENTS:

12 jarred grape vine leaves

1 small Camembert (about 10 ounces)

2 tablespoons olive oil

Coarse salt and coarsely ground black pepper

¼ cup Cranberry Mustard Vinaigrette (page 41)

DIRECTIONS:

Light a grill for direct medium heat, about 350°F (see page 12).

Put one of the largest grape leaves in the center of a small plate and surround with 10 more leaves, overlapping them to create a mat at least 8 inches across. Rub the cheese with 1 tablespoon of the oil and season with salt and pepper. Place the cheese in the center of the leaves and wrap the leaves around it. Top with the remaining grape leaf. Tie with twine to keep the leaves in place using the plate to help you flip the cheese. Coat the whole bundle with the remaining tablespoon olive oil.

Brush a grill grate and coat with oil. Grill the cheese just until it begins to soften, about 3 minutes per side. Cool for 5 minutes before serving.

Untie and unwrap the cheese and serve it on its bed of leaves. Spoon the vinaigrette over top. Serve with crackers or bread for spreading.

FRESH GOAT CHEESE

Grilled Goat Cheese with Za'atar and Balsamic Chocolate Drizzle

MAKES 6 SERVINGS

Goat cheese does not melt, which allows you to grill-bake it without any danger of it collapsing. But it can still overcook. When goat cheese gets too hot, it turns grainy. So it is important to remove it from the heat as soon as it crisps and chars a bit over its surface. Goat's milk contains fats that give it a pungency some people refer to as "barny." That strong flavor goes well with za'atar, a spice mix consisting mostly of thyme and sumac berries (a souring agent similar to tamarind). The warm cheese is accompanied by the sexiest of elixirs—balsamic vinegar that's been reduced to a syrup and then enriched with bittersweet chocolate.

INGREDIENTS:

3 tablespoons extra-virgin olive oil

1 garlic clove, minced

1 round of firm fresh goat cheese (about 8 ounces), about 3½ inches in diameter and 1½ inches thick, chilled

2 tablespoons Za'atar (page 30)

3 pita breads

⅓ cup Balsamic Chocolate Drizzle (page 48)

DIRECTIONS:

Light a grill for direct medium-high heat, about 425°F (see page 12).

Mix the oil and garlic in a small bowl. Coat the cheese with half the oil and press the za'atar all over the cheese. Brush the remaining oil onto the pitas.

Brush a grill grate and coat with oil. Put the bread on the grill grate and grill until blistered and charred, 1 to 2 minutes per side. Transfer to a platter with tongs or a spatula.

Put the cheese on the grill and cook until grill-marked, 1 to 2 minutes per side. The surface will be slightly melted, but the center will still feel firm. Transfer to the platter with a spatula. Drizzle with a tablespoon of the chocolate drizzle. Serve with the remaining drizzle on the side.

ICE CREAM

Grilled Rum Raisin
Ice-Cream Sandwiches

MAKES 4 SERVINGS

Hot and cold—put them together and what you usually get is tepid, but not here. When you grill ice cream, hot and cold meet with a resounding clash. In this recipe, rum raisin ice cream is sandwiched between two rum-soaked oatmeal cookies and coated with sugar. When they hit the grill, the sugar turns instantly into a molten glaze, hopefully before the ice cream gets a chance to melt. When grilling ice cream it's important to purchase the best product you can. The main factor influencing the price of ice cream is the amount of air beaten into the custard as it freezes. The more air, the faster the ice cream will melt. Premium ice cream stays frozen and holds its shape better than budget ice cream because premium ice cream contains less air.

INGREDIENTS:

½ pint rum raisin premium ice cream, softened

8 homemade or bakery-made oatmeal raisin cookies, about 2½ inches in diameter

3 tablespoons dark rum

Cooking spray

1 cup confectioners' sugar

DIRECTIONS:

Sandwich ¼ cup ice cream between 2 cookies. Press the sandwich together firmly until the ice cream spreads to the edges of the cookies. Run the flat part of a knife around the perimeter of the sandwich, flattening the ice cream all around. Brush the cookies with rum, wrap in plastic wrap, and freeze for 2 hours to 2 days.

Light a grill for direct medium heat, about 350°F (see page 12).

Just before grilling set a rack over a sheet pan, coat the cookies with cooking spray, and set them on the rack. Sift or dust the confectioners' sugar over the cookies, turning them so that both sides get liberally coated.

Brush the grill grate and coat with oil. Put the ice-cream sandwiches on the grill and cook until the sugar glazes and browns in spots, about 1 minute on each side. Serve immediately.

EGGS

Smoked Eggs

MAKES 8 EGGS

The slower you can smoke these eggs, the more beautiful and flavorful they will become. Keep the heat low and don't rush them. In fact, if you can double the cooking time without overcooking them, better yet. The smoking compound is a mixture of wood, rice, tea leaves, and sugar, which yields a very dark, colorful smoke and a beautiful tealike fragrance.

INGREDIENTS:

2 cups wood chips,
preferably fruitwood
or hickory, soaked in water
for 30 minutes

⅓ cup white rice

½ cup loose-leaf black tea

⅓ cup dark brown sugar

8 large or extra-large
white-shelled eggs

DIRECTIONS:

Light a grill for indirect medium-high heat, around 400°F (see page 14). Leave the grill grate off the grill.

Drain the chips, reserving the water in a separate bowl. Mix the rice, tea, and sugar with the wood chips. Mound half of the mixture on each end of a disposable aluminum roasting pan, about 9 by 12 inches. Put on the grill with the wood-tea-rice mounds directly over the fire and the open space in the center away from the fire. Cover the grill and wait until the wood mixture starts to smoke, about 15 minutes.

If using a gas grill, turn the heat down to low (about 225°F). If using charcoal or wood, spread out the coal beds to lower the heat. Place the eggs in the center of the pan and pour 1 cup of the wood-chip soaking liquid over the eggs. Cover the pan tightly with heavy-duty aluminum foil.

Cover the grill and cook for 1 hour. Lift the pan from the grill, using pot holders or grill gloves. Carefully remove the foil cover, turn the eggs, and add another cup of the wood-chip

soaking liquid if the pan is dry. Reseal the foil and replace the pan. Add more charcoal to the grill, if needed. Cover and cook for another 2 hours (replenishing the charcoal as needed), until the wood chips are spent and the shells of the eggs are deep amber, with black spots. The grill temperature should stay around 225°F.

Remove the pan, uncover, and transfer the eggs to a bowl of ice water. Cool for a few minutes, then remove from the ice water and run under hot tap water for 10 seconds. Carefully crack the shells and peel. Cool the eggs to room temperature and serve in any way you would serve hard-cooked eggs, or use for Smoked Deviled Eggs (page 368) or in the stuffing for Argentine Stuffed Flank Steak (page 65).

Smoked Deviled Eggs

MAKES 4 SERVINGS

Deviled eggs are one of the great picnic foods. These are similar to other deviled egg recipes you may have had except that the eggs are hard-cooked over a smoky fire, rather than in a pot of water. The method gives them an amber complexion and a smoky redolence, which is enhanced by adding chipotle hot sauce and smoked bacon to the egg yolk filling.

INGREDIENTS:

8 Smoked Eggs (page 367)

3 tablespoons mayonnaise

2 teaspoons chipotle hot pepper sauce

¼ teaspoon smoked salt

2 tablespoons chopped fresh cilantro

1 or 2 drops liquid smoke (optional)

2 strips smoked bacon, cooked until crisp, drained, and crumbled

½ teaspoon smoked paprika

DIRECTIONS:

Cut the eggs in half lengthwise, dipping the knife into a bowl of water before every cut. Remove the yolks to a small mixing bowl. Add the mayonnaise, chipotle hot sauce, smoked salt, cilantro, and liquid smoke (if using) and mix until fluffy.

Fill the hollow of each egg half with the yolk mixture and sprinkle with bacon and smoked paprika. Chill or serve at room temperature.

Chapter 15

BREADS, SANDWICHES, CAKES & COOKIES

All baked goods are a mixture of flour and water. When moistened, protein in flour forms an elastic web of gluten. The higher the protein content and the more mixing that is done, the thicker the gluten becomes. That's why recipes for chewy breads call for high-protein bread flour and long periods of kneading. Cakes and quick breads benefit from low protein high-starch cake flour and a minimum of mixing after the flour is added.

Many grilled flatbreads are little more than these two ingredients (plus a little salt). The earliest breads were baked directly over or in a fire, which means that baking on a grill takes us back to the roots of baking. Chapati are whole grain flatbreads that cook in seconds, emerging from the flames soft and pliable, slightly chewy, and bubbled and blistered, with flecks of charred dough. They are best eaten right off the grill. Allow them to cool, and they will become brittle and cardboard-y. In order to make bread last, its texture has to be leavened.

BREADS, SANDWICHES, CAKES & COOKIES

PREPARATION	DESCRIPTION	HOW TO GRILL
NAAN	Puffy oblong flatbread speckled with brown spots and bubbles, dry flexible surface, soft interior (Near East)	Direct medium-high
FOCACCIA	Chewy, thick, rectangular, dimpled surface, often with herbs or other flavorful garnishes in the dough and on top (Italy)	Direct medium
CHAPATI	Unleavened whole-grain flatbread, usually griddle cooked, 8-inch rounds, flexible when warm, cracker-crisp after cooling (India)	Direct medium-high
PITA / KHUBZ	Circular flatbread, speckled with brown spots, open pocket in center, flexible with dry surface (Middle East, Mediterranean)	Direct medium-high
LAVASH	Very thin and large rectangular bread, chewy and flexible when warm, gets dry with cooling (Caucasus)	Direct medium-high
PIZZA	Flat thin chewy bread with thick rim to hold sauce and condiments on surface. Often topped with cheese (Italy, worldwide)	Direct medium-high
CALZONE OR STROMBOLI	Pizza with filling inside. Calzone—folded; stromboli—rolled like a jelly roll	Direct medium
POLENTA	Coarsely ground cornmeal pudding cut into portions and grilled to develop flavor and crust (Italy)	Direct medium
CORN BREAD	Crusty cakelike bread with soft interior that is slightly gritty from cornmeal, can be sweetened or not (United States)	Indirect high
GRILLED SANDWICHES	Baked bread, usually sliced, layered with filling. Buttered and grilled, often under weight to compress contents (worldwide).	Direct medium
FRENCH TOAST	Custard-dipped bread, grilled until toasted and set (Europe, United States)	Direct medium
TOASTED POUND CAKE	Rich, dense, buttery cake sliced and toasted to mark surface and flavor	Direct medium-high
TOASTED SWEET BREAD	Baked cake slice, wedge, or square, toasted to mark surface and flavor	Direct medium
TOASTED COOKIES	Baked cookies of any variety, toasted to mark surface and flavor	Direct medium-high
TOASTED DOUGHNUTS	Baked or fried doughnut of any variety, toasted to mark surface and flavor	Direct medium-low
TOASTED WAFFLES	Baked or fried doughnut of any variety, toasted to mark surface and flavor	Direct medium
GRILL-BAKED PASTRY	Pastry dough (flaky, sweet, or puffed) baked over fire until browned and crisp	Indirect medium low
GRILL-BAKED SHORTCAKE	Sweet biscuit dough baked over fire until browned, puffed, and crusty	Direct medium-low
GRILL-BAKED CLAFOUTI	Custardlike cake enriched with fruit	Indirect medium
GRILL-BAKED CAKE	Single-layer moist cake, usually with vegetables or fruit in batter	Indirect medium
GRILL-BAKED COOKIES	Chewy cookies made from firm dough	Direct medium-low

About Breads and Grill-Baking

Leavening agents lighten dough. The most basic leavener is air. Air bubbles get trapped in the web of gluten whenever dough is beaten or kneaded. When heated, the air expands and the baked good rises. In addition, as a dough or batter cooks, water is converted into steam, which fills the air bubbles, stretching the gluten even more. The expansion is intensified by adding yeast or chemical leaveners, like baking powder and baking soda, which produce carbon dioxide gas. The gas increases the volume of bubbles. Leaveners don't produce more bubbles, they just make existing bubbles larger, so it is vital to incorporate air into a batter or dough by beating it, kneading it, or adding an aerated substance such as firmly beaten egg whites.

Pita, pizza, focaccia, naan, lavash, and even pretzels are examples of simple leavened flatbreads that bake well on a grill. The thinner the bread, the higher and more direct the heat can be. Lavash, the paper-thin sheet bread of the Caucasus, bakes over a direct high flame for about 30 seconds per side. Medium-thick breads like pizza and naan bake over medium-high flames, while thicker breads like focaccia and pretzels can be grill-baked either over direct low heat or indirect high heat. Because all of the heat for grill-baking radiates from below, you cannot effectively bake fully risen loaf-type breads on a grill. They require even heat radiating from all directions, like the heat distribution in a closed oven.

Adding fat like oil, butter, or rendered bacon drippings makes dough tender. Baked goods made with more fat, such as cakes, biscuits, cookies, pastries, and shortbreads, are softer or flakier than low-fat, yeast-risen flatbreads. Fat keeps water from hydrating the flour proteins that form gluten. Therefore the gluten strands are shorter (hence the term "shortening") and less elastic.

The higher the proportion of fat, the more pronounced its effects will be. Solid saturated fats, such as vegetable shortening and lard, are 100 percent fat, and they make a more tender and flakier piecrust than butter or margarine, which are only about 80 percent fat. Solid fats hold more air bubbles, making them better for aerated cakes. And, since we depend on fat to transport aromatic components into our olfactory sensors, the addition of fat increases all of the flavors in a baked good.

Small pastries like shortbreads and pastry straws, and thin pastries like tarts and quiches, bake on a grill beautifully. Like breads, large or tall pastries have problems baking evenly over a fire, and are not the best choices for grill-baking. Sugar added to dough doesn't just make it sweet. Sugar makes baked goods tender, moist, and crisp, and gives them a rich brown color. Remove sugar from a cake or cookie recipe, and the results will be dense, dry, and pale. Add extra sugar, and the baked good will become crisper and browner.

Very sweet cakes and cookies tend to burn on the grill. For that reason the recipes that work best are moist, not-too-sweet cakes like carrot cake or zucchini bread, and chewy cookies like oatmeal, molasses, or peanut butter. High-rising cakes like sponge cake, or rich cakes with a delicate crumb like pound cakes, rise irregularly on a grill, and have a tendency to burn at the edges before they are fully baked. These cakes need to be baked in an oven, but that doesn't mean they won't benefit from a turn over the fire. Slices of pound cake or banana bread, squares of gingerbread, or doughnuts are all completely delicious when glazed with sweetened butter and toasted over an open fire.

Grilled Chickpea Chapati with Cilantro Sesame Sauce

MAKES 6 SERVINGS

Chapati, unleavened Indian flatbread, are some of the easiest and tastiest breads to bake on a grill. Because they have no yeast, there is no need to rest and raise the dough for hours before baking. These chapati contain chickpea flour, which gives them a rich and slightly sweet flavor. Chapati are best rolled and cooked just before serving. Although you can use any rolling pin, the small Indian rolling pin (*belan*), which bulges in the center and tapers toward the ends, allows you to grasp the dough with one hand and roll with the palm of the other, making thinning and stretching the dough effortless. We serve these chapati right off the grill with a tahini yogurt sauce that's inundated with cilantro.

INGREDIENTS:

¾ cup chickpea (garbanzo) flour

1½ cups bread flour, plus additional flour for kneading

1 teaspoon fine sea salt

1½ teaspoons melted butter or ghee

1 scant cup warm water (110 to 115°F)

⅓ cup tahini

3 tablespoons extra-virgin olive oil

½ cup yogurt, preferably whole milk or Greek

Finely grated zest and juice of ½ lime

1 garlic clove, minced

1 teaspoon hot pepper sauce

½ teaspoon sea salt

¼ cup minced fresh cilantro leaves

DIRECTIONS:

Combine the chickpea flour, bread flour, and salt in a medium mixing bowl. Stir in the melted butter and water and mix long enough to form a cohesive dough.

Flour your hands and a work surface. Scrape the dough out of the bowl and knead until smooth, about 5 minutes, adding only enough flour to keep the dough from sticking to your hands or the work surface. (Try to add as little additional flour as possible.) Cover loosely with plastic wrap and let rest for 1 hour.

Meanwhile mix the tahini and oil in a small bowl with a whisk until thoroughly combined. Mix in the yogurt all at once. The mixture will bind initially and then relax. Stir in the lime zest and juice, garlic, hot pepper sauce, salt, and cilantro. Set aside.

Light a grill for direct medium-high heat, about 425°F (see page 12).

Divide the dough into six portions and roll each into a ball. Coat with flour and pat out into a ¼-inch-thick disk on a clean work surface. Coat a small rolling pin with flour and roll out each disk until very thin, about ¹⁄₁₆ inch, flipping the chapati over halfway through the rolling process to make sure it is not sticking too badly. You can sprinkle the surface of the chapati with flour as you work if needed to keep it from sticking to the pin. Avoid flouring the work surface because it will cause the chapati to slide across the surface rather than stretch and thin. Lightly flour the finished chapati and stack on a plate or cutting board.

Brush the grill grate and rub with oil. Grill the chapati, two or three at a time (or however many fit comfortably on your grill), until blistered and browned on both sides, 45 seconds to 1 minute per side. Serve immediately with the cilantro sesame sauce.

Cumin Naan with Grilled Tomato Chutney

MAKES 4 TO 8 SERVINGS (4 BREADS)

Naan, the yeasted flatbreads of central Asia, are traditionally baked in wood-fired tandoors, large vertical ceramic ovens that get superhot—hot enough to sear the surface of bread in seconds. Although home cooks try to duplicate the effects of a tandoor by lining the floor of a conventional oven with ceramic tiles, the heat is never the same. We think a grill gives more authentic results, especially a charcoal grill. Like all flatbreads, the dough for naan is relatively easy to prepare. It takes about 10 minutes to mix up and 1½ hours for rising. If you need to leave the dough for a few hours (or as long as a day), you can let it rise in the refrigerator. It will taste even better.

INGREDIENTS:

1 teaspoon active dry yeast

¾ cup warm water (110 to 115°F)

½ cup plain yogurt

1½ teaspoons ground toasted cumin seeds (see Know-How, below)

1½ cups bread flour

1 tablespoon canola oil

2 teaspoons sugar

1 teaspoon sea salt

About 1 cup whole-wheat flour

2 teaspoons unsalted butter, softened

2 teaspoons cracked toasted cumin seed

1¼ cups Grilled Tomato Chutney (page 43)

DIRECTIONS:

Mix together the yeast and ¼ cup of the warm water in a large bowl until the yeast is dissolved.

Mix together the yogurt, cumin, and remaining ½ cup water in a medium bowl and add to the yeast mixture, stirring until well blended. Add the bread flour and stir vigorously for 2 minutes. Cover loosely with plastic wrap and set aside at room temperature until bubbly, about 30 minutes.

Stir in the oil, sugar, and salt and enough of the whole-wheat flour to make a kneadable dough. Knead on a clean work surface, using additional flour to keep the dough from sticking, until the dough is smooth and elastic, between 5 and 10 minutes.

Wash out the large bowl and coat it lightly with oil. Turn the dough in the oiled bowl to coat with the oil. Cover with plastic wrap and let rise at room temperature until doubled in bulk, about 1 hour. While the dough is rising, prepare the chutney.

Light a grill for direct medium-high heat, about 425°F (see page 12).

Divide the dough into four pieces. Roll each into a ball and flatten into a ½-inch-thick disk. Cover with a kitchen towel and let rest for 5 minutes. Lightly flour a clean work surface and roll each disk of dough into an oval about 9 inches long and ¼ inch thick. Coat each bread with oil and stack on a plate to transport to the grill.

Brush the grill grate and coat with oil. Put the dough on the grill so the disks are evenly spaced, cover, and cook until grill-marked and charred in spots on the bottom and puffed on top, about 2 minutes. Turn with tongs and cook on the other side until browned and spotted with char, about 1 minute. Remove to a plate, brush with butter, and sprinkle with the cracked cumin. Serve with the chutney.

KNOW-HOW: TOASTING AND CRACKING WHOLE SPICES

You will need to toast about 2 tablespoons cumin seeds to prepare the ground toasted cumin and cracked cumin for the bread and chutney. Toast the seeds (or any whole spice) by heating a small, heavy skillet (such as cast-iron) until very hot. Add the seeds, remove from the heat, and stir until the seeds are aromatic and lightly colored, about 1 minute. You can use the same heavy pan (after it has cooled down) to crack or crush the seeds by carefully pounding them on a solid flat surface (like a butcher block) with the bottom of the pan.

FLATBREAD

Khubz Za'atar

MAKES 6 SERVINGS

Khubz, the Arabic word for bread, is better known as pita in North America. Real khubz is baked in a wood-fired stone oven, which blisters and crisps the surface. The effect is impossible to get in a home oven, but a hot grill works great.

INGREDIENTS:

1 cup warm water (110 to 115°F)

2 teaspoons active dry yeast

1 teaspoon sugar

¼ cup olive oil

2 teaspoons sea salt

1¼ cups whole-wheat flour

1½ cups bread flour, plus more for kneading

1 tablespoon Za'atar (page 30)

DIRECTIONS:

Combine the water, yeast, and sugar in a large bowl, stirring until mixed. Let sit until foamy, about 5 minutes. Stir in 3 tablespoons of the olive oil, the salt, whole-wheat flour, and bread flour and stir into a kneadable dough.

Turn onto a floured surface and knead until the dough is smooth and elastic, about 5 minutes. Add more flour as needed to keep the dough from sticking to your hands or the work surface. Try to add as little flour as possible. Coat a large bowl with the remaining tablespoon of oil and add the dough, turning to coat it with the oil. Cover with plastic wrap and let rise in a warm spot until doubled in bulk, about 1 hour, or overnight in the refrigerator. If refrigerated, allow to come to room temperature before rolling out.

Light a grill for direct medium-high heat, about 425°F (see page 12).

Divide the dough into six pieces. Roll each into a ball and flatten into a ¼-inch-thick disk.

Cover with a kitchen towel and let rest for 5 minutes. Lightly flour a clean work surface and roll each disk of dough until very thin, about ⅛ inch thick. Coat each bread with some of the oil and sprinkle with za'atar. Stack on a plate to transport to the grill.

Brush the grill grate and coat with oil. Put the dough on the grill so the disks are evenly spaced. Cover and cook until grill-marked and charred in spots on the bottom and puffed on top, about 2 minutes. Turn with tongs and cook on the other side until browned, about 1 minute.

FLATBREAD

Grilled Honey Lavash with Curried-Saffron Butter

MAKES 6 SERVINGS

Bread is gigantic in the Caucasus. Start the recipe a day in advance to allow the dough to relax and be rolled.

INGREDIENTS:

2 tablespoons honey

1½ cups warm water (110 to 115°F)

½ teaspoon active dry yeast

2 cups bread flour

1 teaspoon sea salt

1½ to 2 cups unbleached all-purpose flour, plus additional flour for kneading

⅓ cup Curried Saffron Butter (page 51)

DIRECTIONS:

Dissolve 1 tablespoon of the honey in the water in a medium mixing bowl. Stir in the yeast and set aside until foamy, about 5 minutes. Stir in the bread flour and sprinkle the salt over the top. Mix until a thick, rough batter forms. Beat the batter vigorously for about 100 strokes (1 to 2 minutes). It will become smooth and elastic.

Add 1½ cups all-purpose flour and mix until the dough is too stiff to stir. Turn out onto a lightly floured clean work surface and knead until the dough is smooth and elastic, adding just enough additional flour to keep the dough from sticking to your hands and the work surface. Form the kneaded dough into a ball and roll in flour.

Wash out the mixing bowl and dry thoroughly. Put the dough in the bowl, cover with plastic wrap, and refrigerate overnight.

Light a grill for direct medium-high heat, about 425°F (see page 12).

Mix the remaining tablespoon honey with the curry-saffron butter. Divide the dough into six balls and roll each in flour. Flatten each piece into a rough rectangle.

Work with all of the pieces of dough, one at a time. With a floured rolling pin roll each piece of dough as thinly as possible. Keeping the work surface relatively flour free will help the dough stretch better. If it should stick to the surface, carefully peel it up. Flour each rolled-out piece of dough thoroughly and stack on a sheet pan. When all of the dough has been rolled, flip the pile over and roll the pieces again, starting with the top piece, until each piece is rolled into a paper-thin sheet approximately 10 by 15 inches.

Flour each sheet on both sides and stack again. Carry the pan of dough sheets to the grill. Have a large towel ready by the side of the grill.

Brush the grill grate and rub well with oil. Grill the lavash, one at a time, until blistered and lightly browned on both sides and still flexible, about 30 seconds per side. The breads are ready to flip the first time when they appear dry on the edges, but show no signs of browning. It is easiest to turn the breads with your fingers, although you can use tongs if you want. When each bread is done grilling, fold it in half and roll the towel around it to keep it warm.

Serve the warm breads with the curry butter. Store any leftovers in a sealed plastic bag. They will stay flexible for about 24 hours. Warm gently in a low oven before serving.

FLATBREAD

Blue Cheese Pizza with Watercress and Pomegranate Salad

MAKES 4 TO 6 SERVINGS

Chain up the oven, and throw away that pizza-delivery magnet stuck on the fridge. Pizza on the grill is so convenient, versatile, and delicious that it obliterates all previous routes to a crispy, cheesy slice. Use the following all-purpose pizza dough recipe (you can make it up way ahead and pull it out of the fridge or freezer anytime you get a pizza urge), or you can use purchased pizza dough from the freezer or refrigerator case of your food market. The trick to baking pizza on a grill is rolling the dough as thinly as possible, oiling the surface well, and grilling the top side (it only takes 2 minutes) before adding any toppings. The toppings on this pizza are decidedly sophisticated—a layer of grilled red onions and blue cheese is all the pizza gets during grilling. But then a salad of fresh watercress scattered over the warm dough barely wilts before it is garnished with gems of pomegranate seeds and a pungent pomegranate vinaigrette.

continued →

INGREDIENTS:

1 recipe Pizza Dough (recipe follows)

½ cup Pomegranate Vinaigrette (see page 310)

1 garlic clove, minced

1 teaspoon fresh oregano or thyme leaves

1 large red onion, cut into ¼-inch-thick rounds

¼ cup extra-virgin olive oil

8 ounces blue cheese, crumbled

1 large bunch watercress or baby arugula (about 6 ounces), stems removed (about 3 cups leaves)

Seeds from ½ pomegranate

DIRECTIONS:

Mix the vinaigrette, garlic, and oregano in a small bowl and set aside.

Light a grill for direct medium-high heat, about 400°F (see page 12).

Coat the onion slices with a thin film of the olive oil. Brush and oil the grill grate and grill the onion slices until well marked and starting to become soft, about 3 minutes per side. Remove to a cutting board and cut each slice in half to create strips; set aside. Cut two or four pieces of foil, depending on whether you are making two medium pizzas or four individual ones. Coat one of the pieces with oil. Divide the dough into two or four pieces. Put one piece of dough on the prepared foil, and cover the other piece(s) with a clean kitchen towel. Press and stretch the dough on the foil into a circle about ⅛ to ¼ inch thick. Don't bother making a rim around the edge of the crust unless you like it for aesthetics.

Coat the top of the dough round with oil. Repeat with the remaining dough and foil, oiling each dough round well and stacking them up.

Brush the grill grate again and coat it with oil. Invert each circle of dough onto the grate, and carefully remove the foil. Do this in batches if all of the dough won't fit on the grill at once. Cover the grill and cook each dough round until bubbly on the top and nicely grill-marked on the bottom, about 2 minutes. Turn the dough 90 degrees halfway through grilling for more even browning.

Invert the pizza crusts onto a cutting board so that the grilled side is up.

Drizzle with half of the remaining olive oil. Scatter the cheese over them, followed by the grilled onions. Drizzle with the remaining olive oil.

Slide the pizzas back onto the grill, cover, and grill until the cheese melts and the bottom is browned, about 2 minutes, watching carefully so the pizza doesn't burn.

Toss the watercress with ¼ cup of the vinaigrette. Drizzle the pizzas with the remaining ¼ cup. Mound the watercress on the pizzas and scatter the pomegranate seeds over the top.

Cut medium pizzas into 6 to 8 wedges; cut individual pizzas in quarters.

Pizza Dough

MAKES 2 MEDIUM OR 4 INDIVIDUAL PIZZAS

INGREDIENTS:

1 cup warm water (110 to 115°F)

2 teaspoons active dry yeast

1 teaspoon sugar

¼ cup olive oil

2 teaspoons sea salt

2¾ cups bread flour, plus more for kneading

DIRECTIONS:

Combine the water, yeast, and sugar in a large bowl, stirring until mixed. Let sit until foamy, about 5 minutes. Stir in 3 tablespoons of the olive oil, the salt, and flour and stir into a kneadable dough.

Turn onto a floured surface and knead until the dough is smooth and elastic, about 5 minutes. Add more flour as needed to keep the dough from sticking to your hands or the work surface. Try to add as little flour as possible.

Coat a large bowl with the remaining tablespoon oil and add the dough, turning to coat it with the oil. Cover with plastic wrap and let rise in a warm spot until doubled in bulk, about 1 hour, or overnight in the refrigerator. The dough is now ready to roll out according to the directions in the main recipe. (If refrigerated, allow to come to room temp before rolling out.) Gather the dough into a ball, flatten it into a disk, wrap in plastic wrap, and refrigerate for at least 30 minutes (and no more than 2 days) before using in a recipe. Let the dough sit at room temperature for 10 minutes before rolling.

POLENTA

Grilled Hot Pepper Polenta with Grilled Tomato Marmalade

MAKES 6 SERVINGS

Polenta is drowning in culinary myths. Myth number 1: Simmering polenta has to be stirred constantly. That comes from the days before stoves, when polenta was simmered in large copper pots over an open fire and would scorch if you left it for a minute. On the controlled heat of a stove top, stirring every so often works fine. Myth number 2: The cornmeal has to be added to rapidly boiling liquid a grain at a time, lest it lump. True enough, but unnecessary. If you mix everything together while the liquid is still cold and then heat it, no lumps! Some polenta fascists insist on specially ground cornmeal. We've tried them all, and though any cornmeal will suffice, coarse stone-ground cornmeal does have a more interesting texture and a cornier flavor. Sometimes the fascists know what they're talking about.

INGREDIENTS:

1¼ cups milk

1¼ cups water

1 cup coarse stone-ground yellow cornmeal

1 teaspoon sea salt

Dash of ground habanero chile

2 serrano chiles, stems and seeds removed, and finely chopped

3 ounces sharp cheddar cheese, shredded

Cooking spray

¾ cup Grilled Tomato Marmalade (page 43)

DIRECTIONS:

Stir together the milk, water, cornmeal, salt, ground habanero chile, and serrano chiles in a medium saucepan until the cornmeal is moistened. Heat to a simmer, stirring constantly, about 10 minutes.

Reduce the heat to low and simmer until a skin forms across the bottom of the pot and the polenta pulls away from the sides, stirring often, about 30 minutes.

Remove from the heat and stir in the cheese. Spray a pie pan or an 8-inch square baking pan with oil. Scrape the polenta into the prepared pan and smooth the top with a rubber spatula. Cool until firm and cut into wedges or squares.

Light a grill for direct medium heat, 350 to 400°F (see page 12).

Brush the grill grate and coat liberally with oil. Coat the polenta pieces with cooking spray and brown on both sides, 3 to 4 minutes per side.

Serve with the marmalade on the side.

VARIATION:

Basic Grilled Polenta: Omit the ground habanero chile and fresh serrano chiles.

MUFFINS

Grilled Rosemary Corn Sticks

MAKES 6 OR 7 SERVINGS (14 CORN STICKS)

The glory of corn sticks is the sensual counterpoint playing out in your mouth between the crackling crust and the mousse-like interior. A hot oven can get you halfway there, but for truly remarkable results corn sticks should be baked over fire. For this recipe you will need two cast-iron corn stick pans. Cast-iron muffin pans will work, too, but you should only fill the cups half way. Put the pans over the fire while you are mixing the batter. You want them to be searing hot so that a crust starts to set as soon as the batter hits the pan. The heavy cream in the batter makes these corn sticks beautifully light and deceptively rich.

INGREDIENTS:

3 tablespoons unsalted butter

2 tablespoons minced onion

1 tablespoon finely chopped fresh rosemary

¾ cup stone-ground yellow cornmeal

¼ cup unbleached all-purpose flour

½ teaspoon sea salt

Pinch of cayenne pepper

3 tablespoons sugar

1½ teaspoons baking powder

1 extra-large egg, lightly beaten

1 cup heavy cream

2 tablespoons corn or canola oil

½ cup Spicy Orange Honey (page 51), optional

Butter for serving (optional)

DIRECTIONS:

Light a grill for indirect medium-high heat, about 375°F (see page 14). Put two well-seasoned cast-iron corn stick pans (each making 7 corn sticks) on the grill directly over the heat. Leave them while you mix up the batter.

Melt the butter in a small skillet over medium heat. Add the onion and rosemary and cook until the onion is soft and the rosemary is fragrant, about 3 minutes; set aside.

Mix together the cornmeal, flour, salt, cayenne, sugar, and baking powder in a medium mixing bowl. Stir in the onion-rosemary mixture, scraping in all of the melted butter. Add the egg and cream and stir just until the batter is well blended. Take the batter out to the grill.

With a grill mitt on, move the corn stick pans away from the fire. Using a silicone basting brush, coat the corn stick indentations with oil. Carefully spoon the batter into the pre-pared pans, cover the grill, and cook until the corn sticks are puffed and browned, 10 to 12 minutes.

Remove from the grill to a cooling rack, and cool in the pans for 3 to 5 minutes. Loosen each corn stick around the edges with a small knife, and carefully lift out of the pan and trans-fer to a serving plate. Be careful; they're fragile. Serve warm with the spicy orange honey and butter, if desired.

KNOW-HOW: SEASONING CAST IRON

Iron is porous, and must be sealed or seasoned before its first use. Many cast-iron pans come preseasoned. Seasoned cast iron looks shiny and black; before it's seasoned, cast iron is dull and dark gray. To season a cast-iron pan, wash it and dry it well, coat it with a flavorless unsaturated oil like canola oil, and set it upside down in a 350°F oven for 2 hours, removing the pan every 30 minutes to coat it with more oil. Put a sheet pan or a large sheet of foil below the pan to keep dripping oil from getting on the oven floor. Turn off the oven and allow the pan to cool before removing it. Seasoned cast-iron pans can be washed in soap and water, but they should be dried immedi-ately, and never scrubbed with anything abrasive. If they are scrubbed, the seasoning will come off, and you will have to season the pan again.

PASTRY

Grilled Cheese Straws

MAKES 12 SERVINGS (2 DOZEN CHEESE STRAWS)

Pastry grills beautifully. The only trick is coating it with something that will help it keep its shape until the dough sets. Without that, as soon as the dough warms, the fat in it melts and everything falls through the grill grate. In this simple recipe a sheet of pie crust dough is encrusted with cheese and cut into strips. When the crust hits the grill grate, the cheese sets up right away and then quickly browns while the pastry crisps. The resulting cheesy, crunchy pastry straws go great with cocktails.

INGREDIENTS:

1 recipe Flaky Pie Pastry (page 364)

2 tablespoons milk

1 cup grated Parmesan cheese

1 teaspoon cayenne pepper

½ cup finely shredded Cheddar cheese

1 teaspoon paprika

Cooking spray

DIRECTIONS:

Roll the pastry to a thickness of ³⁄₁₆ inch. Trim to a 12-by-6-inch rectangle, and brush with the milk on both sides.

Combine the Parmesan, cayenne, Cheddar, and paprika, and press the mixture into both sides of the pastry. Cut into 24 ½-inch-wide, 6-inch-long strips and arrange in a single layer on a baking sheet. Refrigerate for 30 minutes.

Light a grill for a bilevel medium/low fire, about 375/275°F (see page 13).

Brush the grill grate and coat with oil. Coat the cheese straws on both sides with cooking spray. Grill over the low heat until grill-marked and crisp, about 1½ minutes per side, moving to medium heat if necesary for crisping.

Depending on the size of your grill, you may have to cook several batches. Serve warm or room temperature.

SANDWICH

Ham and Brie Baguette Panino

MAKES 4 SERVINGS

Panino is Italian for "small bread," and *panino imbottito* is a stuffed panino, or a sandwich that is typically compressed to help it hold its shape, and grilled. *Panini* refers to more than one panino, but it has become the worldwide term for any Italian-style sandwich made on a small crusty roll, and grilled under pressure. Panini presses are double-sided grills that compress panini sandwiches as they're grilled, but if you've got a gas or charcoal grill, you can make panini that are far superior to any that come out of an electric press. You will need a brick, a flat stone, or a heavy skillet to weight the sandwich as it grills.

INGREDIENTS:

3 tablespoons unsalted butter, softened

1 tablespoon Dijon mustard

1 tablespoon chopped fresh tarragon leaves

1 garlic clove, minced

1 fresh baguette, 24 inches long, split lengthwise

8 ounces Brie, rind removed, cut into 12 slices

8 ounces thinly sliced baked ham

1 tablespoon olive oil

DIRECTIONS:

Mix together the butter, mustard, tarragon, and garlic in a small bowl.

Open up the baguette like a book and spread the interior with the butter mixture. Lay the Brie slices evenly down both sides of the bread and top with ham, folding each slice of ham loosely before putting it on the bread. Close the bread and compress the sandwich with your hands. Top with a baking sheet filled with canned goods or some other heavy weight. Let stand for 30 minutes while the grill heats up.

Light a grill for direct medium heat, about 375°F (see page 12).

Brush the grill grate and coat with oil. Coat the outside of the sandwich with the olive oil and put on the grill. Top with a sheet of heavy-duty foil and a skillet, rock, or brick that will keep the sandwich compressed. Cover the grill and cook for 5 to 8 minutes, until the bread is toasted and the cheese has melted, flipping and re-compressing the sandwich halfway through cooking.

Remove the sandwich to a cutting board, and cut into 4 servings.

SANDWICH

Grilled Cheese and Tomato Sandwiches

MAKES 2 SERVINGS

It has always seemed odd that a grilled cheese sandwich could be cooked with a skillet, a griddle, a fryer, a broiler, and even a clothes iron, but not a grill. These sandwiches fix that. The bread is coated with garlic butter, the cheese is aged Cheddar, and the tomato is tangy-sweet tomato marmalade—all grilled into an open-faced sandwich. If you prefer, slap two together and close them up.

INGREDIENTS:

3 tablespoons unsalted butter, softened

½ garlic clove, minced

4 slices crusty whole-grain bread

4 ounces sharp Cheddar cheese, thinly sliced

¼ cup Grilled Tomato Marmalade (page 43)

½ cup microgreens (optional)

DIRECTIONS:

Light a grill for direct medium heat, about 375°F (see page 12).

Mix the butter and garlic, and spread on both sides of each slice of bread. Brush the grill grate and coat with oil. Put the bread on the grill and toast one side lightly, about 2 minutes.

Put a layer of cheese on the toasted side of each bread slice and return to the grill. Cover the grill and cook until the cheese is melted and the bottom of the bread is toasted, about 2 minutes. Serve each open-faced sandwich with a tablespoon of marmalade and a small mound of greens.

SANDWICH

Grilled PBBB & J

MAKES 4 SERVINGS

In a salute to Elvis Presley, this revamped PB & J nestles bacon strips, peanut butter, and bananas between slices of bread that have been brushed with bacon fat. The whole thing is grilled and served with a jelly dip spiked with hot sauce.

INGREDIENTS:

4 thick strips bacon

8 slices sandwich bread

¾ cup all-natural peanut butter

2 bananas, peeled and thinly sliced

⅔ cup strawberry preserves

1 teaspoon hot pepper sauce, such as Tabasco

DIRECTIONS:

Light a grill for direct medium heat, about 375°F (see page 12).

Meanwhile, cook the bacon in a skillet over medium heat until cooked through, but still flexible. Drain the bacon on paper towels, and break each piece in half. Reserve the fat in the pan.

Spread 4 slices of the bread with the peanut butter, top with the bacon, bananas, and the remaining 4 slices bread. Brush the outside of all sandwiches with a thin film of the bacon fat.

Grill directly over the fire until the bread is toasted, about 2 minutes per side. To create crosshatch grill marks, position the sandwiches diagonally across the grill grate and rotate them 90 degrees halfway through grilling.

Remove from the grill and cool for 1 to 2 minutes. Mix the preserves and hot sauce. Cut the sandwiches in half and serve with the sauce for dipping.

SANDWICH

Double-Grilled Reuben

MAKES 4 SERVINGS

The Reuben, a bulging, deli-style sandwich loaded with corned beef, sauerkraut, and Swiss cheese cries out for some grilling. We grill the corned beef separately, then toast the whole sandwich on the grill and brush it with mustard butter.

INGREDIENTS:

2 thick slices corned beef (8 ounces total)

1 teaspoon canola oil

1 pound sauerkraut, rinsed and drained

4 ounces Swiss cheese, shredded

3 tablespoons unsalted butter, softened

2 tablespoons spicy brown mustard

1 garlic clove, minced

8 slices rye bread

¼ cup mayonnaise

2 tablespoons ketchup

1 tablespoon sweet relish

continued ⊕

DIRECTIONS:

Light a grill for direct medium heat, about 375°F (see page 12).

Brush the grill grate and coat with oil. Coat the outside of the corned beef with the oil and grill until browned on both sides, about 8 minutes, turning halfway through.

Remove to a cutting board and chop finely. Mix with the sauerkraut and Swiss cheese in a large bowl.

Mix together the butter, mustard, and garlic; spread on both sides of the bread. Sandwich the corned beef mixture between the bread slices. Press down on the sandwiches with your hands, pushing in any stray bits.

Mix the mayonnaise, ketchup and relish and set aside.

Brush the grill grate and coat with oil. Put the sandwiches on the grill, cover the grill, and cook for 5 to 8 minutes, until the bread is grill-marked and the cheese melts, turning once.

Cut each sandwich in half and serve with the Russian dressing.

SANDWICH

Pain au Chocolat French Toast

MAKES 4 SERVINGS

A slab of chocolate sandwiched between slices of French bread is the PB & J of France, and the inspiration for this sensual grilled French toast. A glaze of cinnamon honey butter gilds the lily.

INGREDIENTS:

1 French baguette, about 12 inches long

4 ounces semisweet chocolate

5 large eggs

1½ cups half-and-half or milk

1 teaspoon pure vanilla extract

Pinch of salt

1 tablespoon sugar

2 tablespoons unsalted butter, softened

1 tablespoon honey

½ teaspoon ground cinnamon

Pinch of grated nutmeg

DIRECTIONS:

Cut off and discard a small diagonal slice off each end of the bread. Cut the bread on a diagonal into eight 1½-inch-thick slices. Cut a slit through the top crust of each slice to form a deep pocket. Break the chocolate into pieces and insert a piece in each pocket.

Lay the stuffed slices of bread in a shallow baking dish just large enough to fit all of the slices snugly in a single layer.

Mix the eggs, half-and-half, vanilla, salt, and sugar. Pour the mixture evenly over the bread. Carefully tilt the pan and swirl the egg mixture to completely coat the bread. Let sit for 30 minutes or cover and refrigerate overnight.

Light a grill for direct medium heat, about 375°F (see page 12). While the grill heats mix the butter, honey, cinnamon and nutmeg together. Set aside.

Brush the grill grate and coat with oil. Put the French toast on the grill and cook until nicely browned, about 5 minutes per side. Transfer to a platter and brush both sides with the cinnamon honey butter.

WAFFLE

Fire-Toasted Sour Cream Walnut Waffles with Maple-Grilled Fruit

MAKES 4 SERVINGS (4 LARGE WAFFLES)

Waffles are the most whimsical of fire-flecked breakfast options—a light and crunchy honeycomb cradling puddles of warm syrup, bits of grilled fruit, and melting blobs of butter. We have found that oversized Belgian-style waffles grill best. They toast beautifully over a low fire and have a large honeycomb, which easily holds lots of topping. The waffle batter is exceptionally light and tender because it's made with sour cream. It also contains ground walnuts, which lend these waffles a toasty, crunchy richness that goes great with the maple-glazed fruit accompaniment.

INGREDIENTS:

Sour Cream Walnut Waffles:

1 cup sifted cake flour

1¼ teaspoons baking powder

1 teaspoon baking soda

2 tablespoons sugar

½ cup finely ground walnuts

3 extra-large eggs, separated

2 cups sour cream (not fat-free)

2 tablespoons walnut or canola oil

¼ teaspoon sea salt

Butter for coating waffle iron

Maple-Grilled Fruit:

2 bananas, cut in half lengthwise through the peel

1 crisp apple, peeled, cored, and cut into 16 wedges

1 ripe pear, peeled, cored, and cut into 16 wedges

1 tablespoon walnut or canola oil

¼ cup maple sugar or brown sugar

4 tablespoons unsalted butter, melted

¾ cup maple syrup, warmed

Unsalted butter for serving (optional)

DIRECTIONS:

For the waffles: Preheat a waffle iron. Mix together the sifted flour, baking powder, baking soda, and sugar in a large bowl. Stir in the walnuts.

Beat the egg yolks with the sour cream and oil in a medium bowl, and stir into the dry ingredients just until blended. With an electric mixer, beat the egg whites with the salt until soft peaks form, and then fold into the batter.

Grease the hot waffle iron with butter, and ladle on enough batter to fill three-quarters of the surface. Close the lid, and cook until the waffle is brown and crisp on both sides.

Remove and repeat with the remaining batter.

Light a grill for direct medium heat, about 375°F (see page 12).

For the grilled fruit: Coat the cut surfaces of the bananas and the entire surface of each apple and pear wedge with oil. Sprinkle with maple or brown sugar, and set aside.

Brush the grill grate and coat with oil. Put the apple and pear slices on the grill, cover the grill, and grill until both sides are grill-marked and the fruit is barely tender, about 5 minutes per side. Halfway through cooking, put the bananas on the grill, cut-side down, and cook until grill-marked, about 4 minutes. Peel the bananas and slice ½ inch thick. In a medium bowl, mix half the melted butter with the maple syrup. Add the fruit, toss, and cover with foil to keep warm.

Brush the grill grate again and coat with oil. Brush the waffles with the remaining butter and put on the grill. Cover the grill and cook until the waffles are toasted and heated through, about 3 minutes.

KEEP IT SIMPLE:

Use frozen or refrigerated packaged waffles instead of homemade, preferably Belgian waffles.

DOUGHNUTS

Grilled Glazed Doughnuts with Chocolate Espresso Dunk

MAKES 6 SERVINGS

Ben Cassorla, a member of the eponymous jazz group Cassorla, lives in a small apartment in L.A., where he is a devoted balcony-grill guy. Working with charcoal briquettes and a small (10-inch square) hibachi (no cover, no adjustable grill grates, no vents), he manages to turn out dinner most nights. He told us that his favorite thing to grill is doughnuts—nothing fancy, a box of DD works just fine. He's tried all flavors. Chocolate gets bitter, cream-filled are disastrous, and powdered sugar is pretty good, though not as good as glazed (he's partial to cinnamon glazed). We agree. The notion is brilliant and the technique couldn't be easier. The glaze caramelizes almost on contact with the grill, so keep your fire pretty low. The whole cooking process takes only 1 to 2 minutes. The results are mind-blowing—crispy, subtly charred sugar skin, warm interior, and doughnuts that taste like they just came out of a fryer (by way of a charcoal grill). We have gilded Ben's creation with an awesome dunk made from freshly pulled espresso morphed into hot fudge sauce.

INGREDIENTS:

1½ cups unsweetened cocoa powder

1½ cups brown sugar, light or dark

Pinch of salt

2 cups freshly made espresso or strong coffee

2 tablespoons unsalted butter

6 glazed doughnuts, preferably cinnamon-glazed

Cooking spray

1½ cups half-and-half, warmed (optional)

DIRECTIONS:

Light a grill for direct medium-low heat, about 325°F (see page 12).

Mix together the cocoa powder, brown sugar, and salt in a large heavy saucepan. Whisk in the espresso and continue whisking until the mixture is smooth. Cook over medium heat, stirring constantly with a wooden spoon or heat-resistant spatula, until the sauce comes to a boil. Reduce the heat and simmer for about 2 minutes, until slightly thickened and very smooth. Remove from the heat and add the butter, stirring until melted. Cover and keep warm.

Coat the doughnuts on both sides with cooking spray.

Brush the grill grate and coat with oil. Grill the doughnuts until the glaze melts and the donuts are browned on both sides, 30 seconds to 1 minute per side. Do not allow to burn.

Pour ½ cup warm chocolate dunk into each of 6 small coffee cups and serve one to each guest with a doughnut for dunking. Serve warm half-and-half on the side for adding to the chocolate dunk, if desired.

CAKE

Honey-Crusted Pound Cake with Rum Raisin Hard Sauce

MAKES 4 SERVINGS

A classic pound cake has no added leavening, just the air that gets incorporated into the batter during mixing. The resulting cake is deliciously dense—a cake texture that has fallen out of favor as cake manufacturers attempt to inflate profits by pumping up their pound cakes with leavening gases in place of more expensive butter, eggs, flour, and sugar. Real pound cake is firm enough to toast on a grill; ersatz pound cake is too soft and has a tendency to fall apart during grilling. The pound cake recipe that follows toasts beautifully, but if you've got a favorite recipe or have access to a great bakery pound cake, by all means use that. Once you have the cake, this recipe is effortless. Cake slices are brushed with cardamom honey butter, and after toasting on the grill, they're topped with more of the butter mixed with rum-soaked raisins. Serve with ice cream—rum raisin, of course.

INGREDIENTS:

2 tablespoons raisins, chopped

2 tablespoons dark or golden rum

3 tablespoons honey

½ teaspoon ground cardamom

3 tablespoons unsalted butter

4 slices Real Pound Cake from Scratch, about ½ inch thick (recipe follows)

DIRECTIONS:

Soak the raisins in the rum in a small bowl for 30 minutes.

Meanwhile, heat the honey and cardamom in a small saucepan just until warm, about 20 seconds. Remove from the heat and stir in the butter until melted.

Brush the pound cake slices on both sides with half the butter mixture. Pour the remaining butter mixture into the bowl with the rum and raisins and set aside until the sauce thickens, about 10 minutes.

Light a grill for direct medium-high heat, 375°F (see page 12).

Brush the grill grate and coat with oil. Grill the pound cake slices until grill-marked on both sides, 20 seconds per side, turning the slices 90 degrees halfway through to make crosshatch marks.

Serve the pound cake warm topped with the rum raisin sauce.

Real Pound Cake from Scratch

MAKES 1 CAKE

INGREDIENTS:

Flour-and-oil baking spray

1 cup (2 sticks) unsalted butter, cut into pieces

1½ cups sugar

2 teaspoons pure vanilla extract

5 extra-large eggs

2 cups sifted all-purpose flour

DIRECTIONS:

Preheat the oven to 350°F. Coat a standard loaf pan (8 by 4 by 2½ inches) with the baking spray and set aside.

With an electric mixer, beat the butter with the sugar in a large bowl until light and fluffy.

Then beat in the vanilla and the eggs, one at a time. Add the sifted flour, beating just until the batter is smooth. Pour into the prepared pan.

Bake until a tester comes out clean, about 1 hour. If the top of the cake begins to brown too much, cover loosely with foil.

Let the cake cool in the pan on a rack for 15 minutes. Unmold, and cool on a rack to room temperature.

CAKE

Grilled Cornmeal and Summer Berry Clafouti

MAKES 8 SERVINGS

Clafouti, a traditional country dessert from the Limousin region of France, is half custard and half cake. Loaded with fruit (classically cherries), it has a crispy crust and a moist, mousse-like center, the perfect textural context for the bottom-up baking that happens on a grill. The consistency of this clafouti is further enhanced by a gritty addition of cornmeal, giving it a rustic crumb, well suited to a fire-baked confection.

INGREDIENTS:

Flour-and-oil baking spray

1 cup yellow cornmeal

½ cup all-purpose flour

¾ cup sugar

1½ teaspoons baking powder

½ teaspoon baking soda

½ teaspoon salt

2 large eggs, lightly beaten

1½ cups low-fat buttermilk

2 pints blueberries

1 pint raspberries

3 tablespoons unsalted butter

3 tablespoons rum or fruit brandy

Confectioners' sugar for sprinkling (optional)

½ cup heavy cream, warmed (optional)

DIRECTIONS:

Light a grill for indirect medium heat, about 325°F (see page 14). Coat the interior of a heavy 9-inch round layer-cake pan with the baking spray and set aside.

Mix together the cornmeal, flour, ½ cup of the sugar, the baking powder, baking soda, and salt in a large mixing bowl. Add the eggs and buttermilk and mix together until the dry ingredients are all moistened. Fold in 1 pint of the blueberries and 1 cup of the raspberries just until distributed evenly; do not overmix. Pour and scrape into the prepared cake pan.

Put the pan on the grill away from direct contact with the fire. Cover the grill and bake until the top is browned and a tester inserted in the center of the cake comes out with just a few moist crumbs clinging to it, about 50 minutes. Cool in the pan on a rack for 10 minutes.

If using a gas grill, turn the remaining burner(s) to medium. If using charcoal, spread out the charcoal bed for direct grilling. Melt the butter in a large skillet over medium to medium-high heat (you can do this on a side burner or directly on the grill). Add the remaining 1 pint blueberries, 1 cup raspberries, and ¼ cup sugar to the skillet and stir gently until the sugar is dissolved and the berries are plump and glossy. Remove from the heat and stir in the rum.

Brush the grill grate and coat with oil. Loosen the clafouti from the sides of the pan. Brush the top of the clafouti with some of the liquid from the sautéed berries. With the clafouti still in the pan, invert it onto the grill. (If the cake pan is still too hot to handle, use pot holders or grill gloves.) Grill just long enough to char the surface lightly, about 2 minutes. Use a large spatula (or two medium spatulas) to remove the clafouti (grilled-side down) to a flat plate or baking sheet. Cover with a serving platter and invert.

Sprinkle with confectioners' sugar, if desired, and serve with the sautéed berries and a drizzle of warm cream, if you like.

CAKE

Grilled Banana Bread Foster

MAKES 8 SERVINGS

Bananas Foster—a sauté of bananas, brown sugar, cinnamon, rum, and banana liqueur served over vanilla ice cream—was created at Brennan's restaurant in New Orleans in 1951. Our rendition supercharges the flavor of caramelized banana with grill-toasted sour cream banana bread and grilled bananas crusted with cinnamon sugar. To keep it simple, use store-bought banana bread instead of homemade.

INGREDIENTS:

Sour Cream Banana Bread:

Flour-and-oil baking spray

½ cup (1 stick) unsalted butter, cut into 8 tablespoons

1 cup sugar

3 ripe bananas, peeled and chopped

¼ cup sour cream

1 teaspoon pure vanilla extract

¼ teaspoon salt

2 eggs, extra-large

2 cups all-purpose flour

¾ teaspoon baking powder

½ teaspoon baking soda

1 cup light brown sugar

½ teaspoon ground cinnamon

4 bananas, unpeeled, halved lengthwise

6 tablespoons unsalted butter, softened

Cooking spray

½ cup dark rum

1 teaspoon pure vanilla extract

DIRECTIONS:

For the banana bread: Preheat the oven to 350°F. Coat a standard loaf pan (8 by 4 by 2½ inches) with the baking spray and set aside.

Put the butter and sugar in the work bowl of a food processor set up with a metal blade. Process in pulses until a smooth ball forms. Add the bananas, sour cream, vanilla, salt, and eggs and process in pulses until well combined, scraping down the sides of the bowl as needed. The batter may appear curdled at this point; don't worry.

Mix together the flour, baking powder, and baking soda in a small bowl. Add to the processor and blend in pulses until the batter is smooth, scraping down the sides of the bowl.

Pour the batter into the prepared pan and bake until browned and a tester inserted in the center comes out with only a few moist crumbs clinging to it, about 50 minutes.

Cool the bread in the pan on a cooling rack for 15 minutes. Invert and remove from the pan. Turn right-side up and cool to room temperature on the rack.

Light the grill for direct medium heat, about 375°F (see page 12).

Mix the brown sugar and cinnamon and sprinkle half of it over the cut surfaces of the bananas; set aside for 10 minutes.

Cut a thin slice from each end of the cake (munch on them for a snack). Cut the cake into 8 slices about ¾ inch thick. Melt 2 tablespoons of the butter and use it to brush the cut surfaces of the cake slices. Set aside.

Brush the grill grate and coat with cooking spray. Put the cake slices on the grill and also the bananas, cut-side down. Cover the grill, and cook until they are grill-marked and the bananas are tender, about 2 minutes per side.

Remove the bananas from the peel and arrange a banana half and a slice of cake on a plate for each person. Bring the rum to a boil in a small saucepan or skillet. Add the vanilla, remove from the heat, and stir in the remaining 4 tablespoons butter until melted.

Pour over the bananas and part of the cake and serve.

CAKE

Grilled Black Pepper Gingerbread with Chipotle Chocolate Butter

MAKES 9 SERVINGS

We love the interplay of sweet and spicy—in barbecue sauces, spice rubs, and on the dessert plate. This palate-popping grilled gingerbread explodes with black pepper, chiles, and dark brown sugar (boosted with extra molasses). Then we add a little smoke with chipotle chiles suspended in creamy chocolate butter and by charring the surface of the cake over a hot fire. The combined effect is over-the-top spicy.

INGREDIENTS:

Black Pepper Gingerbread:

Flour-and-oil baking spray

½ cup (1 stick) unsalted butter

½ cup dark brown sugar

1 cup dark molasses

1 teaspoon spicy brown mustard

2 eggs, large or extra-large

1 tablespoon ground ginger

1 teaspoon ground cinnamon

½ teaspoon ground allspice

1 teaspoon ground black pepper

2 teaspoons baking soda

2⅓ cups all-purpose flour

1 cup boiling hot coffee

3 tablespoons unsalted butter, melted

½ cup Chipotle Chocolate Butter (page 48)

DIRECTIONS:

For the gingerbread: Preheat the oven to 375°F. Coat a 9-inch square baking pan with baking spray and set aside.

Melt the butter in a large heavy saucepan. Remove from the heat and add the brown sugar, molasses, mustard, and eggs, beating with a whisk until smooth. Add the ginger, cinnamon, allspice, and black pepper, and then add the baking soda in pinches, breaking up any lumps with your fingers. Stir until well blended. Mix in the flour, stirring just until blended, followed by the hot coffee.

Pour the batter into the prepared pan. Bake for 40 to 45 minutes, until the cake is springy and a tester inserted in the center comes out with just a few crumbs clinging to it.

Cool in the pan on a rack for 10 minutes. Invert and remove from pan, and cool right-side up to room temperature.

Light a grill for direct medium-high heat, about 400°F (see page 12).

Cut the gingerbread into 9 squares and brush the top and bottom of each square with melted butter.

Brush the grill grate and coat with oil. Put the squares on the grill and cook until toasted on both sides, 1 to 2 minutes per side.

Arrange the gingerbread on a platter or plates, and top with the chipotle chocolate butter before serving.

KEEP IT SIMPLE:

Use store-bought gingerbread instead of homemade. To get the spicier flavor, add ½ teaspoon finely ground black pepper and ¼ teaspoon ground mustard to the melted butter used to brush on the gingerbread squares before grilling. Or use a gingerbread cake mix and add the spices to the dry ingredients.

CAKE

Grilled Smoked Sweet Potato Skillet Cake

MAKES 8 SERVINGS

Smoked salt, smoked oil, and the radiating smoke of wood chips smoldering over flame combine to give this cake its unique flavor profile. The sweet potato in the cake plays a role similar to that of carrots in a carrot cake. The vegetable doesn't take over the flavor (the brown sugar, smoked oil, ginger, cinnamon, and allspice take care of that) but it does affect the cake's shelf life helping to keep it fresh for as long as there is moisture left in the potato shards. Vegetable cakes of this type easily stay fresh for over a week.

INGREDIENTS:

2 cups hardwood wood chips, soaked in water for 30 minutes

Flour-and-oil baking spray

4 eggs, large or extra-large

2 cups firmly packed light brown sugar

1 cup hickory-smoked oil, or ¾ cup plus 3 tablespoons canola oil plus 1 tablespoon liquid smoke

1 teaspoon pure vanilla extract

2 cups all-purpose flour

2 teaspoons baking soda

2 teaspoons smoked salt, plus more for sprinkling

2½ teaspoons ground cinnamon

1 teaspoon ground ginger

½ teaspoon ground allspice

1 pound sweet potatoes, peeled and coarsely shredded (about 4 cups)

2 cups chopped pecans (about 8 ounces)

¼ cup confectioners' sugar

DIRECTIONS:

Light a grill for indirect medium heat, about 325°F, with smoke, trying to keep the temperature toward the lower end of the range (see pages 14 and 16).

Coat the interior of a 12-inch cast-iron skillet or a heavy 13-by-9-inch baking pan with the baking spray and set aside.

Whisk the eggs in a large mixing bowl until light and fluffy. Add the brown sugar, stirring until completely moistened. Add and the oil and vanilla and stir until incorporated.

Mix together the flour, baking soda, salt, 2 teaspoons of the cinnamon, the ginger, and allspice in a separate bowl and add to the wet ingredients, stirring just until the batter is smooth and thick. Stir in the shredded sweet potato and chopped pecans.

Pour and scrape the batter into the prepared skillet.

Drain the wood chips and add to the grill.

Put the skillet on the grill away from the fire, cover the grill, and bake until the cake has risen and browned, and a tester inserted in the crack in the center comes out with just a few moist crumbs clinging to it, about 1 hour and 25 minutes.

Remove to a cooling rack, and cool in the pan for 15 minutes. Invert the cake onto another cooling rack, remove the skillet, and sprinkle the cake with smoked salt. Cool to room temperature.

Mix together the remaining ½ teaspoon cinnamon and confectioners' sugar. Dust the top of the cake with this mixture before serving.

Salted Caramel S'mores

MAKES 4 SERVINGS

There are few cookies as puritanically plain as the graham cracker (originally formulated as a digestive aid), which is why when we bite into a s'more, it is always with a wee bit of awe. Although one would be hard pressed to improve upon this campfire icon, we think we've come up with something that aspires to a higher level. Inspired by salted caramels, we take soft caramel candies, sear them over an open fire, scrape them onto a chocolate-capped cracker, and sprinkle with fleur de sel. Because caramel can get outrageously hot without bursting into flames (unlike a marshmallow), they do a great job of melting the chocolate.

INGREDIENTS

4 long bamboo or metal skewers

8 traditional chewy caramel candies, such as Kraft

1 dark chocolate bar (about 3 ounces), broken into 12 squares

8 graham crackers

1 teaspoon fleur de sel or sel gris

DIRECTIONS:

If you are grilling with bamboo skewers, soak them in water for at least 30 minutes. Light a grill for direct high heat, about 475°F (see page 12). Leave the grate off the grill.

Unwrap the caramels and flatten between the heels of your hands to about ¼ inch thick. Thread 2 caramels onto each of the skewers, piercing the caramels through their narrow sides.

On a serving plate, arrange 3 squares of chocolate on each of 4 graham crackers.

Hold the caramels close to the fire of the grill until they brown on both sides and start to collapse, 3 to 4 minutes, turning often. When the caramels are on the verge of collapse, place each skewer on a chocolate-topped graham cracker. Sprinkle with fleur de sel and top with a plain graham cracker. Holding the graham sandwich in place, slide the skewers out from the centers.

Let the s'mores rest for a few minutes before serving to give the chocolate time to melt. Serve with plenty of napkins.

Piggy Oatmeal Whoppers

MAKES 8 SERVINGS

Fresh-baked cookies coming off the grill is a puzzling sight, as if the distinction between cooking indoors and outdoors had suddenly disappeared. The cookies are as good as any that have ever come out of an oven—thick and moist, rich with bacon fat (it makes them exceptionally tender), salty and smoky from bacon pieces, molasses-sweet from lots of brown sugar, and chewy with whole grain and dried fruit. They will stay fresh for 4 to 5 days in a cookie jar.

INGREDIENTS:

3 thick strips bacon, finely chopped

2 cups old-fashioned (rolled) oats

⅔ cup dark brown sugar

3 tablespoons molasses

1 extra-large egg, lightly beaten

2 tablespoons coffee or water

½ cup all-purpose flour

¼ teaspoon baking soda

¼ teaspoon sea salt

½ cup raisins

Flour-and-oil baking spray

DIRECTIONS:

Cook the bacon in a large skillet over medium heat until crisp, about 5 minutes. Add the oats and cook until lightly toasted, about 2 minutes.

Remove from the heat and stir in the brown sugar, molasses, egg, and coffee. Mix together the flour, baking soda, and salt in a separate bowl and stir into the liquid in the frying pan until well blended. Stir in the raisins. Refrigerate for about 30 minutes.

Light a grill for direct medium-low heat, about 275°F (see page 12).

Coat a baking sheet or rectangular grill tray with the baking spray. Wet your hands with cold water and form the dough into 8 balls. Flatten between your palms into cookies, and place about 1 inch apart on the prepared pan.

Put the baking sheet on the grill. Cover the grill and cook just until the cookies in the center of the pan are set around the edges but still soft in the center, 20 minutes. Transfer to a cooling rack with a small spatula and cool before serving.

46 Points of Ingredient Know-How

Sources

We use local farmers, ranchers, butchers, and purveyors whenever possible. If you have trouble finding some of the less common ingredients used in this book, the following purveyors sell good-quality products in their online and/or traditional stores.

MEAT, POULTRY, AND GAME

Niman Ranch

Natural beef, pork, and lamb

www.nimanranch.com

510-808-0330

NFR Natural Beef

Grass-fed and dry-aged beef from the Neff Family Ranch

www.nfrnaturalbeef.com

530-284-6371

Lobel's

High-quality beef, pork, lamb, sausages, and other specialty foods

www.lobels.com

877-783-4512

D'Artagnan

Boar, bison, venison, duck, quail, sausages, and other meats

www.dartagnan.com

800-327-8246

Dean & Deluca

Standing rib roasts, prime beef cuts, venison, pork, lamb, quail, cured meats, seafood, cheese, and other fine foods

www.deandeluca.com

800-999-0306

DiBruno Brothers

High-quality pancetta, prosciutto, and other charcuterie

www.dibruno.com

888-322-4337

Buon Italia

Lardo, cured meats, and other high-quality products imported from Italy

www.buonitalia.com

212-633-9090

Hudson Valley Foie Gras

Duck and foie gras

www.hudsonvalleyfoiegras.com

845-292-2500

Jamison Farm

High-quality lamb, whole or parts

www.jamisonfarm.com

800-237-5262

McReynolds Farms

Frozen whole suckling pigs and other meats

www.mcreynoldsfarms.com

800-981-1854

Goat World

Goat meat

www.goatworldnj.com

908-735-5928

Copeland Family Farms

Goat meat

www.goatmeats.com

530-436-2348

Game Sales International

Boar, bison, rabbit, pheasant, quail, ostrich, and other wild game and game birds

www.gamesalesintl.com

800-729-2090

Fossil Farm

Foie gras, bison, Berkshire pork, venison, boar, ostrich, pheasant, rabbit, and other game meats

www.fossilfarms.com

201-651-1190

Seattle's Finest Exotic Meats

Alligator, yak, snapping turtle, llama, kangaroo, rattlesnake and other exotic meats, poultry, seafood, and sauces

www.exoticmeats.com

800-680-4375

Viva Gourmet

Alligator tail tenderloin and other specialty foods

www.vivagourmet.com

407-855-1119

Broken Arrow Ranch

Game, including antelope and venison fillets, loin, kabobs, stew chunks, sausage, and ground meat

www.brokenarrowranch.com

800-962-4263

SEAFOOD

Prawn Corporation of America

Prawns, conch, octopus, eel, and other seafood

www.prawnco.com

866-772-9626

Cajun Grocer

Crawfish tails and many other foods from Louisiana

www.cajungrocer.com

888-272-9347

Estero Bay Abalone

Abalone steaks

www.esterobayabalone.com

805-962-4313

Catalina Offshore Products

Abalone and other exotic fish and shellfish

www.catalinaop.com

619-297-9797

PRODUCE

Melissa's

Specialty fruits, vegetables, and international produce

www.melissas.com

800-588-0151

Frieda's

Specialty fruits, vegetables, greens, and nuts

www.friedas.com

800-241-1771

SALT, SPICES, CHOCOLATE, AND DRY GOODS

The Meadow

More than 100 kinds of artisanal salts and peppers, salt blocks for grilling, cocoa nibs, and chocolate

www.atthemeadow.com

888-388-4633

Salt Traders

Smoked salt, black salt, and other artisanal salts and peppers

www.salttraders.com

800-641-7258

Penzeys Spices

Massive array of good-quality and hard-to-find spices and seasoning blends

www.penzeys.com

800-741-7787

Vann's Spices

Good-quality spices, both common and hard to find

www.vannsspices.com

800-583-1693

Zamouri Spices

Sumac and other Middle Eastern, Moroccan, Indian, and Asian spices

www.zamourispices.com

866-329-5988

Chocolate Source

A wide variety of good-quality chocolate chips, bars, and blocks

www.chocolatesource.com

800-214-4926

Ethnic Grocer

Pomegranate molasses, chutneys, herbs, spices, and other international ingredients

www.ethnicgrocer.com

630-860-1733

Mustaphas

Harissa, preserved lemons, and other Moroccan foods

www.mustaphas.com

206-382-1706

Index

TABLE OF EQUIVALENTS

The exact equivalents in the following tables have been rounded for convenience.

LIQUID/DRY MEASUREMENTS

U.S. .... Metric

¼ teaspoon ....1.25 milliliters

½ teaspoon ....2.5 milliliters

1 teaspoon ....5 milliliters

1 tablespoon (3 teaspoons).................................15 milliliters

1 fluid ounce (2 tablespoons) ....30 milliliters

¼ cup.. 60 milliliters

⅓ cup...80 milliliters

½ cup...120 milliliters

1 cup...240 milliliters

1 pint (2 cups) .... 480 milliliters

1 quart (4 cups, 32 ounces) .... 960 milliliters

1 gallon (4 quarts)...3.84 liters

1 ounce (by weight) ....28 grams

1 pound .... 448 grams

2.2 pounds ....1 kilogram

LENGTHS

U.S. .... Metric

⅛ inch.. 3 millimeters

¼ inch.. 6 millimeters

½ inch.. 12 millimeters

1 inch..2.5 centimeters

OVEN TEMPERATURE

Fahrenheit......................Celsius ....Gas

250......................................120 ....½

275......................................140 1

300 ....150 2

325......................................160 3

350 ....180 4

375......................................190 5

400 ....200 6

425......................................220 7

450 ....230 8

475......................................240 9

500......................................260 10